Ink

MUSIC IN AMERICAN LIFE

The Music in American Life series documents and celebrates the dynamic and multifaceted relationship between music and American culture. From its first publication in 1972 through its half-century mark and beyond, the series has embraced a wide variety of methodologies, from biography and memoir to history and musical analysis, and spans the full range of musical forms, from classical through all types of vernacular music. The series showcases the wealth of musical practice and expression that characterizes American music, as well as the rich diversity of its stylistic, regional, racial, ethnic, and gendered contexts. Characterized by a firm grounding in material culture, whether archival or ethnographic, and by work that honors the musical activities of ordinary people and their communities, Music in American Life continually redefines and expands the very definition of what constitutes music in American culture, whose voices are heard, and how music and musical practices are understood and valued.

For a list of books in the series, please see our website at www.press.uillinois.edu.

Ink

The Indelible J. Mayo Williams

CLIFFORD R. MURPHY

UNIVERSITY OF ILLINOIS PRESS
Urbana, Chicago, and Springfield

Publication of this book was supported in part by a grant from
the Judith McCulloh Endowment for American Music.

© 2024 by the Board of Trustees
of the University of Illinois
All rights reserved
Manufactured in the United States of America
1 2 3 4 5 C P 5 4 3 2 1
♾ This book is printed on acid-free paper.

Library of Congress Cataloging-in-Publication Data
Names: Murphy, Clifford R, author.
Title: Ink : the indelible J. Mayo Williams / Clifford R Murphy.
Description: Urbana : University of Illinois Press, 2024. | Series:
  Music in American life | Includes bibliographical references
  and index.
Identifiers: LCCN 2023054304 (print) | LCCN 2023054305
  (ebook) | ISBN 9780252045882 (hardback) | ISBN
  9780252087981 (paperback) | ISBN 9780252056765 (ebook)
Subjects: LCSH: Williams, J. M. (J. Mayo), 1894–1980. |
  African American sound recording executives and producers—
  Biography. | Sound recording executives and producers—United
  States—Biography. | Blues (Music—To 1931—History and
  criticism. | Blues (Music—1931–1940—History and criticism.
  | Jazz—1931–1940—History and criticism. | Football—United
  States—History—20th century. | BISAC: MUSIC / Genres
  & Styles / Jazz | MUSIC / Genres & Styles / Blues | LCGFT:
  Biographies.
Classification: LCC ML429.W5507 M87 2024 (print) | LCC
  ML429.W5507 (ebook) | DDC 781.64092 [B—dc23/
  eng/20231208
LC record available at https://lccn.loc.gov/2023054304
LC ebook record available at https://lccn.loc.gov/2023054305

For Jeff Todd Titon, who saw something in me and gave me a shot

And for Monica, who helps me to laugh, to cry, and to feel whole

Contents

Acknowledgments   ix

INTRODUCTION: Black Bottom   1

CHAPTER 1. Ink   5

CHAPTER 2. Howard   14

CHAPTER 3. Brown   23

CHAPTER 4. Buffalo Soldier   37

CHAPTER 5. Williams vs. Yale   42

CHAPTER 6. Alpha   50

CHAPTER 7. Sambo   58

CHAPTER 8. Black Swan   62

CHAPTER 9. Hammond Pro   73

CHAPTER 10. Paramount   87

CHAPTER 11. Bronzeville   95

CHAPTER 12. Madame   107

CHAPTER 13. Bulldog   121

CHAPTER 14. Blind Lemon   129

CHAPTER 15. Black Patti   141

CHAPTER 16. Hokum   159

CHAPTER 17. Bumble Bee   169

CHAPTER 18. Maroon Tiger   182

CHAPTER 19. Sepia   189

CHAPTER 20. Outskirts   209

CHAPTER 21. Kingfish   219

CHAPTER 22. Ebony   226

CHAPTER 23. Pioneer   238

POSTSCRIPT: Indelible   251

Notes   261

References   289

Index   299

Acknowledgments

I've been married to Monica McGrath for over twenty glorious years; Mayo Williams has been a presence in our home for eighteen of those, and for the entirety of the lives of our four vivacious children, Lucy, Mary, Augustine, and Joseph. To all five of you: you fill my life with joy and meaning that is immeasurable. I thank you not just for tolerating my long journey with Mayo Williams, but for always encouraging me to see this project through.

To my editor, Laurie Matheson, at University of Illinois Press—thank you for urging me to complete this project since I first broached the idea with you and the late Judith McCulloh at the American Folklore Society conference in 2005 (!). I am grateful for your bottomless patience. Indeed, the entire editorial and production team at Illinois Press has earned my deepest gratitude: Barbara Curialle showed herself worthy of sainthood with meticulous copyedits that greatly improved my prose; Managing Editor Jennifer Argo shepherded this work along its journey from manuscript to book; Art Director Dustin Hubbart, Content Manager Kevin Cunningham, and Marketing Assistant Roberta Sparenberg have worked to ensure that this book gets read (and not just written); and indexer Martin L. White has made it possible for readers to find what they are looking for.

I am profoundly grateful to Steven Lewis, Amy Stolls, Thomas Grant Richardson, Mark Puryear, Brooks Long, Jeff Todd Titon, Paul Austerlitz, Marc Perlman, and Frank McGrath for reading various drafts of my manuscript, and for being honest and unsparing in your comments.

The late Stephen Calt looms large in this work—both as the person who published the most substantial research about Williams's Paramount and Black Patti years, and also as someone who freely shared his correspondences and interviews with Williams with me. Jim O'Neal at *Living Blues*, likewise, has dedicated his life to illuminating the lives, artistry, and history of the blues.

Jim graciously shared full audio recordings of his interviews with Williams and Little Brother Montgomery with me (as well as the only known photo of Williams in his final decade); his published interviews with other key figures in blues (particularly Thomas A. Dorsey and Muddy Waters) proved invaluable. Without Calt's and O'Neal's documentation of Williams, history would know so very little about him. And Russell E. Malbrough kindly shared his history of the Alpha Gamma chapter of Alpha Phi Alpha Fraternity with me, which also proved enormously helpful.

I am indebted to the world of 78-rpm record collectors and enthusiasts who have constructed useful, accessible, and exhaustive guides to the commercial releases of the early blues, jazz, and hillbilly record industry. In particular, Steven Abrams and Tyrone Settlemier's Online Discographical Project (www.78discography.com) essentially provides a time line for Mayo Williams's professional career through the Decca era. Alex van der Tuuk's exhaustive history of Paramount Records provided significant shape to Williams's Paramount era. The website devoted to Williams's post-Decca career constructed by George Paulus, Robert Campbell, Robert Pruter, Dr. Robert Stallworth, Dave Sax, and Jim O'Neal ("Ebony, Chicago, Southern, and Harlem: The Mayo Williams Indies," https://campber.people.clemson.edu/ebony.html) provides the rest of the time line.

The parallel world of early professional football scholarship has likewise created meticulously researched and freely shared resources of the box scores, schedules, and statistics of the early National Football League. The PFRA (Pro Football Researchers Association) and websites such as www.profootballarchives.com and www.pro-football-reference.com have long been stewards of the facts of the early league and have long illuminated the indelible truth of the league's early Black and Native American stars. My great thanks go to the historian John M. Carroll, who shared notes and ideas regarding Williams's life and whose important biography of Fritz Pollard is foundational not only to this work but also—and more important—to advancing racial equity in the head coaching ranks of the NFL.

Todd Harvey at the American Folklife Center; Steven Weiss at the Southern Folklife Collection; Sonja N. Woods at the Howard University Archives (Moorland-Spingarn Research Center); Dr. Robert L. Harris, national historian for Alpha Phi Alpha Fraternity, Inc.; C. Bird Romano, library media director of the Monmouth High School library; Allison Schein Holmes at the Studs Terkel Radio Archive (Chicago History Museum and WFMT); and Ray Butti Jr. at the Brown University Archives all enthusiastically indulged my requests for archival holdings related to Williams and unearthed fascinating and unexpected correspondences related to him. I am grateful to Elijah Wald, not only for writing terrific books but also for fielding my questions about Josh White's encounters with Mayo and Millie Williams. And the genealogist and

Monmouth community historian Richard Clark generously shared insights and images from Williams's childhood in Illinois and Arkansas.

My brothers of the road, Say ZuZu: Jon Nolan, James Nolan, Tim Nylander, Jon Pistey, and Steve Ruhm, you've inspired my creative self, kept me honest, and have endured an education in the music business with me that informs this work.

To working musicians everywhere—including the eternal souls of those whose struggles and triumphs are chronicled herein—may the world someday value the deep meaning, counsel, and artistry you provide in our everyday lives, and may the world acknowledge what you do as hard work that deserves fair pay.

My parents—Dorothy and Peter Meneghin—have always encouraged my interest in history and music. My mother's stories about her father, Cliff Ronan, serving as Louis Farrakhan's high school track coach in Boston have always piqued my interest and hang in the background of this book. And the echoes of my mother's, father's, brother's, and sister's work as journalists resonate throughout and compel me to keep asking questions.

I'd like to close with thanks to Sidney "Pepper" Smith, my late colleague at the National Endowment for the Arts. Pepper and I sat next to one another at work, and we both had very young sons. We were usually the first to arrive at the office and were often tired. In our last workday before the 2018 new year, we talked about the creative projects we hoped to complete when we emerged from the beautiful exhaustion known as early parenthood. Our lists were long. I told him about my long-languishing Mayo Williams manuscript; he stopped, looked me in the eye, and said, "You can't wait until you're not tired anymore: you need to finish this project now." Pepper died suddenly the following day. I took his last words to me as an order, and I expect that he is looking down, sipping a high-quality pour-over coffee, and smiling—knowing that I am still always tired but that the book is finally done.

Ink

Introduction
Black Bottom

Chicago, at the dawn of the Great Depression, circa 1930

Little Brother Montgomery and Irene Scruggs are dressed for business as they ride in the streetcar, the flickering cinders floating through the dank air along the shore of Lake Michigan. Both are seasoned performers, well versed in the unctuous and underhanded world of the race record business. Scruggs has made a name for herself as a blues singer in St. Louis, sitting in with Joe Oliver's and Kid Ory's jazz bands when they came to town. She has parlayed these gigs into a recording deal with OKeh records in 1924; more recently, she is recording under the pseudonym "Chocolate Brown" for Paramount in order to skirt her contract with OKeh. Irene Scruggs sings straight blues like "Hometown Blues," but Chocolate Brown sings dirty blues like "Must Get Mine in Front."

Little Brother Montgomery follows on her heels as the two step into an elevator to ascend the twenty-one floors of Chicago's massive American Furniture Mart building. They are here to see a man about a record deal. The new global music powerhouse, Decca Records, is headquartered on the top floor of the city's newest skyscraper, the opulent epicenter of the nation's furniture industry at 666 Lake Shore Drive in Chicago—an unusual setting for two Black blues musicians. Scruggs is the one who knows J. Mayo "Ink" Williams, the producer who runs Decca's race records division—a robust entity responsible for recording and marketing music made by and for African Americans. Still in his early twenties, Montgomery isn't used to the gilded world of Chicago's business district; his young life so far has been steeped in the rougher currents of the Great Migration. Born Eurreal Wilford Montgomery in 1906, he bears such a strong resemblance to his father, Harper, that he is called "Little Brother." The biracial Montgomery family, who are Black and Muscogee (Creek), make their home near the Mississippi border in Kentwood,

Louisiana. On the occasions that the visionary Creole jazz pianist Jelly Roll Morton crossed Lake Ponchartrain from New Orleans to play gigs near Kentwood, he would visit the Montgomery house, inspiring Little Brother to take up the piano at age four. By his teens, Montgomery was playing boogie-woogie piano in the steaming, violent world of the lumber and turpentine camps in Louisiana, Mississippi, and Arkansas. He teamed up with Chocolate Brown when he moved north to Chicago in 1928.

The elevator doors open on the twenty-first floor, revealing an all-white staff in the Decca waiting room.

"We'll let you know when you can see Mr. Williams," the secretary politely informs the two.

Montgomery and Scruggs sit fidgeting. An hour passes.

Williams's secretary approaches. Young, female, and white, she says demurely, "All right, you can see Mr. Williams," and leads them through the sprawling Decca complex to an office that smells vaguely of aftershave, liquor, and smoke. A cigar-chomping man in a three-piece suit approaches.

"I'm so glad to see you!" Scruggs exclaims. She and the man embrace. The three ease into chairs on opposite sides of an enormous desk and settle in for a long conversation.

Annoyed, Little Brother keeps asking himself, "Who the hell is that?" He's come to see Mr. Williams. This man can't be Mr. Williams, because—as Montgomery would recount the moment four decades later—he's "Black as night. As Black as these shoes. If he's any Blacker, he's blue. *Jet* Black. *Ugliest* Black."

After what seems an interminable wait, Scruggs gestures to Montgomery. "This is Little Brother. He wants to see you too."

Montgomery corrects her, saying, "I want to see Mister J. Mayo Williams."

"I'm ready," the Black man says, leaning back in his chair.

Confused but playing along, Montgomery talks with the man about a possible record deal before they get up to leave. On the elevator ride down, Little Brother vents his frustration at Chocolate Brown.

"I thought we were going to see Mr. Williams. That's some guy—"

"*That's* Mr. Williams!" says an impatient Scruggs.

Little Brother is stunned. "He sure is Black," he says. "I wasn't used to seeing nobody Black as him sitting behind one of these desks before, down where I come from in Louisiana and Mississippi."

"He's so Black," says Scruggs, "they call him 'Ink.'"[1]

Reintroducing Ink Williams

The playwright August Wilson's masterful *Ma Rainey's Black Bottom* opens with a familiar scene of the racist music industry of the 1920s: a white record producer, disdainful of the Black musicians he has to record, waits with irritation for the "Mother of the Blues," Ma Rainey, to arrive at the studio to cut a new batch of records.

Though it is ostensibly a historically based play about the great blues singer at the height of her commercial power in 1927 Chicago, it is also like a song that is emotionally true but factually incorrect. Yes, many predatory white record producers and executives enriched themselves while holding their noses at the Black artists they recorded—only Ma Rainey's real-life producer was J. Mayo "Ink" Williams, and Williams was Black.

This detail is significant in a number of ways—the opening scene sets the tone for the entire play and sets us up to see Rainey and her band as righteous foils to the producer, a depraved, white supremacist who extracts Black culture to enrich whites. And this, in turn, is a metaphor for American society as a whole.

But how does the emergence of Ink Williams onto the historical stage change our perception of the story of Ma Rainey and, by extension, of American music and society? What if we were to know that Williams was not only Black, but that he was—in 1927—an Ivy League graduate, a former World War I army officer, a nationally celebrated track-and-field athlete, a six-year veteran of the National Football League, and the first Black referee of a National Football League (NFL) game? And what if we were to know that Ma Rainey was just one of many iconic Black artists Williams introduced to records from the 1920s to the 1950s?

Perhaps readers did a double-take there, as it confounds our perception of race, cultural production, and professional sports in the pre–Civil Rights era. Williams's participation in the NFL is perhaps the most striking fact; the integration of professional sports is seen as a symbol of modern racial progress in America. Yet Williams had his NFL career *before* what we understand as the age of professional sports' integration. The story we have learned says that pro football was integrated in 1946 by four Black players: Kenny Washington, Woody Strode, Marion Motley, and Bill Willis; and major league baseball in 1947 by Jackie Robinson and Larry Doby. This version of American history shows us how sports helps move society forward on a path toward racial and cultural equality and justice. Yet how is our understanding of societal progress altered by the fact that pro football originated as an integrated sport only to become segregated in 1933 and *re*-integrated in 1946? The accomplishments of those pioneering 1946 athletes—who were conscious of this now-forgotten history—was a continuation of what Williams, his peers, and his predecessors, sought to accomplish in previous generations. With Williams and his contemporaries erased from the historical record, how is our appreciation and understanding of 1946 and 1947 distorted, enhanced, and diminished?

And what does it mean to be erased? We may ask ourselves *how* someone like Ink Williams was forgotten, but the more important question is *why*, and at what cost?

CHAPTER 1

Ink

Dan Williams was riding a fast train from Pine Bluff to Clio, Arkansas, with a pistol in his coat and his body hurtling toward destiny. A solid citizen of Pine Bluff's Black middle class, Dan had a steady job at the Bluff City Lumber Company's sawmill in Clio. He and his wife—both born in Tennessee at the dawn of Emancipation—were the fully literate parents of four and well respected by their neighbors. Dan was not someone you would expect to find riding a fast train with the intent to kill.[1]

The strong fibers of Williams's life had started to unravel earlier that day: Fred Hiller—Williams's coworker at the Clio sawmill and a resident of that frontier outpost milltown—had traveled to Pine Bluff to tell Dan's wife, Millie, that her husband was the cause of domestic troubles in Clio. Hiller's accusation painted a picture of a double life: Dan and Millie's married bliss in Pine Bluff, where Dan lived on the weekends, and infidelity and carousing over in Clio, where he lived during the workweek.

Dan had been with Millie for over twenty years. They had had their first child, Luther, in 1881. Back then, he had earned a living logging on the Mississippi—working and sleeping in rowdy and violent lumber camps in Tennessee, while Millie lived with her parents upriver in Monmouth, Illinois. They married in Monmouth in 1887 and had a second son that year who died at birth.[2] Although Dan's pay was good, the lifestyle in logging camps was brutal—clearing the stinking swamps and forests of the Mississippi Delta by day, and living in work camps filled with raggedy piano music, booze, and gambling by night. Perhaps in search of a less volatile occupation, or in need of a change of scenery after their infant son's death, the young Williams family moved five hundred miles southwest to Pine Bluff, Arkansas—less than fifty miles south of Little Rock and some one hundred miles due west of Clarksdale, Mississippi.

The Williamses arrived in Pine Bluff only sixty years after the forcible removal of the Indigenous Quapaw Nation. The recent advent of steamboats on the Arkansas River, followed by the expansion of the Cotton Belt Railroad, had opened up the region's prodigious timber reserves to national markets. The booming lumber industry (and related offshoots such as furniture manufacturing) caused the city's population to quintuple between 1870 and 1890.[3] Pine Bluff's ten thousand residents included a thriving Black middle class and a robust Black working class; by the time the Williamses moved there, several local Black men were active in national politics for the Republican party, including the former US congressman Jeremiah Haralson.[4] Like Dan, most people in Pine Bluff seemed to work for either the Sawyer-Austin Lumber Company or the Bluff City Lumber Company. Bluff City Lumber had sawmills in Kearney and Clio, with Pine Bluff serving as its headquarters.

Until Fred Hiller knocked on the Williamses' door in the fall of 1901, Dan's family had thrived in Pine Bluff. In 1894, they had welcomed a son, Mayo Jay Williams. A daughter, Marie, was born in 1897 and a son, Maurice, in 1898. By 1900, both Luther and Mayo were attending school. The family residence at 1206 West Fourth Avenue was on an all-Black street in Pine Bluff's Third Ward. Nearly all of their neighbors had been born elsewhere—Tennessee, Missouri, Kentucky. This included Dan's cousin Mattie, who roomed in the house next door. One street over was West Fifth Avenue, whose all-white residents had either immigrated from Ireland, England, Germany, and Canada, or were first-generation Americans of such descent. Like Dan, most residents in the Third Ward—both Black and white—were laborers.

When Dan Williams ran out the door with his pistol on the morning of November 17, 1901, he left behind thirty-nine-year-old Millie, twenty-year-old Luther, seven-year-old Mayo, five-year-old Marie, and three-year-old Maurice. They would never see him alive again. The *Pine Bluff Daily Graphic* reported that Williams left town to find a man "and came home in a box." When the train pulled in to Clio, Dan headed for Fred Hiller's house. The frontier work camp was carved raw from the Arkansas forest, and the smell of hot, freshly sawn timber filled the air. Hiller saw Williams coming, grabbed his Winchester rifle, and fired three shots. Williams was killed instantly. Hiller disappeared and was never apprehended. Residents of Clio accompanied Dan Williams's body back to Pine Bluff on the train. The incident was covered in three different local papers, most prominently on the front page of the *Pine Bluff Daily Graphic*.[5]

Devastated, humiliated, and in desperate need of income, Millie Williams packed up her four kids and moved back to Monmouth, Illinois. For seven-year-old Mayo Williams, the loss of his father was a cruel and stunning shock: he never spoke of his father or Arkansas again and never acknowledged Pine Bluff as his birthplace. On college transcripts, draft registration cards, social security cards, census forms, and in interviews—and even on his death certificate—Monmouth, Illinois was listed as his place of birth.

Millie moved back to the pastoral calm of Monmouth to be close to her parents, but the family's grief was compounded when Marie died soon after. Millie's mother, Jennie McFall, helped to support the family as a cook; Millie's stepfather, John, ran his own blacksmith shop. And though John and Jennie were both on their second marriage (they wed in 1896), they owned a home together. Both were able to read (John could also write), and they provided a stable presence during the tumultuous years to follow.

Into this mix came Miles Magruder. On the face of it, one might surmise that Millie married Miles (in 1905) to bring some stability to a single-parent household with four kids. Magruder was a potter. Monmouth and nearby Macomb were home to a thriving pottery industry, producing the kinds of storage jugs and drinking vessels that were commonplace and necessary household items at the turn of the century. A skilled laborer like Magruder was in demand, which brought him a decent wage. But Magruder was sketchier than he was stable: local newspaper accounts suggest that he was no stranger to the kinds of trouble chronicled in early blues and hillbilly music.

Magruder had a physical impairment whose origins hinted at a life lived on the fringes. Part of one hand was missing—sliced off while he was riding between boxcars en route to Galesburg in 1893, the same year he was fined five dollars for assaulting a man in Macomb. The following year, 1894, he was arrested and fined five dollars for drunkenness and had to be bailed out of prison. Two years later, in 1896 in the "Whiskey Row" neighborhood of Bushnell, Illinois (near Macomb), Magruder was a person of interest in the killing of Charles Hillyer. Hillyer, who was white, was killed when a brick hit his skull during a street brawl outside an integrated drinking establishment named Korn's, frequented by Black and white potters from the Macomb factory. Magruder was identified as being involved in the fight but was not fingered for the crime.

In 1903, around the time that he met Millie, Magruder was apprehended in what appears to have been a botched robbery on a train. In a series of events seemingly torn from a comedy sketch, Magruder and his friend Fisher Keithley were riding a train from Macomb to Colchester with another passenger. After leaving the train car briefly, the third passenger returned to find his bank roll of one hundred forty dollars missing from his coat. The man reported the crime to the train police, and Magruder and Keithley were interrogated. Keithley, in turn, accused *his* accuser of stealing his ring; after an extensive search, Magruder found most of the cash in Keithley's sock but claimed to have no idea how it got there. Magruder also claimed to have no idea how Keithley's ring showed up on his person. Two years after this incident, in July

1905, Miles Magruder married Millie Williams in a religious ceremony in Macomb; after the wedding, the newlyweds rode the train to Monmouth to begin their married life.

That year, Mayo Williams turned eleven years old. His older brother, Luther, was perpetually out of town working as a Pullman porter. Millie and Miles separated soon after; by 1909, Magruder was working in a pottery factory in Coffeyville, Kansas, some five hundred miles southwest of Monmouth. Magruder's influence on the younger Williams brothers—Mayo and Maurice—is unknown, but his presence in the house added an exclamation point to a period of painful chaos and change in the Williamses' family life.

After Miles Magruder left town, Mayo as we know him—a learned, charming young man who was an exceptionally gifted athlete—emerged against the picturesque backdrop of Monmouth, the seat of Warren County, Illinois. Founded in 1831 on the ancestral land of the Sac and Fox Nation, by the mid-nineteenth century Monmouth was a place of emerging urban development and racial progressivism. Judge Stephen A. Douglas—who gained lasting fame for his fierce debates and his presidential campaign against Abraham Lincoln in 1860—had presided over the 1841 extradition trial of the Mormon faith's founder, Joseph Smith, at the Warren County Courthouse in downtown Monmouth. By the Civil War, when a local man named Wyatt Earp and his family left town to go west, Monmouth was mostly a livestock farming community of about six thousand people fifty miles due south of Davenport, Iowa, and just fifteen miles west of Oquawka on the Mississippi River. Monmouth's local coal and clay mines created nonagricultural work, and their resources drove the growth of a number of industries. By 1869, Monmouth hosted a small manufacturing base of sewer pipe, pottery, paving brick, and cigar factories, claimed some eight churches, a CB&Q (Chicago, Burlington, and Quincy) Railroad depot, a small private academy, Monmouth College, four public schools, and a "colored school" (Ruger 1869).

Mayo Williams was fourteen years old in the spring of 1908 when he started his freshman year at Monmouth High.[6] By then, the town's population had grown to about ten thousand. Millie was supporting the family by doing housework, and Luther's income as a waiter on a Pullman train car helped the family's bottom line considerably. Like Pine Bluff, Monmouth was segregated by street. Also as in Pine Bluff, very few of the Williamses' adult Black neighbors were born in the state where they now lived. This was also the case for many of the Williamses' white neighbors, many of whom had immigrated from the British Isles and Europe. Although the streets were segregated, the Monmouth public schools had been integrated for a quarter of a century.[7] Of the one hundred twenty freshmen at Monmouth High, Mayo emerged as a singular personality. By the end of his first year, he had acquired the nickname that would follow him for the rest of his life: "Ink." Though history has attributed Williams's nickname to a wide (and wild) variety of personal characteristics—from his blurring speed, to his ability to "smear" opponents on the football field, to his tendency to rip off blues artists before the ink on their contracts had dried—the nickname unquestionably predates his accomplishments in athletics and as a record executive. Most likely, the nickname "Ink" (and "Inky") derives from the fact that he was a popular, dark-complexioned Black student at a mostly white school.[8]

In the fall of 1908, Williams exhibited astonishing speed, playing on the Maroon, the school's football team. Though only a substitute player his first year, by the fall of 1909 he was a full-fledged star for the Maroon, playing halfback and end. In those early days of American football, players played "both ways"—that is, they stayed on the field to play both offense and defense. (It wasn't until the mid-twentieth century that teams shifted to having players only on offense or defense.) The end position—which became Williams's position for the rest of his athletic career—required a multiskilled player with speed, strength, agility, and imagination. On offense, an end was eligible to both block and receive, requiring a fluid mindset that allowed improvisation as plays developed unexpectedly.

In June 1910, Williams had his first taste of long-distance travel. As reported in the *Monmouth Daily Atlas*, "Mrs. H. R. Moffet [sic] and party consisting of Leo and Victor Moffet, Leo Ryan, Mayo Williams, and Miss Mary Weed left this afternoon for [Manitou], Colo., where Mrs. Moffet will open up the Sunnyside Hotel which is a popular resort for Monmouth people during the summer months."[9] Mrs. Moffett was the wife of H. R. Moffett, editor of the *Daily Atlas* (which is ironic, given that the paper misspelled her last name); Mayo Williams was the only person of color in an otherwise all-white party that traveled over nine hundred miles together to open up a summer resort. Mayo and his brother Maurice would work at the Sunnyside Hotel during the next three summers, exposing them to the region's stunning red-rock canyons, natural springs, and recently rediscovered thousand-year-old Anasazi cliff dwellings just west of Colorado Springs. Though Williams never mentioned these westward trips in interviews later in life, they were regularly reported each summer in the Monmouth papers.

After returning from Manitou in the fall of 1910, Williams firmly established his reputation as a great football player. After playing one early season game at right halfback, he played left end in nearly every game for the next twenty years. Similarly, the 1910–11 school year chronicled Williams's emergence as a track-and-field powerhouse in the 100-yard, 220-yard, broad jump, and discus, and as a noteworthy member of the school debate team. The 1910 yearbook noted that Williams "was the fastest man on the team.

His offensive and defensive won for him the title of being the best end in this part of the state."

In the spring of 1911, Williams was elected captain of the track team.[10] That the young Black sprinter inspired such confidence in his mostly white teammates is a testament to Ink Williams's ability, charisma, and leadership and would be a harbinger of things to come. By the fall, the five-foot, eleven-inch junior started at left end for the Monmouth High football team, weighing in at a wiry 160 pounds, and helped the Maroon to a 7–2 season record.[11] Among the season highlights was a September exhibition game between Monmouth High and Monmouth College. Williams's dominating play that year prompted his coach to write in the yearbook:

> All, who have seen Williams play, have simply gasped in astonishment and are still wondering how he does it. His equal in dodging, speed, straight-arming, goal-kicking, tackling and grabbing forward-passes cannot be found in the central states.[12]

At eighteen, Williams was a small-town high school celebrity—a debater, a track team captain, a football star, a multisport varsity athlete whose name was regularly in print throughout the region. By these measurements, Monmouth was good to Williams. "I would've remained there," he said in later years, "but I wanted to get out and see the world."[13] Perhaps it was the influence of his older brother who, as a Pullman porter, had seen a bit of the country. Perhaps it was stories his father might have told him of life in a riverboat town. Whatever it was, Williams had ambitions and hungered for adventure.

On a high school football trip in the fall of 1911 to play Rockford High in the Divisional Championships, Williams saw a chance to make a break for it and took it. He remembered thinking, "This is as close to Chicago as I'll ever get." He took the train out of Rockford to Chicago, while the rest of the team headed back to Monmouth. His destination was Luther's place; his older brother was living at the intersection of 39th and State, overlooking the "L" (Chicago's elevated train line), in the neighborhood that became known as Bronzeville. The high schooler's big plans quickly turned into a caricature of a small-town rube act when he found himself mesmerized and paralyzed by big-city life. Years later, he cried with laughter at the memory, remembering, "I spent *all day lookin' at the 'L' go by!*" Luther, quickly growing tired of his wayward teenage brother, told him, "Listen, you, you're goin' back to Monmouth, 'cause you—you're no good up here." As he left the city, Ink thought he would never get so close to Chicago again.[14]

Williams's final track season was legendary, epitomized by his accomplishments in the "big eight" track meet against Monmouth's seven chief rival high schools: Davenport, Galesburg, Canton, Kewanee, Moline, Princeton, and Rock Island. "For Monmouth Williams was as usual the star," reported the

Monmouth Daily Atlas. "He secured fifteen of the twenty-two points and was forced to run ten races, counting heats, semi-finals and finals. The colored athlete won his heat in the two hundred and twenty-yard dash but the finals which was the tenth race in which he was entered proved to be too much of a strain on him and he was defeated."[15]

Though Williams tied his own state record for low hurdles (twenty-seven seconds, which he had set the previous year), his state record in the broad jump (also set his junior year) was broken by a student from Kewanee at twenty-one feet, seven inches. Ink's classmate Earl McKinnon also starred at the meet in the mile and half-mile. Between Williams and McKinnon, the Monmouth team finished third, close behind Davenport and Galesburg. At a schoolwide assembly, Coach Smith presented Ink Williams with a pennant to mark the accomplishment. Smith then readied his track stars for their ultimate meet: the 1912 Illinois State Track Finals in Champaign.

On Thursday, May 17, 1912, Williams and two teammates—Bruce Brady and Earl McKinnon—traveled with Coach Smith to Champaign. Williams, Brady, and McKinnon were all prominent members of the Monmouth student body: Brady was a standout on the debate team and would become a prominent lawyer in Maple City; Williams was the captain of the track team, a noted debater, and a football star; and McKinnon was the captain of the football team, a debater, the track team's best distance runner, and a future mayor of Monmouth. The Monmouth trio's underdog status caused regional news outlets to watch with great anticipation. Saturday morning, the teammates arrived at the track to find a stiff headwind blowing against the runners and a track that was teeming with thousands of competitors. Except for Williams's runaway junket to Chicago the year before, it was likely the biggest crowd he had ever been around in his life.

Though each race featured some seventy-five competitors, Williams singlehandedly helped Monmouth place eighth overall, finishing first in the fiftyyard dash (at 6.2 seconds) and second in the hundred-yard dash, just behind Paul Johnson's winning time of 10.6 seconds. It was a dramatic end to his senior year. He finished the season with an eye-popping twenty-three medals. The evening edition of the *Monmouth Daily Atlas* reported the accomplishments of the "dusky Monmouth athlete," noting that Bruce Brady finished fourth in the hundred-yard dash and that Lane Technical School had taken the top honors of the day.[16]

Lane Tech was a perennial powerhouse in Illinois high school athletics. Unlike Monmouth—which garnered eighth place through the accomplishments of one man—Lane Tech had an entire team of standout stars. Undoubtedly, the biggest star of the team was a young Black man named Fritz Pollard. At the state finals, Williams and Pollard forged the bonds of a lifelong friendship that defined the course of Ink's adult life. Frederick Douglass "Fritz"

Pollard hailed from Chicago—some two hundred miles east of Monmouth. Though he was also a gifted runner—finishing the 1912 Illinois State Track Finals with one of the top five best times in both the 440-yard dash and the 220-yard low hurdles—it was his explosive speed and startling agility on the football field that would propel Fritz to the Ivy League and eventually to the NFL.[17] Williams and Pollard spent some time together over the course of the long day and agreed to stay in touch.

After such excitement, graduation from high school must have felt anticlimactic. Williams spent the summer of 1912 working in Manitou, Colorado with three other Black kids from Monmouth, including his younger brother, Maurice ("Sam"). The Williams brothers had some excitement in late August when the helpers' quarters at the Sunnyside Hotel caught fire; Mayo and Sam were safe, but they lost their clothes in the fire.[18] They returned to Monmouth at the close of the summer to the familiar rhythm of life in Monmouth. Mayo's grandparents, John and Jennie McFall, still lived at 634 East Eleventh Avenue. John was still working as a blacksmith; Jennie was now the chef at Monmouth's Colonial Hotel. Ink's Aunt Hanna and Uncle Thomas Wallace—a house cleaner and a janitor at the local plow factory, respectively—lived nearby with Ink's cousin Elmer, who was a molder at the town's pottery and jug works. When John McFall passed away on February 28, 1914, Jennie moved to 509 South Fifth Street, where she ran a catering business just down the street from Ink and Millie Williams's home at 417 South Fifth Street.[19]

Mayo Williams was fond of his mother, Millie, whose down-to-earth personality made a lasting impression. "Because of my mother," Williams recalled, "I couldn't be what they called an uppity nigger."[20] And it was through his mother that Ink was first exposed to blues musicians in Monmouth, telling the historians Jim O'Neal and George Paulus:

> **WILLIAMS:** My first exposure to blues was I was a kid down in Monmouth, Illinois. That's all they could play, you see? Everybody could play *blues*. They couldn't play anything else *but* the blues, you see? And those twelve-bar blues was about the only thing that you ever heard.
> **O'NEAL/PAULUS:** You remember the names of some of the guys you heard who were playing around the time you were young?
> **WILLIAMS:** Yeah. One was named Ed Payne, a wonderful piano player . . . and there was Hazlee Wallace, Everett Murphy, and Frank Gray. All of them had little bands, you see? And they were all piano players.[21]

Wallace, Murphy, and Gray were musicians who would have been personally known to Williams and other members of the tight-knit Black community of Monmouth. Two were neighbors and coworkers to Williams's cousins, and one was established enough to list "bandleader" as his occupation in the 1910 census. None of them recorded, but the piano-driven dance rhythms of Monmouth blues—which Williams grew up clogging to—were what he would seek out in the sounds of virtually all of the blues musicians he recorded later in life. But it would still be an entire decade after Williams's high school graduation before the first commercial blues recording was made by Black musicians; in other words, "blues record producer"—which became Williams's lifelong occupation—was a nonexistent career choice as he pondered his future. Whatever the future held for Williams, he believed it was in the East.

CHAPTER 2

Howard

In the autumn of 1915, Mayo Williams enrolled as a third-year student at Howard University's Commercial College. From the moment Williams looked out the window as his train arrived in Washington, DC—past Union Station's coal- and ash-strewn train yards, past the gleaming dome of the nation's capital, to the stately townhouses of the political classes, and down through the humbler, mostly Black neighborhoods that encircled the city—everything was new.

All around Williams—from the urban enclave of DC through the rolling tobacco fields and towns of the Virginia and Maryland Tidewater—was a context of American life that was different from Monmouth. Not since he was seven and leaving Pine Bluff had Williams been in the former slaveholding section of the country, with its codified segregation and the backbreaking sharecropping carried out by poor tenant farmers. In Arkansas, the landscape was defined by money crops such as cotton that ran right up against the heavily timbered Ozarks. Monmouth, although rural and surrounded by farmland, small industry, riverboats, and trainyards, wasn't a cash-crop region. The Tidewater region of Virginia, along the Potomac, and the farms of Maryland to the east and north, was hardcore cash-crop country—tobacco, all the way west to the Piedmont and the Appalachian Blue Ridge—with scattered tenant farmers and the old, landed gentry—and the scourge of Jim Crow.

Williams had landed himself at Howard after an intense and extensive college search. He had watched his track, football, and debate teammates go off to college to pursue careers in business and law—a future he felt he could actualize despite the obstacles of institutionalized racism. He considered his possibilities while reading through hundreds of college catalogs. He was also reading the *Crisis*, the journal of the National Association for the Advancement of Colored People (NAACP), edited (and often penned) by W. E. B. Du Bois, and realized he was hungry for a deeper engagement with an Afrocentric experience. "I'd never gone to a colored school," Williams later told the music historian Bill Russell, "and I wanted to get some of that background in my whole system."[1]

If an Afrocentric college education inspired by the *Crisis* was what Williams was after, he had come to the right place. When the integrationist gains of Reconstruction crumbled in 1877, one of the enduring legacies of abolition was what are now known as Historically Black Colleges and Universities, or HBCUs. The first HBCUs—Cheyney (1834) and Lincoln (1854) in Pennsylvania, and Wilberforce (1856) in Ohio—were in northern destinations along the Underground Railroad. During and just after the Civil War, Southern HBCUs were founded in former Confederate states, where racial segregation was legally enforced until the 1960s. The first HBCUs—North and South—have long been considered the most prestigious. By 1915 those early HBCUs closest to either side of the Mason-Dixon Line—Lincoln, Howard (1867), Morgan (1867), and Hampton (1868) had established strong athletic rivalries.

Howard's Commercial College was the predecessor to Howard's School of Business and also appears to have been a kind of college preparatory school. On his 1915 school forms, Williams is listed as both a third-year student and as "unclassified." The possibility remains that he was enrolled elsewhere in the 1913–14 and 1914–15 academic years, but Williams's papers at Howard list his previous residence as both Monmouth and Chicago, and news accounts of him during those years reflect the same. Regardless, at Howard, Williams set himself on course for higher education, with an interest in business, at a prestigious Black university with a noteworthy athletic program.

Williams's enrollment at Howard in 1915 made him one of fewer than 1,694 Black students (about .0002 percent of the overall Black population of the United States, roughly 10 million) who were enrolled in what the US Department of Education considered "college grade" universities.[2] Most of those 1,694 students were male, and most were enrolled at either Howard University, Fisk University, or Meharry Medical College. (Both Fisk and Meharry are in Nashville, Tennessee.) Williams was part of a relative surge in Black college enrollment, compared with the previous three centuries. From the time the first college was founded in North America (Harvard College, 1636), no Blacks are known to have received a college degree until Alexander Lucius Twilight graduated from Middlebury College in Vermont in 1823. By the close of the Civil War, the total number of Black college graduates ever was forty. By 1900, the historical total was still fewer than five hundred.[3] The rise of HBCUs such as Howard University changed Black access to higher education in fundamental ways. By the time of Williams's arrival at Howard, a handful of noteworthy Black men and women had received PhDs from some of the nation's most prestigious institutions, a Black football player had been awarded All-American status, and the first Black fraternity and sorority had been established. Williams benefited directly from these pioneering efforts.

Howard University, a coeducational institution, was founded in 1867 by an act of Congress and named after General Oliver Otis Howard. A Medal of Honor recipient who had lost an arm in the Civil War, General Howard was a Radical Republican and an evangelical Christian dedicated to voting rights for Black Americans throughout the South. The "Christian General" (as he was known throughout the US Army) served as the commissioner of the Freedmen's Bureau, a branch of the War Department that was created to assist emancipated Blacks and other people displaced by the Civil War. General Howard was the university's first president. In 1873, he left to command the brutal US Army campaigns against the Apache peoples in the Arizona Territory.

Known in later decades as "Chocolate City" on account of its majority African American population, in 1915 Washington, DC was still a mid-sized city of just over three hundred thousand, about a third of whom were Black, and teeming with ideas and expressive culture of Black America. Williams enrolled in the last year of Alain Locke's first stint as a professor of English at Howard, during the formative years of Locke's ideas of cultural pluralism and ten years before publication of his groundbreaking book *The New Negro*. The Black neighborhoods north of the capitol and surrounding Howard's campus were home to a sixteen-year-old DC native named Edward Kennedy (later "Duke") Ellington, who was working just a half mile from Howard's main quadrangle (the "Yard") as a soda jerk at the Poodle Dog Café.

At Howard, Williams was thrust into the influential orbit of the NAACP, founded in 1909. Williams encountered the fledgling civil rights organization up close at a flashpoint in its evolution. Indeed, the segregationist policies of President Woodrow Wilson and the sensational popularity of the film *The Birth of a Nation*—which was released in February 1915 and romanticized the Ku Klux Klan while portraying southern Blacks as sexual predators—galvanized the NAACP, causing its membership, political influence, and profile (particularly that of its philosophical leader, W. E. B. Du Bois) to soar. Within Ink's first few months in Washington, the campus chapter of the NAACP sponsored lectures on campus by the educator and orator William Pickens, the muckraking journalist and NAACP cofounder Charles Edward Russell, the mathematician and NAACP *Crisis* editor (and dean of Howard's College of Arts and Sciences) Kelly Miller, and the activist Archibald Grimké.

Grimké's presence on campus illustrates the span of history that Mayo Williams had stepped into at Howard. Born into slavery in Charleston, South Carolina in 1849, Grimké was enslaved by both his biological father, Henry, and his own half-brother, Montague. Grimké—who also was a relative of the abolitionist Grimké sisters—went on to graduate from Lincoln and received a law degree from Harvard. He eventually became involved with Frederick Douglass's National Council of Colored People, developed public disagreements with Booker T. Washington, was a founding member of the NAACP, and ultimately navigated an intellectual space between Washington's and Du Bois's positions on the strategy for racial progress in America. Grimké served as the US consul to Santo Domingo (now the Dominican Republic) and was the president of the NAACP chapter in Washington when Williams enrolled at Howard.

The college chapter of the NAACP also sponsored a series of lectures by Alain Locke, "Race Contacts and Inter-Racial Relations." The famed African American sociologist E. Franklin Frazier, a native of nearby Baltimore, was finishing his senior year at Howard when Williams arrived. The trajectory of both Locke's and Frazier's careers and intellectual concepts suggests that in 1915 Howard was a place where historical and contemporary Black culture was considered to have both merit and value in its vernacular forms, not solely as a source of potential that might be gentrified and uplifted. Williams would later apply this concept to his work in recording and marketing Black vernacular music, but those days were still unimaginable to him and his peers in 1915.

The NAACP chapter at Howard circulated a campuswide petition during the fall, signed by most of the students, that sought to prevent local screenings of *The Birth of a Nation*. It is not known if Williams signed the petition, but it is clear that discourse about racial progress and justice was the steady intellectual diet at Howard and would have been difficult for Williams to avoid. After spending the first two decades of his life as a racial minority in the small cities of Pine Bluff and Monmouth, Mayo Williams's sudden immersion in majority Black life at Howard must have been a revelation. It is also possible that it was disorienting and overwhelming: the newspapers of Williams's adolescence suggest that most conversations about racial progress and justice were held behind church doors, in small living-room gatherings for church societies, or in social settings within the Black community. And despite the fact that Williams, his teammates, and his coaches chose to travel to long-distance games and meets together in high school, the likelihood that classrooms at Monmouth High, or even Monmouth College, ever had open discussions about racial justice in the United States is very slim.

Williams's comfort zone was athletics, and he very quickly established himself as one of the most prominent members of the Howard football team, holding down the position of left end. Howard employed what was then considered the new, "modern" style of football—emphasizing speed and an open field of play. In this way, Howard's approach to the game marked a significant evolution from the game's earliest days, when it was still emerging from the raw stuff of rugby on the fields of Princeton College in 1869. Those first few decades of the game would be mostly unrecognizable to modern-day fans, with formations that favored brute force without sophistication. Forward passing did not exist, slugging opponents in the face was commonplace, broken bones were a regular occurrence, and mass plays such as the flying wedge and the haymaker proved so deadly that in 1905, eighteen deaths resulted from football games, twice the average of the previous five seasons. President Theodore Roosevelt—himself a fan of the game's manly brawn—intervened. In October, he summoned the leadership of several major football programs (Princeton, Yale, and Harvard) to the White House and pushed them to make the game less violent, but deaths and injuries continued. In December, the chancellor of New York University called together thirteen institutions to reform the rules. Later that month, sixty-two colleges and universities founded the precursor to the National Collegiate Athletic Association (NCAA).

The big four—Princeton, Harvard, Yale, and Columbia—dominated the early game in both the news and the national imagination. Inspired by the collegiate game, municipal athletic clubs spawned amateur football teams in the urban Northeast and Midwest by the late 1800s—a network that, in time, became the framework of the professional game. The physicality of early football was seen as an extension of Christian fortitude, and the popularity of the college game and of the municipal athletic clubs flourished in schools and communities well beyond the Ivy League. This included HBCUs such as Howard as well as government boarding schools for Native Americans. And it was the latter—specifically the Carlisle Indian Industrial School in south-central Pennsylvania—whose resourcefulness and creative play making, borne of necessity on account of the Carlisle students' relatively leaner builds, revolutionized the game in the first years of the twentieth century. The extraordinary feats of Carlisle's star players—Jim Thorpe, Pete Calac, Joe Guyon, and Gus Welch—and the strategic wizardry of Carlisle's head coach, Glenn "Pop" Warner, opened the field of play, introduced forward passing, reliable drop kicking, men in motion, and trick plays. In 1912, when Thorpe and his Carlisle team stunned the nation with an upset of Army (West Point's team included the young Dwight D. Eisenhower), the Carlisle style of play was widely adopted, making the game smarter, faster, safer, and far more interesting to watch.

Though elements of Carlisle's innovative style of play—specifically the forward pass—had already reached Illinois high school squads like Williams's at Monmouth, Howard's 1915 team was built in Carlisle's image. Given this new system of play on Howard's football team, the heady intellectual atmosphere on campus, the Afrocentric worldview in the classroom, the political sophistication of classmates, and the very real social class status and aspirations of many of Howard's students, Williams was on unfamiliar turf.

The fighting spirit of the Howard football team was in question by November: they had lost to Lincoln and defeated Morgan early in the 1915 season, but the school's opinion of its team would be formed by how it fared against its chief rival, Hampton, in their annual Thanksgiving Day showdown. The Howard newsletter promoted the game for weeks. Students traveled by steamship from Washington down the Potomac, well past Mount Vernon, into the Chesapeake Bay, and south to Hampton, Virginia. Hampton—founded in 1868 near the 1619 landing site of the first ship bearing enslaved Africans—had emerged directly out of educational programs for Blacks who had sought refuge at Fort Monroe for the duration of the Civil War. (Fort Monroe remained a Union stronghold in Virginia.) Hampton's most influential student—Booker T. Washington—graduated in 1875.

As Howard's steamship pulled into the harbor at Hampton, Williams, who was interested in colonial history, must have been intrigued by the proximity of Hampton to Yorktown—and to the celebrated Black nightlife of Norfolk and Newport News. But on Thanksgiving Day, he had no time for sightseeing. By 2:15 pm, five thousand jovial fans were crowded along the sidelines as dueling marching bands played. The players took the field for a crisp set of warmup drills, and the crowd—noted for an atypically large turnout of female specta- tors—began to cheer as the team captains met at midfield with the referees for a coin toss. Howard won the toss, opted to defend, and absorbed relentless hits from the Hampton running backs. By 2:35, Hampton had scored its first of three unanswered touchdowns. The final score of 18–0 could have been worse, as Hampton missed all three of its extra-point kicks and was stopped just short of the end zone several times. Williams—who had two different end runs for twelve yards each—garnered praise from Howard's scribes for being one of the few standouts on a forgettable squad. It was a long boat ride home for Howard; the loss cast a pall on campus that would linger for the rest of the school year.

With the football season over, Williams's focus turned back to academics. During the year, students attended guest lectures at chapel services by speak- ers such as Cecilia Carolyn Kennedy (the wife of William J. Yerby, a Black physician who was the American consul in Dakar) on the state of affairs in West Africa. The campus included five Black fraternities, including a chapter of Alpha Phi Alpha. Whether Williams joined Alpha Phi Alpha at Howard is unknown, but his acquaintance with the first Black fraternity would blossom in later years.

By mid-February, Williams and the indoor track team were training hard for what was expected to be the largest gathering ever of Black track-and- field athletes in Washington, DC. The meet—which brought together Black colleges, high schools, and amateur clubs from the mid-Atlantic and upper South—had the added buzz that Howard P. Drew would be the featured star. Drew's name has largely faded from popular memory today, but at the time he was one of the best-known Black athletes in any sport, often heralded by both the Black and white press as the "world's fastest human." Unlike football, track and field was then America's most racially integrated sport and enjoyed a level of attention in the popular press that is inconceivable today. Drew—who made the famed 1912 Olympic team (along with the gold-medal decathlete and pentathlete Jim Thorpe)—brought a stature to the DC meet that must have filled Williams with great excitement.

Nevertheless, bad feelings from Howard's loss to Hampton lingered for months. Essays in the *Howard University Journal* (the school newspaper) lambasted the team well into the spring, critiquing everything from school spirit to the flaws of the football, track, basketball, and baseball programs. Underclassmen were excoriated for failing to attend games in large numbers (and for failing to cheer when they did show up). Sports writers and zealous alumni wrote editorials that ranged from scathing to motivational. One late April article in the *Journal* expressed admiration for Hampton's athletic program—which was considered to be the best of all HBCUs—while singling out the football team for its failings.

If Howard's sports writers made Ink Williams wish he could play elsewhere, that wish was granted late in his freshman year. Howard's students and faculty were playing a long game, working to change the national discourse about race in America over the course of a century. Williams's character—like his instincts as a sprinter, his surprising explosiveness as a left end, or his growing inclination to gamble—was defined by a high-risk, high-yield short game. In the spring of 1916, he took a low-risk, high-yield gamble on a contact from an old friend.

Since last they met four years earlier, Fritz Pollard had become Brown University's most famous undergraduate since John D. Rockefeller Jr. and arguably the most famous Black college student of the early twentieth century. Pollard had left Chicago after high school in 1913 in search of an eastern football powerhouse to play for. His older brother Leslie had starred in football for Dartmouth College in Hanover, New Hampshire, and the younger Fritz aspired to no less. In those days, accomplished football players could readily bypass the typical admission processes, even at elite private colleges, if the head coach chose to take them on. Between the fall of 1913 and 1915, Pollard made the squad and enrolled (in that order) at Dartmouth, then Harvard, then Bates college before settling in at Brown in 1915.[4] Pollard's performance grabbed national headlines that fall as the first Black halfback to achieve All-American status and propelled Brown to the second Tournament of Roses (the Rose Bowl, played in January 1916). In one short year, he had become the closest thing college football had to a celebrity.

Brown University's assistant football coach, Archie Hahn, worked closely with Pollard to maximize the explosive speed that garnered Pollard his nickname, the "Human Torpedo." Hahn—known as the "Milwaukee Meteor"—knew more than a little about both speed and celebrity. Born in Dodgeville, Wisconsin in 1880, Hahn starred in football and track at Michigan State. He earned three gold medals at the 1904 Summer Olympics in St. Louis (sixty-meter, hundred-meter, and two-hundred-meter sprints), and again won the hundred-meter sprint at the 1906 Intercalated Olympic Games in Athens, Greece.

Brown had recruited Hahn away from Whitman College to serve as its track coach and assistant football coach in 1915. He held a law degree from Michigan State, and was deadly serious about running. (He eventually authored the original bible of sprinting, *How to Sprint: The Theory of Sprint Racing*, in 1925.) As the Milwaukee Meteor got to know the Human Torpedo, the two men realized they had a shared history in Illinois; Hahn had worked for one year in Monmouth, Illinois as the athletic director of Monmouth College, where he was also the head coach of the football team.

Hahn asked Pollard if he knew a player who had impressed him in football scrimmages between Monmouth College and Monmouth High School: Ink Williams. Pollard explained that they were friends and that Williams was currently at Howard University. Hahn asked Pollard to track Williams down with an invitation to come to Brown on a football scholarship.

To Williams, this was exciting news. Although he was happy at Howard, "I just dropped everything": an Ivy League education on an athletic scholarship fit the ambitious Williams's aspirations. Although he would still be required to take Brown's entrance exams, Williams was not concerned. "There were two Grade A schools, colleges in the country that didn't require mathematics as an entrance course," Williams later recounted: one was Oberlin College, and one was Brown. Additionally, Hahn and Pollard told Williams that Brown was one of the few Ivy League schools where freshman could play varsity football.[5]

The Ivy League schools of the Northeast tended to admit only the smallest number of exceptional Black applicants. One Black applicant to Brown in 1927 recalled being told by the registrar that Brown accepted students "if they are black, blue, brown or pink. If they do the work, they stay."[6] However, there was an understanding between the administration and alumni that Blacks, Jews, and other minorities would never be admitted in sizable numbers. Brown University had been closed to African Americans before the Civil War, after which abolitionists began to have an impact on school policy. The first African American students—Inman Page and George Milford—graduated in 1877. Like Williams, Page attended Howard before enrolling at Brown. (Milford went to Howard for law school after graduating from Brown.) Still, Black enrollment was very low in 1916 when Williams was accepted as a member of the Brown University class of 1920.[7]

For reasons we may never know, Williams's year at Howard University would be, like his time in Pine Bluff, a well-guarded secret. Howard is not listed on his transcripts at Brown, and he acknowledged his enrollment there in only one of the five known recorded interviews he gave in his life. Two small articles in Boston newspapers previewing Williams's debut track meets for

Brown make brief reference to his year at Howard (one article was reprinted in the *Kansas City Star*), but otherwise his year at Howard was a mystery. History may never reveal why Williams kept so quiet about it—perhaps he was concerned it would limit his athletic eligibility at Brown. But Williams's time at Howard expanded his awareness of Black intellectual discourse, oriented him to the foremost thinkers in Black progressive thought, illuminated a sense of the African diaspora, and gave him a taste of the athletic landscape of the HBCUs. All of these experiences would prove very valuable down the road.

CHAPTER 3

Brown

When Mayo Williams got off the train at Union Station in Providence, Rhode Island, he walked into a wall of coastal humidity and industrial smog. Autumn weather in the heart of the city's manufacturing center was not always pretty, a sooty counterpoint to the nearby Rhode Island State House, which loomed over thrumming mills and clanging machine shops. Williams probably did a double take: completed just eleven years earlier, the State House, with its gleaming white neoclassical design and enormous marble dome, was strikingly similar to the US Capitol and the fourth largest in the world, and said much about Providence's economic vitality as an international textile center. Walking past the shops at the confluence of the Moshassuck and Providence Rivers, Williams slowly climbed up College Hill towards the boarding house at 72 Meeting Street where he would live during his freshman year.[1] Looking westward from the towering hillside, Williams had a panoramic view of massive red-brick mills surrounded by neighborhoods teeming with new immigrants from Italy, Ireland, Portugal, Russia, Armenia, and French Canada. The only similarity with Monmouth or Pine Bluff, was that Williams's new residence was nestled in a thin sliver of homes and churches that comprised the heart of Providence's Black community.

Three blocks away from Williams's boardinghouse was the Brown University campus, which radiated a very different energy. Brown's faculty and student body brimmed with a white, Protestant, upper-middle-class, gentlemanly veneer that belied a nation deeply troubled by domestic and international anxiety and trauma: trench warfare in Europe, the courting of America by Allied and Central powers, blood-soaked labor strikes, intense xenophobia, rising socialist and anarchist movements, widespread corruption in professional sports, revolution brewing in Russia, genocide in Armenia, and a soaring cost of living. Largely insulated from these concerns, Brown's all-male student body of one thousand was mainly focused on two subjects, both covered ad nauseam on the pages of the *Brown Daily Herald*: football and the presidential campaign of 1916. Charles Evans Hughes, a Republican and an 1881 graduate of Brown, had strong national support in his bid for the presidency against the incumbent, Woodrow Wilson. In striking counterpoint to campus discourse at Howard, President Wilson's domestic policies were never discussed—rather, the campus seemed to favor Hughes mainly because he was an alumnus of Brown. Moreover, students favored discussion of Ivy League football over debates about *The Birth of a Nation*.

To excel in football at Brown University was to achieve renown on campus, and a place of importance in the minds of alumni and fans of the college game. In those pre–National Football League (NFL) days, college football *was* football in the minds of the American public. Students at Brown were interested in all angles of the game: detailed accounts of daily practices, developments in tackle-dummy designs, and weekly predictions. Brown was coming off the most successful season in its history, and great things were expected of the sophomores Fritz Pollard and Clair Purdy—who had carried the 1915 Brown squad to the second Tournament of Roses game just nine months earlier.

Like all football players at Brown, Williams was required to arrive several weeks before the start of classes for preseason training. Black, midwestern, and from a family of laborers, Williams stood out in the small student body, most of whom hailed from white, wealthy New England or mid-Atlantic families. Williams's presence was an early indicator of changing tides in Providence and in Brown University's racial history.

Founded on the tribal homelands of the Narragansett and Wampanoag peoples, Providence Plantations—Roger Williams's free religious colony—was nestled between the colonies of Massachusetts and Rhode Island. (Eventually Rhode Island and Providence Plantations were consolidated.) Rhode Island became a major import-export hub of southern New England. Although Rhode Island was the first of the thirteen colonies to outlaw slavery, it was a hearty participant in the international slave trade. Over one thousand transatlantic slave-trade routes originated from Rhode Island ports. Ultimately over one hundred thousand human captives were brought to the United States from Africa prior to 1808. The slave trade enriched local merchants and their families. One of these families—the Brown family—used their financial largesse to found Brown University. And although Williams was almost certainly unaware of Brown's direct connection to the slave trade, his racial outsider status stood in stark contrast to his experience during the previous year at Howard.

Immediately, Williams steeled himself against the indignity of being unlikely to make the varsity football squad, despite being one of the best players anywhere around Providence. Although Fritz Pollard had made the

Brown eleven in his first year, Pollard and Williams sensed the school was unlikely to make room for more than one Black player on varsity. Nevertheless, Williams fought relentlessly all fall to make the team. Tryouts were exhausting and vicious. Freshmen and others vying to make the squad were often brutalized to the brink of mutilation. For the few Black college athletes like Pollard and Williams who played for otherwise white teams, the combative nature of the tryouts was greatly magnified. Paul Robeson, a Black freshman at Rutgers University in 1915, recalled his first football scrimmage:

> One boy slugged me in the face and smashed my nose, just smashed it. That's been a trouble to me as a singer every day since. And then when I was down, flat on my back, another boy got me with his knee, just came over and fell on me. He managed to dislocate my right shoulder.[2]

Still, Fritz Pollard remembered that the gridiron was also the one place where retaliatory violence against whites could go unpunished:

> The football field was really the only place where you could do anything that amounted to retaliation—beating up on those white boys. When you got mad about the racial thing it sure made you play all the harder.[3]

Williams, like other Black players, employed tactics of self-defense, which generally included the tackled player lying on his back and pedaling his spiked shoes in the air to deter any late hits by opposing players.[4] Williams also displayed a kind of self-defense that was interpreted as an infectious enthusiasm for the game: he was noted for his tendency to emerge from a pile of bodies with a whoop and a smile. Williams's excellent preseason play was noticed by the *Brown Daily Herald*, which believed he deserved a place at end on the A team in scrimmages. The head coach, Ed "Robbie" Robinson—a former football star at Brown and the former head coach at Nebraska—certainly would have noticed Williams's talent but did not select him for the varsity squad come opening day against Rhode Island State.[5]

Between practices, Williams could plainly see nepotism at work during the freshman orientation activities. In a reception for freshmen at the student union, he heard rhetoric from upperclassmen about Brown being a "democracy where every man starts even" and where students must "cast aside all matters of birth, family or former record and start with a clean slate." The university president, William H. P. Faunce, then spoke to the students about the wonder of meeting the "sons of my old college friends as if the generations were all woven together." Such would be the brackish waters of legacy and opportunity that Williams would learn to swim in over the next four years. The following morning at chapel service, Williams and the other freshmen received the beanies they were required to wear daily for the duration of their first year.[6]

On and off the field, Williams took his cues from Fritz Pollard, who subscribed to the belief that an athlete of his caliber should not have to worry about keeping up academically. Ink Williams's first semester course load included English, French, Latin, political science, and physics.[7] Fritz had a family to support (his wife and young son lived eighty miles west in Springfield, Massachusetts), so he opened his own clothes-pressing shop out of his Hope College dorm room. (Rhode Island is known as the "Hope State"; Hope College is the name of one of the original dormitories at Brown where Pollard lived in a single room.) Ink Williams spent much of his time hanging out in Pollard's dorm room and quickly became a partner in the business. Their customers were their classmates.

Ink Williams, Fritz Pollard, and Rudolph Fischer were the only Black students at Brown University in 1916. Their presence on campus struck classmates as curious and exotic.[8] When Pollard had debuted on the practice field the previous year, throngs had turned out for their first glimpse of a Black man playing football.[9] The biographies or autobiographies of three Black students enrolled at Brown between 1915 and 1927, and the history of the Providence chapter of the Black fraternity Alpha Phi Alpha, note an absence of overt racial hostility directed toward Black students.[10] (Incidents of hostile antisemitic acts committed by students against their Jewish classmates are recorded, however.) Black students attended integrated theaters, dined in integrated restaurants, spoke in integrated classrooms, showered in integrated locker rooms, and sat with whomever they wished in the integrated dining hall. And although all of this was unusual compared with Williams's year in Washington, DC, Black southerners who attended Brown during the Jim Crow era noted with bitter irony that northern pretenses to freedom and equality fell far short of ideal. The social life of Brown revolved almost entirely around fraternity life (as did the "old boys network"), but Black students were entirely excluded from joining fraternities. Thus Blacks were effectively barred from mainstream social life at Brown. Additionally, social avenues that did not explicitly bar Blacks from attending often did so implicitly by exceeding Black students' financial means. Williams, Pollard, and other Blacks at Brown had to seek out off-campus social events in Providence and Boston. Campus rumor had it that Williams and Pollard wore their customers' clothing to these events.

Athletics did provide an avenue for Williams to forge friendships across racial lines, most notably with his classmate Dunc Annan. Like Williams, Annan hailed from Illinois. But like many of his white classmates, Annan had attended boarding school, excelling in football at Keewatin Academy in Prairie du Chien, Wisconsin.[11] Williams's and Annan's experiences as freshmen demonstrate how racial discrimination manifested itself at Brown. Williams was regularly pitted against the Brown starting eleven in practices—typically charged with covering Fritz Pollard, the team's best player—but he was relegated to the role of substitute on the lowly Brown seconds (junior varsity).[12] When Brown thumped Amherst on October 14, 1916 by a score of 69–0 (Pollard scored three touchdowns), a tide of replacements—including the freshman Dunc Annan in his first varsity appearance—scored thirty-five points.[13] Williams—though able, willing, and talented—did not play.

In this racial environment, it is ironic, then, that the campus was rocked by a rumor that Fritz Pollard was scheduled to speak on Woodrow Wilson's behalf at an upcoming presidential campaign rally—a rumor made all the more profound by Wilson's pro–Jim Crow policies. But that rumor was squashed on October 19:

POLLARD DENIES THAT HE WILL SPEAK FOR WILSON

"Fritz" Pollard '19, comes out with a flat denial that he has been engaged by the Brown Wilson Club as a member of its speaking staff and furthermore he says he is a Hughes man. An article appeared in several dailies Tuesday reporting his addition to the speaking staff of the Wilson Club.[14]

Williams marveled at Pollard's trailblazing at Brown. A single issue of the *Brown Daily Herald* reported that Fritz Pollard was a political player, a stellar athlete, and an entertainer who played trombone with the student band at a recent freshman smoker.[15] One can only imagine the mixture of amusement and admiration Ink Williams had for Pollard while the two men washed and pressed their classmates' clothes together in Pollard's dorm room.

Ink Williams did have one small victory, though. In a late October campuswide interclass track meet, he was the only freshman to score points for the class of 1920, beating out Brown's star sprinter, William Albrecht, in the hundred-yard dash. Adding to the luster of the day, Williams came in second in the two-hundred-twenty-yard dash, just behind Albrecht's 24.6 seconds. The freshman class came in fourth with nine points—all scored by Williams.[16]

On October 28, Brown faced off against Rutgers. The Rutgers game was of no athletic consequence to Ink Williams, but it presented another personal encounter that would help shape his adult life.[17] That day, Fritz Pollard introduced Williams to Rutgers' star end, Paul Robeson. As Williams remembered, "We were friends from then on."[18] Robeson and Pollard had become friends during the summer while working at the nearby Narragansett Pier, a popular seaside destination in Narraganset, Rhode Island. Of the game, Pollard recalled Robeson "staring me down with that smile of his, and joking as he came at me, 'Now Fritz be careful. Look out! Fritz, I don't want to hurt you.'"[19] Robeson's taunts were not enough to stop Pollard, however, and Brown won, 21–3.[20]

On Election Day—Tuesday, November 7—the *Brown Daily Herald* announced that Charles Evans Hughes had won the presidency. The newspaper never ran a retraction or a correction or mentioned the fact that President

Woodrow Wilson—despite conceding victory to Hughes—had narrowly carried California and in doing so, won both the popular and electoral votes.²¹ Despite Hughes's loss, campus enthusiasm for the Brown football team remained at an all-time high. Brown was undefeated as it rolled into New Haven, Connecticut on November 11, fresh off a 42–0 victory over Vermont the week before.²² Some five hundred students boarded the train in Providence for New Haven to watch the game firsthand.

Given the proximity of Yale to New York City and Yale's enormous importance in the evolution of the sport's popularity, Yale football was the darling of the New York press, and its star players were the vaunted heroes of football fans across the United States. A football powerhouse famed for its huge, muscular players, Yale typically drew capacity crowds at its forty-thousand-seat Yale Bowl. Yale was one of the few Ivy League schools that had not integrated its football team, and the alumni who had enabled segregation filled the stands. The year before, Fritz Pollard had stunned a hostile Yale crowd with his dramatic long gains. Pollard played with grim determination and the awareness that he carried the aspirations of other Black students and athletes on his back. By this time, Black students at New England universities had developed a strong intercollegiate social network that was beginning to coalesce in the formation of Black fraternities such as Alpha Phi Alpha. William H. Ashby, a Black student at Yale, recalled meeting Fritz Pollard at one of these gatherings prior to the 1916 Brown–Yale game. Ashby and his friends had followed Pollard's athletic exploits through the campus newspaper, where he had been described as a "burly Negro," so they were wholly unprepared for the Brown star's diminutive appearance:

> This couldn't be, it simply couldn't. At most, this fellow could not weigh more than 145 pounds. Our shock was beyond words. The fellow had lied. He was playing a trick on us.
> On our way to the field we were depressed, literally and honestly scared to death. We knew the size of the men on the Yale line. They would murder this little man.
> We went to the Brown side of the field wanting to give Pollard as much moral support as possible, but also because we knew that there would be animosity towards us in the Yale stands. We would be baited with the foulest and vilest epithets hurled right into our teeth, and we could do nothing about it.²³

As Ashby and his friends stood in solidarity on the Brown sidelines, the Yale Bowl filled with chants of "Catch that nigger! Kill that nigger!"²⁴ Pollard was undeterred. With Brown trailing at the end of the first half, Pollard rose to the occasion. The *Brown Daily Herald* reported:

Pollard did it. It was a few minutes after the start of the second half: the score, Yale 6, Brown 0. Brown's ball on Yale's 40-yard line. The signals rang out; the lines crashed together; and out of the confusion there emerged with the ball a streak of lightning sprinting for the Yale goal-line.[25]

Pollard and Brown scored three unanswered touchdowns in the second half, making for a major upset by thumping Yale, 21–6. "For Brown, Fritz Pollard was the hero of the day," proclaimed the *Brown Daily Herald*.

Brown's victory captivated the nation. On November 14, George "Herbert" Daley—the then-famous football critic for the *New York World*—arrived in Providence to watch the team work out.[26] The *New York World* scribe had some interesting observations regarding the status of football at Brown, telling a reporter for the *Brown Daily Herald*:

> Some things struck me forcibly. . . . In the first place, Freshmen are eligible for the [varsity] eleven, but the scholastic requirements, both for coming and staying are such that the team is made up of real students. Further than that, football gets too little consideration from the faculty, not too much. It is hard to get all of the men together even for one afternoon a week. Team play must be developed in spots. In plain words, biology is playing the dickens with football rightly or wrongly, depending on the point of view.[27]

On November 15, with the team preparing for the Harvard game, Williams grabbed Herbert's attention:

> One of the features of the scrimmage was the playing of J. M. Williams at halfback. He made gain after gain around Team A's ends, twisting and side stepping his way through the defence [sic]. His work on the defence [sic] was also very good.[28]

Brown's varsity squad had sustained a number of injuries against Yale, increasing the need for another quality player from the bench. In Herbert's eyes, Williams was quality starting material. Herbert's position on racial politics is unknown, but it is clear that in pure football terms, he thought that Williams should have been playing varsity. At the time, there were only about fifteen Black men playing for predominantly white universities. That Brown had two Black men on its squad was so unusual as to be remarkable in 1916. Coach Robbie, who had been a celebrated coach at Nebraska, Maine, and Brown, was no fool; Williams had not been playing because the coach, the college, the alumni, or some combination of the three, believed that one Black player on varsity was as much as would be tolerated.

The day before the November 18 varsity match, the *Brown Daily Herald* reported that Williams "was the star of the game," although the junior varsity matchup between Brown and Harvard ended in a 0–0 tie.[29] Brown's varsity squad fared better, upsetting Harvard 21–0 in front of thirty-two thousand, and the team clinched the Eastern Division championship.[30] Quite surprisingly, one of Brown's touchdowns was scored after Ink Williams—inserted as a substitute—blocked a Harvard punt at the nine-yard line. That highlight—along with the fact that referees repeatedly stopped the game for Harvard's unnecessary roughness on Pollard—was splashed across the pages of the national edition of the *Chicago Defender*.[31] Speaking at a bonfire alongside the coaches and the college president, Pollard told the crowd: "I can say that we have a wonderful student body, faculty and coaches. I know that if the students give us the support next year which they gave us this year that we shall beat Harvard by a score of 61–0 instead of 21–0."[32] Perhaps such a score would have been possible if Brown had elected to start all of its best players. Weeks later, the school held a banquet for the football team, where season highlight films were shown and varsity Bs awarded. Ink Williams received a decorative emblem denoting his place on the Brown second team.[33]

Williams's second semester at Brown presented him with a course load consisting of botany, English, French, Greek, and economics. With the demands of football over, the focus shifted to winter track, where Williams grabbed headlines immediately. On Wednesday, January 17, 1917, Williams starred in an interclass track competition, displaying a technique that would characterize how he conducted himself in both athletics and business in the years to come: hanging back in the early heats, only to overwhelm his unsuspecting competitors with a burst of speed at the end.[34] At Mechanics Hall in Boston on February 3, Williams made a name for himself at the Twenty-Eighth Annual Indoor Invitation Games of the Boston Athletic Association (B. A. A.), finishing first in the forty-yard dash. One month later, on March 3, he finished second at the prestigious Amateur Athletic Union (AAU) winter track meet.[35] With that, the short season came to an end. Williams's accomplishments on the track caught the eye of the Boston media and spread quickly across the country, even landing on the pages of the *Monmouth Daily Atlas*, alerting Williams's hometown that he had become a collegiate track star.[36]

At that moment in American history, when baseball was the only major-league professional sport, track and field held a very high place in the popular interest. Local, regional, and national track meets received the kind of reporting that is afforded major-league sports today. Brown's reputation in track and field was strong: Norman Taber won gold and bronze medals at the 1912 Olympics in Stockholm while still a junior at Brown. The B. A. A. invitational was particularly prestigious. Indoor facilities such as Mechanics Hall were unusual at the time. Winter track was typically held outdoors and often canceled due to bad weather. The B. A. A., which was even then one of the oldest amateur athletic associations in the nation, was noteworthy for its high national profile and relatively luxurious facilities. (The B. A. A. remains strong today and is the facilitator of the Boston Marathon.) The nationwide coverage announced Williams as a man to watch among sports enthusiasts but also caused some confusion about his background. After his B. A. A. win, the *Boston Globe* reported that Williams had come to Brown from Missoula, Montana, a reference as intriguing as it is perplexing. The following week, the *Kansas City Star* reported that Williams had attended Howard University prior to Brown. Two weeks later, in reporting on Williams's indoor track accomplishments, the *Missoulian* (Missoula, Montana) reported that Williams had been a standout at the state track meet in Missoula a few years before. On the face of it, this storyline suggests an answer to the question of what Williams did between his high school graduation in 1912 and his enrollment at Howard in 1915. But the *Missoulian* storyline appears to be a stunningly lazy gaffe, re-reporting the story that originally ran in the *Boston Globe*. Local Black athletes in Montana were an exceptional news item that most Montana sports reporters likely would have been aware of. A thorough review of the track rosters of Montana State University and the University of Montana between 1912 and 1915 shows that Williams was never a member of either team. A thorough review of the annual Montana state track meet (which included high school and collegiate teams as well as athletic associations and schools visiting from out of state) produced one possibility: reporters may have confused Williams with Buster Phelps, a prominent Black high school track star from Butte, Montana. Williams never mentioned Montana in his interviews (though, of course, he also never mentioned living in Pine Bluff, working in Colorado, or attending Howard).

By March 1917, anticipation of America's entry into the Great War was rising; campus life at Brown featured boy-soldier scenes. Brown's students held organized military training—their own idea, not the faculty's—and the *Brown Daily Herald* excitedly reported the arrival of hats, boots, belts, and other accoutrements of the US army uniform. By March, over two hundred forty students had enrolled in military drills. Ink Williams and Fritz Pollard were not among them.

It was in this atmosphere of pending war that the 1916–17 school year came to a climax. The annual Union Vaudeville Show was announced for March 27, and the organizing committee consisted mainly of Brown football stars—notably Jimmy Murphy and Fritz Pollard. On March 19, the paper reported that dancing by Jimmie Murphy and Ink Williams would be "some of the more promising acts."[37] Over the course of the week, Murphy boasted of his "world-famed band of vaudevillites."[38] He peppered the newspaper with comical updates about the addition of a trained hippopotamus and comically lauded cast members for their "success as egg targets."[39]

On March 27, the *Brown Daily Herald* announced the program, which consisted of a play featuring the following cast:

Act I., Scene: A room in the Waldorf Astoria, N.Y., occupied by Miss Dillpickle Dollie.

   Cast, in order of entering:
   Eagle Beak Sprudder—Mr. Ralph Mullane
   Johnny McGraw, Manager of the Giants—Mr. Ken Sprague
   Prof. Fred Gorham, of Brown—Mr. J.P. Murphy
   Ink Williams—Mr. Fred Pollard
   Fritz Pollard—Mr. Ink Williams
   Ex-Czar Nicholas of Russia—Mr. G. W. Kowalski
   Theodore Roosevelt—Mr. Ray Walsh
   General Trobatsiniky—Mr. Stan Ward
   The College Widow—Mr. Ralph Gordon
   Miss Maria Slats—Mr. Cliff Munroe

Act II., Scene: Same as Scene 1, only located in Paris at the Rouge Moulin. Same cast, but new line of stuff.[40]

Act VI featured a piece titled "Dancing Now and Then," featuring Ink Williams and Jimmy Murphy.

The *Brown Daily Herald* reported that the vaudeville show was a rousing success:

> The Brown Union Opera House and all the adjacent doorways and balconies were crammed to overflowing last evening at the presentation by Mr. Belasco Murphy of his long-heralded "Dillpickle Dollies," the most uproariously successful of annual theatrical farces.

The *Herald* reviewer noted that "Fritz Pollard appeared with his trombone, followed by members of the Glee Club in a ridiculous opera of 'The Burning House'" and that "The clog-dance tableau by Ink Williams and Jimmy Murphy was another major hit."[41] Ink Williams recalled in later years that he had danced and sung the blues in skits at Brown. It is likely that this was one such occasion. The casting of the central skit is a fascinating look at a student group seeking to adjust minstrelsy to fit a racially integrated cast. In the annual minstrel shows that marked St. Patrick's Day at Brown, students typically performed "mammy"-style minstrel songs in blackface. But students did not black up for the 1917 show, which instead featured only two Black characters, played by Black students who were playing each other. That "Ink Williams" and "Fritz Pollard" were alongside the baseball legend John McGraw, the former president Teddy Roosevelt, and the deposed tsar Nicholas II shows that they were larger-than-life fixtures at Brown whose presence demanded a greater deal of respect than had otherwise been accorded to Blacks in a brutally racist genre of performance.

Six days after the show, the United States entered the Great War. Students and faculty called for athletic schedules to be curtailed, which meant the end of the spring track season.[42] Despite this, Williams and Pollard participated in the Smart Set Athletic Club's national invitational track meet at the Regiment Armory in Brooklyn. The Smart Set was founded by William W. Lattimore, a Black attorney who also was the manager of the composer Will Marion Cook's Southern Syncopated Orchestra. The national headline for the Smart Set event was the return of Howard P. Drew, who was then at Drake University in Iowa; the *Des Moines Register* breathlessly reported Drew's return, stating that he would be racing against the "fastest men in the world"—including Ink Williams.[43] Drew acquitted himself well, though he lost the hundred-yard dash to Andrew Kelly of Holy Cross (who would star in the 1919 Inter-Allied Games); Williams did not place. However, Fritz Pollard surprised everybody by winning the hundred-yard hurdles. The Smart Set Athletic Club was known far and wide for its magnificent medallions for the victors—a tactic many understood then (and now) as a vehicle for paying amateur athletes without cash. For his efforts, Pollard received a diamond medallion.[44]

A celebration followed the meet—an opulent evening for Black society members in New York, featuring women in their Easter best. Williams's crossing paths with Lattimore put him in heady company at the intersection of Black and white entertainment: Lattimore's partner, Will Marion Cook, had been a student of the composer Antonín Dvořák, who also had mentored the trailblazing soprano Sissieretta Jones. Both Lattimore and Cook worked with Bert Williams and George Walker, the two most prominent figures in Black vaudeville. Cook was a mentor to Edward Kennedy "Duke" Ellington and James Hubert "Eubie" Blake. Most of Cook's compositions drew from Black vernacular music, culture, and cultural critique. Whether Williams and Lattimore actually spoke, or what they might have discussed, is unknown. But it is likely they did meet and that Williams was surrounded by lively discussions during his evening in Brooklyn. Two weeks later, Williams and Pollard were with their Brown track teammates at University of Pennsylvania's Franklin Field for the Penn Relays, where they watched Dubuque's Black collegiate track and football star Solomon "Sol" Butler win a gold watch for taking first in the broad jump.[45]

Back at Brown, the ranks of students and athletes were rapidly depleted by departures for the armed services and for various supporting roles in the war effort. By mid-May, the school had excused 207 students (roughly 20 percent of the student body) to take up nonmilitary roles.[46] On May 29, Williams and the rest of the freshmen class, led by a fifty-piece band, marched through the city of Providence, fired off Roman candles, and ceremonially threw the beanies they had worn all year into a bonfire. It was supposed to be a celebration of pending manhood, but as the embers of the bonfire died, students stared at a future that was uncertain and, for many, deeply troubling.⁴⁷

Ink Williams did not return home to Monmouth for the summer. Instead, it is likely he spent part of his summer with Fritz Pollard on the Narragansett Pier. The Pier was a hot spot for wealthy white socialites who summered along the Rhode Island coast; many of the town's restaurants and hotels recruited Black college students to staff service positions. Williams had had experience with such work in Colorado during high school. The Black collegiate community at the Narragansett Pier—where Pollard and Paul Robeson had met the previous summer—was a tight-knit one. Robeson was often called on to sing in informal settings, with Pollard backing him up on piano. It was likely there that Williams, too, deepened his lasting friendship with Robeson. Whatever Williams's situation was, he found time to compete as a member of the Pittsburgh Independents—an all-Black track team that vied with all-white track teams at Forbes Field in Pittsburgh. Williams and his teammate Harry Martin won their sprinting events and propelled the Independents to a second-place finish.⁴⁸ Despite these high points, at the end of the summer Williams received his grades: a dismal 1.2 grade point average (GPA) for his freshman year.

Back on campus in the autumn, a star had fallen to earth. Fritz Pollard had had been declared academically ineligible to play football for the 1917 season, and Williams's eligibility was under review. Pollard and Williams responded by stepping up their tailoring business, advertising pickup and delivery in the school paper:

> Drop in and see Pollard
> the official student tailor
> will keep you looking neat all year by
> Pollard's Pressing Club Plan
> 18 Hope College Hall
> clothes called for and delivered. Prompt
> and good service. Single Suits
> taken care of⁴⁹

The campus tailor was none other than the man whose on-field brilliance had made him the second Black player named by Walter Camp—the legendary player, coach, and sportswriter known as the "Father of American Football"—to the All-American squad in the *New York Times*.⁵⁰ This was the same tailor who had almost singlehandedly enabled Brown to win its divisional championships, generating enough demand for public speaking engagements to make for a very tenuous academic status. Pollard would watch all of Brown's games from the sidelines in 1917. He was not the only star missing from the 1916 team; between matriculation and war enlistments, only two varsity players had returned.⁵¹ Of the other returning students, two hundred fifty had enrolled in the Reserve Officers Training Corps (ROTC). Brown University's President Faunce warned that "if we came to college 'to avoid sacrifice and labor' we were unworthy of our college and traitors to 'our brothers at the front.'"⁵²

Though Williams was a partner in the tailoring business, he did not live at the "clothes pressing shop" (Pollard's dorm room). Instead, he moved from the boardinghouse at 72 Meeting Street to an apartment at 144 Westminster Street, adjacent to the stunning Westminster Arcade—the first indoor shopping mall in the nation—in downtown Providence. His living quarters were improved, but his academic warning, discussed on the pages of the *Brown Daily Herald*, hung in the background of a course load consisting of biology, chemistry, English, and French. It also prevented him from playing in the season opener against Holy Cross, though his eligibility was affirmed in time to make his varsity debut in a win over Boston College on October 21, resulting in a permanent starting position.⁵³ Williams would play the entire game against Colgate the following week; the Bears squeezed out a 7–6 victory. The *Brown Daily Herald* called it "one of the hardest fought and best played game ever staged at Andrews Field," noting that "time and time again Williams downed the Colgate backs for losses."⁵⁴ Following the game, students marched from College Hill, past Williams's apartment on Westminster Street, to Empire Street, on to Weybosset Street, down to City Hall, and back to campus "singing, cheering, and yelling," and ending with a rousing 10:00 p.m. bonfire, where speeches were delivered (though none by Ink Williams).⁵⁵

In mid-November, a crowd of five thousand—including one thousand sailors—watched Brown face off against the Naval Military Reserves, an all-star team of naval enlistees who featured six All-Americans in their starting lineup. Brown was trounced 35–0, and Williams was thrown for a seven-yard loss on the final play of the game at the goal line. He also strained a hamstring, causing him to miss the next two games, including Brown's final home game.⁵⁶ The final game of the season was held at Braves Field, the new, cavernous home of the Boston Braves major-league baseball team. Opened in 1915, the ballpark was so large that no player hit a home run there for five years; its forty thousand seats made it feel all the more spacious. (The Red Sox had held the World Series at Braves Field the previous two seasons, because it could accommodate more fans than Fenway Park.)

The game did not disappoint. Brown and Dartmouth held one another scoreless throughout the first half. The *Brown Daily Herald* noted that Mayo Williams's "speed was such that he repeatedly brought down the ball or prevented the execution of plays behind the Dartmouth front trenches." Thirteen unanswered points by Brown with only eight minutes to go in the game stunned the Dartmouth eleven, and Brown's repeated forcing of fumbles prevented Dartmouth from scoring at all.[57] It was a tremendous end to a season that far exceeded expectations.

The following week, Ink Williams and the other starters on the Brown football team received their varsity Bs, and the major New York newspapers began announcing their lists of All-Stars and All-Americans. The first list, from the *New York Sun*, indicated the way all of the nationwide lists of all-stars would go regarding Ink Williams. Paul Robeson had turned in an outstanding year at Rutgers and was named one of the two ends. In the prestigious Walter Camp All-American listing, Walter Weeks—the other end at Brown—was named the second end for the squad.[58] Although Weeks was popular and talented enough to win the title of captain for the following football season, his name appears only a fraction of the times Williams's does in the game recaps in the *Daily Herald*. It is fair to speculate that America's football writers were not yet ready to name two Black players to their "best of" polls. One Black end was enough for 1917.

While Brown spent the fall winning on the football field, it was fighting a losing battle to retain its student body. The slow trickle of students leaving to join the military or to offer their services in noncombatant roles on the home front became a mass exodus by late 1917. By December 1, 262 students were serving in the war effort.[59] Among the lost students was Fritz Pollard, who had continued to suffer academically. "I was young and foolish and crazy," Pollard would later tell his biographer John Carroll. "I was Fritz Pollard, All-American, and my head was getting a little bit big then."[60] Even a surprise visit to Pollard and Williams's clothes-pressing shop by the Brown alumnus John D. Rockefeller Jr. (who bought Fritz a new clothes-pressing machine and offered to pay all of his tuition and expenses) was not enough to keep Pollard from dropping out.[61] Ink Williams was not far behind, struggling academically and failing both English and French, causing his GPA to dip to a precarious 1.13.

CHAPTER 4

Buffalo Soldier

Ink Williams reported for Officer Training School (OTS) at Camp Sherman, Ohio in the spring of 1918. A so-called soldier factory, the camp was built on the ancient mounds of the indigenous Hopewell people, in modern-day Chillicothe, about seventy-five miles west of Dayton. On the face of things, Williams—along with an elite group of mostly college-educated Black men—was training to be an officer in the 325th Field Signal Battalion, a unit of the Ninety-Second Division of the US Army.

Beneath the surface, however, was a military experiment in civil rights progress. In 1917, the United States Army was almost entirely segregated. Although Native Americans and Asian Americans served in integrated units, Latino soldiers and Black soldiers served in segregated ones. The inclusion of Black men in the draft had been a hard-fought civil rights battle, pitting prominent racial progressives against white supremacist members of Congress who objected to arming Black Americans. W. E. B. Du Bois and other NAACP leaders, as well as the Alpha Phi Alpha fraternity, argued that Black leadership in the Great War—including dangerous roles in combat situations—would lead to breakthroughs in civil rights. Over the course of the war, 350,000 Black Americans served on the Western Front, mostly in support roles. The notable exceptions were the two Black combat units: the Ninety-Second and Ninety-Third Infantry Divisions. The contention over Black combat roles led the army to hand-pick Black collegiate leaders for the OTS, which fed into the two Black combat units.

White recruiting officers and Black civic leaders were involved in identifying OTS candidates, as were the local chapters and the national office of Alpha Phi Alpha. Fritz Pollard and Charles Wesley, both stationed at Camp Meade in Maryland, were particularly influential in pointing recruiting efforts toward Black college students and athletes. Roughly twenty miles equidistant between

Baltimore and Washington, DC, Camp Meade was a major training ground for soldiers awaiting combat deployment. (Some four hundred thousand soldiers and twenty-two thousand horses and mules passed through the camp during the war.) Neither Pollard nor Wesley were actually *in* the army—their employer was the YMCA, which provided nonmilitary services for (and to) the army, including morale, welfare, and recreational (MWR) programs; and rest and relaxation (R & R) programs. Wesley was a man of strong political convictions in keeping with Du Bois's and served as the education secretary at Camp Meade's YMCA.[1] Pollard and Wesley used their access to high-ranking white officers—and Pollard's celebrity—to advocate for placement of elite Black college athletes such as Ink Williams into OTS programs at Camp Sherman and at Fort Des Moines in Iowa.[2]

At home in Monmouth, on campus at Brown, and in national news, Williams's pathway to the armed services had been a source of public speculation. The *Brown Daily Herald* reported in early February that Williams had left school and was waiting to be called up in the draft.[3] (This was two weeks before Pollard's appointment as YMCA Physical Director at Camp Meade was announced.) When Williams's grandmother Jennie McFall died in April 1918, Williams was unable to attend the funeral in Monmouth because he was in the service.[4] Williams appears to have registered for the draft in Providence along with his Black classmate Maynard Wartman, although their draft cards were not processed until late May. At that point Brown's commencement program (May 1918) reported Williams as stationed with the Signal Corps.[5] By July, the *Monmouth Daily Atlas* had caught wind that Williams had registered for the draft. The paper speculated that he was headed to Germany, on account of the unlucky thirteens that seemed to be following him: his draft number (13), exemption number (13), the number of letters in his name (13), the number of letters and numerals in his mother's street address (417 South Fifth), and the number of letters in "Atlantic Ocean" and "Allied Nations." "Plenty of other 'thirteens' could probably be connected with Williams," wrote the paper in a distastefully goofy front-page article about Williams's potential combat deployment, "but the young man probably thinks the array mentioned is enough."[6] By August 1918, Williams's military service was a matter of national news, with papers such as the *Los Angeles Times* reporting that Ink Williams was at Camp Sherman, Ohio with the Signal Corps.[7]

One likely pathway for Williams to Camp Sherman was through Major Thomas C. Spencer, the white US Army officer charged with recruiting members into the 325th Field Signal Battalion. Spencer, who became the lieutenant colonel in charge of the 325th in France, was reported to have toured the major colleges and HBCUs of the East and the South, "enlisting only those that he felt could and would make good."[8] Given that Maynard Wartman, Williams's only other Black classmate at Brown, served with the 325th Field

Signal Battalion (Company C), it seems likely that Major Spencer had visited Brown's campus in late 1917, in time for Williams to withdraw for the Spring 1918 semester and for Wartman to land in France by June. If so, it might also reflect Spencer's inclination to place a star college athlete in officer training, whereas Wartman—four years older than Williams and not an athlete—served as a private.

The Signal Corps was responsible for communication and observation systems on the battlefield. The 325th, which consisted of about five hundred men, was divided into three different companies: Company A focused on radio, Company B on wire (stringing and maintaining telegraph wire in the trenches), and Company C on outpost. The Signal Corps encompassed a wide variety of responsibilities, from piloting hot air balloons that observed enemy troop movements, to managing carrier pigeons, to communication with semaphore flags. Training provided Signal Corps members with fluency in electronics. But officers such as Williams also needed to be proficient in machine gunning.

Most of the approximately four hundred thousand Black soldiers who served on active duty during World War I were given labor and supply assignments. But the "Buffalo Divisions" of the US Army—the Ninety-Second and Ninety-Third—consisted of Black combat troops. Along with progressives such as Du Bois, General John J. ("Black Jack") Pershing—the commander of the American Expeditionary Forces (AEF) on the Western Front—had actively lobbied for Black combat roles. Du Bois believed this was an important step toward mutual respect, and Pershing noted Black soldiers' historic reputation for volunteering for difficult and dangerous work. Pershing, who was white, was the commanding officer of the Tenth Cavalry in the late 1890s in Montana. The Tenth Cavalry was an all-Black unit, nicknamed "Buffalo Soldiers" during the prolonged Indian wars on the Plains and in the Southwest that followed the Civil War; the nickname of the Ninety-Second and Ninety-Third Divisions came from this association.

The Ninety-Second was dispatched to the Western Front; by the summer of 1918 they were on the front lines near the Argonne Forest. White US Army officers strenuously resisted accepting the Buffalo Divisions as fellow combatants. Such attitudes were not surprising to Pershing: when he served briefly as an instructor at West Point, the cadets insultingly referred to him as "Nigger Jack" because of his service with the Tenth Cavalry. By World War I, that nickname had morphed into "Black Jack," which was widely used in the military and in the popular press. Given Pershing's extensive combat experiences with the Tenth Cavalry in Montana and Cuba, it is not surprising that he would have advocated for combat roles for Black troops during World War I. Nevertheless, Pershing capitulated to racist attitudes among US Army officers, and the Buffalo Divisions were placed under the command of the French army. The French, in turn, attached the Ninety-Second Division to their Thirty-Eighth Division of Infantry, which was drawn from France's African colonies in Algeria, Tunisia, Morocco, and Senegal.

While Private Wartman traveled to the Western Front with the Buffalo Divisions, Williams was instead sent to Camp Dodge in Johnston, Iowa. Camp Dodge received most of its Black officers from Fort Des Moines, a Black OTS that had been created under pressure from the NAACP and Alpha Phi Alpha. Although Howard University had lobbied to be the site of the officer training program, racist expectations of high-profile failure at an eastern location led to the selection of a rural midwestern location instead. In May 1917, one thousand Black men—drawn significantly from HBCUs and Ivy League schools—reported to Fort Des Moines under the command of Lieutenant Colonel Charles C. Ballou, a controversial white officer with a noted disdain for General Pershing.

Most of the men at Fort Des Moines were eventually transferred to Camp Dodge, just ten miles away. Many would ship out to France in June 1918 as members of the Third Battalion of the Ninety-Second Division of the AEF.[9] However, fifty-six Black soldiers in officer training at Camp Dodge—including Ink Williams—were transferred instead to Camp Hancock, five miles outside Augusta, Georgia, near the South Carolina state line.

As a southern institution, Camp Hancock was noteworthy in that it comprised both Black and White troops and was the first place in Georgia where Black soldiers were promoted to ranking officers. Overseen by Brigadier General Oliver Edwards, the Machine Gun Training Center was the first stop for officers and troops prior to transfer to the Western Front, where General Edwards had also established a machine gun training center, earning him a Distinguished Service Medal. For both Black and white officers in training, a transfer from the Signal Corps program at Camp Sherman to machine gun training at Camp Hancock was not unusual.[10] In one year, Camp Hancock ballooned from a small National Guard training center to the "machine gun training center of the world."

Williams was in the first class enrolled in Camp Hancock's machine-gun officers' training school, which was commanded by Lieutenant Colonel Wade H. Westmoreland. Westmoreland, a white officer, was a friend of Colonel Charles Young, a Black officer who was then stationed at Camp Sherman in Ohio to assist in the recruitment and training of Black soldiers. With Young's blessing, Westmoreland was happy to receive Black trainees who had passed through Camp Sherman. Colonel Young was then the most celebrated Black veteran of the US military: just the third Black officer to graduate from West Point, Young had distinguished himself as a second lieutenant in the Ninth Calvary Buffalo Soldiers during the Indian wars and the Philippine-American

War. Later he became the first Black US National Park superintendent; a military attaché to Haiti, the Dominican Republic, and Liberia under President Theodore Roosevelt; and a noted veteran of the (failed) Mexican campaign to capture Pancho Villa. All of this was in addition to his stature as one of the foremost faculty members at Wilberforce University, where he worked closely with W. E. B. Du Bois.[11]

In short, Colonel Young—who most believed should have been made the commanding officer at Fort Des Moines—played a strong role in recommending men from Camp Sherman (including a number of Wilberforce students) for consideration at Camp Hancock. The OTS at Camp Hancock began on June 20, 1918, with eight hundred white and Black enlisted men. By the conclusion of officer training, on September 16, 1918, six hundred remained, including forty-two Black men who were commissioned as second lieutenants, including Mayo Williams. All forty-two Black officers were assigned to the Seventh Group, Main Training Depot, where they trained Black soldiers in machine gunnery.

Of the eight companies of Black troops at Camp Hancock, seven were commanded by Black officers. Among his fellow officers, Williams was the most prominent athlete, named as one of Walter Camp's All-American honorable mentions. The Ohio State University cross-country runner Daniel Ferguson was another noteworthy officer-athlete among the ranks of the Seventh Group.[12]

Williams served as a second lieutenant at Camp Hancock for the duration of the war, training troops in machine gunning, until he was discharged from the service in early 1919, several months after the armistice ending the war was signed. Instead of the civil rights gains that the NAACP hoped would result from wartime service, returning Black servicemen faced a sickening spasm of violence and outright terrorism. Lynchings surged throughout the South. Williams left Georgia for his hometown of Monmouth and was spared a violent homecoming. After visiting with friends and family for a few weeks, he left for Washington, DC before returning to campus in Providence.[13] Back at Brown, the sports equipment company Wright & Ditson announced it would present a tablet to the Brown Athletic Association inscribed with the names of the men of the 1916 and 1917 football squads who had served in the war, including that of Ink Williams.[14]

CHAPTER 5

Williams vs. Yale

Ink Williams knew he was a marked man. The jeers of the Yale fans grew louder as he walked from the locker room across the quad under a canopy of fall colors. The air was crisp on this Saturday afternoon in November 1919, nearly one year to the day after the armistice had been signed, ending the World War. Spilling over the massive earthen berm that gave the Yale Bowl its name were the chants of the tens of thousands of fans inside. Clad in chocolate-brown leggings, shoes with long-spiked cleats, white-striped socks, and brown wool jerseys pulled over thin leather pads, the Brown football team jogged out of the tunnel as chants of "Catch that nigger! Kill that nigger!" washed over them.

Unlike most of his teammates, Williams eschewed a helmet, meeting the hostile gaze of the forty-five thousand spectators with an electric grin. He had anticipated this moment, having witnessed Fritz Pollard endure it in 1916. Racism wasn't unique to Yale. Williams encountered it everywhere, most often in quiet ways—such as having to ride the bench despite being the best player on the team. But here on football's biggest stage in 1919, it was brutally loud.

Across the gridiron, Yale's coaches were nervous about the threat Williams posed to their dominance. The head coach, Albert "Doc" Sharpe—who would later recall Williams as the fastest end who ever played in the Yale Bowl—asked his coaching staff to develop a plan to neutralize Williams. At least one of the assistants translated this in his own way, telling the players that "no colored man should finish the first half of a game in the [Yale] Bowl." Williams was the only Black player on either team. As Yale's backup center, Bill Galvin, later recalled:

> One of our assistant coaches—and he was not a Southerner—had a pet peeve against "Inky" Williams. He got me, the fullback and one tackle together and ordered us to be "on" Inky every play. This coach put the whole thing

on a "color" basis. He apparently didn't realize we were northerners and had no feeling of discrimination along color lines.[1]

Although Galvin idealized race relations in the North, much of the Yale squad had played in integrated games before. Galvin, for one, had played on integrated high school teams in Massachusetts and had played against Howard P. Drew, before Drew quit football to focus exclusively on sprinting. To Galvin's thinking, the assistant coach was still angry about Fritz Pollard's 1916 game against Yale, which had ended in a stunning 21–6 upset in favor of Brown. Because of the war, the 1919 game was the first time the two teams had met since the upset, and Doc Sharpe's assistant did not want to be embarrassed again.

In 1919, many postwar football players were bundles of nerves. Like Williams, most of the players had been discharged from the military just six months before. Many had seen combat, and college football only added to their "shell shock"—which we now recognize as posttraumatic stress disorder. Brown's coaches acknowledged this issue to reporters that September.[2]

Postwar football was also rife with competition. Returning veterans had caused enrollment to swell to historic proportions. Coach Edward "Robbie" Robinson had the challenge of managing a massive football squad—essentially five years' worth of students. Returning seniors who had gone to the war after their junior year expected to return to their starting positions—only to find two new waves of starters with similar expectations.

Now twenty-three years old, J. Mayo Williams had returned from wartime service with a newfound maturity: he had an officer's commission, veteran status, a military service credit of twenty-one semester hours (covering the cost of seven courses at Brown), and renewed energy for both athletics and academics. His fall-semester courses included economics and philosophy, as well as three courses (two English and one French) that were makeup classes for those he had failed in previous semesters. After failing four courses in his first three semesters, Williams would not fail another class.[3]

Even before the war, the coaching squad had been reluctant to start Black players, so once more Williams started the season on the bench. He had already endured the indignity of riding the bench his first year at Brown after being recruited away from Howard University. Perhaps his experience in Office Training School made Brown's bad decision making more transparent, as well as more frustrating to bear.

Whatever segregationist pressure the coaching staff was under, they were under greater pressure to win. But the team's great expectations were unrealized as they stumbled into the Yale Bowl with a 3–3 record. They had thumped lesser squads such as Bowdoin, Rhode Island State, and Norwich, but had been shut out by Colgate, Syracuse, and Harvard. After the Harvard game, Coach Robinson handed Williams the starting job at left end. Curly Oden, another junior who became a lifelong friend, was also given the starting job at quarterback.

The press seemed split on whether to embrace or reject Williams. Week after week, scribes detailed his speed, agility, and electrifying play—even stating that he was one of the few competent Brown players in an embarrassing loss against Syracuse. The *Brown Daily Herald* writers—who were never given a byline—appeared divided in their treatment of Williams, one advocating for All-American consideration one day, another calling him "barely varsity caliber" the next.

Williams and other Black players who found space on otherwise white teams *had* to be disproportionately excellent. Thus, Williams was almost always among the most heralded players in printed recaps—just as he was noticeably absent from the annual All-American lists. Journalists and fans periodically grew giddy over the exotic idea of Black players in the Ivy League. Before one matchup with Dartmouth, rumors swirled that Williams and Johnny Shelbourne—Dartmouth's lone Black player—were dating the same woman. (The schools are nearly two hundred miles apart.)

Articles presented Williams as if he were Fritz Pollard's shadow, even when the two were no longer teammates. Most Native American football stars of that time similarly stood in the shadow of Jim Thorpe. The trouble—for Black and Indigenous players alike—was that even when they stood head and shoulders above their peers of other races, they were cast as disappointments in the press because they were not Pollard or Thorpe, arguably two of the greatest athletes of any era. When Pollard and Thorpe turned professional, it was seen as an inevitable failure of character, and cast a pall on their fellow Black and Ingenous athletes.

But the Yale players knew elite skill when they saw it on the field, regardless of what the papers said. So whereas their fans chanted about killing Williams, Galvin and his Yale teammates respected him as a force to be reckoned with:

> Needless to say, we knew that "Inky" was the key to a Brown victory. His end around play was something to watch. That afternoon we watched "Inky" every second and we layed [sic] it on pretty stiff in a legitimate way, but "Inky" could take it. He was not only a top star but he knew that most of his opponents would be on his neck most of the game to keep him from scoring. Like all top men, he could take it, and with a big smile.

Williams, as he nearly always did, remained in the game without substitution—and without a helmet—for every play on offense and defense. With the game tied at halftime, Yale's assistant coach screamed at Galvin, Walker, and Stearn, who were confident that their coach "didn't seem to realize that his 'color' talk had been ignored by us."

Within earshot of the fans, players, and coaches were the referees. Being a referee requires a certain amount of bravery, enforcing rules even when they are unpopular; but the presence of racism at the highest levels of the game made it hard to take these calls at face value. We know that many of the forty-five thousand hometown fans were screaming about killing Williams and that a Yale assistant coach was telling his players to hurt Williams. A referee could neutralize Williams without physically injuring him. Perhaps this happened—or perhaps not. It was brave of Williams to be on the field at all.

• • •

Hometown fans typically look the other way when their coaches or team play dirty. But for both home and away fans, questioning the judgment and impartiality of officials is universal and timeless, even when racism is not a factor. The fall of 1919 was the era of the Chicago Black Sox scandal in major league baseball, marking the twentieth-century apex of gambling corruption in professional sports. The *Brown Daily Herald* reported, "We hear that more money is being wagered on Brown than has been put on the Yale game in some years."[4] We know the assistant coaches were trying to bend the rules, but we simply cannot know if the officials afforded Williams a level playing field. In Williams's final appearance at the Yale Bowl in the fall of 1920, Curly Oden received the opening kickoff and lateraled to Williams, who ran for a sixty-yard gain. In what was reported as "one of the doubtful decisions of the game," the referees called the ball back. In that contest, the hostile Yale crowd cheered as Brown received a rash of penalties. Williams played the entire game with a bad knee: "Crippled as he was, [he] reeled off yards on end around plays." Although the 1920 Brown-Yale contest ended in a loss and effectively ended his collegiate football career, it was "his finest game of the season," despite the questionable judgment of the referees.[5]

• • •

This same uncertainty intruded on Williams's career in other sports. Some months after the 1919 Yale game, the winter track season began. Williams and J. F. S. Carter—another Black student at Brown—emerged as the stars of the team. At the B. A. A. meet in Boston, Williams made national news when he finished in the top three in the preliminary heats of the forty-yard dash, qualifying him for an intense final against four of the greatest sprinters of the time: Loren Murchison of the New York Athletic Club, Charley Paddock of the University of Southern California (USC), William Hayes of Notre Dame, and Jackson Scholz of the University of Missouri. Of the group, all eyes were on Paddock, who had made a name for himself during the Inter-Allied Games in France during the spring of 1919. The starter's pistol cracked, and then it was over in a flash. The *Boston Globe* reported breathlessly:

Little Scholz just streaked through the field in the final heat, his stooped body showing to the fore at half the distance. Murchison, running steadily, forced the Missouri star to the tape, and then came the dusky Williams, well up. Scholz' time was 4 4/5 seconds.[6]

In beating Paddock to the finish, Williams was hailed by college scribes as "one of the best sprinters in the college world."[7] Just a few months later, Paddock, Murchison, and Scholz, along with Morris Kirksey of Stanford, set a world record while winning gold in the 4 × 100-meter relay at the 1920 Summer Olympics in Antwerp. Paddock won two gold medals in the 1920 Olympics; in 1921, he became the first person to run the hundred-yard dash in under ten seconds.[8] Murchison won gold on the relay team again at the 1924 Olympics in Paris, and Scholz won gold and silver at the 1924 games. Whether Williams was ever considered for the Olympic team is unclear: only two Black athletes participated for the United States in the 1920 Summer Olympics, including Sol Butler, whose path Williams would cross later on the gridiron. The 1920 Olympic trials were held up the road at Harvard Stadium in Cambridge, making Williams's absence all the more noticeable. (Howard P. Drew competed in the trials, but failed to make the team.) In the process of winning third at the B. A. A. meet, Williams was injured and was forced to sit out of competitions until the end of the month, when Brown again went to Boston to compete in the New England Indoor Championships (NEIC) in late February. There, Ink dominated: following six heats and two semifinals, he won the forty-yard dash in 4.8 seconds. J. F. S. Carter placed third. Williams's race saw him nose out the local favorite, Johnny Barr of the Boston Athletic Association team. Apparently, the decision to award the medal to Williams was controversial enough that several days after the meet, the *Boston Globe* speculated that Williams's NEIC medal might be revoked and awarded to Barr instead.[9] So in this instance, we see the hometown fans feeling that the referees got the call wrong, this time to Williams's benefit. But we also see one of the world's fastest men being excluded from the Olympic Trials after two high-profile victories on two of the biggest track-and-field stages. It is possible that Williams had experienced a recurrence of the injury that followed his B. A. A. bronze. But in light of the racial atmosphere of the time, it is fair to speculate that discrimination barred Williams from participating in the Olympic trials.

• • •

Back out on the Yale Bowl field after halftime, Brown was still tenacious against the bigger, deeper Yale squad. But with a starting lineup that played almost entirely without substitution, Brown simply ran out of gas. As the *Brown Daily Herald* reported, "After smashing the Bulldog completely off his feet for two periods, Brown's defense finally broke before the fierce advance of Eli's backfield." "Rats" Albright and Ink Williams played brilliantly throughout the game. Albright blocked two Yale dropkicks, and Williams gained seventeen yards on a pass play from Oden. The school paper noted:

> "Ink" Williams tore off gain after gain in end around plays and had the interference been better, the fast end would have broken away more than once. . . . Yale kicked off at the outset of the second half and Armstrong punted a long sailing one to Eli's 35-yard line, where "Ink" Williams dropped Neville in his tracks.

Albright went down late in the game with a dislocated shoulder, and Brown didn't have enough energy against a heavier and well-reinforced Yale team. Brown lost 14–0, dropping their season record to 3–4.[10]

Yale's Bill Galvin would never forget what he witnessed: thirty years later, he told the *Hartford Courant* how Williams had played the entire game without substitution, all while subjected to fierce racial epithets, violent opposition, and triple coverage. With both teams sharing the same locker room, Galvin recalled that "in the showers after the game [Williams] kidded us to the effect that if we had not been bearing down all afternoon he probably would have gone the distance" on one of his long runs. Williams and the three Yale players who had triple-teamed him—Galvin, Stearn, and Walker—"had a good laugh among ourselves in the showers after the game, with 'Inky' being the best sport of all."[11]

Although Williams would have a strong showing again as a senior in 1920, his brilliant play at the Yale Bowl in 1919 put him on the map. The *Hartford Courant* reported that he "completely fooled the Yale defense on four occasions," each time having to be dragged down from behind. In a story by the Associated Press that appeared in the *Baltimore Sun* and in virtually every other major newspaper nationwide, Williams's and Albright's defensive play against Yale was described as "deadly."[12] The *Boston Globe* stated:

> Outside of Williams, Brown could boast of no stars. Offensively, and defensively, this left end put up a fine game. The much heralded Brooks and Armstrong could make nothing through the line, but it was on Williams' end run and the forward passes he took for Fox and Crowther, brother of the ex-All-American quarter, that Brown made almost all of its gains.[13]

The Black media took notice of Williams, too. The *Chicago Whip* introduced its readers to "Mayo Williams, the pride of New Negro sports!"

> Williams is as fast as "mercury poisoning," and in 1917 won the 50-yard indoor B. A. A. race. Williams is a sure tackler, an eel-like broken field runner, and follows up the plays of his opponents like a hawk. He is also an excellent field general and is always in the game.

The *Whip* also reported that Williams was benched for the 1916 season—while Fritz Pollard was still active—as a matter of "athletic policy" at Brown. Nevertheless, Williams's play in the 1919 Yale game "proved the superiority of the colored athlete."[14]

Considering the difficult Jim Crow–era news features and opinion pieces that filled the pages of the *Chicago Defender* and the *Chicago Whip* alike, it is no wonder that the accomplishments of Black athletes in white America were embraced as a point of pride and a sign of optimism. Mixed in with news articles detailing multiple lynchings of returning black veterans, Ku Klux Klan (KKK) uprisings in the Midwest, and the murderous rampage of white supremacists who destroyed Tulsa's Black Wall Street district were descriptions of Black athletes such as Ink Williams ("this copper-colored hero bids fair to carve a new niche in archives of athletic fame") and Duke Slater ("nature was kind to Slater, molding him in gigantic stature and Herculean strength"). The *Whip* declared that Williams and Slater "are a credit to the athletic world and the race feels proud of them."[15]

The *Whip*'s editor, Joe Bibb, had met Williams at a party while Bibb was still enrolled at Yale University Law School. The two men kept in touch, even sharing their enthusiasm for Mamie Smith's "Crazy Blues" (the first known commercial recording of a Black person singing the blues) when it was released in August 1920.[16] Bibb recognized something in Williams—friendship, talent, or both—and devoted space on the pages of the *Whip* to promote (and sometimes inflate) Williams's accomplishments and to use him as the embodiment of racial advancement:

> Williams states that he was roughed in the last Yale game and that he was called a Nigger. He feels that by supreme ability that the colored athlete will break down the prejudice that exists against him on account of his race and color.[17]

J. Mayo Williams rarely, if ever, promoted himself as a race "pioneer." But he was most certainly aware of the paper's opinion that he and Pollard were pioneers and public examples of a Black man's ability to succeed in a white world. He also knew that Bibb might help him advance his postcollege career: Bibb told Williams to look him up in Chicago after graduation.

Whatever idealized portrait of Williams appeared on the pages of the *Whip*, his life at Brown wasn't entirely pretty. He participated in a "dance tableau" at Brown's 1920 St. Patrick's Day minstrel show, in which the cast was roasted by the student paper for being drunk and distasteful. Williams performed a clog dance routine for his classmates and maybe sang blues. He also continued running the clothes pressing shop for Brown students with his fellow Black war veteran Maynard Wartman.

Williams's final season of collegiate football began in the fall of 1920 with rules that made the fledgling sport resemble the game we watch today: the new "man in motion" rule required players in motion to have both feet stationary on the ground when arriving at their position; "unnecessary roughness," or "roughing the passer," brought greater protection to quarterbacks, enabling offenses to increase their aerial game without sacrificing the health of their quarterback; time would now be called in the event of incomplete passes; false starts would be called with greater frequency; the "fair catch" came into play during kickoff and punt receptions; and the "punt out" was entirely abolished. The biggest rule change was that the "side making the touchdown, no matter where the touchdown is made, may bring the ball out straight in front of the goal." This made it considerably easier for teams to kick the extra point successfully.[18]

Williams's teams—at Monmouth High, at Howard, and in his three previous seasons at Brown—had been on the cutting edge of these innovations, and had been working toward a more aerial style of play. Just the previous fall, Brown had spent a week learning the innovative passing game of the University of New Hampshire (where Williams scored the only touchdown of his college career). So although the rules were new, the team was ready for the concepts, and they jumped out to a 6–0 start. But the team's fortunes faltered on Williams's injured legs. They stumbled badly, losing the last three games of the season to Yale, Harvard, and Dartmouth, respectively.

Williams played a spectacular, if difficult, game against Yale on a hurt knee. (The *Whip* described it as "Williams vs. Yale.") The following week, against Harvard, he injured his knee and left the game early, dashing Brown's hopes for a storybook season and causing resentment among some of his classmates. Brown's *Daily Herald*'s scribes—typically more generous to its hometown favorites—listed Williams as a Third Team All-American selection, behind the Second Team selection Rats Albright, Brown's other end, and described him as having "more than average ability."[19]

The *New York Times* named Williams a Third Team All-American after the 1920 season. The esteemed Walter Camp gave Williams an honorable mention, as did the *Boston Post* (which only selected a First Team All-American list).[20] Back home, the *Monmouth Daily Atlas* reported on Walter Camp's praise for both Williams and another Monmouthian—Rex Wray, who was Bert Bell's successor at quarterback for the University of Pennsylvania—saying that "the many friends of both of those boys in this city, will be greatly pleased to hear of their success."[21] Other papers in the region—the *Dispatch* in Moline, Illinois, and the *Daily Times* in Davenport, Iowa—celebrated Williams's receipt of a varsity B.

CHAPTER 6

Alpha

As Ink Williams spent the Christmas of 1920 in Providence nursing a swollen knee, perhaps he wondered if playing through injury while en route to his *New York Times* Third Team All-American nod was worth the price: disappointing his classmates and fans at season's end and preventing one of the nation's fastest sprinters from running his final season of winter track.[1] And as Williams convalesced, his name receded from the pages of local papers; indeed, the frequency of Williams's and Pollard's names on the pages of local papers from 1914 to 1920 had created an exaggerated impression of Brown's progressivism with regard to racial integration—an irony certainly not lost on Williams. Though classrooms, dormitories, dining halls, and playing fields were open to Black students, the segregation of fraternities in turn segregated social behavior. Blacks were not only a strikingly small—if prominent—minority on campus, but in Providence and Rhode Island, too. In 1920, there were just over 5 million African Americans in the United States, of whom only 5,096 lived in Rhode Island (out of a total population of 613,000), and 3,660 of whom resided in Providence (237,500 total population).[2] This was during the height of Jim Crow, when lynching of Blacks had surged following World War I: fifty-nine Blacks were lynched nationwide in 1921. And although no Blacks were ever lynched in any of the six New England states, it was a region where blackface minstrelsy would continue—including in the theaters in Williams's Providence neighborhood—in urban centers until the early 1960s and in some small towns until the 1980s.[3]

Black students such as Williams had long participated with other Black collegians in informal social networks; this is how Williams befriended Joe Bibb of the *Chicago Whip*. But in the face of growing racial hostility in the nation, momentum arose to establish a more secure, formal fraternal network. Williams had learned about Alpha Phi Alpha, the nation's first Black fraternity, six years earlier at Howard; many of the Black college athletes and army officers he had met were members. Alpha Phi Alpha was founded in 1906 at Cornell University in Ithaca, New York, and counted W. E. B. Du Bois and Paul Robeson among its members. In early 1921, Williams and other Black students at Brown reached out to Alpha Phi Alpha's headquarters in Baltimore to request the creation of a chapter at Brown. J. H. Hilburn, a fraternity member and lawyer from Baltimore, traveled to Brown to meet with the students and spoke with the Brown administration about establishing a chapter on campus. The administration was not receptive to Hilburn's proposal, as was noted in a report given to the 1921 Alpha Phi Alpha General Convention:

> On February 2, 1921 an application was filed from students at Brown University for the establishment of a chapter there. The application was approved and steps were taken to install the chapter.
>
> However the faculty of the university objected to the installation of another fraternity because of the large number already established there. The seat of the chapter was changed to the city of Providence, Rhode Island.[4]

President Faunce and the Brown administration rejected the establishment of Black, Italian, and Jewish fraternities in the early 1920s on the grounds of not allowing fraternities based on race, religion, and nationality, and claiming that the university already had enough fraternities.[5] And yet Faunce and the administration *did* allow all the existing fraternities to remain on campus despite the fact that they barred membership to students based on race, religion, and nationality—including the very Black, Italian, and Jewish students who had petitioned to start their own fraternities on campus.

Alpha Phi Alpha sidestepped Brown's refusal, founding a chapter based in the city of Providence—the Alpha Gamma chapter—on February 2, 1921. J. Mayo Williams was a founding member of the Alpha Gamma chapter, which issued the following mission statement:

> The objectives of Alpha Phi Alpha Fraternity, Inc. are to stimulate the ambition of its members to prepare them for the greatest usefulness in the cause of humanity, freedom and dignity of the individual; to encourage the highest and noblest form of manhood; and to aid downtrodden humanity in its efforts to achieve higher social, economic and intellectual status.[6]

The founding of the Alpha Phi Alpha chapter in Providence redefined Black social life at Brown. From 1921 to 1932, most Black students at Brown were members of the fraternity. The chapter played an integral part in building community on campus and in Providence—playing football and basketball against local Black city teams—and within the larger constructs of the fraternity, enabling fraternity brothers to establish a widespread network of business contacts that would prove helpful for Williams and others on graduation.[7] The Alpha Gamma Chapter promoted academic excellence—offering cash prizes to students with the highest grades—conducted plays, hosted parties for Providence's Black community, and would plan a reunion in 1923 of all living Black graduates of Brown. The Alpha Gamma chapter promoted the national fraternity's "Go to High School, Go to College" program at Providence's schools, sponsored oratorical contests, and brought notable speakers to Black community events in the city.[8]

Black students at the university needed solidarity amid an environment that was generally silent—or cavalier—about race matters. In his autobiographical work *No Day of Triumph*, the Brown graduate J. Saunders Redding is scathing in his assessment of life for Black students at Brown. Redding (the younger brother of the Alpha Gamma chapter founder Lorenzo Redding) attended Brown from 1924 through graduation in 1928. Dramatic and bleak when compared with his Alpha Gamma brother Russell Adrian Lane's reminiscences of Brown life, Redding wrote that Black students were suffocated by a white world that was not open to them, causing their spiritual and social lives to atrophy from neglect. Desperate to break out, Black students attended parties with other collegiate Black students in Boston and other neighboring cities where debauchery ran rampant. The hangover of guilt from these manic escapades, Redding claimed, caused him and his fellow Black students at Brown to view themselves with nausea and contempt.[9] However, J. Saunders Redding's wife, Ester, recalled things differently, remembering that Redding did not have a difficult time at Brown—at least relative to the experience of Jewish students at Brown, who she said were segregated into their own living space.[10] Her recollections temper those of her husband's in *No Day of Triumph*, in which Redding said that he "raged with secret hatred and fear" during his time at Brown.[11]

It is worth noting that in four years' worth of nearly daily accounts of his football, track, military, and other school activities at Brown, Ink Williams's race and color are never once mentioned in the *Brown Daily Herald*. And whereas the *Providence Journal* certainly displayed a great deal of insensitivity in news accounts of "midget" boxing, "Japs" (during World War II), and so forth, both Providence papers seem to have made a point of treating Brown's Black athletes with greater sensitivity than most other media outlets did. This was highly unusual by journalistic standards of the time: in comparison, news accounts of Fritz Pollard's, Paul Robeson's, and Ink Williams's football activities in major papers of the day frequently described the men as "burly negroes," "Ethiopians," or "African," or affixed "dusky," "bronze," "Negroid," or other racialized adjectives to their names.

Still, glimpses of embarrassing insensitivity can be found in the *Brown Daily Herald*, particularly in the annual St. Patrick's Day minstrel show. Evenings of minstrelsy at Brown appear to have consisted mostly of white students strumming on banjos and singing songs about "darkies" in the "sleepy" South. Shows during Williams's time at Brown were punctuated with a blackface routine that proved the high point of the evening's hilarity.[12] It is tempting, therefore, to sum up minstrelsy at Brown as a purely racist form of entertainment. However, Ink Williams's and Fritz Pollard's willing—even enthusiastic—participation each year in the minstrel show suggests a deeper complexity.

The paradoxical culture of integration and minstrelsy can be read in accounts of Williams's locker room encounters. Despite the popular caricature of varsity athletes as ignorant meatheads, athletics was—as it is now—a place of considerable interracial socializing, where friendships—and conflicts—across racial lines were normalized. In the days when visitors shared the home team's locker room, the scene at Yale in 1919 was a revelation for Yale's players, whose coach had attempted to use race baiting as a motivator in limiting Williams's play. Locker rooms also were a place where athletes socialized. On March 8, Brown's basketball team (of which Williams was not a member) played a home game against the Colonels of Centre College—a small, liberal arts college based in Danville, Kentucky that was enjoying a period where it was considered a national athletic powerhouse. It was unusual for Brown to play southern schools, but Centre College was on a lengthy road trip through the Northeast, showcasing the talents of its star players, Bo McMillan and George Maver, whose prowess on the court had shone a spotlight on to a relatively new sport that was only then starting to garner widespread attention. Following the game against Brown, which Centre won 40–28, Williams stopped by the locker room to meet McMillan. McMillan, like Williams, was a multisport star, being Centre's right forward in basketball as well as its quarterback in football. Williams was eager to meet the man who had earned All-American status three times.

McMillan had also earned a reputation as a team leader and a prominent forerunner to demonstrative prayer in public sporting matches. McMillan was known for being stone-cold sober, playing hard, and praying harder. Prior to games, McMillan—who was Roman Catholic—would round up his teammates for a (public) group prayer, eventually earning the team the nickname of the "Praying Colonels." Ink Williams had a penchant for gambling, and McMillan's fondness for gambling was well known, even then. The Brown and Centre players showered and dressed in the same locker room, and none of the players is reported to have objected to Williams's presence. While McMillan showered in plain sight of visitors and reporters, Jim Barrett—one of Williams's football teammates—overheard Ink comment on McMillan's physique. According to the *Kansas City Times*, Williams said of McMillan, "Well, if I had the build of that boy I sure wouldn't waste my time prayin' for heavenly succor. I'd wade in with both arms flyin' and let the other team do the prayin.'"

It was a funny quip, and apparently it had made the rounds for a full month before first appearing in print on April 9 in Kansas City.[13] The story was subsequently retold in numerous papers coast to coast, beginning with a near-verbatim account in the *Oregon Daily Journal*. Whereas none of the reports dwell on the subject of the integrated locker room, Williams's portrayal is minstrelized in various accounts. Details such as McMillan's hairy chest and tree-trunk-like legs are mentioned, and, in what reads like a 1920s blackface routine, Williams's wide-eyed double-take at the showering McMillan's body is added for comic effect. The *Boston Globe* ran the story with a similar quote attributed to Williams, adding "Yes sir!" at the end of it, and a postscript intended to underscore McMillan's manliness by stating that "Williams is no weakling by any means. Quite the contrary."[14] When the story appeared on April 25 in the *Dayton Daily News*, Williams—a former standout high school debater and orator, Howard and Brown University student, and US Army lieutenant—is reported as saying:

> Well, if ah-all had dat dar kinda build I sho' wouldn't waste mah time praying foh aid and succor before a game. Ah'd just tatchelly wade right in wid both arms flying and let de udder team do de prayin.' Yassuh.[15]

The McMillan-Williams encounter demonstrates the paradox of Williams's unique privilege on the one hand (a star athlete being welcomed into white social spaces not usually open to Black men), while showing how such privilege opened Williams up to public, racist ridicule. Likewise, these stories illuminate how college athletes appear far more comfortable with interracial mixing than the people paid to coach and write about them. Williams and McMillan would encounter one another again in the NFL; McMillan would go on to a legendary collegiate and professional coaching career.

For many Black students, Brown may not have had an ideal racial climate, but it was recognized as an improvement over the overtly racist environments of the South. Williams's classmate and fraternity brother Russell Adrian Lane, who was not on any athletic team, lamented that he and other Black students "had very little contacts with whites—certainly none with the white fraternities."[16] Still, Lane was impressed by Brown, and by what he called the "outstanding" people there. Lane lived in a dormitory with wealthy white students, even showering in the same place as they did. For Lane, this was a revelation:

> These boys thought nothing about it because they had never had any problems with Negroes. In Baltimore, [Blacks] made me stay clear of [whites], so I began to think Brown was a wonderful school for a Negro to come to after being kept back and being segregated all of my life. I marveled at the many professors there—they were so high class—so well trained. I didn't have any problems. Brown was a very high-class school. They took in

millions of dollars. They turned out some famous people, and I thought it was just lovely to be there among them—rubbing off some of that on me.[17]

Of the mission of Alpha Phi Alpha at Brown, Louis L. Redding said,

> What we were doing was not addressed to the purpose of singularly changing lives. We were trying to change the status and experience of a minority of Americans that happened to be black. We were not trying to change our lives, we were trying to change the opportunities of American citizens.[18]

Louis L. Redding—the first president of the Alpha Gamma chapter of Alpha Phi Alpha—went on to give the commencement oration in 1923. Most members—including Redding—went on to graduate school and prestigious careers in law, medicine, and academia. J. F. S. Carter and Heber E. Wharton III attended Howard Medical School and graduated in 1928. Louis Redding taught at Morehouse College for two years before graduating from Harvard Law in 1928. Russell Adrian Lane went to Howard Law and received four separate degrees.[19] Roscoe E. Lewis, class of '24, taught sociology at Fisk, Tuskegee, and Hampton, was a folklorist for the Works Progress Administration, where he directed sixteen Black scholars who conducted over three hundred interviews with formerly enslaved people. Lewis eventually became the chair of the social science department at Hampton.[20]

Seemingly just as the Alpha Gamma chapter established itself in Providence, the spring semester—Williams's final semester of college—began to wind down. At the beginning of spring break, the college asked ex-servicemen to bring their uniforms and sidearms back to campus with them, to be worn at the dedication of Soldier's Gate—the World War memorial arch, which had been under construction on Brown's campus since the 1918 armistice. The university promised to supply all students with rifles for the dedication, which was held on April 6, the four-year anniversary of the United States' entrance into the Great War. Over twenty-five hundred people attended the ceremony, which featured speeches from Brown veteran officers and a delegate officer from the French military.[21] Etched into the arch were the names of twenty-two men with whom Ink Williams had gone to school at Brown (classes of 1916 through 1922) but who had died in or as a result of the war. Lieutenant Colonel Noble B. Judah Jr., class of '04, delivered an address in which he lauded the two thousand Brown students, alumni, and faculty for their wartime service.[22]

Spring track held some promise for Williams to shine one last time as a college athlete, with prestigious meets scheduled in New York, Philadelphia, and Cambridge, Massachusetts. Archie Hahn, who had recruited Williams to Brown and had coached him since 1916, had left Brown following the 1920 season for a job at Michigan State; his replacement, A. W. Haddleton, had coached Italy's Olympic track team.²³ In his four years at Brown, Williams had always been the fastest man, but following his knee injury, he was edged out by his Alpha Phi Alpha fraternity brother J. F. S. Carter. Carter and Williams frequently placed—in that order—in sprints and hurdles, and both were the undisputed stars of the track team.²⁴ In a mid-May meet in New York City against Wesleyan and Columbia, Carter tied the Columbia track record for fastest time in the 100-yard dash, while Williams came in third.²⁵ In Brown's preparation for the international Penn Relays in Philadelphia, Williams suffered the indignity of being left off the relay team, despite being one of the two fastest men on it and one of the fastest men in college track nationally. Carter would be the only Black runner on the Brown relay team. At Penn, Williams saw Dartmouth's Johnny Shelbourne compete, as well as Harvard's E. O. Gourdin and the Olympian Charley Paddock.²⁶ Brown's quota system hamstrung its aspirations: the team placed fifth, just a yard behind the Paris team, a gap that certainly could have been closed by the speedy Williams.²⁷

Williams's final snub came on the heels of the Intercollegiate Championships in Cambridge, Massachusetts. Williams and Carter were competing in the 100- and 220-yard dash, with Williams also competing in the 220 hurdles, running high jump, and broad jump. Western Union telegrams updated the *Brown Daily Herald* staff on the preliminary heats, reporting that Carter had qualified in the 100- and 200-yard dash, J. West in the pole vault, and Williams in the broad jump. Carter won the 100-yard dash with a time of 10.2 seconds. Williams did not place, finishing fourth overall in the broad jump. Carter's accomplishment gained Brown enough points to tie for fifth place at the meet.²⁸ When the Brown Athletic Association awarded its varsity B to college athletes, Williams was denied a varsity letter because he failed to place at the Intercollegiate Championships. And, despite Carter's and Williams's star status, neither was among the four track athletes profiled in the spring's *Brown Daily Herald Weekly Alumni Supplement*. For Williams, it had to be a disappointing end to a noteworthy college athletic career.²⁹

While considered part of the class of 1920, Williams graduated with the class of 1921, with a cumulative 1.41 GPA.³⁰ His time at Brown was summed up in the yearbook:

JAY MAYO WILLIAMS, Monmouth, Ill.
"Ink" "Duke" "Speed"
Football (2) (3) (4); Track (2) (3) (4)

    Introducing "Ink," the star end. We have seldom seen him miss a tackle, and have never seen him emerge from scrimmage without a 5 inch grin. Not only does he excel in making his way thru interference, but also in executing end around plays. He has a warhoop [sic] that defies description.

This dusky warrior is as fast on the cinders as he is on the gridiron. In the dashes he shakes a fleet pair of heels. Au revoir, "Ink."[31]

Graduating along with Williams was his Alpha Phi Alpha brother Russell Adrian Lane, who was newly married. Lane's mother and new wife could not afford the expense of the train trip from Baltimore to Providence for commencement.[32] Along with Williams and Lane, Maynard Jones Wartman also graduated. Wartman, from Tilton, New Hampshire and a fellow Black veteran of World War I, had been assisting Ink Williams with what was left of Fritz Pollard's old clothes-pressing shop, helping their classmates with "'pressing' engagements."[33]

A better future was in the wind for both Wartman and Williams. Stepping out of the audience on Brown's college green was John Hope, the first Black president of Morehouse College and a graduate of Brown (1894). Hope introduced himself to both men, inviting them to come to Atlanta to take teaching positions at Morehouse.[34] Wartman accepted Hope's offer. Williams, however, told Hope that he would consider the offer and left Providence for Chicago to be reunited with his family. Williams was also weighing offers from Talladega College in Alabama, a Black high school in Evansville, Indiana, and an intriguing offer from Joe Bibb to work for the *Chicago Whip*. The Williams family had not made the trip to Providence for Williams's graduation. In the years since Williams had last seen his family, they had migrated to Chicago after Mayo's baby brother, Maurice, had landed himself in prison.

CHAPTER 7

Sambo

Mayo Williams, the fleet-footed Black kid from Monmouth, the captain of his integrated high school football team, the kid from the debate team, the Ivy League graduate and nationally famous college football star, had masterfully navigated systems of racial oppression and white supremacist culture. His older brother, Luther, had taken a more conventional path toward Black middle-class security by becoming a Pullman porter. But brutal systems of racial oppression still crushed the lives of young Black men back home in Monmouth, Illinois—an unavoidable truth when comparing the storied life of Mayo Williams with the turbulent life of his little brother, Maurice.

Everybody back in Monmouth called Mayo Williams "Ink." The nickname was indelible, coloring his life for its duration. Monmouth had been good to Ink and proud of his accomplishments, chronicling his track, football, and debate exploits in the daily papers of his youth, and keeping tabs on his collegiate, military, and professional endeavors as an adult. But although Ink spoke fondly of Monmouth later in life, the town was a paradox of opportunity and inequity. Miraculously, Ink Williams came out on the winning side of that equation.

In contrast, Maurice Williams came out on the losing side. Everybody back in Monmouth called Maurice Williams "Sambo," except for those who just called him "Sam." The nickname was dehumanizing, and systemic racism crippled his life for its duration. Monmouth was cruel to Sam, laughed at his missteps and chronicled them in detail in the daily papers. Six years younger than Ink, Sam was well liked but was not endowed with the same athletic gifts as Ink or with the same responsible constitution as his much older brother, Luther. Maybe Maurice lacked his brothers' intellectual skills, or their discipline, or maybe he just couldn't sit still, stay out of trouble, and steer clear of the drink.

When Mayo was a junior in high school, fifteen-year-old Sam was already living in a boardinghouse and working as a laborer. Perhaps the older Williams brothers kept Sam out of trouble while they still lived in town, but within a year of Ink's departure for Howard, Sam was already in the kind of trouble that could drag a man down: in September 1916, he was arrested by the Monmouth police for selling bootleg liquor. Brought before the local magistrate, Sam pled guilty and was fined two hundred dollars, roughly equivalent to five thousand dollars in today's currency. Eighteen years old at the time, Sam Williams was unable to pay the fine. According to the *Monmouth Daily Atlas*:

> Not having the money necessary to liquidate the fine, Williams was given a position on the street sweeping gang and unless a satisfactory settlement is made between now and a year from next November the prisoner will still be pushing a broom.[1]

The legal system of the day deemed it appropriate to sentence Williams to a street-sweeping gang for fourteen months for selling bootleg liquor. Sam Williams never quite recovered. In June 1919, he was arrested for vagrancy, a condition that meant he was homeless, unemployed, or both. Sam's mother and grandparents were still living and working in Monmouth, and he appears to have been close to all of them—so it is probable that he was earning money illegally. In court, Sam pled guilty; the authorities told reporters this was the first time they could recall someone pleading guilty to vagrancy.[2] Sam was fined one hundred dollars; again, he was unable to pay. Instead, he was sent to the county jail for three months.

In March 1920, just seven months after being released from the county jail, Sam was involved in a series of events that would land him in prison and influence his brother Ink's post-collegiate career decision. Sam was working at the Colonial Hotel in Monmouth, when he and a coworker named Spec Moore hatched a plan to steal and sell whiskey and gin. Moore broke into the home of a Monmouth resident named E. C. Hardin, stealing a case of whiskey, a case of gin, and a jug of gin from the basement. A cab driver named Wayne Ray waited outside, with Sam Williams in the back seat. Ray drove Moore, Williams, and the liquor to the outskirts of town, where they sold the cases of whiskey and gin for $225. One of the buyers was Carl Wallace, a relative of Sam Williams who worked at the pottery factory. Ray drove the cab with Williams, Moore, and the jug of gin to nearby Galesburg.

Carl Wallace got busted for buying the stolen liquor, all of which had Hardin's address printed on it. Wallace fingered Williams and Moore as the sellers, who were off getting "well oiled" on the remaining gin in Galesburg. Drunk and feeling confident, Sam Williams hired another cab to take him to Monmouth, where a night watchman found him attempting to break into a local hardware store; evading capture, Williams took off for Galesburg on foot. A manhunt ensued, and the police and townspeople searched for Williams—described as "Sambo Williams, well-known police character"—and Moore in a major sweep of "all of the dives" in Galesburg.[3]

Williams and Moore were now wanted for burglary and grand larceny, and both were still evading capture. Local officials believed that Williams was tied to a spree of ensuing robberies in the downtown district of Monmouth, including a break-in at the Chapin South First grocery store. On May 31, a man named Claude Davis was arrested for the Chapin South First break-in when police used fingerprints—then a new, revolutionary technique—to prove his involvement. Davis, in turn, reported Sam Williams as his accomplice, "thus adding another black mark against the already bad record of the fugitive Sambo. While talking to the officers Davis stated that he had been Invited by Sambo to take part in the robbery at the Hardin home but that he declined and stayed straight that night."[4] Sensing that the jig was nearly up, Spec Moore left Galesburg for Nebraska, and Sam took off for Chicago where he assumed the alias Sam McFall, a combination of his nickname and his grandmother Jennie McFall's last name.

Over in Chicago, it did not take long for trouble to find Sam. In late May (about two months after the gin-stealing caper), during an argument about a debt, Sam smashed a bottle over a man's head and ran through a plate glass window trying to escape. He was arrested and sentenced to time in Cook County Jail (nicknamed "Bridewell" after the notorious London jail), where he was given the bewildering news that his fingerprints revealed his true identity and connected him to the robbery in Monmouth.[5] For his crime in Chicago, Williams was sentenced to a year of prison time and slapped with a one-thousand-dollar fine, which he would have to work off.[6] After he served his time in Cook County Jail, he would have to report to Monmouth County Courthouse, where he would be arraigned for sentencing at the state penitentiary in Joliet for stealing and selling liquor in Monmouth.

Sam's flair for the dramatic and his wry sense of humor were on display the night of April 29, 1921. Following his release after eleven months in Bridewell, he appeared on the Monmouth train platform, escorted by a deputy sheriff, and announced to reporters, "It's the beginning of the end." Williams had to have been a character well known to Monmouth residents; it was rare for petty criminals (or most everyday citizens) to be quoted in news accounts. But reporters wanted to know what Williams thought of his pending trip to the state penitentiary in Joliet: compared with eleven months in Chicago's Cook County Jail, where he was fed "soup, soup, soup, everyday," Williams said Joliet would be relatively easy.[7]

First, however, Sam would need to go to the Warren County Courthouse for his arraignment related to the theft and resale of the whiskey and gin and for the break-in at the grocer's the previous year. He arrived in court on May

1 without an attorney and prepared to plead guilty in front of a grand jury of twenty-two white men. But Williams balked on learning that the charges of burglary and grand larceny meant he could face up to twenty years at Joliet, and asked to confer with an attorney.[8] Back in court on May 3 with a court-appointed attorney, Williams pled guilty; also in court that day were two of Williams's accomplices, Carl Wallace and James Friel, who were represented by Ink's old high school track teammate Bruce Brady. Brady attempted to get Wallace a period of probation in return for a guilty plea to burglary and grand larceny, but this was denied. Carl Wallace and Sam Williams were sentenced to one to twenty years each at Joliet. Friel, a minor, was sentenced to reform school.[9]

For the Williams family, the die was cast. While Sam was in prison at Cook County Jail, his mother, Millie, moved to Chicago to be close by. Luther had been living in Chicago for eight years with his wife, Agnes, working for the Pullman Company and for the Canadian National Railway. The transfer to Joliet placed Maurice fifty miles southwest of Chicago—one hundred fifty miles closer than Monmouth. Millie stayed in Chicago, making it the new hometown of the Williams family.

CHAPTER 8

Black Swan

In May 1921, following his graduation from Brown, Mayo Williams caught a train from Providence to Chicago, where he encountered a city that was experiencing its most celebrated age. Chicago's assembly-line factories were booming, luring millions of newcomers from across Europe and the rural and urban South. This latter group included the first massive wave of the Great Migration, which eventually saw six million Blacks leave the South for urban centers in the North and the West. Such was the process by which a critical mass of Black folkways—culinary, musical, devotional, craft, and otherwise—were transplanted to Chicago, and where traditions such as blues and jazz took on the terroir of their new soil. Ink's older brother, Luther, had migrated nine years earlier; his younger brother, Maurice, was incarcerated there for a time in Cook County Jail; his mother, Millie, followed in 1920, and Mayo completed the family migration after graduation in the spring of 1921.

Williams was weighing job offers to coach football in the fall of 1921 at several all-Black schools: Morehouse College in Atlanta; Paul Quinn College in Waco, Texas; Talladega College in Talladega, Alabama; and a high school in Evansville, Indiana. These were solid job offers for clearly defined positions of some prestige in their respective communities. But Ink Williams was ambitious and not shy about pursuing more speculative careers in Chicago. He was interested in the possibility of working in insurance. Fritz Pollard had recently moved to Chicago to try his hand at banking, which also piqued Williams's interest, but he was disappointed to learn that bank salaries started at just twenty-five dollars a week. In addition to college and high school coaching jobs, Ink also had a vague offer of work from the editor of the *Chicago Whip*, Joe Bibb, who had been responsible for the paper's regular (and flattering) coverage of Williams's athletic exploits. At an Alpha Phi Alpha gathering in Boston, Williams remembered Bibb telling him, "'When you come to Chicago, look us up.' So I *did*."[1]

The *Chicago Whip* was a weekly tabloid newspaper with a circulation of over sixty-five thousand. It was one of five newspapers in the city aimed at Black readers, and it was second in circulation to the more famous *Chicago Defender*. William Linton, Bill Bottoms, Virgil Williams, and Frank Preer had launched the *Whip* in 1919, and the tabloid distinguished itself through its emphasis on entertainment. As the heavyweight boxer Jack Johnson's former personal chef and sidekick, Bill Bottoms had a high profile in Chicago. He had opened Chicago's Dreamland Café in 1917 and had hired the blues singer Alberta Hunter for her first substantial gig, as well as the jazz pioneer Joe Oliver, who at that time was providing music in the grandstand at Chicago White Sox games at nearby Comiskey Park. Bottoms also helped Virgil Williams open the Royal Gardens in 1918. Preer was the owner of the DeLuxe Gardens. Bottoms, (Virgil) Williams, and Preer saw the *Whip* as a vehicle for weekly cabaret and club entertainment advertising. But it was William Linton who was the main actor behind the *Whip*'s content, which was otherwise modeled after the *Defender*.

Each issue of the *Whip* published by Linton—from 1919 until his death in 1922, when Arthur Clement MacNeal and Joe Bibb assumed leadership—displayed this banner: "With due regard for right, with purity of motive in our expression, with conscientious compassion for stricken humanity, with unstinted credit to those who merit, with truth as our guide post and love as our inspiration, we have committed ourselves to the world of journalism. We have dedicated ourselves to public service."[2] Although the paper had some noble motives, the entertainment venues that supported the paper were spaces where Chicago's notorious organized crime syndicates gathered to do business, developing elaborate workarounds so that alcohol consumption (and profits) would be uninterrupted during the height of Prohibition. This intertwined world of mobsters and musicians was unavoidable for anybody involved in the business end of blues and jazz in Chicago in the 1920s.

Most of the clubs that advertised in the *Whip* were Black owned and employed a "black and tan" tradition of welcoming all shades of all races to shows. Yet under Bibb's influence, the *Whip* was transformed into a radical paper, a mouthpiece of Marcus Garvey–inspired separatist politics. It appears that Bibb and the music and theater editor Dave Peyton—who eventually went on to some prominence as a writer for the *Defender*—were both active in Marcus Garvey's Universal Negro Improvement Association (UNIA). Despite the paper's pro-Garvey/UNIA sympathies, some articles still celebrated "how well the 'blacks and tans' get along after midnight" and lamented city efforts to segregate clubs and disenfranchise Black entrepreneurs. This celebration of racial mingling suggests that separatist philosophies had yet to be fully embraced by the time of Williams's arrival in 1921, and that encouraging all races to frequent Black-owned establishments was simply good business policy. The Dreamland Café and the Royal Gardens were closed temporarily in May 1921, and many Black-owned clubs on Chicago's South Side were subsequently bought up by whites. Thus, what the historian Ted Vincent has called the early twentieth-century high point of racial integration in Chicago's clubs had passed at the very moment of Williams's arrival in the city.[3]

Faced with the choice between working for the *Whip* in Chicago or as a football coach at several of the most prestigious Black colleges in the deep south, Mayo Williams did what many other college graduates before and since have done: he asked his mother what to do. "I told her what I was confronted with," he recalled. She asked him, "Why not stay around here a while?" Mayo's answer suggests he asked his mother because he knew she would recommend the choice he wanted to make: "I said, 'Oh, why not?'"[4] Taking a job at the *Whip* provided Mayo Williams with a basic network of people within the Black intellectual elite, the entertainment business, and the athletic community. (*Whip* readers were mostly working-class Blacks, but the paper was run entirely by Black college graduates.)

Williams made his journalistic debut on August 27, 1921, with an article that could best be described as a post-mortem essay on his experience as a collegiate football player.

FOOTBALL PROSPECTS IN THE EAST

Ink Williams, last season's brilliant star writing exclusively for the *Whip*

by Mayo "Ink" Williams—Brown University's All Eastern End

With so many inquiries regarding the colored boys in eastern intercollegiate football circles this fall, the writer is only too glad to give to the public some hope for an enthusiastic anticipation for the coming season. Almost daily some big eastern school publishes its schedule for its first call for candidates; and lovers of the sport wonder if we will be represented in the big games where hundreds of thousands of spectators gather each Saturday to witness the greatest of all outdoor sports, football. However, before going into detail it is altogether proper that a tribute of praise be given to [Fritz] Pollard, of Brown, [William Henry] Lewis of Harvard, [Paul] Robeson of Rutgers, [Matthew] Bullock of Dartmouth, [John] Shelbourne of Dartmouth, Courney of Maine, Eller [*sic*, Herbert Ayler] of Brown and [Joseph Edward "Joe"] Trigg of Syracuse for breaking down the bars of prejudice in their respective schools, not only by excelling in football, but also by gentlemanly conduct and sportsmanship, and paving the way for any who are capable of representing the big eastern schools.[5] One of the questions that the colored public asks the most is this: "Well, how do they treat you." In answer, I might say, different athletes meet with different situations, and duly the individual athletes can answer.

However, every colored athlete in white schools meets with barriers which are common to all. The colored athlete must not only stand head and shoulders above every man who tries for the position which he is after but he must also satisfy the critical eye of the coaches, the vacillating dispositions of the various alumni associations, which in reality are the schools, the various players with whom he must fight with and against and the student body from which lifelong friends from all over the world are either lost or made. The fraternities, and lastly the press, which controls the sentiment of all other obstacles.

Thus it is obvious that the colored athlete in big intercollegiate circles must not only possess super-athletic ability but a thorough understanding of human nature, the most complex and fickle of all mechanisms.

The Big Three

We are all familiar with the history of Princeton and Yale, as well as Cornell and Pennsylvania, as regards colored athletes, no encouragement or support whatsoever is given at any of the schools and consequently no colored athlete has ever won the Princeton P, the Yale Y, the Cornell C, or the Pennsylvania P in football. At Harvard, however, the situation is different, as was shown last spring when Harvard refused to schedule track meets with schools that would not show courtesy to [Ned] Gourdin, who recently brought the world's highest broad-jumping honors to Harvard and himself.[6] But even at fair Harvard a colored athlete must be capable and able to display his ability under trying circumstances for competition is keen and lonely the man with the iron nerve survives at "Fair Harvard," where the slogan is "Fair Play, and May the Best Man Win." Very recently a colored boy tried out for the varsity at Harvard; his past record in one of our colored schools warranted a trial and consideration. Suddenly he was dropped from the squad. A committee of men, headed by Drs. [William] Latimore and Taylor, who have seen every game in the stadium for the last eight years, obtained this information from the coaches: "Harvard knows no prejudice; a man must possess the goods when he comes to Harvard to try for the football team; he must know the game and have ability; we haven't time to teach the fundamentals to anyone." This is the sentiment of Harvard and all other eastern schools where colored boys have made and shall make records for themselves and the schools.

Colored Schools vs White

Having played on and against the best, both colored and white teams, I can safely offer an unbiased comparison. The large colored universities possess wonderful material individually. On almost every colored team will be found one or more men who might make the varsity on any team in the country. But the teams as a whole, man for man, would not measure up properly with the large eastern or western university teams. This fact is not due to the coaches or individual players, but to the lack of funds with which to develop the men. When we think of a large eastern team carrying eight coaches and assistants; three doctors, five trainers and innumerable rubbers who are always ready to offer suggestions for individual and team work, we can easily see how hard it would be to compare the schools favorably. However, a just comparison cannot be made until a big inter-racial game is played.[7]

Ink Williams's article reveals the mind of an athlete who is keenly aware of his environment and actively questioning his role in it. It shows that he was part of a network of connected Black men like William Lattimore, who monitored the progress of Black athletes in college and professional sports. Lattimore, it should be remembered, was the founder of the Smart Set Athletic Club, the hosts of the integrated track competition in Brooklyn where Williams and Pollard had competed in 1917. This essay answers some questions about what life was like for a Black athlete playing in a mostly white league. Williams also alludes to his year at Howard University, saying that he had "played on and against the best, both colored and white teams."

Despite this robust opening statement from Williams in the *Whip*, his journalistic contributions are hard to find, because articles appeared without bylines. Which articles Williams contributed to the paper—in hard news, sports, or entertainment—is an open question.

However, Joe Bibb had a purpose for Ink Williams entirely unrelated to journalism: as a collection agent for, and distributor of, Black Swan Records. In addition to his role at the *Whip*, Bibb served as executive treasurer for Black Swan, the first fully functional Black-owned and operated record label in the nation. The label was the entrepreneurial brainchild of the NAACP and the song publisher Harry Pace of the Pace & Handy Music Publishing Company.[8]

Joe Bibb was Pace's brother-in-law and was in charge of Black Swan's distribution warehouse.[9] Bibb was getting overwhelmed trying to keep the *Whip* afloat and run the Black Swan distributorship. Bibb leveled with Williams about the precarious finances of both enterprises and the nature of his relationship with Pace. Explaining that he and his *Whip* associates were too busy to deal with Black Swan, Bibb asked Williams, "You want to take this distributorship over?"[10] The fledgling business of race records appealed to Williams on an organizational level. He remembered years later, "I wanted to go into something where I could be the organizer; show people how to do it."[11] Williams wired his regrets to Morehouse, Talladega, and Evansville, saying that he had found employment elsewhere and that "I'm gonna devote my time to the record business."[12]

The historical timing of the launch of Black Swan Records was not accidental. Black servicemen returned from World War I only to be met with outright hostility, lynch mobs, and the same ignorant racist policies that had clouded the thinking of many white Americans for centuries. A wave of violent and destructive riots—the Red Summer of 1919—was splashed across the pages of Black newspapers such as the *Chicago Whip*, the *Chicago Defender*, the *Pittsburgh Courier*, the *Boston Guardian*, and others. Black activists worked with renewed vigor toward changing a social system that was heavily armed against them. Out of this quagmire of frustration and neglect rose the ideas that became Black Swan Records—a Black-owned and operated company making "music *by* and *for* African-Americans."[13] The record industry itself had only recently become an important player in American business, dealing mainly in popular and concert styles, mainly serving the tastes of the middle class. But as technology became more affordable, companies began catering to white, rural, working-class and immigrant groups, releasing hundreds of titles aimed at ethnic groups ranging from French-Canadian to Macedonian. The tastes of Black consumers, however, were largely ignored. What little space Black performers were allotted on shellac was reserved for the comic, novelty, and minstrel "coon" songs that were the mainstays of the cross-racial vaudeville and minstrel world. There were few exceptions—most notably recordings made by jubilee-style singers and the bandleader James Reese Europe. In short, Black musicians and consumers were systematically excluded from the record business—as executives, performers, and customers. Black Swan Records was founded to combat this exclusion.

The music columns of Chicago's Black newspapers of this time show a community fully aware of its musical heritage as well as the spectrum of styles ultimately enfolded by the Black Swan catalog. Articles in the music pages of the *Chicago Whip* ranged from who "brings it" best in jazz circles to hailing the cultural-historical origins of jazz as early as 1919 (reflecting the typical from New Orleans, up the Mississippi, to Chicago narrative). These articles revealed a fully developed music scene, eagerly debating its own merits by its own cultural standards. These articles are sprinkled with advertisements announcing countless theater and club dates for jazz and blues concerts, and other advertisements for sheet music of local blues and jazz hits (always sold by Pace & Handy)—further evidence that, prior to the arrival of Black Swan Records, the Black music community only lacked a record label willing to record music of and for a wide range of Black musical styles and tastes.[14]

The oligopoly that ran the phonograph and record business of the late nineteenth and early twentieth centuries began to lose its stranglehold on record-making patents shortly after World War I, and a number of small labels began springing up. As early as 1919, the *Chicago Defender* encouraged its readers to write to phonograph companies demanding the release of records by Black artists. The ironic reality of this particular moment of American cultural history, as plainly demonstrated by the popularity of jazz and minstrel songs among whites in 1917 (profoundly observed at the time by Williams's former Howard professor Alain Locke), is that Black Americans already exerted significant influence over the general complexion of American culture. But Black musicians and consumers had no place of their own in the commercial cultural marketplace, and high-profile Black entertainers such as Perry Bradford, Bert Williams, and Bill "Bojangles" Robinson campaigned tirelessly for labels to record music by Black performers for Black audiences. In 1920, OKeh Records responded by issuing two records by the Black blues singer Mamie Smith—including "Crazy Blues," for which Mayo Williams and Joe Bibb shared an affinity. Smith's first recording for OKeh was "That Thing Called Love," written by Perry Bradford and published by Pace & Handy. Pace & Handy urged Black consumers—via the *Chicago Defender*—to buy her record:

> Lovers of music everywhere, and those who desire to help in any advance of the Race should be sure to buy this record as encouragement to the manufacturers for their liberal policy and to encourage other manufacturers who may not believe that the Race will buy records sung by its own singers.[15]

The incredible success of these records—particularly Mamie Smith's "Crazy Blues"—spawned the "blues craze" of the 1920s, and a market for records by Black artists was firmly established. Later that year, Harry Pace organized the business that became Black Swan Records.[16]

Pace planned for Black Swan to issue a wide spectrum of music by Black artists—opera, spirituals, classical, jazz, blues, and comic songs—in an effort to challenge the racist stereotypes that had historically led Columbia, Victor, and Edison to release recordings demeaning to Blacks. Black Swan was to be a fully self-sufficient Black business entity whose purpose was to financially empower the Black community, "uplift" the tastes of its Black consumers, and improve the public's perception of Black artists and consumers. Pace did not act alone in the development of Black Swan; indeed, he had a long history with W. E. B. Du Bois. Pace also was closely associated with the NAACP, which carefully monitored the progress of the company. The development of Black-owned businesses was a high priority for all three of the era's foremost Black social-political thinkers (Du Bois, Booker T. Washington, and Marcus Garvey); thus the arrival of Black Swan met with overwhelming approval by Black intellectuals. The creation of the Black Swan company was, according to the historian David Suisman, an attempt to make Blacks the "co-workers in the kingdom of culture," as Du Bois had called for in *The Souls of Black Folk*.[17]

Harry Pace had the right résumé for the job. Born in 1884, the son of a blacksmith in Covington, Georgia, Pace had studied under Du Bois at Atlanta University and graduated, the valedictorian of his class, in 1903. He then worked as the business manager for Du Bois's newsletter, *Moon Illustrated*

Weekly, in Memphis. Over the next several years, Pace shuttled back and forth between business interests in Memphis and Atlanta. For six years he was the head of the most prominent and well-respected Black-owned business of the era—the Standard Life Insurance Company—and was president of the Pace & Handy Music Publishing Company.[18] Pace & Handy moved from Memphis to New York City at Pace's behest. There both men encountered constant opposition to their operation—particularly in their quest to have white-owned record labels record Black musicians and in their efforts to entice white performers to perform music written by Black composers and songwriters. Pace later recalled, "It was my job as president of the company to contact all phonograph companies so that our own numbers might be recorded from time to time. I ran up against a color line that was very severe."[19]

Pace himself had parted ways with Handy in 1919, largely to begin organizing Black Swan Records. The newly formed Pace Recording Company, of which Black Swan was a subsidiary, boasted a board of directors that reflected Pace's shrewd business sense and valuable political contacts, including W. E. B. Du Bois and several members of the NAACP. Du Bois publicly endorsed the Black Swan project in the NAACP publication, *Crisis*, telling readers that "until the art of the black folk compels recognition they will not be rated as human. And when through art they compel recognition then let the world discover if it will that their art is as new as it is old and as old as new."[20] With respect to choosing someone to oversee the "uplift" of Black America through Black music, Du Bois found a natural leader in Harry Pace. Pace named the label after the nineteenth-century Black opera singer Elizabeth Taylor Greenfield, whose nickname, the "Black Swan," was a reference to a popular white performer, Jenny Lind, the "Swedish Nightingale." The label's name reflected Pace's musical tastes: the composed, sentimental ballads popular among the Black upper crust, rather than the earthy blues and jazz orientation of Pace's longtime partner, W. C. Handy.

Pace was a well-known figure in Chicago's Black community. Readers of the *Chicago Whip* and the *Chicago Defender* followed notices of which Black artists had signed sheet music contracts with Pace & Handy. Thus, the pending arrival of Black Swan was met with popular fanfare. This excitement did not necessarily spill out beyond the Black community: many whites in the record industry were aggressively anti–Pace & Handy and anti–Black Swan. By the time the label was launched, white-owned record labels threatened to boycott Pace & Handy's music if Pace did not fully sever ties with his publishing company. Though this sort of publishing tie-in was commonplace in the recording industry, technically it was against the law. Pace was forced to fully withdraw from Handy's publishing company, thereby depriving Black Swan of an important revenue stream of profit from song publishing. Pace left with most of the Pace & Handy staff, and the publishing company's advertisements in Black newspapers were replaced with Black Swan ads. Handy's health failed him at this time; he reportedly went blind for several years on account of the resulting mental tension.[21] Pace faced difficulty locating pressing plants to manufacture Black Swan Records, settling on a solution that would have long-term consequences:

> It took me a long time to find a place where records could be pressed. All of the bigger companies refused to press records for outsiders and I finally learned of the New York Recording Laboratory located in Port Washington, Wisconsin, who was willing to press the records for me if I would have them recorded and furnish them a complete master.[22]

Pace and Black Swan persevered and, with the notable assistance of the Wisconsin-based New York Recording Laboratory, released their first record in May 1921—"At Dawning" backed with "Thank God for a Garden"—a sentimental recording by the concert singer Revella Hughes. Hughes was active in the Marcus Garvey movement, performing at many pro-Garvey functions. Pace's decision to make her the first Black Swan release reflects the unifying potential music possessed for the Black intellectual community at that time. Black Swan would ultimately release over one hundred eighty records, forty-five of which were "serious" music (sacred, secular, arias, carols, composed music).[23]

The *Chicago Defender* lauded Black Swan's arrival with a lengthy article. The *Defender*'s description of both Harry Pace and his staff arranger, Fletcher Henderson, highlights the genteel inclinations of that newspaper's editorial staff:

> Mr. Pace is a graduate of Atlanta University as is also his music director, Mr. [Fletcher] Henderson. Both are possessed of regular, refined features, and the poise of the educated and cultured and that of trained musicians.[24]

That the article takes the time to mention Harry Pace and Fletcher Henderson's "refined features" is a sign that Pace's Black Swan endeavor—and the reaction of the writer, Tony Langston, to it—is not in keeping with the agendas of either Marcus Garvey or Booker T. Washington. It should be noted that the *Defender* frequently featured ads for skin-lightening creams, hair straighteners, and other products intended to de-emphasize Black features. In retrospect, critics such as Amiri Baraka have pointed to Black Swan's eclectic catalog as aspiring to elitist trends: the *Defender* article corroborates this, and its citation of Pace and Henderson's academic pedigree is also telling. But the fact remains that Black performers of "serious" music remained entirely unserved until Black Swan's arrival; furthermore, although Black Swan helped solve that particular problem, an actual market for such recordings proved elusive. Black Swan was clear in its public statements that its attention to "serious" music was not an attempt to demean folk-based styles such as blues, jazz, and comedy but rather to create opportunities for a broad stylistic range of Black musicians and to present a catalog representing all styles of music performed and composed by Blacks. In this regard, Pace's agenda differed from that of Du Bois and many bourgeois Blacks who viewed blues as "degraded" music. Despite the remarkable fact that Black Swan had an unproven young jazz arranger in Fletcher Henderson (recording manager, pianist) working with the classical composer William Grant Still (music director), the blues and jazz records released by Black Swan quickly became the financial mainstays of the company. The singer Ethel Waters recalled she, Pace, and Henderson had debated whether she should sing "popular or 'cultural' numbers."[25] Waters sang "Down Home Blues" and "Oh Daddy" and was paid one hundred dollars for the two songs. Her success proved an economic boon to the cash-strapped company; Black Swan finished 1921 turning a profit of $3,100 on revenues of over $104,000. By the spring of 1922, Black Swan had sold approximately four hundred thousand records.[26]

Despite Black Swan's successful first year of business, Pace felt the need to defend the label's inclusion of popular music in a report to members of the NAACP. "We have to give the people what many of them wanted to get them to buy what we wanted them to want," he stated. "I believe that we want every kind of music other people want and it behooves some of us to undertake the job of elevating the musical taste of the race. . . . Black Swan Records are trying to do their part."[27] With non-blues sales falling far short of the success of blues sides by Alberta Hunter and Ethel Waters, it is easy to conclude that Black Swan simply should have tied up less capital in styles that did not sell. And although Black Swan's insistence on *not* doing just that reflected Pace's staying true to his vision of a label that spanned the fullness of Black musical expression, Black Swan's very success was causing the company to push its credit to the breaking point.

The more quickly Black Swan succeeded—selling large numbers of records in a short amount of time—the more capital it invested in producing records that were sold on credit. This arrangement meant that the company was perpetually short of disposable cash. Such is the irony that ruled the world of small record businesses over the entire course of the twentieth century, where quick success often led to bankruptcy. When a company such as Black Swan relied on a network of independently owned record stores to sell its physical products, it was crucial for the label to make sure its purchasers paid their bills in full and on time. A company in such a predicament needs a good collection agent. Enter Mayo Williams.

Harry Pace's office was in Harlem, but Black Swan's records were pressed in Wisconsin and distributed from Chicago. When Joe Bibb hired Williams to take over as Black Swan's distributor and collection agent, he gave Williams responsibility over the label's most significant market. Williams's ability to get record dealers to pay their bills in full and on time was critical to Pace's getting the cash he needed to keep up with orders, produce and press new records, and pay Black Swan's bills. Williams threw himself into this work, quickly becoming immersed in the social and economic life of Chicago's South Side, developing strong contacts with influential record dealers and club owners. Williams was also selling some of these same clients his own home-brewed bathtub gin on the side (something his brother Maurice was likely advising on).

But although business was brisk and invigorating, it was not long before Williams began noticing serious problems with Joe Bibb's business practices. "The records would be sold on credit," Williams recalled. "I'd go around and collect the money, and pay it all to Joe Bibb. And instead of Joe Bibb paying Pace, he would take the money and put it into his paper."[28] Bibb's embezzlement of his own brother-in-law's monies was clipping Black Swan's wings just as the label was getting ready to take flight.

CHAPTER 9

Hammond Pro

On December 4, 1921, a cold Sunday afternoon in Chicago, at a slick, rectangular mud patch named Normal Field, about thirty-five hundred brave souls had turned out to watch a professional football game between the Chicago Cardinals and the Akron Pros.

For a factory worker, this one-year-old pro football league—known in 1921 as the American Professional Football Association (APFA), but in 1922 renamed the National Football League—was a cheap, fun way to spend a couple of hours on your only day off from work. Unlike college games, which took place during the Saturday workday, pro games took place on Sunday afternoons after church. For the price of a dollar, you got beyond the wooden barricades and could take a seat in what passed for a grandstand. It was hardly grand, but you could yell your lungs out at some former college stars and maybe even place some side bets. It was a good time, provided you didn't mind being uncomfortable.

The Cardinals always promised to be exciting, and their backfield featured the electrifying Paddy Driscoll, as well as the brothers Ralph and Arnold McMahon, making them favorites of Chicago's booming Irish community.

The visiting Akron Pros were the real reason to be here. Akron's success was driven by two famous All-Americans, Fritz Pollard and Paul Robeson, both of whom were Black. Pollard was a Chicago kid who rarely played games in town; he shared head coaching duties for Akron with Elgie Tobin.

Akron had won the league's inaugural championship the previous season. As reigning champs with marquee names in their lineup, Akron drew large crowds everywhere they went—particularly on Chicago's South Side. This accounted for today's crowd—about fifteen hundred more than usual, even bigger than when the Cardinals played their crosstown rivals, the Decatur

Staleys. A quarter of the faces there were likely Black and had come from South Side neighborhoods to see Pollard and Robeson.[1]

History was being made that day—not by Pollard, or Robeson, or another player on the field—but by one of the referees officiating at the game.

Weather and a season of hard play had killed almost all of the grass on the muddy field. The colors of the players' ragged uniforms—Chicago in red, white, and brown; Akron in blue, gold, and brown—were muted by weeks of relentless mudslinging. But the crisp starched whites worn by the officials in those days were hard to miss.

Of note was the fact that one of the three officials—the head linesman—was a Black man.

Known today as the "down judge," the head linesman was the official responsible for watching pre-snap encroachment on the line of scrimmage, marking the forward progress of the ball, and marking first-down progress with the measuring chains. In everyday modern NFL circumstances, the head linesman is a target of complaints from fans, players, and coaches. In the highly racially charged atmosphere of 1921, a Black head linesman could be said to be performing under extreme duress.

The head linesman was J. Mayo "Ink" Williams.

Williams's trailblazing role as an NFL official on December 4, 1921 was something the *Chicago Defender* hoped would "set a precedent" for the league to include Black officials.[2] It would be the first and only documented time prior to 1988 that a Black man officiated an NFL game.

It hadn't taken Ink Williams long to realize that he wanted to augment his modest Black Swan earnings with some football income. The upstart NFL seemed like a good place to begin—an option he was aware of through Fritz Pollard. Nor had he signed on to work as a league official—this was just something he was happy to do on a weekend off for the Hammond Pros.

Ink Williams's road to professional football led directly from Brown. Clair J. Purdy had encouraged Pollard to turn pro in 1919. Purdy had been the first student to befriend Pollard at Brown in 1915, telling Fritz that Catholics and Blacks were the last two kinds of players their WASP classmates wanted to see make the team.[3] Purdy and Pollard had carried Brown to the "Tournament East-West football game" (the first annual Rose Bowl game) in 1916. Following graduation, Purdy landed a job playing for the Akron Pros—a professional team in the Ohio League. Purdy convinced Pollard he could make him a star at Akron by setting him up for plays using Brown's system of play. The plan worked, Pollard said, in part because Purdy created an atmosphere of acceptance in Akron.[4] This was in 1919, the year before the creation of what became the NFL.

In 1920, fourteen owners of pro football teams from Ohio, Indiana, Illinois, and New York gathered at a Hupmobile car dealership in Canton, Ohio, and agreed to create a new league called the American Professional Football Association (APFA), a name they changed to the National Football League (NFL) two years later. The team owners could have easily been mistaken for a chamber of commerce with a few gamblers mixed in: they ran car dealerships, tire factories, and laundries—with some doctors and lawyers who speculated on boxing and other sports. Of those original franchises, which included the Dayton Triangles and the Rock Island Independents, only two—the Decatur Staleys (now the Chicago Bears) and the Racine Cardinals (now the Arizona Cardinals)—remain.

The owners selected Jim Thorpe to serve as the league's first president.[5] Then the sport's most high-profile player, the thirty-two year-old Thorpe was a twice-celebrated All-American collegiate football player (at Carlisle Indian Industrial School); a recipient of two gold medals in the 1912 Olympics (decathlon, pentathlon); a six-year veteran of major-league baseball (outfielder with the New York Giants, the Boston Braves, and the Cincinnati Reds); and a five-year veteran of the pre-NFL Canton Bulldogs. He was also the most prominent citizen of the Sac and Fox Nation. His selection as league president was a calculated choice by the team owners, who hoped that Thorpe's fame as the nation's greatest all-around athlete might elevate the profile of a league whose very professionalization sullied the game's reputation in the minds of the general public.

At Normal Field, Williams could see vivid evidence of pro football's bad reputation in the form of the Cardinals' celebrated Irish American backfield. Williams knew the McMahon brothers personally, by their *actual* names: Ralph and Arnold Horween, two Ukrainian American brothers who had run roughshod over Williams and Brown University on their way to Harvard football's back-to-back undefeated seasons in 1919 and 1920. The legendary All-American Horween twins were celebrated officers in the navy during World War I; Arnold was elected the first Jewish captain of the Harvard football team. The "McMahon Brothers" was effective local cover for these sons of the Chicago leather tannery titan Isidore Horween. (Horween Leather Company is the longtime supplier of leather for NFL footballs and NBA basketballs.) Isidore was proud of his sons' college football exploits, even though professional football was regarded as a violent, unregulated, crude brawl among unrefined men. Many other early NFL players played under assumed names in order to protect their off-field reputations.

The team owners did think that the creation of this new league might boost the professional game's respectability. But mainly they were businessmen who wanted to develop a more consistent and profitable product. They knew spectators would turn out to see former collegiate stars such as Thorpe, Pollard, and Driscoll. These stars were mostly reliable, but the quality of games was not, and this limited the appeal of the professional game.

Pollard's experience with Akron was a microcosm of the league's considerable promise and of the obstacles it needed to address. The 1919 iteration of the Akron Pros was "mostly sandlot" guys, according to Pollard, and the team practiced only on Sunday mornings, two hours prior to game time. Like Purdy, Pollard and others began recruiting more college graduates into the league—because it was an opportunity to play for pay, but also to improve the overall quality of the league. By the 1920 season, twenty of the twenty-three Akron men had played in college. The Akron Pros won the first league championship in 1920, and Pollard became the new league's first Black star.[6]

Pollard succeeded in recruiting Paul Robeson to join the 1921 Akron team, telling him it was "easy money." Robeson recalled earning between $75 and $300 per game for Akron; Pollard claimed to have gotten as much as $1,500.[7] Williams was eager to play professional ball as well, but he seemed to want a less demanding situation—fitting football into his professional life, rather than fitting his professional life into football. This desire would lead him to join an NFL team that had the opposite trajectory of Akron—the Hammond Pros of Hammond, Indiana.

Sizing up the line of scrimmage at Normal Field, Ink Williams got a good look at the Cardinals' wiry leader, Paddy Driscoll. Widely considered one of the greatest players in NFL history, Paddy Driscoll also started his journey to the NFL in Hammond. An Evansville, Illinois native, Driscoll starred in baseball and football at Northwestern University before turning professional in 1917, playing football with Hammond and minor-league baseball with the Chicago Cubs. He met the future football great George Halas in the navy during World War I while both men were part of the 1918 Great Lakes Navy Bluejackets football team, the winners of the 1919 Rose Bowl.

After the war, Driscoll had a short-lived major-league baseball career—eighteen games as a light-hitting Cubs infielder—but made his mark in pro football with Halas at Hammond in 1919. Although Hammond was located just beyond Chicago's city limits in Indiana, the team played many of its games in Chicago. On Thanksgiving Day, 1919, Hammond played Jim Thorpe's Canton Bulldogs at Cubs Park in front of twelve thousand spectators. The large turnout is said to have inspired the creation of the American Professional Football Association in 1920.

After the triumphant 1919 Hammond-Canton Thanksgiving Day game, Halas and Driscoll were poached by other franchises prior to the inaugural APFA season. Halas became the player-coach of the Staleys—owned by the Staley Manufacturing Company, which made food starch in Decatur, Illinois. Halas bought the team, moved them to the North Side of Chicago, and renamed them the Chicago Bears in 1921. Driscoll signed on with the Chicago Cardinals, who played at Normal Park, off Racine Avenue (why they are sometimes referred to as the Racine Cardinals), on Chicago's South Side. Halas's and Driscoll's football fortunes skyrocketed; Hammond's never recovered.

When Ink Williams first settled into his new job at Black Swan in the late summer of 1921, he contemplated his football future. The Bears and the Cardinals were his closest options, but both—the Bears in particular—were in the vanguard of professionalization. Early football franchises such as Hammond and Dayton had players who worked full-time jobs nearby, sometimes for the company that owned the team, fitting practices in when they could. (The Green Bay Packers' name is a legacy of this kind of arrangement.) Teams such as the Bears, the Cardinals, and the Akron Pros placed significant demands on players' time during the season. They played better, were paid better, and drew more fans—factors that are interrelated. None of those teams would have tolerated the time demands of Williams's Black Swan day job.

Hammond, however, operated on the old model. The man who offered Williams a spot on the Hammond squad was its owner, Alvah Andrew "Doc" Young. Young was a physician, a Mormon (a nephew of Brigham Young), a boxing promoter, and a gambler. His record as an owner is more distinguished by his history of racial inclusion than by his ability to field a winning team. Doc was "not a civil rights activist as we know them today," wrote his son Harry in later years, "he was simply color blind."[8] As a student at the University of Indiana, Doc Young was a member of the wrestling and baseball teams. When he became a surgeon and settled in Hammond, Indiana, he developed an interest in professional sports—not just football but also horse racing and boxing—prompting his friends to call him the "gambling sporting doctor."

After Driscoll's and Halas's departures before the 1920 season, the team functioned like the mom-and-pop operation it was. Doc Young's son, Harry, traveled everywhere with the Pros starting at age five; according to Harry, "Mother washed the uniforms." Hammond's financial struggles were magnified by its lack of any hometown advantage. The team did not draw well in Hammond (the home of Purdue University), so the Pros played most of their games on the road, even when they were at "home" at Cubs Park (later Wrigley Field) or Normal Field. Doc Young was generally pleased with a turnout of five or six thousand fans, which meant gate receipts of approximately sixty-five hundred dollars. The team was not profitable, however, and rarely made that much; put quite plainly by Doc Young's son, Harry, "We lost our butts."[9]

Hammond held practices on the Thursdays, Fridays, or Saturdays prior to Sunday games. In the eyes of their opponents, they appeared a ragtag bunch, even if capable of stealing occasional victories. The flexibility of the Hammond situation suited Williams.

The 1921 Hammond Pros were all young men, ranging in age from twenty-two to thirty-one (the exception being Ralph Jones, who played one game at tailback that season at the age of forty-one). Of the twenty-five men on the roster, at least nineteen were college educated. Some of the faces on the squad were familiar to Williams—he had played against the fullbacks Dick King and Hank Gillo at Harvard and Colgate, respectively. Ben Derr, a South Dakota native, had starred at the 1917 Rose Bowl in the University of Pennsylvania's backfield along with the future Philadelphia Eagles owner and NFL president Bert Bell. Williams had also played against the guards Tommy Tomlin and Lou Usher while both were at Syracuse. (Usher had been an All-American.) But the majority of the Hammond squad was from midwestern schools, such as the Indiana University star quarterback (and former Hammond high school football captain) Wally Hess or the All-American center Jack Depler of the University of Illinois.

But although most of the players were college educated, most of their fans were not, and the style of play was often violent, startling, and ugly. Fields were not well tended, resembling mud baths or dust storms on game days. On-field scrums were dirty, with players in the pile often biting and maiming opponents with their cleats. Players from larger midwestern universities were often physically bigger than eastern college players were used to. The gentlemanly veneer that marked the game and its fans at the college level was stripped off the pro game. Bob Nash, an Irish immigrant who spent six seasons in the NFL from 1920 to 1925, remembered those early league games as a working-class-friendly spectator sport:

> We didn't have much of a backing in the Eastern Seaboard cities where they rooted for their Harvards, Yales, and Princetons. They thought we were some kind of outcasts giving football a bad name because we played the sport for money. But those Midwestern towns, maybe a cut below Cambridge or New Haven, with their iron and coal and rubber workers, they took a liking to us. Most of those folks in Akron, Canton, or Milwaukee had never seen a college football game. Hell, they were working on Saturday. But they came out to see us on Sunday.[10]

The birth of the NFL marks an interesting shift in the culture of sport, from genteel to working class: the game of football evolved out of college rugby in 1874 at Princeton and Yale. The allure of Ivy League football stimulated the development of football teams affiliated with amateur athletic associations in cities across the industrial North. It was from these amateur athletic associations that the professional game evolved. Clubs that were born as vehicles for physical fitness and social advancement framed amateur sport as the pinnacle of gentlemanly behavior and Christian fortitude. However, as these associations became increasingly identified with local municipalities, the stakes for victory grew. Increasingly, teams began luring "ringers" to play for them in exchange for trophies and awards that could easily be exchanged for cash. And, increasingly, the matches between associations became vehicles for wagers.

The colleges and universities of the Northeast, in particular, the Ivy League schools—Princeton, Yale, Harvard, Columbia, and the University of Pennsylvania—became sources of ringers for amateur associations wanting to gain a competitive edge. By the late 1890s, the competitive football hotbed of western Pennsylvania began paying ringers—particularly from Princeton and Yale—to compete, and the professional game was officially born. By the first decade of the twentieth century, central Ohio and Indiana had become the epicenter of professional football. The founding of the NFL in Canton is no accident, and the placement of the Pro Football Hall of Fame in Canton is a reminder of the region's importance as the birthplace of the professional game. Significant existential debates began, and continue unabated today, about how it is that a team can represent a town or a city when the players come from somewhere else: are we rooting for our neighbors, or are we rooting for the laundry?

When the head linesman Ink Williams again sized up the line of scrimmage between Akron and Chicago, he was aware of three Black men on the field, himself being one of them. This, too, marked the beginnings of a shift in the culture of sport. The early amateur athletic associations were predominantly white social institutions. However, as high schools and colleges across the country adopted the sport as an extracurricular activity, Native American and Black participation became noteworthy, if primarily segregated. By 1912, the Carlisle Indian Industrial School had become a major football powerhouse, and athletes such as Jim Thorpe grabbed the attention of the nation. Carlisle's strategic creativity on the field and on the sidelines forever transformed the game. Working with his players' unorthodox style and strengths, Carlisle's legendary coach Glenn "Pop" Warner helped shape the evolution of the sport (for example, the development of the spiral pass) in ways that still matter today. And although historically Black colleges and universities such as Howard, Lincoln, Tuskegee, Morehouse, and Morgan had football teams, the Black stars of integrated northern high schools and the few Black students who were allowed to matriculate at Ivy League schools and major midwestern universities began to find their way into the professional ranks. By the late 1910s, on the eve of the founding of the American Professional Football Association, Native American and Black players—though decidedly in the minority—had become important drawing cards of professional football.

The first Black pro football player was Charles W. Follis, who played for the Shelby Athletic Association (the Shelby Blues) of Shelby, Ohio from 1902 to 1906. One of Follis's teammates on the Shelby Blues was Branch Rickey, who admired Follis's remarkable ability to maintain composure in the face of racial hostility.[11]

In Hammond, Doc Young had never hired a Black football player prior to Ink Williams, but his proclivity for hiring Black players would become his defining mark on the history of the game. Of the thirteen Black men who played in the early NFL from its founding as the APFA in 1920 until it became segregated in 1933, five played for Hammond. Young claimed no integrationist agenda, instead seizing an opportunity to hire great players who were available solely because they were Black. Of the five Black men who played for the Hammond Pros—Ink Williams, Fritz Pollard, Dick Hudson, John Shelburne, and Solomon "Sol" Butler—four were collegiate all-stars before arriving in Hammond. (Only Hudson did not attend college.) Their willingness to play for one of the worst teams in the league is an indication of how impossible it was for Blacks to find employment on most teams, as well as a testament to Young's dedication to cultivating a tolerant environment in the Hammond club. Williams felt accepted by the other men on the Hammond Pros, but the road was filled with ugly racism. Doc Young's son Harry remembered:

> The black players had a rough time in Indiana. The Christian Church next to my grammar school had a fiery cross burning from its steeple. Many times, I would see a KKK funeral after school with the white robes and masks.[12]

The fact that Hammond rarely played any games at home in Indiana was not without its benefits.

Doc Young also had a very laissez-faire attitude about players "jumping" to other franchises on weeks when Hammond didn't have league games scheduled. ("League games" were those against other NFL teams; teams could schedule as many exhibitions against non-NFL teams as they wished.) In those early years of the league, a team could hire players away from other teams for specific games. This policy maddened some team owners, who felt that it wasn't fair play and that it destabilized the league. It also caused a dynamic where players—college athletes, or pro athletes under contract to other teams—often played under assumed names. White players such as the Horween brothers might be able to pass as the McMahon brothers, but assumed names would not work for Black players, whose presence in the league was so rare. Williams was fine with Hammond's lend-lease arrangement, which suited his sense of adventure.

Such was the backdrop of Williams's appearance at Normal Field on December 4, 1921. He had had an exciting—if oft-losing—rookie season playing for Doc Young's Hammond Pros and had spent the previous weekend on loan to the Canton Bulldogs in their matchup against Akron. The Akron press had been displeased to see Williams show up in front of four thousand at League Park on November 24, because he had already appeared for Canton against Akron on October 23. In that game, seven thousand spectators turned out at Canton's Lakeside Park to watch the visitors win, 3–0. The game was noteworthy because it involved Black players on both teams.[13] After the October matchup, Williams and the Bulldogs went out for a postgame dinner in Canton. "When we sat down," Williams recounted to Studs Terkel, "they put a *screen* around the table."[14]

Akron didn't object to Williams on account of his race; they hated the lend-lease policy, which allowed Canton to also hire Swede Youngstrom on loan from the Buffalo All-Americans. Akron announced that they would tolerate Williams's and Youngstrom's presence. Before the game (which Canton won, 14–0), the *Akron Beacon Journal* announced that league owners would meet in January 1922 to establish a more powerful league office with more strictly enforced rules.[15]

Here at Normal Park on December 4, with that game firmly behind him, Williams had intended simply to watch his friends play. But the Cardinals needed to secure enough officials for the game, and the key people involved—Driscoll, the McMahon brothers, and Pollard—all knew and respected Williams. A month earlier, Williams had impressed Driscoll, his teammates, and the Cardinals' fans alike in his first game at Normal Park:

"INK" WILLIAMS STARS IN CARDINAL-HAMMOND GAME

"Ink" Williams, fleet end of the Hammond pro team, startled the stands on last Sunday afternoon at Normal Park by his dashing play and unerring tackling. Paddy Driscoll, star player of the Chicago Cardinals, was nailed in his tracks time and again by the dark-skinned, fleet-footed end, who seemed to dart with the aid of wings. Although the Hammond team was defeated by a score of 7 to 0, which score was made in the first quarter, the Cardinal team found out that the man to be feared was Williams, who managed to get in every play and who outstripped even the ball in its flight.[16]

The story of Hammond versus Chicago foreshadows most of Williams's six-year NFL career. When he had debuted in the league on October 2, Hammond lost, 17–0, to the Buffalo All-Americans. But the papers were full of praise for Williams. The *Times* of Muncie, Indiana, which followed the Hammond Pros most closely, called Ink a "sensation," compared his evasiveness with "greased lightning," and proclaimed him the "greatest football player of the age."[17] The *Whip* stated that Williams displayed the "speed of an antelope and the strength of a tiger," finding victory in Williams's play even in Hammond's defeat.[18]

Opponents were always impressed by Williams's tenacity. At the close of the 1921 season, Bob "Duke" Osborn, a tough former Penn State star who played guard and center for the Canton Bulldogs, told the *Whip* that Williams was the single greatest opponent he had faced that season:

Williams . . . gets my vote [for greatest pro player faced in 1921]. He played against us on one of the Chicago pro teams and was a flash all the way.

Although Williams weighs but 135 pounds, he hit our biggest tackles and backs like a 200-pounder.[19]

Osborn, who was noted for his disregard for personal safety on the field (usually wearing only a baseball cap to protect his head), likely recognized a kindred spirit in Williams, who rarely wore a helmet in games. The *Whip* reported that the Chicago Cardinals fans recognized—and admired—Williams's thick skin, writing, "Spectators who scoffed at him upon his appearance on the field rooted for him continually after his splendid tackles and his handling of forward passes."[20]

This same mix of razzing and admiration returned over the course of the Akron-Chicago game that Williams officiated. As reported by the *Whip*:

"INK WILLIAMS" WAS OFFICIAL AT BIG GAME

Aside from the individual play of Pollard last Sunday when Akron met and defeated the Chicago Cardinals on a local gridiron, the officiating of "Ink" Williams amazed, yet pleased the many South Side followers of the game. Williams was head linesman, and the other officials and captains appealed to him on several occasions to render decisions which were regarded as final. Despite the hoots and jeers from the big crowd Williams was cool at all times and proved himself capable of mastering in football in uniform or out, as the management of both teams were satisfied with his officiating though both teams were white.[21]

It is erroneous of the *Whip* to say that "both teams were white" (Pollard was co-head coach of Akron, and his team featured two Black players in significant roles), but the portrait of Williams's officiating role is otherwise stunning. Williams was an active player who had played *against* Chicago just four weeks earlier; he was known to be friends with at least two members of the visiting team; and one of the central underpinnings of racist paranoia is that members of a racial minority cannot render impartial judgment when it comes to other members of their own race. The largest Chicago Cardinals crowd of the season turned out for this game, the home team *lost* with Williams officiating, eighteen months after the Red Summer of 1919, and there was no reported violence or disagreement in a sport known for both. It is a testament not only to Williams's disposition but also to the players and fans involved on December 4, 1921. Ink Williams had cemented his place as a respected figure in the NFL.

In its 1921 year-end review, the *Chicago Defender* listed the Olympic silver medalist Ned Gourdin, Fritz Pollard, and Ink Williams—along with the boxer Harry "the Black Panther" Wills (then just three years into his legendary eight-year reign as World Colored Heavyweight Champion), among others—as the most outstanding and accomplished Black athletes of 1921.[22]

After the close of the NFL season, Williams, Pollard, and their old friend Dunc Annan helped to develop an indoor football league in Chicago. The league never quite took off, but it gave some old college friends a chance to mix with players from other teams. Williams kept working at Black Swan and as a journalist for the *Whip*—the latter was even reported in the *Macomb Daily By-stander*. Macomb was a town adjacent to Williams's old hometown of Monmouth, Illinois, where the press continued to keep tabs on him.[23] Williams also got to work recruiting John Shelburne—Dartmouth's star Black player and Williams's old nemesis—to join Hammond for the 1922 season. It would be Shelburne's only season in the league, but he remembered it fondly:

> Our white teammates, many of them from the South, didn't resent our presence on the team. It was a lesson in fellowship that most of them were glad to have. They got the type of contact never open to them before and liked it. Remember that all of us were college graduates and thus on the same educational level.[24]

The Hammond Pros were trying to evolve to meet the new standards of the NFL. Of the twenty-two players on the roster that season, Shelburne was one of thirteen rookies. The team had turned away from hiring local talent: only six members of the Pros were not products of major collegiate football programs, and only one of the college graduates—the quarterback Wally Hess—actually was from Hammond. Many of the team's original fans lamented the rise of ringers, those paid players from out of town. Doc Young had a published exchange in the *Times* (Munster, Indiana) after the 1921 season with a disgruntled fan who wanted to see only local talent on the field for Hammond—an exchange that showed some nostalgia for the game's roots in local amateur associations.[25]

Some of this nostalgia was rooted in the idea that players who felt a sense of hometown pride could always be counted on to try their hardest. The Hammond Pros were perennial losers in the NFL. Williams and his teammates made ten dollars apiece per game when turnout was low—and at home games, turnout often was low. Williams later joked—perhaps with a kernel of truth—that teams played harder for larger crowds. Climbing into the stands prior to game time, Williams and his teammates joked that if "it was $10 crowd, $10 game, $20 crowd, $20 game they get!"[26] Still, Hammond's 1922 season—which was entirely on the road—presents strong evidence that despite larger crowds and supreme effort, the team was still greatly outmatched.

Whatever evolution Hammond was going through, it was not evolving as fast as the rest of the league. Hammond's 1922 season was one of the worst on record of any team in the history of the NFL: they scored zero points all season on their way to a 0-5-1 record. It was marked by a pattern—in Buffalo, Toledo, Dayton, Milwaukee, Akron, and Racine (Wisconsin)—where the local press focused significant pregame attention on Williams, resulting in strong showings at the gate. The *Buffalo Morning Express* reported that other teams had been trying to sign Williams prior to the 1922 season.[27] Prominent pregame praise in the *Buffalo Times, Enquirer, Courier*, and *Commercial* all indicate how much Williams was used as a drawing card for attendance at games. Hammond lost 7–0 in front of thirty-five hundred fans at the Buffalo Baseball Park on October 1, and 14–0 in front of twenty-five hundred against the Toledo Maroons at Swayne Field in Toledo, Ohio.[28] Following the Toledo game, the *News-Messenger* (published about forty miles outside of Toledo in Fremont, Ohio) ran a piece lamenting the difficulties Ink Williams faced in pro football:

> "Inky" Williams, leader of the Hammond, Ind. Professional football team is a colored boy whose sable hue is so dark that a touch of charcoal would make a white mark on his complexion. "Inky" is said to be a better man than Fritz Pollard, famous colored star from Brown University, if such a thing is possible. A colored man sure has one hard row to hoe in the grid sport. If he stars everybody tries to get him and if he gums a few shots the crowd is sure to give him the "bird" as Lord Mountbaten [sic] is want [sic] to say in times of great excitement.[29]

Fans and curious onlookers alike were turning out to see Williams, and some were giving him loud raspberries (this is Mountbatten's "bird") or worse. From Toledo, Hammond went to play the Dayton Triangles, whose name referred to the three different General Motors manufacturing subsidiaries in Dayton, where most of the players worked (Dayton Engineering Lab, Dayton-Wright Aeroplane Manufacturing, and Dayton Metal Products).[30] Dayton double-covered Williams to prevent him from scoring, and Hammond lost, 20–0.[31] Up in Milwaukee, the Pros saw their largest crowd—four thousand—who had turned out to see a singular moment in early NFL history: four Black players (Williams and Shelbourne for Hammond, Pollard and Robeson for Milwaukee) were on the field at one time. Pollard was the head coach for the Badgers' inaugural season in the NFL. Injuries and clashing egos on the Badgers squad helped Hammond squeeze out an unlikely 0–0 tie. Hammond marched onward to Akron, where pregame press called Williams "brilliant" while reminding readers he had "set up a furor" the previous season when he "jumped Hammond to play with the Canton Bulldogs against Akron."[32] The Akron Pros took out two days of print ads in the *Akron Beacon Journal*, urging fans to come see Hammond, "With Inky Williams—Famous Colored Star." Williams was heavily covered by Akron "and unable to do his stuff." Hammond lost, 22–0.[33] After a pair of non-league games (one win, in which Williams scored on a seventy-yard run; and one loss, both against the Gary Elks), Hammond's season ended with a thud on

November 26 in Racine, Wisconsin, where 1,084 freezing cold fans saw their team beat Hammond, 6–0.

Two days before the Racine game, Ink Williams and Fritz Pollard hightailed it to Washington, DC, to watch Howard University lose to Lincoln University, 13–12, in front of fifteen thousand people at American League Park on Thanksgiving Day. The game was preceded by a parade through Northwest Washington, DC and was followed by a reception at the Howard Coliseum. On Friday, celebrations continued with fraternity receptions, including one for Alpha Phi Alpha. The *New York Age* reported on the festivities, noting a crème-de-la-crème guest list of Black intellectuals and public figures, including Black Swan Records' owner, Harry Pace, as well as W. E. B. Du Bois, James Weldon Johnson, Bill Pickens, Adam Clayton Powell Sr., Oscar De Priest, Fritz Pollard, and J. Mayo Williams. Although it is clear that Ink Williams's life intersected those of Pace and Du Bois, and that his future career in music would color the cultural worlds of men such as Johnson, Pickens, Powell, and De Priest, it is nevertheless astonishing to read a newspaper account that places them at the same social gathering.[34]

Back in Chicago, Fritz Pollard assembled an all-Black exhibition squad called the Fritz Pollard's All-Stars. It was the first time that Paul Robeson, Fritz Pollard, Sol Butler, Duke Slater, Dick Hudson, John Shelburne, and Mayo Williams played for the same professional team at the same time.[35] Pollard filled out his All-Star team with members of Chicago's Lincoln Athletic Club 11 (which included the future NFL players Hudson and Butler, as well as Napoleon and Virgil Blueitt, and Fritz Pollard's brother, Frank). The Fritz Pollard All-Stars won an exhibition game in Chicago on December 16 against what was billed as an all-white team of college stars (they appear to have been drawn mainly from teams Pollard and Williams had played for), organized by Pollard's former teammate, Dick "Rip" King of Akron, and including Paddy Sullivan and Oscar Knop of Hammond, and Festus Tierney of Hammond and Toledo.[36] The game, played on a frozen Schorling Field in Chicago, prompted one scribe to report in the *Iowa Press Citizen* that "never in the history of football has so strong a Negro aggregation gathered on a gridiron as this bunch of all-stars."[37] The frozen ground led to tentative play, but Pollard secured a 6–0 victory with a touchdown pass to Paul Robeson.[38] Following the game, Pollard's All-Stars hit the road for a barnstorming tour of the West Coast. The friendships among Pollard, Williams, Robeson, Slater, and Butler would develop during this adventure and deepen and endure well into the next three decades.

For Robeson, 1922 was his last year in professional football. Balancing football with law school and acting in New York City was simply untenable. In the summer of 1922, Robeson had joined the cast of Eubie Blake's musical *Shuffle Along*, and he now wanted to do little more than act—to the extent that his law school studies suffered. Adding football to the mix only made things worse: on an average football weekend, Robeson boarded the train in New York on Friday night, arrived wherever the Badgers were playing in time for the game, played, and returned home on Sunday night or Monday morning in time for class at Columbia University Law School. His average train time was twenty-five hours, round trip. Nevertheless, some of his Badgers teammates resented his absence from daily practices.[39] It has been said that athletes hate to retire, and although this was likely a reason for Robeson's decision to participate in such a grueling schedule, money was also a factor. Robeson was married, had heavy tuition fees, and as a Black man in America—even one with a college degree and a promising acting career—was facing a limited financial future.

CHAPTER 10

Paramount

Back at his day job, Ink Williams was making connections and doing collections as he made the rounds for Black Swan at Chicago's record stores. Down on the street, he could see that Black Swan's records, particularly the blues records, were landing with buyers. But he could also see that they had growing competition from OKeh, Columbia, and Victor. While collecting payments, Williams talked up record-store owners, got a sense of what was hot, befriended the in-house pianists who helped sell sheet music, and schmoozed with customers. Then he took the cash back to the *Chicago Whip* and gave it to his boss, Black Swan's executive treasurer, Joe Bibb.

From this vantage point, Williams could see better than anyone what the race record market looked like. He could see that Black Swan had helped create an industrywide change in the way record companies did business by forging a space in the market for Black music. But he could also see Black Swan was not alone. By late 1922, major labels were releasing enough race records that Harry Pace worried it was a strategy: competing labels could be trying saturate the market in order to wipe out Black Swan. Given the coordinated hostility that music publishers had shown Pace & Handy, Harry Pace might be forgiven for being a bit paranoid. The reality was that the record industry was just beginning to meet a very real demand for Black music. Presciently, Black Swan responded with an ad campaign telling Black record buyers to "Go to your Record Dealer and ask for the Better Class of Records by Colored Artists." Their advertisements were also deliberate game changers, depicting Blacks with dignity and respect. This approach, the historian David Suisman writes, helped Black consumers "understand the connection between cultural achievement and market relations."[1]

A new threat to Black Swan's business emerged in 1922 in the form of the radio industry. Harry Pace dubiously recalled that "radio broadcasting broke and this spelled doom" for Black Swan.[2] It is true that nationwide record sales dropped by 15 percent in 1922 on account of radio, but Pace ignores the fact that Black Swan's artists were never on the radio to begin with. Pace recalled that "immediately dealers began to cancel orders that they had placed, records were returned unaccepted, many record stores became radio stores."[3] Again, this was widely true for the industry, and perhaps it was true to some extent for Black Swan (if so, Williams never recounted such incidents), but the fact was that Black music wasn't broadcast on the radio. Instead the race-record side of the industry was starting to boom.

Black Swan's real problem was cash flow. The company was expanding in exciting ways: marketing its own phonograph (the "Swanola"), enlarging its office space, and creating new distributorships beyond Chicago and New York. With strong demand for its titles throughout the United States, Europe, and the Caribbean, Pace was convinced—and not unreasonably so—that Black Swan could outlast the strain of a budget stretched just short of its breaking point.

But Pace's quest to make Black Swan self-sufficient proved too much, too soon. For the duration of its short life, Black Swan Records lived under the shadow of the debt it owed to the company that pressed all its records: the tiny, Wisconsin-based New York Recording Laboratory (NYRL). Pace wanted to be free of this dynamic, so in the fall of 1921 Black Swan purchased Olympic Records—a defunct New York–based label with an in-house record-pressing operation. A clause in the purchase had Black Swan repressing the old Olympic titles with the Black Swan label. (For example, the white recording artist Aileen Stanley was repackaged as "Black" with a name like "Mamie Jones.") This arrangement began in November 1921. These repackaged Olympic recordings eventually made up one third of all Black Swan releases. It was a philosophical backslide for a company whose advertisements claimed, "All others are only passing as colored." However, the buying public never seemed to notice.[4]

The Olympic gamble didn't pay off fast enough. Black Swan simply owed too much to NYRL, forcing Pace to sell the pressers a stake in Black Swan in 1922. Black Swan ceased advertising itself as all-Black owned, but it did continue to advertise (falsely) the racial homogeneity of its catalog.[5] Despite these setbacks, Black Swan continued to be a significant producer of music by Black artists. But although it had successes with artists such as Alberta Hunter and Trixie Smith, Black Swan turned down an opportunity to record Bessie Smith on account of her rougher approach to the blues.

Black Swan also had a more serious problem that Harry Pace was unaware of: its executive treasurer, Joe Bibb, was embezzling the funds that Mayo Williams had been collecting across Chicago. Williams did not report to Pace and Black Swan's Harlem-based front office; his only contact with management was Joe Bibb at the *Chicago Whip* office. Through his relationship with

Bibb, Ink Williams was acutely aware of Black Swan's financial woes—which may have also included federal tax problems (an unconfirmed implication by Williams). Through his regular conversations with Bibb, Williams knew that "Pace was gradually going down, the federals coming on, and everything was going down for him."[6] Williams also knew that the *Whip* also was in tough financial straits and how Bibb was addressing that—with Black Swan funds.

Joe Bibb was Harry Pace's brother-in-law and the son of the Black Swan board member Viola Bibb. They should have been able to trust him. Instead, Joe Bibb watched Black Swan sink while he kept his *Chicago Whip* newspaper afloat with Black Swan's profits. It is safe to say that in Black Swan's first year of business—during which it made a slim profit margin of $3,100—and in every year following, it could have used every cent it was owed. Considering that Chicago—the region for which Williams served as distributor and collection agent—was Black Swan's primary market, losing its embezzled funds from its home region certainly contributed to Black Swan's economic collapse. There is no other known evidence to corroborate Williams's claims about Bibb's practices, except that he repeated the story in at least two separate interviews conducted some fifty years after the alleged crimes took place and several years after Bibb's death in 1966. Nor is there evidence that Williams had an axe to grind against Bibb. One can only speculate that the unscrupulous Bibb thought the *Whip* was more important than Black Swan.

Black Swan finally declared bankruptcy at the end of 1923. As part of the agreement, the Black Swan masters were leased to the NYRL's subsidiary label, Paramount Records, in return for "no less than $50,000." Thus, Black Swan's catalog was folded into the Paramount catalog.[7] Previously, Paramount's own recordings had consisted mainly of white regional polka bands from Wisconsin; in fact, most of its business came from pressing Black Swan's records and issuing some of Black Swan's blues artists on the Paramount label. As Paramount's chief executive officer, Otto Moeser, recalled rather matter-of-factly, Paramount "could not compete for high class talent with Edison, Columbia, and Victor, and we had inferior records so we went to race records."[8]

The acquisition of Black Swan's catalog and name recognition positioned Paramount to enter the race-record industry with credibility and impact. According to another Paramount executive, Art Satherly, "We made a deal with [Pace] to buy him out, lock, stock and barrel. That's how we got the Black Swan label and with it came the artists. That's how we got into the race business very big."[9] Prior to its dealings with Black Swan, Paramount had worked with only two Black artists—Lucille Hegamin (four of her six Paramount sides had been leased from Black Swan and Arto) and W. C. Handy's daughter Katherine (whose recordings were never released).[10] Paramount's executives knew little about Black music, but Paramount's general manager,

Maurice A. Supper, could tell from Black Swan's pressing numbers that blues records sold well. "If they'd stuck with blues," Williams speculated about Black Swan, "they would have been more successful."[11]

Pace attempted to spin the sale of Black Swan as a merger, but he faced significant criticism from Black political leaders who had expected much of Black Swan.[12] Even Williams questioned Pace's emotional investment in Black Swan years later: "I don't think Pace was as dedicated to the record business as he was interested in insurance."[13] In a tone both defensive and frustrated, Pace explained the deal in a letter to the NAACP, asking, "How could we survive with a meager capital of about $40,000 and a limited market when concerns with millions . . . either died or were mortally wounded?" In all, the label released one hundred eighty records that sold worldwide. It also launched the noteworthy recording careers of Ethel Waters, Trixie Smith, Alberta Hunter, and Fletcher Henderson.[14]

Though Black Swan declared bankruptcy in late 1923 and was sold in the spring of 1924, Mayo Williams foresaw its downfall much sooner: Black Swan had issued its last record in the summer of 1923. "I could see what was going to happen. They was going to take [Pace] over, take over his masters."[15] Williams had invested his first two post-collegiate years in the race-record business and felt he needed to make it count. So he boarded a train running from the North Shore of Chicago to Milwaukee (the same train he had taken for football games against the Milwaukee Badgers), catching a connecting train that ran the forty miles north to the Lake Michigan town of Port Washington, where the Wisconsin Chair Company and Paramount headquarters were located. The Wisconsin Chair Company had become involved in the music business by way of manufacturing phonograph cabinets—essentially record players enclosed in period furniture. So they also manufactured records to be played on their record players.

The parochial town of Port Washington, population just over three thousand, made sense for a furniture business but was an unlikely fit for the headquarters of a record company that was going all in on Black music. When Ink Williams got off the train in Port Washington and struck out on foot through the town for the Paramount headquarters, curious white children followed him from the train station to the company offices:

> Listen, they didn't know anything about the blues. And I'd go up to Port Washington and the kids 'round there would follow me around like I was something [laughs]. I don't think there were *any* blacks living in Port Washington, nor around there.[16]

When he arrived, the company's executives were likely as surprised and curious as the kids around Port Washington about this handsome young Black man with a French-style mustache. Williams was confident the executives needed a man on the inside, so he was unsurprised when they agreed to meet. "I believed that a college man could sweep a floor better than anybody," Williams told Stephen Calt a half century later. "I just jived my way into the whole situation."[17]

In truth, Williams was clear headed and ambitious: "There's no need for me getting started in this and not getting in on the ground floor. So, I went to Port Washington, told them that I was the distributor down in Chicago for Harry Pace of the Black Swan Records. And they said, 'Well, yes. Why, we'd be glad to work with you.'"[18]

The Paramount executives told Williams their concerns about the viability of the race-record market, citing Black Swan's lack of funds. Williams assured them things were not as they seemed, explaining, "There was no money available for this reason: they were takin' the money that I'd bring in from the distributing of Pace's records, and *put it in their newspaper* to get their paper out." According to Williams, his first visit convinced Paramount to take over Black Swan entirely; thus Black Swan's last recordings of Ethel Waters came out as Paramount releases. Emboldened by this success, Williams took a second trip to Port Washington to make the case for the label to hire him as a talent scout and producer, stressing the insights he had gained from working the clubs and record stores of metropolitan Chicago for Black Swan. According to Williams, Paramount responded enthusiastically, and "that was the beginnings of Paramount Records and the artists that I got."[19]

It is stunning to consider that Williams chose to make a direct appeal to the Wisconsin Chair Company executives but never mentioned doing the same (or even making an in-person visit) to the Black Swan offices in Harlem. Nor did he seem to alert Harry Pace to Joe Bibb's theft of Black Swan's Chicago-based revenues. Indeed, Williams's first encounter with the Wisconsin Chair Company executives suggests that Bibb was stealing a sizeable amount of funds. Perhaps Williams felt a sense of loyalty to Bibb, or perhaps he simply knew the die had been cast in Paramount's favor. Either way, Williams's two trips to Wisconsin are as significant as they are unscrupulous. Williams reveals his true character: smart, charismatic, with a keen sense of human nature, and utterly self-interested. And like a football player who has broken through the defensive line, he would make an incredibly long gain for Black vernacular music.

Officially, Williams was offered the job of administering copyrights of Paramount material; unofficially, he supervised their race-record catalog, recruiting and recording new talent in Chicago—and, to a lesser degree, New York. In a deal evocative of the one Ralph Peer would later famously secure at Victor, Williams drew no salary but would receive two cents (the publisher's share) for each record sold that he had copyrighted.[20] He also had a comfortable expense account so that he could scout talent on the road and pay artists a flat fee for recording. Williams brought important organizational skills and vision to Paramount along with a strong grasp of the commercial issues that had challenged Black Swan's viability—mainly, Black Swan's disinclination to "give the people what they want." And in Williams's estimation, what the people wanted was blues music that they could dance to.

The blues historian Stephen Calt posited that it was "doubtful that any other black employee could have succeeded in Williams's position, which required consummate skill as a job politician." More to the point, wrote Calt:

> Williams was tactful and circumspect. Although he was better-educated than his superiors at Paramount, "I never made any attempt to show it," [Williams] said. Nor did he attempt to advance his own hobby-horses at the expense of Paramount's interests. His own tastes in music ran to cultivated singers like his ex-fraternity mate Paul Robeson, whom he considered far greater than any blues singer.[21]

Williams's grasp of the market, his familiarity with blues from childhood, and the personal relationships he had developed with South Side musicians, coupled with his years at Howard and Brown University, made him particularly adept at navigating the racial and cultural politics of Paramount Records and its white personnel. Williams was working on the very plausible premise that Paramount's executives in Wisconsin were so far removed from Black America that they would bestow an inordinate amount of responsibility and trust in him. And he was right.

Paramount was also motivated to use Williams to address the problems the company had been encountering with lost copyright revenues. In late 1922, Paramount had bungled an opportunity to license Alberta Hunter's "Down Hearted Blues," which in turn caused the company to miss out on profits from Bessie Smith's more successful cover version of the same song. In January 1923, just before Williams's first train trip up to Port Washington, the Paramount executive Maurice Albert Supper founded a song-publishing satellite company named Chicago Music. Supper was the president and treasurer; he set up a Chicago Music office for Williams to run at the Overton Hygienic Building at 36th and State Street in Chicago.[22] "I was an officer, but my title was A&R blues and jazz man," said Williams.[23] The Overton Hygienic Building was a hive of Black businesses. Commissioned by the prominent Black attorney Anthony Overton, the building housed Overton's cosmetics manufacturing company, his bank (Douglass National Bank), the Victory Life Insurance Company, and the Theater Owners Booking Association (T.O.B.A.).[24] The arrangement matched two key aspects of Williams's ascent in business: Overton was a fellow Alpha Phi Alpha fraternity brother, and successful T.O.B.A. artists would make up the core of talent Williams recorded for Paramount.

Williams employed a staff of three or four arrangers to notate melodies for copyright registration and to help aspiring singers and songwriters arrange their own blues-based compositions. At Black Swan, Fletcher Henderson took on the role of musical arranger. It was significant that Williams hired a young man named Tom Dorsey—better known today as Thomas A. Dorsey—to be Paramount's chief song arranger. Years later, when the blues historian Jim O'Neal asked Dorsey how he met Ink Williams, Dorsey responded:

> He met me. I was playing piano in one of the music stores there on State Street. I don't know which one it was now, Lloyd Smith or I don't know, there were about half a dozen music stores up and down State Street. Didn't sell so many records, but they sold sheet music and piano rolls. And he used to promote so many singers. He's the one that handled the recording contracts and everything.[25]

For reasons unknown, Williams never aspired to build Chicago Music into a Pace & Handy–style publishing house. But like Ralph Peer at OKeh (and later Victor) in the hillbilly music business, Williams recognized there was money to be made from originals cut from familiar cloth. Dorsey did, too, and used his bench at Chicago Music arranging for piano as a platform to pitch his own songs to prospective takers. In 1923, several Paramount artists would record Dorsey's songs—most notably King Oliver's recording of "Riverside Blues."[26] For blues musicians like Dorsey, Williams's arrival at Paramount marked a turning point in the financial viability of blues music. Before Williams hired Dorsey at Paramount, Dorsey had always had to hold a steady job outside of music. Chicago song publishers such as Ink Williams and Lester Melrose (who ran a music shop on Chicago's South Side and was a significant music publisher and blues producer and promoter) changed that. Dorsey credited Black Swan and Paramount with creating a space in the market for blues music and musicians to thrive:

> Wasn't much of the blues then. Ragtime. See, you didn't have the blues singers. The blues wasn't recognized much until the blues singers got a break, till they got a chance, see. And then blues began to spread. Blues singers began to come in by the score. Well, they had them before, but they had no place to sing them, to exhibit what they had. And when they started to making these records, of blues singers, that was all we all needed, the piano players, and the musicians and all. You'd do a session, didn't get much for it, but it was good, and you had a steady job; whenever there was a session, you knew where you had to go and what you had to do. You knew you'd get paid for it.[27]

Supported by a strong staff, Williams used the Black Swan castoff Alberta Hunter to form the bedrock of Paramount's new catalog of Black music. Fourteen of Williams's first twenty race releases on Paramount were Alberta Hunter records, and the woman Eubie Blake once called a "flea in Ethel Waters' collar" became a star in her own right.[28]

Race talent at Paramount was subject to Williams's approval; he supervised nearly every Chicago recording session and chose the songs from each session that the label would release. Williams's boss, M. A. Supper, was virtually uninvolved in the musical aspects of Chicago Music. "Anything that sold was all right with him," Williams recounted, "and these blues were selling." Williams told Stephen Calt that Supper never listened to any of the talent Williams signed, simply stipulating that only singers who sold upward of ten thousand copies were eligible for follow-up sessions. Supper and Williams got along well, and Supper even asked Williams to suggest a name for a hair straightener he wanted to sell to Black women. Williams suggested the name "Black Patti."[29]

CHAPTER 11

Bronzeville

Ink Williams's new Chicago Music office was in the heart of the "Stroll," the Black nightlife district in Chicago's Bronzeville neighborhood. "Friday night to Monday morning that place was just like an Easter parade," he remembered, "or a promenade down the boardwalk in Atlantic City." Nearby on the Stroll, at 35th and State, was the five-hundred-seat Dreamland Cafe. Farther down the street was the DeLuxe Gardens. Close proximity to such places meant that Williams did not need to visit the Black Belt, which he knew to be rough and dangerous. With a population of one hundred thousand at that time, it was the largest Black neighborhood in the country after New York City's Harlem, Philadelphia's Seventh Ward, and Washington, DC's U Street corridor—and packed with street musicians "playing for chickenfeed."[1]

Despite his tough, muscular build, honed by football, Williams did not like to go to South Side clubs. "Now, tell you the truth," he admitted years later, "I was kind of afraid to go in places myself. I was scared." The Apex Club, where the clarinetist Jimmy Noone's band held court, was one such venue Williams would not visit alone because he feared its unpredictable violence. But after football games in Chicago, Williams and his Hammond teammates would go nightclubbing on the South Side—showing up in force, and sometimes "turning them out." "And we used to celebrate in those places after the football games on Sunday. But I had my crowd with me. . . . When you're with someone, you're not so afraid."[2]

Next to the DeLuxe Gardens and the Dreamland Cafe was the Monogram Theater. "Nothin' but the low-life ever went to the *Monogram*," recalled Williams. "The upper crust went to the *Grand*."[3] The leader of the Monogram's house band was Lovie Austin, a gifted pianist, songwriter (she was a cowriter of Alberta Hunter's 1922 "Down Hearted Blues") and arranger who also worked as a de facto talent scout for Williams.

In setting up the Chicago Music office for his new Paramount gig, Williams drew inspiration from his tour of duty as a US army officer, noting, "Generals surrounded themselves with assistants and subordinates." He repurposed this idea brilliantly, surrounding himself with talented assistants and scouts while maintaining a cool remove. Later, he would admit, "I didn't know anything about music, so I used assistants, and I never relied on any one person too much for anything."[4] In addition to hiring the then unknown Thomas A. Dorsey as his chief arranger, Williams hired the musicians Tiny Parham, Kid Austin, and Aletha Dickerson and her husband, Alex Robinson. Aletha Dickerson also served as Williams's secretary. Dickerson and Robinson ran Dickerson's Record Shop, a popular hangout for Chicago musicians.[5] It is likely there that Williams met Dickerson, Robinson, Parham, and Austin while working for Black Swan.

Lovie Austin and Aletha Dickerson were—in Williams's estimation—very capable arrangers. Both were musically trained but were also able to speak and arrange in the vernacular. In the orchestra pit at the Monogram theater, Williams had watched Austin tell the pit musicians who couldn't read sheet music, "'All you got to do is *say dada dadadada bum da*!' They'd start singing it!"[6]

Of the whole group of scouts and arrangers, Dorsey and Dickerson were the most talented and indispensable to Chicago Music. Like Dorsey, Dickerson was a trained pianist and a songwriter. She was responsible for typing out the lyrics to Paramount recordings and filing them with the Library of Congress copyright office. Dickerson was also, in Williams's estimation, "a pretty good hustler herself," who occasionally played on Paramount sides, and occasionally co-wrote songs.

Williams never cultivated close relationships with any of his staff. He was aloof at the office and kept at a remove from both his subordinates and his superiors.[7] While this did not make him well liked in the workplace or with recording artists, it did make for a long career in the music business. Paramount executives did not know Williams relied on others as talent scouts, and Williams's subordinates had no idea what or who was pulling the strings back in Wisconsin. Self-preservation was his intent:

> I didn't tell *anybody* all I knew—there are very few people you can trust in this business; very few. From the top to the bottom everybody's trying to screw everybody else; get in on the "pie."[8]

Ink Williams knew that the record industry was cutthroat—from the executive level to the street, where singers refused to perform original songs in the presence of other singers for fear that competitors would beat them to recording studios with their own material. Aletha Dickerson, too, recalled being aloof and detached from the artists who frequented the Chicago Music office:

As a secretary, it wasn't necessary for me to either talk to the artists who were constantly coming into the office, or even listen to them when they were talking among themselves. To say I thought them "odd" is the understatement of the ages. (It's possible they held the same opinion of me.) I neither liked nor disliked these people. I was merely indifferent to them.[9]

In later years, Aletha Dickerson would express shame and regret for her snobbish attitude toward blues musicians. Dickerson, the daughter of two trained musicians, had received formal music training growing up; she was only about twenty when she began working for Williams. She felt that blues—and the musicians who wrote and played the blues—were uneducated and uninteresting. She later credited W. C. Handy with changing her perspective:

On one occasion when I gave forth with my undiluted opinion of what I termed "alleged artists," Handy laughed and said: "You should learn something about them. THEY have something TOO." Time has proved him correct. Eventually, I learned how utterly stupid it was to judge everyone by my own standards.[10]

Williams's brilliance as Paramount's race-records director was precisely this kind of self-awareness: that his own tastes were not a reflection of the broader public's tastes, that a great many Black record buyers were interested in a more vernacular style of music, and that their tastes had value—both monetary and cultural.

For Black musicians, all roads to Paramount—and its money—led through Ink Williams. Williams paid artists personally, typically offering them flat fees from expense accounts and not offering royalties. Williams was aware that Paramount charged a one-cent royalty on every record sold, after expenses, yet nine out of ten Paramount artists never received *any* royalties in Williams's recollection. Instead, Williams served as a black hole of information to protect Paramount from its own artists. When artists requested copies of their contracts, Williams lied and promised to put them in the mail. He regularly shortchanged artists who borrowed money against future recordings or sales, saying, "You made up with one hand what you paid out with the other."[11] Such practices made Williams's position at Paramount strong, but many artists could see that he was deliberately cheating them and resented it.

Williams felt that every angle of the music business was underhanded and rarely allowed this fact to bother him. Of Lester Melrose—his main competition in Chicago, Williams joked, "Melrose took everybody that I ever recorded. . . . He would just take them out from under me," which Williams said, "was no trouble."[12] Artists weren't loyal to labels (with the notable exception of Lil Hardin), so labels didn't have to be loyal to artists. Plus, Williams was confident in the nonstop flow of recording talent.

Though his undefined job gave him many freedoms, Williams felt that the label "race music" was constraining, even while it created a home for Black music and musicians in the commercial market. Having been founded during the height of the Jim Crow era, the record industry and its myriad marketing categories reflected Jim Crow policies and philosophies. Even while he had masterfully navigated Jim Crow America, Williams was forever irked by the music business's very real policies of segregating sound.[13] In particular, Williams was annoyed that he was not allowed to seek out white talent and was made to feel uncomfortable by Paramount's executives about allowing Blacks to record "white" material (hillbilly music, ballads, pop, light opera). Instead, Williams asked talented ballad singers to compose blues. "I would very quickly say: 'Well, we can't use it . . . write me a blues.' In doing it that way I'd save a lot of embarrassment for myself, the company, and the person."[14] Williams recalled that Alberta Hunter knew as many popular ballads as blues songs, but Paramount discouraged Williams from recording the ballads. Throughout his life, Williams chafed at the false division between Black and white repertoires that marred the recorded cultural output of American music in the first half of the twentieth century, creating the false impression that Blacks only sang blues and jazz, whereas Whites sang whatever they pleased.[15]

Early on at Paramount, Williams tended to correct the grammar of blues singers, but was hands off about lyrical content otherwise. Despite the contempt that many upwardly mobile Blacks held for the vernacular styles of blues and jazz, J. Mayo Williams said he recognized the cultural importance of those styles. Of Williams, Steven Calt wrote:

> Williams held the heretical belief that blues represented an important aspect of his racial heritage. When his friends sneeringly referred to him and his retinue of blues singers as "Mayo Williams and his dogs," he replied: "My dogs are thoroughbreds."[16]

Williams's need to defend his blues singers to his friends provides insight to Black American class differences in the early 1920s. His impressive upward mobility, coupled with his upbringing in Pine Bluff, Arkansas, and Monmouth, Illinois—where his father had worked in a saw mill and logging on the Mississippi River, and his mother worked as a domestic—put Ink in a position uniquely suited to straddling two separate classes in Black Chicago. Additionally, the legal troubles of his former stepfather, as well as of his brother Sam, opened Williams's life up to the very content of so many blues songs, creating a necessary empathy.

Because Ink Williams maintained a certain distance from lower-class Blacks, he relied heavily on the suggestions of subordinates such as Dickerson and Dorsey. He approached each artist as unique, favoring danceability and strong lyrics and vocals over musical accompaniment, virtuosity, and good looks. But such a sedentary style of scouting also meant that some quality artists never got a chance to be recorded. For instance, Williams was living at 4946 South Michigan, just three blocks south of the former heavyweight boxing champion Jack Johnson. Though Johnson famously brought his upright bass to all of his bouts and was the leader of a Chicago jazz band, Williams never sought him out, saying, "We just weren't on the alert."[17] Williams said that the business of finding race recording artists was located "just around a few places."[18] He made a practice of checking in at the local black theater houses of the T.O.B.A. (Theater Owners Booking Association—or as Count Basie and others called it, "Tough On Black Asses"). Several T.O.B.A. theaters located close to Williams's State Street office yielded most of Paramount's artists. Williams had a favorable view of vaudeville veterans, saying, "The artist with a reputation in show business like the T.O.B.A. was always welcome at Paramount."[19] Williams also scouted nearby jazz clubs like the Dreamland Cafe and the DeLuxe Gardens, where he found singers who possessed two characteristics he deemed important: "Deep contralto voices made the best singers. . . . and ninety percent of the ones that were good were black, jet-black."[20]

Ink Williams also cultivated the curious practice of attending blues-singing competitions and offering contracts to the second-place finishers. He reasoned that first-place finishers were likely to possess difficult egos that would embroil Paramount in expensive bidding wars with competing companies. As a result, Williams passed up first-place finishers in favor of the runners-up, who often lost on account of a lack of stage presence or good looks rather than vocal ability. Williams understood his medium—sound recordings—and focused only on vocal style: "In recording they had to sing from the soul, instead of just shaking and dancing," he said. Williams's biggest find early on was the statuesque Ida Cox, who "stood flat-footed and sang; she didn't need any motion at all to put her song over."[21]

Williams generally showed an interest in all things that could help him make money, including buying and installing several jukeboxes in local houses of prostitution. "I went in two, three houses of prostitution, put my own jukeboxes in there, and spent my money right in the place," he once boasted.[22] Williams's involvement in the jukebox business suggests he had familiarity (if not associations) with organized crime. Business with coin-operated machines—particularly jukeboxes—had strong connections to the mob and money laundering. Additionally, Williams was no stranger to brothels, claiming that he had accompanied Paul Robeson to a brothel in college in a visit that would mark the future actor's first sexual encounter.[23] This familiarity with prostitution illustrates an interesting personal dynamic that clouds Williams's otherwise rigid standards of propriety. At Paramount, Williams often encouraged his blues-singing "thoroughbreds" to use clever euphemisms rather than blunt sexual imagery. In addition, Williams maintained a strict ban on Black singers' recording "coon songs" for Paramount, despite their popularity at the time.[24] It is tempting to see this as Williams's maintaining some sense of Black Swan's vision of cultural "uplift"; however, it more likely reflects the fact that Black record buyers had no interest in spending their money on minstrel songs.

Williams's entrepreneurial spirit and ability to speak the language of the Black middle class proved valuable in the marketing and distribution of Paramount's race records. With limited distribution, performers were encouraged to sell their records at shows and had little choice but to perform their hit material. Williams had also arranged a deal with railroad porters, selling them stacks of Paramount race records at seventy-five cents per disc; the porters would in turn sell them for one dollar per disc.[25] Williams recalled, "The railroad porters and waiters had a network of distributors all over the country, from coast to coast. . . . You could put in an order with a porter who was running to New York, or running to Chicago, and he'd take your order all over the country."[26]

Williams's "network" likely was the Brotherhood of Sleeping Car Porters, which was formally organized by the American Federation of Labor in 1925 and headquartered in Chicago; some fifteen thousand men worked in this historically Black occupation.[27] Williams's familiarity with the network of porters was through his brother, Luther, who had worked as a porter for over a decade by 1923. (Maurice, too, would go to work as a railroad porter after his release from Joliet.) Armed with Paramount catalogs and order forms, porters carried out a guerilla marketing campaign across the United States and Canada.

In addition to his lieutenants, Williams also had informal advisors who recommended artists for Paramount. Fritz Pollard—who claimed that Ink Williams "didn't know a damn thing about music"—kept an ear out for artists that might suit Williams. Pollard succeeded in landing Jelly Roll Morton (Ferdinand Joseph Lamothe), a Creole pianist from New Orleans who came to Chicago by way of Los Angeles, where he had been working as a performer and a songwriter for a sheet-music company. In 1923, Morton learned that his "Wolverine Blues" had become a hit for King Oliver on Gennett, prompting him to move to Chicago to cash in on his success.[28] Morton told the folklorist Alan Lomax, "Fritz Pollard introduced me to Ink Williams who was then a scout for the Paramount Recording Company. I got together a band . . . and those records sold very big. I was to be paid by the side and I never have got all the money yet."[29] In reality, it was a while before Morton had a follow-up session with Paramount, an indication that his first sides had not sold as well as he imagined.

If ever there was an artist who was "pitching a curve," it was Morton. Morton bragged to Alan Lomax, "I was recording for just about everybody else under different pseudonyms. Those days I used to call myself almost anything for a disguise and go on in and make the records. Naturally [Gennett] didn't like this too well."[30] Between Morton's first session for Paramount in June

1923 and his follow-up session in July 1924, Jelly Roll recorded under various pseudonyms for Paramount, Gennett, OKeh, Paramount (again), Rialto, Autograph, Champion, and Gennett (again). Morton's label hopping didn't seem to bother either Williams or Morton all that much. Williams called Morton a "freelancer" and may have helped him record for Gennett right after recording for Paramount.

Morton never allowed his devout Catholicism to be a barrier to a life fully lived in the dark corners of society. Williams possessed a similar ability to compartmentalize his unsavory practices (a growing gambling habit, working with houses of prostitution, predatory and unscrupulous business practices) from his life as a middle-class, philanthropic fraternity man. Morton was astute enough to see both sides of Williams and to know when he could be trusted. On one occasion in 1925, Morton's younger sister, Frances, was visiting from Louisiana. Morton asked Williams to escort her around Chicago to "see the sights"—including a museum and some college campuses—and to keep her away from his musician friends and the red-light districts where Morton usually played. Frances was delighted to have Williams as an escort—she knew him as a famous football player and had no idea he was involved in the music business prior to coming to Chicago.[31]

Williams admired Jelly Roll's style and the fact that he could play four bars on the piano and anyone would know it was him. But he also described him as a "braggart" who tried to claim that he had invented jazz: "Everything that came out of New Orleans, he'd make you believe that he did it, he brought it out, he did this, he did that. Nobody else did anything down there in New Orleans but Jelly Roll. That was the thing that got wheezy."[32]

Although Pollard had helped connect Morton and Williams, Morton's Paramount sides never sold particularly well. As for Pollard's claim that Williams didn't know "a damn thing about music," Williams unknowingly presented a convincing argument to the contrary in an interview with the researchers Jim O'Neal and George Paulus:

> **PAULUS**: Okay. First let me ask you, what are your personal feelings about blues? How much did you like blues, or were you just in it for the business?
>
> **WILLIAMS**: Well, I will answer that in this way. You see, in college I had an appreciation for music which was, naturally, of a different kind. My classmates . . . didn't appreciate blues. But I had always *heard* blues, and it became a kind of second nature to me. But I had no idea that I would end up recording in the blues business. . . . I remember while in school [at Brown University], we used to have little skits. And I'd get up and I'd *dance*. Sing 'em the blues. *Try* to sing. I had had a little funny thing about my home situation. I never could play an instrument of *any* kind.

> I *never studied music.* That's the most unusual thing in this whole setup. But the way I used to audition bands, if they played music and I found myself tappin' my foot [taps a steady 4/4], that's the one I'd take, see? If I could dance to it—I could always dance, I did all them funny steps that they used to do, not like the dancing now. [laughs] One of the questions they'd ask me was, "How could I record bands?" . . . It's because of the way it would move me. [taps steady 4/4 on floor].[33]

In addition to danceability, Williams felt that a simple and singable melody was equally important to the success of a blues song. He would say to musicians, "Listen, don't make it too *hard*. Just make it simple and easy [so that] *anybody* can sing it. But if you put all them chromatics and ninths and tenths and elevenths and twelfths and thirteenths in there, other things, a million things, . . . ain't nobody gonna *try* to sing it, or try the melody."[34]

With his team of lieutenants and talent scouts, Williams could depend on being presented with quality talent. Once the talent was in front of him, Williams was adept at recognizing what would sell and getting it out to the interested public.

His first year at Paramount was busier and more profitable than his previous job at Black Swan. But Williams still chose to moonlight as an NFL player with Doc Young's Hammond Pros in the fall of 1923. By this point he had forged a lifelong friendship with the Young family and was a regularly invited guest at their home. Doc Young expanded his integration of the Pros, employing three Black players on the 1923 team: Williams, Fritz Pollard, and Sol Butler. Williams's old friend from Brown, Dunc Annan, also signed on with the Hammond team.[35] Doc Young's racial outlook stood in increasingly defiant opposition to the strong KKK presence in and around Hammond, as well as the growing anti-integration sentiments of many NFL team owners. Young felt optimistic about the 1923 season and set up an ambitious schedule—even scheduling four home games for the team at A. Murray Turner Field in Hammond. (Hammond typically held its home games in Chicago.)

Young's ambitious vision was not realized—the season proved rife with cancellations, and the games that took place were crushingly bad. Still, the season was not without notable highlights. Fritz Pollard coached the team, though he played only when he deemed it absolutely necessary. (Their record suggests Pollard was always needed, but he only appeared in a handful of games.) At the season opener against the Canton Bulldogs, who were the previous season's league champions, five thousand were on hand at Canton's Lakeside Park, as was Pathé News, to film the season's opening festivities. Doc Young's six-year-old son, Harry, recalled "leading a parade around the field at Canton, Ohio. . . . I wore number seven which was Ink Williams, my buddy and hero."[36] Though Canton manhandled Hammond, the *Evening Review* noted that "'Inky' Williams was the big noise for Hammond. He was the only visitor who could halt the Cantonians."[37] Hammond lost the game 14–0.

The following week, the Pros went home to face the Dayton Triangles, a game that they won, 7–0, in front of two thousand fans. This was their only home game that season and marked one half of the points the Pros scored all season. All seven points were scored by Williams and Pollard. Dayton fumbled a punt at their own ten-yard line in the fourth quarter, which Williams grabbed and ran back for a touchdown, his only touchdown during his six-year NFL career.[38] Pollard kicked the extra point, putting a rare seven points on the board for Hammond. When the team traveled to Missouri the following week to play the St. Louis All-Stars to a 0–0 tie, Williams and Pollard did not play. Their absence was most likely due to the NFL's practice of not bringing Black players to games in Missouri. This policy famously cost the Rock Island Independents the 1924 league championship. Rock Island, whose 1924 lineup featured two Native American players (Jim Thorpe and Joe Little Twig) and one Black player (Duke Slater) tested Missouri's segregationist policy that season in a game against the Kansas City Blues. Although Thorpe and Little Twig were allowed to play, Kansas City refused to allow Slater to take the field. So far, Slater had played all sixty minutes of nineteen consecutive games and was the team's key player in their dominating season. Without Slater, Rock Island went down to defeat, ultimately costing them the league title.[39]

Fritz Pollard did not appear in another game for Hammond that season, and the team suffered a four-game losing streak, even traveling all the way to Duluth, Minnesota only to lose to the Kelleys, 3–0. Thirty-five hundred watched Williams and the Pros lose 6–0 against Paddy Driscoll's Chicago Cardinals at Comiskey Park, a game that marked the Hammond debut of Sol Butler.[40] Butler was an all-star quarterback for Dubuque (1915–20), had won five track-and-field medals at the Inter-Allied Games in Montenegro in 1919, and had competed in the long jump at the 1920 Olympic Games in Antwerp. (He injured himself in his first long-jump attempt but still finished seventh overall.)[41] Butler—who had met Pollard and Williams at the 1917 Penn Relays, and who had become friends with both in Pollard's off-season All-Star teams—started the season with the Rock Island Independents (his hometown team), appearing in three games before Doc Young acquired his services from Rock Island for Hammond. Young told the *Chicago Defender* that ten thousand dollars was "close to the amount paid" for Butler's contract (a dubious figure, given how little money Hammond seemed to earn).[42]

Doubtless Doc Young had taken note that Black former collegiate stars caused a significant uptick in gate receipts for Hammond. The Black media in Chicago—with which Young was in contact—had been advocating for the reintegration of pro boxing and the integration of major league baseball, not just as a civil rights issue but also as economic common sense. In a furious piece in the *Chicago Defender*, the sports writer Frank Young estimated that eight hundred of the attendees at the Cardinals' game against Hammond were Black, drawn out to see Ink Williams and Sol Butler. Young speculated that many of the white spectators had also come specifically to see Williams and Butler play. Young used this point as evidence of the economic idiocy of segregationist white boxing promoters' refusal to schedule a match between the Black heavyweight champ Harry Wills against the white heavyweight champ Jack Dempsey. Black athletes should be acknowledged as peers in sports, most Black and white sports fans wished to see the best compete with the best regardless of race, and promoters harnessing the buying power of Black spectators was simple common sense.[43]

Tragedy struck the Williams family in November 1923. Ink went to Monmouth, Illinois for the funeral of his older brother, Luther. Luther had been working as a dining-car waiter for the Lake Shore Railway in Chicago when he died from an intestinal blockage, a health problem that had plagued him for several years. Ink paid for Luther's funeral at St. James AME Church in Monmouth, his burial, and the headstone—an indication that his finances had become solid.

On November 25, during Thanksgiving weekend, Hammond faced off against George Halas and the Chicago Bears at Cubs Park. Halas, the team's owner-coach, also worked as the Bears' public-relations advance man, planting stories in area newspapers, and making sure that games were well promoted. Before the Chicago-Hammond matchup, the *Chicago Tribune* ran a preview of the game, which demonstrates Halas's awareness of the drawing power of Black players in the early NFL: "Two great Negro stars, 'Ink' Williams of Brown, and Sol Butler of Dubuque, are among the aces the Hoosiers will send in against the north side team."[44]

Hammond lost to the Bears, 14–7, in front of thirty-five hundred at Cubs Park (Wrigley Field). It was a close-fought game, and Williams was the star of the visiting team:

> "Ink" Williams, ex-Brown end, was one of the features of the engagement. He is one of the best wingmen seen at the North Side park in years. Early in the battle he spilled end runs, tackled men catching punts, nailing them in their tracks, and created havoc generally. It got so the Bears finally sent two men against him.
>
> There was little to mark the first quarter except Williams' superb play.[45]

Lining up across from Williams all day for the Bears was George Halas. Only three years later, Halas would be party to the NFL owners' gentleman's agreement to purge Black players from the league, a thirteen-year stain on the league's history. The NFL owners' party line in 1927 was that Black players were simply uninterested in playing or were afraid of getting hurt. In light of Halas's advance promotional work prior to the Hammond-Chicago contest, the fact that Halas saw Williams line up against him all game, and his decision as head coach to apply double coverage against Williams, it's difficult to accept Halas's silence on ownership's segregationist stance. In later decades, Halas's close association with major Black sports figures such as Gale Sayers and Walter Payton has caused him to be seen as a positive force for integration. But early Black NFL players never forgave Halas for his silence—mainly because he had witnessed the skill, bravery, and tenacity of men such as Williams and Butler on the field yet remained silent on the question of segregating the league in 1933.

Four days after the Chicago game, Hammond traveled to Wisconsin for a frustrating 19–0 loss to the Green Bay Packers at Bellevue Field. Snapping the ball that day to Curly Lambeau for Green Bay was Williams's fellow Monmouth, Illinois native Francis Louis "Jug" Earp.[46] The *Green Bay Press-Gazette* wrote that Hammond appeared flat, and Williams "didn't perform with his usual brilliance."[47] Hammond then limped to Kokomo, Indiana to close out their season with an exhibition against the Kokomo Legion on December 21. The townspeople knew that Williams and Butler would be coming and posted KKK propaganda to scare them out of town. It didn't work. Harry Young recalled:

> I remember we once played a game in Kokomo and the restaurants had signs that said "This is a 100 percent American establishment—no Koons, Kikes, or Katholics." They refused to feed our black players. I don't know what Dad did, but I know he cussed all the apple knockers. Ink Williams kept his helmet on the whole game.[48]

Hammond beat Kokomo, 14–0. Williams almost never wore a helmet, but he made an exception for this game. The bravery of Williams, Butler, and their Hammond teammates in playing an integrated game of football was very real. Kokomo's klansmen—whom Doc Young called "apple knockers"—meant what they said. In 1930, nearby Marion, Indiana was the site of the high-profile lynching of Thomas Shipp and Abram Smith.[49]

Sports writers were taking notice of Ink Williams. George Calhoun of the *Green Bay Press Gazette* picked Williams as an end on his All-American Pro First Team, then the most prestigious recognition in pro football journalism. To put Williams's accomplishments in perspective, he was on the First Team alongside Jim Thorpe and Paddy Driscoll—arguably two of the greatest players of the age—despite playing for the abysmal Hammond team. Calhoun's All-American list was actually the product of a balloting system, with journalists from Pittsburgh, Milwaukee, Duluth, Rock Island, Akron, Cleveland, Canton, Dayton, Minneapolis, St. Louis, and Green Bay casting votes. According to Calhoun, there was stiff competition for the end position, but "Ink Williams was picked by nearly every critic for the first team."[50]

Herb Sies—the head coach of the Rock Island Independents—had also taken notice and tried to hire Williams for the Independents' final game against the Chicago Bears at Cubs Park in Chicago on December 9. Rock Island had employed Black players since Bobby Marshall and Rock Island won the first game in the NFL's inaugural 1920 season. Sol Butler had played for Rock Island, and Duke Slater was the team's standout star. Williams's decision not to play for the Independents would prove to be a minor moment in NFL history, but a seismic moment in American music.

For nearly a week, newspapers in Davenport and Rock Island filed daily reports on Williams's availability. Ink was willing to play the game but couldn't travel to Rock Island for weekday practices. If Rock Island was willing to practice in Chicago, Ink would be there. Rock Island wasn't willing to pay for boarding its players in Chicago for a week.[51] Ultimately, Williams decided to stand pat and not play. It wasn't about ego, it was a work thing: instead of playing in front of six thousand people at Cubs Park on December 7, Williams would be recording history in a Chicago studio, cutting the first records of Gertrude "Ma" Rainey for Paramount.

CHAPTER 12

Madame

Ink Williams was excited. As he arrived at the Marsh Laboratory recording studio, he had no regrets about missing Rock Island's game against Chicago. He was about to make the first recordings of Ma Rainey, and he knew these records would be great.

His engineer, Otto Marsh, had picked an unlikely spot to build a recording studio. The five-story Marsh Laboratory building was right up against Chicago's elevated train, the L, which meant some takes would be ruined by the roaring of passing trains. But that location meant Marsh's services were affordable, and that meant Williams did business with Marsh.

Just a few nights before, Williams saw Ma Rainey perform at the Monogram Theater. Only six years Williams's senior, Rainey appeared considerably older. There was nothing subtle about her: she was loud, made no bones about her bisexuality, wore a giant necklace made of gold dollars, and flashed a smile full of gold teeth. To Williams, all of this was extraneous. As he sat in the Monogram, Williams heard and felt Rainey's performance more than he saw it. The visceral connection between Rainey and the audience—not the flamboyant stage persona but the emotional directness of a profoundly gifted singer—was Rainey's timeless gift. Records could deliver that gift to thousands of Black homes. After the show, Williams asked her to record for Paramount.

At thirty-six, Ma Rainey was considered the grand dame of southern Black music. Like so many of Williams's artists, she was not the headliner at the Monogram. Rainey's protégé, Bessie Smith, had been signed by Columbia Records earlier in the year, and Smith's successful run of hit records revealed a market hungry for classic blues. Black and white record buyers saw Bessie Smith as young and exciting; Ma Rainey was understood to be a throwback to a rougher time, place, and sound rooted in the rural Black South. The musicologist John Wesley Work Jr. described Rainey's singing style as "authentic."[1]

The young Thomas A. Dorsey called her "an old-timer." However others might describe her, Williams was impressed.

Ma Rainey was born Gertrude Pridgett in 1886, grew up in Columbus, Georgia, and started in show business as a young teenager around 1900. She claimed to have coined the term "the blues," a style of music she first heard at a tent show in Missouri in 1902. In 1904, the eighteen-year-old Pridgett became known as Ma Rainey after marrying William "Pa" Rainey, a dancer, comedian, and singer. They had met as touring members of the Rabbit Foot Minstrels. Graced with a figure that was as earthy as her stage persona, Rainey used her powerful voice to deliver songs, often original material, with either lean accompaniment or full, raucous backing bands in equally effective measure. Of all the vaudevillian (or "classic") blues singers who made recordings, Rainey stuck closest to strict blues, frequently recording classic twelve-bar blues and pairing new songs with familiar tunes like "Boll Weevil Blues" from the folk-blues canon.

Though she was possibly the most experienced show business performer Williams had ever met, Rainey had never been inside a recording studio before. But Williams was confident Rainey would adjust quickly. Backing her at the session was the house band from the Monogram: Lovie Austin and Her Blues Serenaders, consisting of Austin on piano, Jimmy O'Bryant on clarinet, and Tommy Ladnier on cornet. Three months earlier, the Blues Serenaders had backed another soon-to-be-marquee Paramount blues singer, Ida Cox, on a session produced by Williams, resulting in the single "Graveyard Dream Blues" (with the B-side "Come Right In"). Like Rainey, Cox was a Georgia-born singer who had cut her teeth on the rural minstrel circuit. And, like Bessie Smith, Ida Cox had toured with—and idolized and emulated—Ma Rainey.

When Rainey and her group arrived at Marsh, Williams directed them to the twenty-by-twenty-foot padded room where they would play. Recording in those days was a strictly mechanical process: the singer and the musicians played into an acoustic horn (think of a Victrola morning-glory speaker), causing a stylus to vibrate. The stylus cut these vibrations into a wax disc that moved clockwise on a turntable beneath the disc. Driving the turntable was a heavy counterweight: a stone that slowly descended on a rope. The turntable spun at a rate of seventy-eight rotations per minute (78 rpm). The discs were ten inches in diameter, so at 78 rpm, they could fit only three minutes of sound. The band needed to conclude its performance within that time. The technology did not yet exist for achieving "fadeouts," a technique whereby the sound engineer gradually lowers the volume to silence. At the top of the session, Williams would tell the performers to watch a series of lights—one that indicated the recording was in process, one that indicated it was coming to an end.

False starts, flubbed lyrics, musical "clams" (missed notes)—all were cut into the disc. If a take was bad, the fragile wax disc was irretrievably ruined.

(Each disc could be cut only once.) Though the final format had evolved from Edison's wax cylinders to flat shellac discs, every sound recording, from Edison's first in 1877 until electric recording was introduced in 1925, was made by this acoustic, mechanical process—a horn, and a stylus that cut into wax, either a cylinder or, after about 1920, a disc.

All performers—particularly first-time recording artists like Ma Rainey—had to do considerable work to prepare a mistake-free, three-minute performance. From time immemorial until Thomas Edison unleashed acoustic sound recording technology on the world, musicians had played songs for however long they—or the audience—wished. An instrumental country fiddle tune, such as "Devil's Dream," played for dancing could—at a house party—stretch for thirty minutes. A slow-drag blues song by Ma Rainey might—at a tent show in rural Alabama—go for ten minutes or longer. But when the same musicians entered the twenty-by-twenty-foot cell at Marsh Laboratory, they had to arrange their music to fit within three minutes—making sometimes hard decisions about which verses to cut, which musicians to play solos, and how to arrange an ending.

Performers made these decisions at Williams's Chicago Music office prior to arriving at the studio. Williams, the musicians, and the Chicago Music staff gathered there and listened through possible song choices. Depending on what he heard, Williams chose the songs to be recorded on the session. Then Tom Dorsey and/or Aletha Dickerson would help the musicians arrange and rehearse a three-minute (or shorter) version of the song; Dickerson typed up the lyrics. For first-time Paramount artists, this process typically involved two or four songs to test the market, with each record having a different song on each side. Ma Rainey's first session included at least eight songs. This required significant preparation time, indicating that Williams felt sure Ma Rainey's records would sell.

When Rainey arrived at the Chicago Music office, it was not the first time Dorsey had seen her:

> I'd heard and I had seen her, years ago when she used to come to Atlanta. She and Pa [Rainey] was there when I was a boy sellin' pop around the theater, see. So, I met her there, but she didn't know nothin' about me, and I didn't care that much about her, for all I was worried about 'em payin' me for that pop I was sellin.' She was always a great star.[2]

Dorsey was somewhat baffled by Williams's enthusiasm for Ma Rainey. Most of the acts Paramount recorded were young. Rainey, in Dorsey's estimation, was an old-timer stepping out of the past.

Now that Rainey, Austin, Ladnier, and O'Bryant were at Marsh Laboratory in the small, padded sound room, Williams and Marsh sat in the engineer's room upstairs and listened to them perform all eight songs, not yet cutting a disc. During the performances, Marsh and Williams would come in and out of the recording room to physically group the players. With a single acoustic horn to pick up the sound, the performers had to be positioned closer to or farther from the horn depending on how the sound waves from any particular instrument or voice affected the stylus. Some instruments, such as drums, overpowered the stylus and made it jump off the disc; others created a distorted signal; still others needed to be close to the horn (or even partly inside it) to be audible over the other instruments. In other words, the musicians had to adapt to a physical arrangement that was entirely foreign to them.

As Marsh worked on the acoustic arrangements, Williams may have suggested changes that were lyrical or musical. He was mainly concerned about the words: he knew the words mattered to listeners, and he did not want mistakes that would waste wax discs. If singers could read, Williams gave them a copy of the lyric sheet typed up by Aletha Dickerson. If a singer was blind—and many who recorded for Paramount were—Williams sat behind them and whispered prompts. Ma Rainey, who was illiterate, brought her own ideograms, mapping out the lyrics in pictures she had drawn to ensure that she didn't make any stumbles while cutting records—a technique Williams would ultimately require of other illiterate singers.

From this very first session for Paramount, Rainey proved she was thoroughly prepared, utterly dependable, and stone-cold sober. Offstage, she was low-key and professional, and Williams claimed Rainey was the only blues singer he worked with who didn't drink alcohol. In Williams's assessment, she was "a shrewd businessman. We never tried to put any swindles over on her."[3]

Producers often told vaudeville blues singers what to sing. Ma Rainey was an exception to that rule, which reflects her triumphant power as an artist and a businesswoman. It also reflects Williams's innate trust in Rainey's instincts and vision. With Ma Rainey, Williams even threw out his grammatical rulebook. "What do you want," he once asked rhetorically, "good grammar or good blues?"[4]

When it came time to cut the songs onto wax, Williams and Marsh did not use an earphone to listen to the recordings. Nor did they listen to the delicate wax masters before packing them and shipping them from Chicago to the pressing plant in Port Washington, Wisconsin. Instead, Williams listened intensely as the musicians performed in real time and had Marsh make three recordings of each song. Chicago was notoriously cold in December, which made it easier for Marsh to pack and ship the wax masters to the pressing plant. (During the summer, Marsh had to pack the wax masters in ice.) Even then, there was no guarantee a single would emerge: in at least one instance, mice nibbled on the masters and ruined a shipment of Paramount recordings.

Williams then had to wait for the pressing plant to create metal masters from the wax masters; the metal masters were then used to make test pressings of each recording on shellac. The shellac discs were then shipped to Williams's office so that he could finally hear the results of the session. Listening to the test pressings, he selected the best of the A, B, and C takes, which Paramount would then mass-produce as the official release. From a twenty-first-century vantage point, it is astonishing to see that there was no instant gratification for any of the musicians, producers, or engineers involved in this work. Many of them never had the satisfaction of hearing their recordings at all.

When Williams heard the test pressings of Ma Rainey with Lovie Austin and Her Blues Syncopaters, the results were electrifying. Rainey sings "Bad Luck Blues" in a soulful, bold, confessional style; her phrasing moves into each measure like someone sliding into a booth at a nightclub. Ladiner's cornet appears to join in conversation with Rainey's voice. And while O'Bryant's clarinet adds a plaintive third melodic line, Lovie Austin's piano provides a rhythmic anchor that holds the piece swingingly together. "Bad Luck Blues" would appear on the A-side of Rainey's first Paramount release—the B-side being a gut-bucket rendition of the folk song "Boll Weevil Blues." Something new was paired with something old—a coupling that announced Ma Rainey as a commercial powerhouse for Paramount.

With Ma Rainey's first record released into the world, Paramount's prolific advertisements praised her as the "Mother of the Blues," and the "legendary Ma Rainey." Whereas Black Swan had tried to "uplift" the blues by changing the music, Williams's approach was to inject a sense of pride into advertisements of the music and musicians. Such was the case with Ma Rainey, of whom Williams claimed "I gave her the name Madame in order to dignify the blues."[5] Williams's signing and recording of Ma Rainey enabled him to succeed at Paramount where Fletcher Henderson couldn't at Black Swan. The blues that Mayo Williams was recording at Paramount was, he claimed, "not only contemporary but what had been our heritage from birth."[6]

Ma Rainey's music resonated with the public. In 1924, Williams decided to turn his quest to record what the people wanted into an overt marketing appeal. On the cover of the 1924 Paramount Records catalog is a photo of a handsome, well-dressed thirty-year-old Black artists and repertoire (A&R) man, and a question for the masses:

WHAT DOES THE PUBLIC WANT?

What will you have? If your preferences are not listed in our catalog, we will make them for you, as Paramount must please the buying public. There is always room for more good material and more talented artists. Any suggestion or recommendations that you may have to offer will be greatly appreciated by J. Mayo Williams, Manager of the "Race Artists Series."[7]

Paramount brilliantly deployed Williams's photo as a marker of racial authenticity. It telegraphs to customers that Paramount wasn't just some white executives guessing at what Black listeners wanted to hear. Paramount's race records were being managed by a famous Black athlete. Williams's face appeared again later in 1924 on Paramount's thirty-page *Book of Blues*, in which a solicitous Williams again stated that Paramount was open to "every phase of music from Blues to grand opera and everything that comes between. What will you have?"[8]

In asking the public, "What will you have?" Williams signaled an approach that was strikingly different from that of Harry Pace and Black Swan. Whereas Pace promoted the Black vernacular styles of blues and jazz to try to entice customers to ultimately buy "what we wanted them to buy," Williams sought to please the public while also dignifying Black vernacular music on its own terms. Perhaps Williams hoped the public would ask for Paul Robeson records, but he refused to allow that hope to drive his agenda. Instead, 90 percent of the public's responses called for Paramount to issue more blues.[9] To his credit, Williams had learned a lesson from watching Black Swan in the marketplace, and he went hard after rugged blues.

Williams wasn't seeing live blues music only in T.O.B.A. theaters such as the Monogram: he was also seeing it on the street. One day, Williams was struck by the rhythmic playing of a banjo-wielding street performer named Papa Charlie Jackson. "I was lookin' for somethin' like that," Williams said, "somethin' different. He was a hell of a banjo player. I could just see myself dancing to Papa Charlie, but not to those other artists."[10]

Jackson was a long, lanky Creole from New Orleans who played the six-string banjo. On recording for Paramount in August 1924, he became the first male blues recording star in what was then a nearly all-female commercial genre. In Jackson's playing, Williams heard a dance-band soloist and was confident his sound would develop an audience. "If you follow Papa Charlie, you find that he had good rhythm—you could dance by nearly every song Papa Charlie made," said Williams. "He was a one-man band."[11] Like Ma Rainey, Jackson was the rare artist whose repertoire consisted almost entirely of original material, much of it cheery-sounding, up-tempo music. "He did lean towards comedy," said Williams.[12] Much of his catalog reflected minstrel, vaudeville, and popular influences.

Williams's intuition paid off. Not only was Papa Charlie Jackson's recording of "Salty Dog Blues" enormously successful but his fifth single, "Shake That Thing," proved to be a sensation. Williams accompanied Charlie Jackson to Mardi Gras in New Orleans twice, "and each time, we had the hit song of the Mardi Gras, and one of 'em was that 'Shake That Thing.'"[13] Williams told Jim O'Neal, "Everybody in the street with tin bands, and tub bands, and washboard bands and everything, were all in this Mardi Gras parade singin' nothin' but 'Shake That Thing.'"[14]

After one Mardi Gras trip, Williams booked Jackson into a T.O.B.A. theater in New Orleans before making a side trip (at Jackson's sister's request) to visit

Jackson's relatives. This meant going to Algiers, Louisiana, which Williams did, "like a damn fool. . . . In Algiers, they drink anything! I went over there and didn't know what I was doin' for two or three days and when I came to I got myself outta Algiers and got myself outta New Orleans."[15]

Papa Charlie was what Williams called a "liquorhead"—someone who was always drunk—and said that "the more he drank, the more he showed off. You couldn't tell when he was gonna 'tear his drawers.'" Still, Papa Charlie kept people guessing by generally *appearing* sober. "You might say to him: 'Why don't you come by and record?' and he might show up today or tomorrow or the next day, just disregard everything. He'd get out on a drunk, and wasn't physically able to make it." Williams believed Papa Charlie's early death at age fifty-one in 1938 was due to alcoholism, but "if you got a few drinks in him he'd do anything you wanted." This proved a common trait among Williams's blues singers: "I never had any male singers who didn't drink, and that was one thing you had to guard against."[16]

As Williams recorded more male blues singers, he was concerned about the toxic combination of alcoholism and competitiveness. He made sure never to schedule two male artists in the studio on the same day. He also refused to allow artists to bring an entourage with them in the studio for fear of fights breaking out and damaging studio equipment. Most singers started drinking heavily during rehearsals at the Chicago Music office, seemingly unaware when too much liquor diminished their performances.[17]

Ink Williams never shared his positive feelings with Papa Charlie Jackson or any other musician for fear that success might drive them to get what he called a "big head." Instead, Williams was nonchalant, telling artists, "We only know how good you are by what the sales figures tell us."[18] With the success of Rainey, Jackson, Ida Cox, and others whom Williams signed to Paramount, his power grew: "My word was final in anything that I wanted to do."[19]

On July 1, 1924, Paramount's general manager, M. A. Supper, secretly dissolved Chicago Music in order to disassociate the label from the publishing money Williams had rolling in.[20] Supper and Paramount's CEO, Otto Moeser, "didn't challenge [me] because they was makin' so much money . . . but I never asked for anything that was out of proportion to what I was earning for them." It's stunning to consider how quickly Williams achieved success for Paramount—Black Swan had released its last record only a year before. Yet Williams was successful enough in 1924 to receive a Paramount company car; he made a comfortable living by padding his expense accounts: "If anyone was pitching a curve, I was pitching it in padding my expense accounts."[21] Despite this success, Williams still had to take the back entrance and the freight elevator on the rare occasions he attended meetings at Paramount headquarters in Wisconsin or in the hotel rooms of executives on their visits to Chicago.[22]

In both personal and professional terms, 1924 proved to be a milestone year for Williams: in addition to his success with Ma Rainey and Papa Charlie

Jackson, he married a Chicago public school teacher named Aleta Carolyn Stokes.[23] Aleta Stokes was born in 1895 in Illinois—most likely in Danville, where her older sisters, Stella (1882) and Pearl (1889), also were born. The county seat of Vermilion County, Danville was one hundred twenty miles south of Chicago, ninety miles west of Indianapolis, and at the epicenter of Illinois-Indiana coal country. When Aleta was sixteen in 1910, Danville's population hovered around twenty-seven thousand people—more than double what it had been twenty years earlier.[24] Danville may be little known today, but it was a booming coal-production center in the early 1900s. Its most prominent citizen, Joseph Gurney Cannon, served as United States Speaker of the House from 1903 to 1911.

Aleta's father, Cassius, was born in Kentucky in 1850; her mother, Julia, was born in Hickman, Kentucky in 1864 to John Lewis and Martha Jackson. Julia married Cassius when she was just fifteen and Cassius was twenty-nine. Aleta, Stella, and Pearl grew up on North Street in Danville, where—in 1910—most of their neighbors were Black and had moved to Danville from Indiana, Kentucky, Missouri, Virginia, and North Carolina. Significant numbers of the Stokes's Black neighbors claimed on the census not to know where in the United States their parents were born; one neighbor, Vassals Spragur, claimed that his father was born in Africa and his mother in Holland. The white families nearby were mostly immigrants from Germany and Syria. All five of the Stokeses were fully literate. Cassius worked as a laborer, Julia maintained the family home, and they rented a spare room to a boarder. As for Aleta, she must have resembled her father: everybody called her Cass.

By 1920, Cassius had died, Stella and Pearl had moved out, and Aleta—now twenty-four years old—had accomplished the extraordinary: her father was born enslaved, yet she attended Illinois State Normal School (in 1912 and 1918) and both the Teachers' Institute for Southern Illinois and a summer graduate program at University of Chicago in 1917.[25] She then worked as a public school teacher in Mount Vernon, Illinois. About ninety miles east of St. Louis, Mount Vernon was a small town (nine thousand) with an even smaller Black population; Julia and Aleta's home was one of three Black households on an otherwise all-white street. After Aleta's sister Stella married Eugene Sykes, a waiter from Tennessee, and settled in Chicago in 1922, Aleta and Julia joined them within a year.

Aleta Stokes was a member of the Delta Sigma Theta sorority, most likely joining Chicago's citywide chapter after its founding in 1921. Her marriage to Williams at the Carters Temple CME (Christian Methodist Episcopal) Church in Bronzeville was reported as "one of the outstanding social events of the season."[26] Aleta was resplendent in a white crepe romaine dress beaded with pearls, a tulle veil with orange blossoms, and a bouquet of roses and lilies of the valley. Her brother-in-law, Eugene Sykes, walked Aleta up the aisle; her sister Pearl was a bridesmaid in a maize taffeta frock with pink rosebud trim and a large matching hat. Williams's best man was William H. Temple, a former football teammate at Howard. Temple was a native of Vicksburg, Mississippi who was voted "most eloquent" in his graduating class at Howard, where he and E. Franklin Frazier had served as class president and vice president, respectively, during their junior year. Temple served as a lieutenant in World War I before moving to Chicago to study law at Northwestern. After graduating in 1921, he opened a practice on the South Side.[27] Both men were members of Alpha Phi Alpha, and several of their fraternity brothers were in attendance, along with some friends from Brown.[28] Following the wedding, Mayo and Aleta went to Boston for their honeymoon.[29]

Williams's status as a "company man" was on full display: his engagement ring for Aleta came from Bostwick's jewelry store in Port Washington. (John M. Bostwick made a fortune as a diamond broker, which is what made him the most powerful investor in Paramount.) Likewise, when Mayo and Aleta moved in together, they furnished their apartment with furniture made by the Wisconsin Chair Company.[30] Aleta's social life as Mrs. Mayo Williams—particularly her bridge parties, which were widely reported in the Black press—showed her to be part of a close-knit group of educated Black socialites.

History suggests that Aleta and Mayo had a happy marriage—or, at the very least, a long and durable one. They remained married until Aleta's death nearly fifty years later. Aleta's personal style may have brought some moral firmness into Ink's life. By all accounts Mayo wrestled with his own moral code and ideas of self-improvement. He insisted that he refused constant advances by would-be female blues singers, abstaining from casting-couch techniques prevalent in the entertainment industry. He struggled on and off with drinking. Finding that his grammar and sobriety slipped when he hung around with musicians, he tried to keep his distance.[31]

Musicians did not like Williams's aloofness, but they hated him for his tendency to fleece performers out of their money. Alberta Hunter, in particular, loathed Williams—both for his own underhanded practices and for his willingness to enable Paramount's. This hatred, in turn, irritated Williams, who defended his transgressions by pointing a finger at the bad behavior of artists. Hunter angrily said Williams would pay for his sins.[32] Of his own deceits, Williams once said, "I've got a bit of Shylock in me," a decidedly antisemitic reference to the central character in Shakespeare's *Merchant of Venice*. In fact, although Williams had many Jewish friends, teammates, and colleagues, he delighted in making antisemitic remarks intended to show off his ruthless business style.

Williams never pretended to be anything other than what he was, declaring, "I was better than fifty percent honest, and in this business that's pretty good." Stephen Calt assessed Williams's practices as reflecting the widespread exploitation in the race-record industry rather than being invented by Williams himself.[33]

However, Williams's practices were downright predatory—except when they were simply consistent with standard industry exploitation. Williams lined his own pockets—and those of Chicago Music—by regularly purchasing songs from songwriters. In music publishing, each cent derived from royalties is divided equally between the writer and the publisher. Williams often purchased both the writer's and publisher's shares for fifty or sixty dollars per song. Many performers bought into Williams's scheme, saying, "Give me mine now, Mister Williams; whatever you make beyond that, that's yours." Williams was frank in explaining how this payoff worked in his favor:

> I'll say this, 35 percent of the artists sold their compositions outright for a flat proposition. They didn't want to wait and see what they might earn on royalties. They'd say: "Give me fifty dollars, seventy-five dollars, or a hundred dollars, and forget about it." That's where the publishing company made money. Not only did the publishing company receive all the royalties from the compositions that they owned outright, but they stood to make a lot if another company made a record using that composition.[34]

The musicians' choice here—to sell the song immediately and take the money up front—seems clearly wrong in hindsight. The events of the so-called British invasion of the 1960s and its explosive commercial relationship with early blues records was simply unimaginable in 1924. The entire idea of British bands such as the Rolling Stones, Led Zeppelin, or Cream bringing early blues songs to a cross-racial international market and netting song publishers millions of dollars in the process would have seemed absolutely ludicrous. But even if blues singers had had a crystal ball in 1924, most of them lived hand to mouth, and they needed money now. Williams knowingly, even enthusiastically, took advantage of their situation.

It's true that the world of commercial recording is a gamble. No matter how good a song or a performance may seem, nobody knows if (or why) a song will become a hit. Most of Williams's purchases did not "hit," so it is true that he was taking a modest risk in buying unproven songs. But *how* Williams came to own these songs is telling. He admittedly made a practice of loosening artists up with alcohol, cutting records, and then seeing that those artists signed their rights away in contracts. Williams did this to Big Bill Broonzy, who was unsparing in his disdain for Williams. Broonzy said that to Williams, blues singers were just "a meal ticket for the man or woman who wears dollar-signs for eyes."[35]

Like Williams, Broonzy was raised near Pine Bluff, Arkansas; they were of similar age, and Broonzy had served two years in the army in Europe during World War I. The men were peers, yet Broonzy referred to Mayo as "Mister Williams"—which is how Williams remembered many of the artists addressing him. In the Jim Crow era, Black Americans of all ages were generally expected to address white males (even if they were younger white men) as "Mister," so it is disquieting that Broonzy and many others would refer to Williams in the same manner.

As defenders of Williams point out, not only was Bill Broonzy's disenfranchising experience common in those days—and in getting drunk and breaking recording equipment, he was not exactly a model citizen—but the lump sums of money Broonzy and others received from Williams was often the only money they would ever see from their recordings and often more than the royalties they could have received in their initial commercial life. Tom Dorsey remembered that Williams's mindset was, "'Well, let's make the record now. We may not get 'em back.' Well, you know that spelled this: they'd make the record, didn't have to pay for it like that, see. The artist was glad to make the record, get a chance to hear themselves."[36]

The amount of money most blues artists could have received from their recordings prior to the folk and blues revivals of the 1950s and '60s was negligible. But some top-selling artists stood to reap significant payments. Williams was involved in copyrighting material—each song, in fact—so he *knew* money was at stake, even if many songs were short-term losses. To put it plainly, Williams was self-aware of his speculative and deceptive practices.

Williams once laughed, "It was 'screw the artist before the artist screws you.'"[37] For instance, when Ethel Waters approached Williams about a sizeable cash advance for an entrepreneurial investment her boyfriend was making, Williams recalled, "I gave her the five hundred dollars and recorded her." In the meantime, unknown to Williams and Paramount, Waters had already recorded the same material for Columbia, and Paramount "couldn't get the record out, and we lose the five hundred dollars."[38]

In considering how Williams worked with Ma Rainey as opposed to Big Bill Broonzy or Alberta Hunter, it appears that he approached the process like a football player eyeing his opponent: he sized his artists up and dealt with them according to whatever advantage he could find. Broonzy fit the "we may not get 'em back" category of musicians with turbulent, dangerous lives. Ma Rainey's dependable, long-term professional relationship with Williams galvanized the label and demanded care and respect. Artists such as Alberta Hunter and Big Bill Broonzy quite accurately identified recording as a sort of money grab; thus each all too knowingly signed disenfranchising recording deals. Ink Williams did not invent this lopsided game, but that does not excuse his enthusiasm for always winning it.

As Dorsey recalled it, the stakes were so low that the word "steal" wrongly implies there was actual money to be made:

> What're you gonna steal? Nothin' you could do with it if you steal it. Unless you stole a sheet of music or a book, something, go and sing it. See, they

just started to copyrightin' that stuff like blues and church music about 1915. Well, all blues sounded alike for a while anyway, so we never bothered about the other fellow. If he got something' out, that's OK. I'd just let him take me out to dinner or somethin' like that. And if he thought I infringed on him, there never was no money transaction, no.[39]

Mayo Williams planted himself firmly in the middle of this low-stakes world of song ownership, usually crediting songwriters for their own compositions but also claiming songwriting credit on occasion. "I didn't exactly write 'em," Williams explained years later. "I touched 'em up lyric-wise, and put my name on some I wrote under a pseudonym."[40] Williams's pen name, intended to avoid the scrutiny of Paramount executives, was "Everett Murphy," the name of a childhood friend and piano–blues band leader from his hometown of Monmouth, Illinois. One of the songs that "Everett Murphy" claimed partial songwriting credit for was "Freight Train Blues," which Trixie Smith recorded for Paramount in 1924 and again years later with Sidney Bechet for Vocalion. Williams explained his cowrite on "Freight Train Blues" to the historians Jim O'Neal and George Paulus:

> That is the greatest song, greatest *blues*, it was one of the greatest blues that was ever written in that day! See? . . . And here she's got this song all outlined. And I just helped her finish it up lyric-wise and claimed the copyright right along with her, and so forth and so on. Now, we paid all of these people flat payments.
>
> **PAULUS:** As soon as they made a record, they were paid?
> **WILLIAMS:** They were paid. Yeah. They didn't wait for any royalties. See? . . . Bing Crosby was one of the *first* artists to get a royalty contract on sales in this whole business. See? And, but the black artists didn't have sense enough to ask for a royalty because they were so *poor*, they wanted their money, yeah, right quick, see? [laughs] As soon as they got it. And some of the ones we paid them on was never released. Never released, see, because we just didn't feel as though it would be worthwhile, see?[41]

Williams is correct about Bing Crosby and royalties. But his glib characterization of poor, Black artists as witless is simply disgusting. Paramount's practices—indeed the widespread practice in the hillbilly and race record industry prior to World War II—ensured that even after the folk and blues revivals of the second half of the twentieth century, when old race and hillbilly recordings were reissued for a global market, and international stars made millions by performing the songs of relatively obscure blues and hillbilly artists of the 1920s and '30s, corporations and/or the estates of long-dead corporate executives were the beneficiaries of royalty payments, not the estates of the actual songwriters and performers.

It is distressing that Williams continued to defend these practices until the end of his life. In contrast, Thomas A. Dorsey, who assisted Williams in harnessing the royalties of so many artists for Chicago Music, looked back with regret, feeling he should have organized the musicians into a union.[42]

Nevertheless, Paramount's business chugged along, and Williams had some fun along the way, deciding to run a mail-order competition in the summer of 1924 to name Ma Rainey's "Mystery Record." Customers mailed proposed names to Williams's office. Williams and Harry Pace judged the proposals on September 14, 1924. This marked the first time we know that Williams met Pace in person, despite having worked for him for two years with Black Swan (and attending at least one party with him at Howard), and only after Pace had left the music business for the insurance industry.[43]

Williams's work with Ma Rainey brought him into contact with an even wider circle of musicians beyond Chicago. In 1924, Ma Rainey recorded eighteen sides for Paramount, including several in New York ("Jelly Bean Blues," "Countin' the Blues," "See, See Rider"). Williams worked with Black Swan's former musical director, Fletcher Henderson, to line up a session band for Rainey—one of several musical experiments Williams had started to tinker with. Joe Smith, the trumpeter who regularly backed Bessie Smith, was intended to be on the session. Williams told the story: "Now, when I got there with Ma Rainey . . . Fletcher Henderson says, 'I can't give you Joe Smith, but I can give you my second trumpet player.'" Henderson's second trumpet player was Louis Armstrong.[44]

• • •

Nineteen twenty-four was Williams's busiest year in the music business, but it was his quietest in the NFL. Back on the Hammond Pros with Williams were Sol Butler and Dunc Annan. Hammond's shortest season (five games) would result in a .500 record, good enough for tenth in the league. Season highlights included opening day in Racine Wisconsin, where three thousand watched Hammond lose 10–0 behind Racine's quarterback, Milton "Mitt" Romney. (The namesake of the US senator Mitt Romney was a first cousin of Senator Romney's father, George.) Once again, Ma Rainey's recording schedule threw a wrench into the Rock Island Independents' schedule. The media hyped Williams's arrival with Hammond in Rock Island. It was supposed to be a big day, with Jim Thorpe playing halfback for Rock Island and the Illinois governor, Len Small, making a halftime appearance. However, "Many fans were disappointed when the great colored star failed to put in an appearance. At last it was stated that he was sick and was unable to make the trip."[45] Williams wasn't sick—he was in New York with Ma Rainey for the session with Fletcher Henderson and Louis Armstrong.

Williams's decision to go to New York with Ma Rainey rather than playing in Rock Island meant he didn't get to see players he doubtless admired

(Guyon, Thorpe, and Slater). But it is indicative of his growing responsibilities at Paramount and the important place that Ma Rainey had gained in the Paramount catalog. Rainey was now Paramount's undisputable star artist and the centerpiece of the label's extensive print advertisements. Her continued success guaranteed Williams's continued success in the record business.

Four days after Ma Rainey's New York session, Williams and the Hammond Pros were back on the road in Wisconsin, tying the Kenosha Maroons in front of an anemic crowd of six hundred. Hammond then returned to Chicago to face the Cardinals in front of twenty-five hundred at Comiskey Park, surprising Paddy Driscoll's team with a 6–3 victory. The Chicago game marked only the second time in his NFL career that Williams didn't play the entire game. The Pros' season wrapped up against the Kansas City Blues, but neither Ink Williams nor Sol Butler made the trip because of Missouri's color bar—a decision that the *Chicago Defender* reported it was "sorry to see."[46] With time off, Williams was contracted by the Dayton Triangles to play the Cleveland Bulldogs at Cleveland's Dunn Field.[47] But Williams and the Triangles proved no match for the Bulldogs, losing to the league champions 35–0.[48]

As in seasons past, Williams spent his Thanksgiving Day on a football field, this time playing with a mashup of the Kenosha and Hammond teams against Rock Island.[49] Dunc Annan, Sol Butler, and Alfred Earl "Greasy" Neale would join him for the trip. Williams likely needed a ride to Rock Island: four days prior to the game, two men jumped him in Bronzeville, near the intersection of 54th and Calumet, robbing him of eight dollars and stealing his car.[50] Game day proved frigid; despite a hard-fought game and a performance at halftime by the Evans Orchestra, only fifteen hundred brave souls watched Kenosha-Hammond lose to Rock Island.

Williams had concluded his most accomplished year to date in the record business. He had signed a number of highly successful acts to Paramount and had been given free rein by the label's executives. His professional football career had attracted the attention and respect of players and coaches throughout the league. However, as Williams's power and income grew at Paramount, he caught the attention of Art Laibly, a white executive at Paramount who began actively to undermine Williams in an attempt to usurp his role and harness his earning power. That battle would begin in 1925 with the arrival of a test pressing of a Texas blues guitarist named Lemon Jefferson.

CHAPTER 13

Bulldog

With the release of Paramount's two catalogs in 1924—and the question, What will you have?—Williams began receiving letters and recommendations from customers and distributors across the country. In late 1924, Williams received an inquiry from Guy B. Johnson, a scholar of Black music at University of North Carolina, Chapel Hill. Dr. Johnson had asked Williams to identify those records from the Paramount/Black Swan catalog that he deemed most culturally significant. Williams responded in January 1925 with a short note, including thirteen records of his choosing, and billing Johnson fifty cents per record. (Sadly, no record of *which* thirteen records is known to exist.) The bulk of Johnson's work had focused on Black sacred music, but in early 1925, he was considering including a brief history of the blues in his forthcoming collaboration with the sociologist Howard T. Odum, *Negro Workaday Songs*, a follow-up to their 1925 publication, *The Negro and His Songs: A Study of Typical Negro Songs in the South*.

In July 1925, Williams told Johnson that if he wanted to "compile the history of Negro blues, it will be necessary for you to obtain records of our entire colored catalog, which, as you mentioned, would be quite an expense." Williams marked up a Paramount catalog for Johnson, checking off the records he deemed essential—regardless of the "business end of the whole matter." Of the 214 records that appeared in the catalog, Williams checked off 113 records for Johnson; Johnson checked off 24 of Williams's recommendations. Williams also pointed out that this might be a mutually beneficial correspondence relationship, whereby Dr. Johnson might recommend groups and spirituals to be recorded by Paramount. Johnson seems to have taken this to heart—in his marked up Paramount catalog, Johnson wrote "Send words and music to our 'Pharoh's [sic] Army,'" later noting "probably already recorded." Johnson replied a week later with an agreement that he would send Williams a copy of

The Negro and His Songs as a kind of guidebook to songs worth recording on Paramount, in exchange for Williams's guidance on which Paramount records were deemed essential for blues research.

Neither the scholar nor the producer would quite receive what he wanted. Johnson was clearly hoping Williams could provide him with a narrower set of recommended recordings, whereas Williams clearly wanted Johnson to recommend specific groups rather than specific songs. Nevertheless, the spirit of the letters is highly collegial. Doubtless it was unusual for Williams and Johnson to be having such a correspondence at all. On August 12, Williams mailed a copy of the 1924 Paramount "Book of the Blues" catalog to Johnson, along with circulars for newer Paramount releases. However, Johnson's name was erroneously dictated to—or mistyped by—Aletha Dickerson as "Guy P. Brown," causing the letter to be returned. Williams re-sent the letter, along with more circulars on September 21, the day he was participating in the season-opening NFL game between the Hammond Pros and the Green Bay Packers.

Nineteen twenty-five was largely a year of momentum, impelled by groups that had begun recording for Williams and Paramount in 1924. The continued success of Ma Rainey had become Williams's chief concern. But he had also amassed a significant stable of additional artists. Williams had recorded forty or so blues and gospel singers at Paramount in 1924. Of these, half sold well enough to get a follow-up recording session. Ma Rainey, Papa Charlie Jackson, and Ida Cox were company staples by the start of 1925, selling recordings in the tens of thousands. Williams was so successful at establishing Paramount's race catalog in Chicago that the company would close its New York studio in 1926.[1]

Chicago's Bronzeville music venues and connections continued to be the primary places where Williams found talent, particularly the venues that were a part of the T.O.B.A. circuit, where people such as Lovie Austin continued to recommend most of the artists that Williams recorded.[2] Williams also checked in on Clarence Williams (no relation), a Black session musician, talent scout, song publisher, and versatile performer who courted and recommended talent for record labels such as OKeh and Columbia. Primarily situated in New York, Clarence Williams also operated an office in Chicago on Thirty-First and State, and he had more talent there than places to put them. As Mayo Williams recalled, Clarence "had artists, and I could go down there and pick up artists" for Paramount.[3]

With Paramount's business going so smoothly, perhaps Williams felt he could coast—if by "coast" we mean dive into the busiest football season of his life.

Both Williams and Fritz Pollard were back with Hammond at the start of the 1925 season. Pollard had returned as the head coach of the Pros, though by this time he was considered a somewhat controversial figure in the football world. Harry Young said that Pollard was aggressive and pushy, a man possessed of great talent but hampered by great arrogance and unreliability. While playing in the NFL, Pollard was also playing in the Coal League in Pennsylvania, running a private business in Chicago, and—in name at least—coaching football at Lincoln University in Philadelphia. He was at once overcommitted and not entirely dependable.

The season got off to an ominous start. When they arrived in Green Bay, Williams and Pollard were confronted with segregated hotel policies:

> We stopped at the only hotel of any consequence in Green Bay. But after we were sitting down in the *dining room*, in Green Bay, we were paged—Fritz Pollard and I—we were paged out of the dining room in Green Bay, Wisconsin. I'll give you an example: We're sitting there, enjoying ourselves, and all of a sudden a bellboy comes through the dining room. "Call for Mister Williams! Call for Mister Pollard!" Well, we think we're big, you know, and somebody wants to get in touch with us. And lo and behold, the bellboy says, "They want you at the office." And in going to the office, they said, "We don't *allow* colored people to eat at *our* dining room.[4]

Although the Green Bay press complimented Williams and Pollard as an electric passing-receiving duo and reminded readers that Williams was named to the *Gazette*'s 1923 All-Pro Team, the two were also referred to as the "Gold Dust Twins."[5] This racist nickname came from Gold Dust Powder, a laundry powder whose label featured two grinning Black Sambo–like boys.

After a town parade and a 14–0 loss to Green Bay, Pollard and Annan quit the team to join the Akron Pros.[6] Doc Young assumed head coaching duties and brought another Black player onto the team—Dick "Super Six" Hudson—to replace Pollard in the backfield. The immediate result was a surprise 10–6 Hammond defeat of Paddy Driscoll's Chicago Cardinals. But the momentum stopped there. Hammond fell to Toronto (Ohio), where Williams faced off against Sol Butler for the first time.[7] Next they lost to the Chicago Bears, where Butler rejoined the Hammond squad.

The *Chicago Tribune* reported that Hammond was pounded by the Bears, 28–7, though it credited Williams and Len Sachs—Hammond's two ends—with hard tackles that kept the losing score from being even higher.[8] Williams lined up across from Halas, though unlike Halas, Williams played the entire game without substitution.

The following week, at Cubs Park in Chicago, when Halas looked up at the line of scrimmage against the Cleveland Bulldogs, he again found Ink Williams staring back at him. The Bulldogs had hired Williams as a substitute for their starting left end, Joe Baldwin; Williams's departure from Hammond was lamented by the *Rock Island Argus* as part of a wholesale unloading of the team's talent by Doc Young.[9] (The former Texas A&M quarterback Jim Kendrick and the right end Harry Curzon had left for Buffalo; Fritz Pollard,

Dunc Annan, and the fullback Guil Falcon had left to play for Akron.) Williams's addition to the Bulldogs' roster wasn't enough, however, and Halas's Bears beat Cleveland, 7–0.

Back in the Chicago Music office, just four days after the Bulldogs-Bears game, Williams received a letter of regret from the sociologist Guy Johnson. Johnson was sorry the materials Williams had sent were so long delayed—he assumed Williams was "off taking a rest" or was swamped with work. Either way, he had received the materials too late to include in his book. Howard W. Odum had decided that the pair of scholars could not wait, and *Negro Workaday Songs* was slotted for publication in November. Johnson still hoped to research and publish a history of the blues and promised to send an order for Paramount and Black Swan recordings for that purpose. As a token of his commitment, Johnson included a copy of *The Negro and His Songs*, which Johnson and Odum had documented between 1908 and 1910, drawing Williams's attention to the spiritual "All My Sins Done Taken Away," recommending that Williams have a Paramount artist record it. Johnson and Odum were still visiting Black churches in the region and asked Williams to recommend a portable recording unit they might use. Williams responded to Johnson just four days later. He expressed regret over Johnson and Odum's publication schedule, told him that he looked forward to receiving the books, and disabused him of the idea that a portable recording device was at all practical. Instead, Williams proposed that Johnson bring singers up to New York so that they could be recorded in a studio. Williams proposed an ambitious idea to Johnson regarding the spirituals in his collection:

> Concerning the song "All My Sins Done Taken Away" I wish to say that this is a new one to me, and I will be pleased to receive a copy of this number together with the melody as the title seems to be very striking. No doubt it can be made up into a very good spiritual. It would be a good idea if you could have your entire catalog made into records as a means of preserving them in a form that would be very novel. Also, it could be arranged to have this done as a special set of records which you could merchandise yourself. Concerning this, I will be pleased to have you write and let me know what you finally decide as to having your numbers recorded, as it will be to your personal advantage if you are willing to spend some money.[10]

In short, Williams wasn't proposing that these records—essentially field recordings—be recorded and pressed for Paramount, but rather specifically for Johnson and Odum (at the professors' expense). Williams was making an entrepreneurial attempt at cultural documentation. At this date, very few ethnographers outside of the US Bureau of American Ethnology (the precursor to the Department of Anthropology at the Smithsonian's National Museum of Natural History) were making field recordings, though Johnson already had made cylinder field recordings of Black music. Johnson and Odum passed on Williams's suggestion.

Williams wasn't done with Hammond—at least not yet. On November 1, Williams and the Pros traveled to Navin Field in Detroit to take on the Detroit Panthers—a new and impressive team formed by the future Hall of Famer Jimmy Conzelman. Detroit handed Hammond a 26–6 loss; at game time, Detroit was in first place and had shut out all of its opponents. Hammond distinguished itself only by being the first team to score against Detroit all season. Detroit fans were unimpressed with Hammond and seemed puzzled by the fact that Hammond had managed to score at all. The *Detroit Free Press* considered Williams and Sachs the only two bright spots on the team. The paper made no reference to Williams's or Hudson's race—remarkable, considering that in the Detroit mayoral campaign then going on, one of the leading candidates was a self-identified member of the KKK.[11] However, when the team checked in at the Bach Cadillac Hotel, Williams was told he couldn't ride the passenger elevator with the rest of the team. "I had to go around to the freight elevator."[12]

It is curious that the same day that Williams was playing in Detroit for Hammond, the New York *Daily News* and the *Brooklyn Daily Eagle* reported him as playing for the New York Football Giants in front of eighteen thousand at the Polo Grounds, where the Giants defeated the Cleveland Bulldogs, 19–0. It was the Giants' first season in the NFL. Oddly, the *Brooklyn Daily Eagle*, a Black newspaper, mistook the Giants' large (white) guard Joe Williams for the wiry (Black) Ink Williams (who was far away in Detroit).

However, after the Detroit game, Hammond loaned Williams out to the Cleveland Bulldogs for most of the remainder of the 1925 season. The Bulldogs, featuring the future Hall of Fame tackle Steve Owen, were the reigning league champions. Williams played nine games for Cleveland in 1925 in his busiest season in professional football (twelve official games).[13] Williams rejoined the *Cleveland* Bulldogs for a game against the *Canton* Bulldogs on November 8 at Canton's Lakeside Park in front of two thousand fans.[14] Three days later, in front of a surprisingly large Wednesday crowd (five thousand) who were likely off work for Armistice Day, Williams was back at Navin Field in Detroit, where the (Cleveland) Bulldogs fought and lost to the Panthers, 22–13. (Again, Williams had to take the hotel's freight elevator.) From Detroit, the Bulldogs embarked on an East Coast "1924 World Champions" tour, starting on November 21 in Philadelphia at Frankford Stadium against the Frankford (Philadelphia) Yellow Jackets. Seven thousand saw the Bulldogs beat the impressive home team, 14–0, in a rare Saturday game. The following day, the team headed eighty miles northwest to Minersville, in the coal country of Pennsylvania, to take on the Pottsville Maroons.[15] Williams and the Bulldogs played games on back-to-back days against two of the strongest teams in the

NFL. Williams and Baldwin again swapped back and forth at left end, and the 1924 champions (Cleveland) lost 24–6 to the disputed 1925 champions. Four days later, on November 26, in Hartford, Connecticut, Cleveland played the Kansas City Cowboys, losing 17–0 on Thanksgiving Day. (The Cowboys were from Kansas City in name only—all of their games were played on the road.) Two days after Hartford, Cleveland was down in Atlantic City, New Jersey to play a Saturday exhibition against the non-NFL (but New Jersey professional football champions) Atlantic City Roses, winning 12–0 in front of twenty-five hundred at the Dog Race Track Park. Though he played the whole game without replacement, just one day after Hartford, Williams's play was described as "dazzling."[16] The team finally ended up in Providence, Rhode Island to take on the Steam Roller on November 29.

The matchup against Providence was a homecoming for Ink Williams. Playing for the Steam Roller that day were his former Brown teammates Fritz Pollard, Curley Oden, Mike Gulian, Dolph Eckstein, John Pohlman, Bert Shurtleff, Jack Spellman, and Fred Sweet, as well as a rogues' gallery of former collegiate opponents such as Dutch Connor and Cy Wentworth from New Hampshire, Red Maloney from Dartmouth, and Jim Laird of Colgate.[17] The *Providence Journal* gave a great deal of attention to the Bulldogs–Steam Roller game. The day was rainy and cold. The field—set in the middle of the Providence Velodrome (a cycling oval)—was an ocean of mud. The paper noted that Williams's speed and talent had not diminished any since his departure from Providence four years earlier. Pollard entered the game partway through the second quarter to huge applause. The game ended in a 7–7 tie as the Bulldogs' barnstorming tour of the East Coast came to a mud-caked conclusion.[18]

Williams and the Bulldogs had played five games in five cities over the eight days of the tour, including two against the preeminent teams in the league. Williams was, it should be noted, now thirty-two years old. From Providence, Williams accompanied the Bulldogs back to Dunn Field in Cleveland to face the Canton Bulldogs on December 6. It was one of the few games in Williams's career that he did not start. Cleveland beat Canton, 6–0 in front of a crowd of fifteen hundred. After the game, Williams returned to Chicago and hung up his spikes for the remainder of the 1925 season.

In a sign of things to come, the Chicago Bears signed the Notre Dame phenom Red Grange to a lucrative contract. Grange's star power proved to be the catalyst pro football needed to surpass the collegiate game as the American public's preferred sport. Part of Grange's contractual agreement with Chicago involved a barnstorming tour of the East in late 1925. Grange played most days of the week for the greater part of a month against NFL, semiprofessional, and college teams. By December 9, Grange and the Bears were at Braves Field in Boston to take on the Providence Steam Roller in front of fifteen thousand fans. When Fritz Pollard and the Steam Roller took the field, they saw that Grange was playing with severely swollen arms and lasted only twenty minutes. Nonetheless, Grange's ascent to professional football stardom brought a close to the lunch-pail era of the working-class football player.[19]

Back at the Chicago Music office, Williams found a letter waiting for him from Guy B. Johnson at the University of North Carolina. Johnson had some surprising news: he and Odum had spent the past several weeks collaborating with Dr. Carl Seashore, a noted speech pathologist, music educator, and psychologist from the University of Iowa, on a series of photophonographic records of Black singers.[20] Johnson and Odum believed these photophonographic records would definitively show that Black singers' voices were physically superior to those of other races. The work, Johnson said, had been so tedious that he had "scarcely had time to think of blues" and would be back in touch shortly with "all sorts of questions" for Williams. In the meantime, he apologized for being able to supply only a fragment of the song "All My Sins Done Taken Away."[21] Williams responded on December 14, stating he would have responded sooner had he not been "away on a business trip" (the Cleveland Bulldogs' East Coast World Champion barnstorming tour). He let Johnson know that he looked forward to the full transcript of "All My Sins," as Paramount intended to expand its catalog of spirituals at the beginning of 1926.[22]

Williams also commented on Johnson's work, informing him that he found the "filming" of Negro voices to be intriguing, and that Johnson had no doubt "come in contact with some unusual situations." Williams also congratulated Johnson on the book, which he had evidently shared with a number of people who had offered up some criticisms (perhaps these were Williams's own criticisms). Williams told Johnson, "I am in hopes that in the near future I will be able to write you with regard to the criticisms that have been made in regard to your publication." This was a bold move by Williams. The correspondence between Johnson and Williams was somewhat extraordinary for that time period, with a white, southern university professor asking a Black record executive for his cultural expertise and insight into Black music. Nevertheless, Williams softened his critique by concluding his letter by reiterating that he looked forward to sharing whatever information might be useful with regard to Johnson's future research.

Two days after mailing his letter to Johnson, Williams received another letter from Johnson—meaning that Williams's letter mentioning the "criticisms" of Johnson and Odum's work had still not arrived in Chapel Hill. This December 12 letter from Johnson included the professor's list of records he wanted to order, apologizing that Dr. Odum was restricting his purchases to just those titles that bore some resemblance to titles in their publications.

Johnson included an additional request, however, sharing two lines from a blues that he hoped Williams was familiar with and would include in the order if Paramount had recorded it:

> Sweet mama, tree-top tall,
> Won't you please turn your damper down.

Unknown to Johnson, the snippet of song he quoted was from a blackface minstrel song, "Sweet Mama Tree Top Tall," which had been published and copyrighted by the minstrel singer Lee "Lasses" White (of the famed WSM Grand Ole Opry duo Honey and Lasses). Ida Cox recorded "Sweet Mama Tree Top Tall" for Paramount in 1928. Though Williams had left Paramount by this time, it opens the possibility that he had suggested she record the tune, due to Johnson's suggestion.

One month later, on January 12, 1926, Johnson responded to Williams's December 14 "criticisms" letter, which had clearly struck a nerve. Johnson intended to write Williams a letter letting him know that the records had arrived, that a check was in the mail, and that he would look forward to hearing the criticisms of the book that Williams had to share. It is there that Johnson's letter takes a hard detour, delineating the Black newspapers he subscribed to and lamenting that not all reviews in the Black press had been positive. Johnson's letter shows a surprising vulnerability for the time:

> I sometimes despair of trying to work for better feeling and good will between the races, for there is always a certain group which refuses to see anything good in what a white man does.[23]

Johnson then addresses a raft of specific criticisms of the book that he felt were unkind or showed that the reviewers had not really read the book closely. He then apologized for his tangent, and asked Williams to please forward his criticisms. It is the last known correspondence between the two men.

CHAPTER 14

Blind Lemon

In early 1926, a short, chubby, well-dressed Black man wearing thick, wire-rimmed glasses was guided into Mayo Williams's Chicago Music office by a white record-store owner from Dallas named R. T. Ashford. The man Ashford was guiding was a songster and bluesman known in Dallas as Blind Lemon Jefferson. Mayo Williams had been expecting the two: Ashford had sent a test record of Jefferson's music to Paramount earlier in 1925, and the label invited them up to Chicago to make records. Lemon's music would not be the first document of a solo blues guitarist and singer, but his records would become the first to launch the medium into the Black commercial mainstream and be foundational elements of rhythm and blues and rock and roll.

Lemon Henry Jefferson had just turned thirty-one a few weeks before arriving at Williams's office. Born the son of cotton farmers near the town of Coutchman, Texas, about sixty miles south of Dallas, Jefferson wore clear glasses, rather than dark glasses, suggesting he had partial vision. Jefferson took to the guitar at an early age and ranged throughout the South, playing regularly in Texas, Louisiana, and Arkansas, often hoboing alone via train, and becoming widely known as Blind Lemon. A number of white country blues singers from North Carolina, including Clarence Ashley, claimed to have met and learned from Blind Lemon in the Blue Ridge Mountains during the Depression. Whether this was true or the claim of some other songster pretending to be Lemon is unknown, but his reputation was expansive.

Blind Lemon's home base was Dallas, where the Black district known as Deep Ellum fostered a lively and lucrative environment for a blues singer. In Dallas, Jefferson made the acquaintance of another Black musician, Huddie Ledbetter, better known as Lead Belly, and the two men performed as a duo from 1912 to 1915. Jefferson was five years younger than Ledbetter, yet Huddie considered Lemon the more masterful guitarist. Huddie's strong, rhythmic playing of dance tunes, ballads, and blues drew deeply from playing at dances in his hometown of Caddo Lake, Louisiana, and in the brothels of Shreveport. His music also was influenced by Jelly Roll Morton (whom he heard in New Orleans), as well as other jazz and vaudeville musicians. Ledbetter recalled Sissieretta "Black Patti" Jones's Black Patti Troubadours as "the first jazz band I heard."[1] Yet despite Ledbetter's own considerable musical experience, he credited Jefferson as his great teacher. Both Jefferson and Ledbetter were peripatetic in their musical wanderings—playing in churches and brothels, on street corners and at parties—and drew large crowds of admirers by playing dance music on guitars.[2] Jefferson, in particular, was a master of what was called "booger-rooger" or "booga-rooga" (later recoined "boogie-woogie"), which the pianist Sammy Price recalled seeing Lemon play in Waco, Texas as early as 1917 or 1918. Ledbetter regularly danced a soft shoe on the streets of Dallas while Jefferson played a tune called "Hot Dogs." On Jefferson's 1927 Paramount recording of the song, you can hear a foot tapping in the background—perhaps by Lemon, but more likely by Ink Williams.

Lemon was a proud and dapper dresser, according to Price, who took issue with later characterizations of the singer:

> "I have heard some critics say that Blind Lemon was fat and greasy and dirty. Well, maybe we're talking about two different people. . . . I'm glad that I was around when Lemon was alive so that I can defend this great American troubadour whose voice used to ring out through the crowd."[3]

Price was living in Dallas by 1920 and remembered Lemon walking from one end of the city to the other, playing on the street, and singing for tips in taverns. According to an interview Price gave later to the blues historian Robert Palmer, Price was working in Dallas at R. T. Ashford's record store in the spring of 1925 when he wrote to Mayo Williams at Paramount to tell him about Lemon. With the letter, Price included a test pressing of Lemon's singing that had been made on a portable recording device set up in the rug department of a Dallas furniture store. Paramount invited Jefferson north to Chicago to record.[4]

Williams, however, recalled that he "discovered" Blind Lemon while visiting friends in Dallas in 1924, saying "I got [Blind Lemon Jefferson] down in Dallas, Texas, playing his guitar by himself on the railroad tracks."[5] Although it is possible Williams had friends in Dallas, we do know he had connections at Paul Quinn College in nearby Waco. Vivian Hillburn, a resident of Cedar Top the Black neighborhood in Kilgore, Texas, was a teacher at Paul Quinn College during the 1920s and remembered seeing Jefferson sing locally. On Saturday nights, Hillburn went to Cedar Top beer joints, which were jammed with locals after a week of selling cotton and pulpwood, to dance to jukeboxes and live music. Hillburn saw Jefferson sing "Loveless Love" at a Cedar Top beer joint, noting that he made a practice of staying in Cedar Top's flophouses on his way between Dallas and Shreveport.[6] Mayo Williams coached football at Paul Quinn College just two years after Jefferson first recorded for Paramount, which gives some plausibility to his claim of "visiting a friend" in the area.

Williams's and Price's versions of the story have been a source of ongoing debate among blues historians. Samuel B. Charters's seminal work, *The Country Blues* (1959), attributed Jefferson's discovery to J. Mayo Williams. But as blues scholarship developed in the 1960s, a competing narrative emerged that offers a glimpse of the internal power struggles at Paramount. Art Laibly, who in 1925 became Paramount's sales manager (and nominal recording director), scooped Williams on the claim to Blind Lemon's "discovery": Price and Ashford mailed their test pressing of Blind Lemon to Paramount's main office in Wisconsin (not to Williams's office in Chicago). Laibly intercepted the letter and, wanting to placate Ashford (a loyal Paramount record distributor in Dallas), invited Lemon to record in Chicago with Williams producing the session. The result of the recording was that Blind Lemon became Paramount's most successful recording artist and the most influential solo country blues guitarist to record in the early blues era.

The first two Jefferson songs released by Paramount, "Booster Blues" and "Dry Southern Blues," were a double shot of pathos about unrequited love. Lemon's soulful tenor moans, swoops, and pleads over an acoustic guitar that is equal parts duet partner, dance band, and lightning-fast soloist. The single's meteoric success ushered in a new genre of commercial blues recordings—the country blues. Prior to Blind Lemon Jefferson, the realm of commercial blues had been exclusively inhabited by vaudeville and tent-show-influenced (so-called classic blues) singers like Ma Rainey, Papa Charlie Jackson, Ethel Waters, and the big four Smiths (Bessie, Mamie, Clara, and Trixie). The country blues—which is primarily the domain of the acoustic guitar player and includes the important strains of Delta blues and Piedmont blues—was mostly a southern phenomenon. Mayo Williams remembered that waves of migrating southern Blacks brought a sudden influx of country blues guitarists to the North:

> Most of the guitar players were coming from the South. . . . We had what was known as an exodus from the South. And in that exodus, the IC [Illinois Central] train—railroad—was running excursions from down Memphis, and even New Orleans, once or twice a month. And those people were anxious to get out of the South anyways. And they would build these excursions and come to Chicago and never go back. Come from the South to St. Louis and other places and never go back south. All the guitar players came from down that way. . . . We didn't hold auditions. I brought 'em in here from Texas, I brought 'em in from St. Louis, and I brought 'em in from further

down south in around Memphis and so forth. And in doing it that way, we would just hold a recording engagement hoping to get something. And as it turned out, we got some of the best blues in the world.[7]

Despite any competitive animosity Jefferson's success may have elicited in Williams by way of Art Laibly, Williams's personal relationship with Blind Lemon appears to have been positive. Jefferson was pleasant to work with, but his alcoholism was problematic. Williams told Jim O'Neal and George Paulus in a 1972 interview:

> WILLIAMS: Blind Lemon was as docile as a kitten. He never did anything but drink to excess. And it was strange how [blues singers] could always get something to drink. They could find it and *I* couldn't find it. And this was all, most of their recordings were during Prohibition anyway, you see? They had that, what do you call it, "white lightinin'"?
> PAULUS: Yup.
> WILLIAMS: And home brew. And bathtub gin, and all that kind of stuff. . . .
> PAULUS: Did any of those guys get married and have children or anything? Like Blind Lemon?
> WILLIAMS: [laughs] If they had them, they didn't claim them! [laughs] I didn't hear of any of them having any they'd claimed. But they all had *girlfriends*. . . .
> PAULUS: What was Blind Lemon like? Was he, you know, most of the guys, were they real friendly?
> WILLIAMS: *Very* friendly. Now. And drank a lot. I mean hide that moonshine whisky and all of that.
> PAULUS: Blind Lemon was [an alcoholic]?
> WILLIAMS: Yeah. *All* the artists were. I never met one that didn't drink. That's how I happened to start drinking it and so forth and so on. And supposing these artists, you see, sometimes they would provoke you to the point of *having to take a drink to bear with them*.[8]

Blind Lemon Jefferson entrusted his Paramount earnings to Williams, who created a bank account for the blues star and bought him (at Jefferson's request) an automobile. When Lemon died in 1929—the rumor was his driver abandoned him in a snowstorm in Chicago and he subsequently died of myocarditis—Williams hadn't worked at Paramount for over a year. However, Williams's relationship with Jefferson was such that he claimed to have emptied Lemon's bank account to give to the Jefferson family when his body was shipped back to Texas by train.[9]

It was ironic that Blind Lemon's commercial success destabilized Williams's position of unquestioned authority at Paramount. The general manager Maurice Supper likely recognized that Mayo Williams was personally responsible for the success of the Paramount race series, because he never interfered with Williams's business. But despite many successes, Williams was still not on an equal footing with Paramount's white executives. For one, he had no official title. Otto Moeser, the CEO of Paramount, never visited Williams's Chicago Music office. Instead, Williams was summoned to business meetings in Chicago (at the Palmer House Hotel in the Loop), where as usual he had to take the freight elevator to Moeser's hotel room. He thought of himself as a semi-welcome member of the race-record endeavor. Although Moeser and Supper did not deal with him as an equal, Williams did not think them racist. Status was not so important to him as his royalty payments, which were substantial. Most Paramount customers knew who Williams was. They didn't know Art Laibly, but Lemon's success helped Laibly build a campaign to usurp Williams and destabilize his job.

With the release of six Blind Lemon Jefferson records in 1926, the singer was on his way to becoming Paramount's major blues artist of the decade. But Ink Williams had still another stroke of good fortune in 1926. By this time, Paramount had become so identified with Williams that it appended the suffix "de Mayo 1923" to its trademark on every record he produced, and other Paramount dealers (not just Ashford) sent singers to him to record for Paramount. Likely this network of record dealers and distributors was responsible for sending Williams's next big "find," Arthur Blake, to his Chicago Music office. Blake began recording for Paramount in mid-1926 under the name Blind Blake, and the success of his first release in October of that year ("West Coast Blues"/"Early Morning Blues") helped extend Mayo Williams's tenure at Paramount while deepening Paramount's development of the country blues market.[10]

Born Arthur Blake in Newport News, Virginia in 1896, Blake was primarily a street performer. He was possibly living in Jacksonville, Florida when he began recording for Paramount. A technically remarkable finger-style guitarist, Blake lived and died in obscurity despite the popularity of many of his records. Blake's style often featured a ragtime-influenced thumb-dragging of the bass strings and embodied the feel of an ensemble dance band—a characteristic that made his music—and that of Blind Lemon and Charlie Jackson—appealing to Mayo Williams. Blake's first recording, "West Coast Blues," was not technically a blues but influenced later country bluesmen like Reverend Gary Davis. In Ink Williams's opinion, Blind Blake was the only bluesman he considered to be an "artist." Blake's records marked the first time the race-record-buying public embraced virtuoso ability over lyrical/vocal impact.

Williams took on the role of Blake's booking agent for white parties in Indiana, which was no small task to manage. "Blake was always getting into something," Williams recalled,[11] including one occasion on which Blake arrived at a recording session with a swollen face:

> One morning, Blind [Blake] walked into the office, all beat up. Eyes black and blue, and scarred. I says, "what's the matter?" . . . He says, "I been shootin' craps." I says, [in a low voice] "*Whaddaya mean, shootin' craps?* A blind man shootin' craps?" And he says, "Yes, and I got in a fight, and they clubbed me." And I says, "How could you be shootin' craps when you're blind?" And he says, "We take the dice, roll 'em out, and nobody touch them until I, being blind, would put my finger on 'em." And that's the way they read the craps. And I says, "Well that's strange to me." Now, he says, "We not only shootin' craps, but we play cards too!" I says, "*Whaddaya mean, play cards?*" I say, "How ya play cards when you can't see?" He says, "We have a deck of cards, and in having this deck of cards, we take pins and prick holes in the corner of each one of 'em, and put a hole in the center of the card, and one near the edge, which would indicate the suit that it is, [laughs] and in that way, we just feel and know how to follow and play this card," and so forth and so on. Now that was the strangest thing that I had ever heard. A blind man playin' cards and shootin' craps.[12]

The edgy reality of Blind Blake's life on the periphery provides an ironic foil to Paramount's description of him in their 1927 promotional *Book of Blues*:

> We have all heard expression of people "singing in the rain" or "laughing in the face of adversity," but we never saw such a good example of it, until we came upon the history of Blind Blake. Born in Jacksonville, in sunny Florida, he seems to have absorbed some of the sunny atmosphere—disregarding the fact that nature had cruelly denied him a vision of outer things. He could not see the things that others saw—but he had a better gift. A Gift of an inner vision, that allowed him to see things more beautiful. The pictures that he alone could see made him long to express them in some way—so he turned to music. He studied long and earnestly, listening to talented pianists and guitar players, and began to gradually draw out harmonious tunes to fit every mood. Now that he is recording exclusively for Paramount, the public has the benefit of his talent, and agrees, as one body, that he has an unexplainable gift of making one laugh or cry as he feels, and sweet chords and tones that come from his talking guitar express a feeling of his mood.[13]

Paramount's copy is pure drivel, but an excellent example of how Williams sought to gentrify the perception of blues through marketing instead of imposing genteel aesthetics onto the arrangements. Williams's assistant, Aletha Dickerson, was unusually impressed with Blake:

> Although my conversations with the various artists were only those I was forced to have with them, I did talk with Blind Blake a lot. I was much impressed by both his sense of humor and his self-reliance.[14]

By the late 1920s, Blake was living at 34th and Cottage Grove in Chicago, playing house parties with the pianists Charlie Spand and Little Brother Montgomery. His recording career ultimately encompassed seventy-nine issued recordings, ending in 1932 when Paramount folded. Blake died soon after.[15]

• • •

When Ink Williams first arrived in Chicago in 1921, he got in on the ground floor of two new professional enterprises: the race-record industry and the National Football League. Although he was the combustion engine driving the success of race records to newer and greater heights, his trajectory in professional football was the exact opposite. As the race-record industry evolved, Williams adapted and evolved with it. As the NFL evolved, Williams was boxed out. Nineteen twenty-six marked a painful moment in the league's history. Ultimately Williams and other Black players were banished, along with most of the midsize midwestern cities that had given birth to the league.

Over the course of six games during the 1926 season, there was every indication that Hammond's future in the league—indeed, the future of all small-city teams like Hammond—was untenable. Big-city teams in New York and Philadelphia were drawing crowds that were five, ten, sometimes twenty times the size of Hammond's average turnout of two thousand. Ragtag groups such as Hammond, Dayton, and even the once-great Akron drew the ire of big-city papers, which complained about the pathetic, unreliable quality of their home teams' competitors. Added to this, some teams padded their schedules, playing more games against weak opponents such as Hammond. The stronger teams would chalk up more wins, boosting their place in the league standings and generating resentment. Stronger, wealthier teams now had greater power within the NFL ownership group; they were only waiting for their moment to exercise it. Hammond gave them plenty of good reasons to do so in 1926.

Dunc Annan had the ignominious role of head coach for Hammond's last NFL season. Per usual, the season started with a whimper: Hammond lost to the Racine Tornados, 6–3. The *Journal Times* of Racine assessed Hammond's performance as terrible. The team made only four first downs the whole game and completed only one of thirteen passes. The one completion from Curzon to Williams resulted in a fifty-five-yard gain for the "famous" Williams; Williams also recovered a Racine fumble. One gruesome moment came when Racine's right guard, Frank Linnan, collided with Hammond's right end, Roy Hahn. The game stopped while the players searched the muddy field for three of Hahn's molars.[16]

The local fans in Hammond were unimpressed with their hometown team, and the (Munster, Indiana) *Times* reported that even the head coach, Dunc Annan, was unimpressed. Only Curzon and Williams received any praise.[17] Hammond wasn't the only franchise struggling. Prior to Hammond's game against Akron, Akron's owner, Frank Nied, vented his frustration to the *Akron Beacon Journal*. Local support for pro football had dwindled over the past six seasons, turning Akron into mostly a road team, jeopardizing their viability in the NFL. Akron's ability to compete in growing markets such as Frankford (a working-class neighborhood in northeast Philadelphia, where—even then—the city's fans were noted for being verbose) only compounded Nied's concerns. Both Nied and Doc Young were getting desperate: Nied hired the local Veterans of Foreign Wars (VFW) band to perform during the game, hoping to pull a bigger crowd. Doc Young even lied to the *Beacon Journal* that the "best team I have ever had" was coming to Akron.[18] The Akron team even changed its name for the 1926 season to the "Indians" in order to draw attention to the three Native American players on the squad: Joe Little Twig (a member of the Mohawk nation), Nat McCombs, and Alvro Casey (both of the Muscogee Creek Nation). All three had starred at Haskell Institute (now Indian Nations University) and the Carlisle Indian Industrial Schools.

Hammond's players still found a way to have fun. On the bus ride to Akron, it came to light that one of the Hammond players was wanted at a jail in Michigan City, Indiana. When the Pros drove by Michigan City, Ink Williams and Dick "Super Six" Hudson led the rest of the team in an improvised song about the player being on the lam.[19] Their good spirits fizzled after a 17–0 loss to Akron.

The next week, on October 10, Hammond played the Duluth Eskimos at Gleason Park in Gary, Indiana. Two thousand people watched Duluth pound Hammond, 26–0. The game is noteworthy for two reasons: it was Williams's final NFL game, and it was where he met Duluth's halfback, Ernie Nevers, the NFLs newest and most electrifying player. Nevers passed for one touchdown, rushed for another, and kicked two extra points for Duluth. Williams would later call on Nevers to assist him in a campaign to reintegrate the NFL.

When the Hammond Pros left for their November 21 game against the Pottsville Maroons in Minersville, Pennsylvania, Ink Williams stayed home. Perhaps he knew the jig was up, and the long trip simply wasn't worth it. November was also a prolific month of recording sessions for Paramount—so it is possible Williams stayed behind to produce sessions with the preacher and gospel singer Reverend J. M. Gates, the classic blues singer Leola Wilson, the Norfolk Jubilee gospel group, and an experimental session—likely Williams's idea—pairing Ma Rainey with Blind Blake on guitar and Jimmy Blythe at the piano for "Morning Hour Blues." That session marks one of Williams's attempts to use the studio as a kind of stylistic laboratory, blending Rainey's classic blues with Blake's Piedmont country blues style. The results weren't revolutionary, but they wouldn't deter Williams from trying again.

Williams wasn't the only member of the Hammond team who chose not to travel to Minersville. The papers reported that Hammond had lost considerable money over the course of the season; league schedules had been set in July, and several teams had dropped out of the league before the season began in September. This accounted for Hammond's four-game season and its deepening financial problems. The *Pottsville Republican* was optimistic: "Although the team was losing money, the loyal citizens of Hammond backed the club to the limit in the hope that the team will go big during the season of 1927, which in all probability it will do." In fact, the paper was trying to gin up a crowd for the game by assuring readers that Hammond was not "soft." The *Republican* said that Ink Williams was coming to town and repeated the claim of Dr. Al Sharpe—Yale's former coach—that "without reserve" Ink Williams "was the best end rush who ever exhibited his wares in the Yale bowl."[20]

Instead of Williams, however, fans in Minersville got a mashup of Hammond and Akron. Ed A. Zweibel Jr., the sports editor for the *Pottsville Republican*, was furious. According to Zweibel, Pottsville's 7–0 victory was pathetic, and Hammond wasn't even really Hammond:

> The Hammond team, a weak sister in the league, came here with about half the Akron team and put on a football game to collect the guarantee. This team had not practiced together, and the Akron players were picked up. Akron was not scheduled yesterday and the stars from the Ohio town were brought here to bolster up the tailenders and came near tying the champs of last year.

Zweibel then made a case for NFL reform—a case that likely was on the minds of many within the league's ownership group:

> It is known that the maroon management did not want to play Hammond. It was considered too poor a club to stack up against the Maroons and an effort was made to get another club so that the Maroons would have some real opposition, but the league officers would not stand for the cancellation of the Hammond game. The league officers did us a big favor when they did so. Had a good club been against the Maroons yesterday we would most likely have another mark in the lost column today.
>
> There were no bright spots in the game unless the fist fight, a regrettable incident, can be so classed.[21]

Hammond had reached the end of its rope. Though the team had put up a good fight against Pottsville—which was just one game out of first place—Zweibel's piece reflected a growing fury about the lack of parity among the teams in the league, as evidenced by the Pottsville owners' request to cancel the game. It proved to be Hammond's final NFL game.

Sol Butler, who was playing that season for the Canton Bulldogs, was one of the players who joined Hammond for the Pottsville game, a sorry counterpoint to a game earlier in the month. On November 2, the Canton Bulldogs met the New York Giants at the Polo Grounds in Brooklyn. This game is referred to as an embarrassing turning point for race relations in NFL history and more broadly for the United States. At the center of the story was Sol Butler, who was starting for Canton at quarterback. In an often-repeated story—typically attributed to the to the *Chicago Defender* and the *Amsterdam News*—a remarkable crowd of forty thousand fans stood watching and restless as the New York Giants refused to take the field until Butler, the only Black player on the Canton team, withdrew—which he is said to have done after ten minutes.[22] However, in its summary of the game, the New York *Daily News* reported that Butler played the entire game at fullback without substitution, resulting in a 7–7 tie.[23] Was the story of Butler's withdrawal from the Giants game hearsay? Fritz Pollard bore lifelong animosity toward the Giants' owner, Tim Mara, who he believed was party to what came next.

In April 1927, the NFL commissioner convened team owners to address the league's future. By the end of the meeting, ten of the league's twenty-two franchises were cut loose, including the Hammond Pros. From a league perspective, it was a hard but sensible decision. Interest in pro football had never been so high—as proven by the forty thousand fans who came out to see the Giants play the Bulldogs at the Polo Grounds. But although the twenty-two-team league exemplified broad geographic interest in the game, it diluted the fan base and stretched logistics and finances to everybody's detriment. The NFL also had new competition: a rival league called the American Football League (not to be confused with the AFL that merged with the NFL in the 1960s), which had snared the NFL's newest superstar, Red Grange. The NFL's credibility with fans and players was further undermined by the disputed 1925 league championship between the Chicago Bears and the Pottsville Maroons.

Unspoken—at least publicly—was the toxic issue of race. The league commissioner, Joseph Carr, pared the league down to its twelve most financially stable teams. Those remaining clubs were free to absorb players from the eliminated clubs, fortifying the league by consolidating talent. With both Hammond and Akron out of the league, four of the league's five Black players from the 1926 season—Williams, Pollard, Butler, and Dick Hudson—were now without jobs and would never play another game in the NFL. Duke Slater of the Chicago Cardinals was the only remaining Black player in the NFL; Slater remained on the Cardinals until 1931. The following year, 1932, the Boston Braves (later known as the Boston Redskins, Washington Redskins, and now the Washington Commanders) entered the league, bringing George Preston Marshall, the NFL's most overtly segregationist owner, into the fold. From 1934 until 1946, the NFL had no Black players.

It is widely believed that NFL owners had a silent gentleman's agreement barring Black players from the league. (Segregationist policy seems to have been restricted to Black players; Native American, Latino, and Asian players were still admitted during this time.) This policy was driven by the team owners Tim Mara (New York Giants) and George Preston Marshall. Marshall was a staunch racist, infamously holding out on integration until 1962, when the US attorney general, Robert F. Kennedy, forced the team to integrate under threat of revoking the team's license to play in the nation's capital. Fritz Pollard was outspoken in his disdain for George Halas, then the coach and manager of the Chicago Bears, who he insisted was complicit in the owners' color bar. Indeed, although Halas did advocate for Black players later in the century, he toed the NFL ownership's party line, insisting many times until after the Second World War that Blacks simply were not interested in playing in the NFL. Other owners, such as Marshall, preposterously claimed that Blacks were excluded for their own safety, even saying that white southern players would try to injure Black players.[24] If anything, the personal testimonies of Williams, Pollard, Shelburne, and other Black players of the day suggests that white players were far more comfortable with integration than white owners and fans, finding commonality in their shared collegiate backgrounds and higher education. Nevertheless, white ownership's racist policy held up until 1946. The Pittsburgh Steelers and the Arizona Cardinals (then of Chicago) are the only two active NFL franchises who employed Black players prior to 1946.

Doc Young's Hammond Pros finished their existence with a grand total of five wins against twenty-six losses and four ties in their seven NFL seasons between 1920 and 1926. Williams's friendship with the Young family outlasted the demise of the team, as Harry Young recalled:

> I'd see Ink at the paddock sometimes when we had a horse running. Ink stayed at our home many times and he visited as a friend after he was done playing football. Dad would shake his head sometimes and say to mother, "Lill, do you know that Ink spent $25,000 on cars last year?"[25]

Ink Williams had a robust NFL career—six seasons in which he dominated the field of play. Of the thirty-eight official NFL games that Williams played in, he started in thirty-five. He played thirty-one of those games without substitution, playing every minute of the game on both offense and defense. He occupied a statistically unglamorous position (offensive and defensive end), but opposing teams knew, feared, and respected him, as did the media in every town where he played. Today, Ink Williams's importance as a professional football player remains overlooked. By Williams's own estimation, "[Robeson] and Fritz Pollard, Duke Slater, and I are the pioneers in the National Professional Football League."[26] This is especially true when considering that Williams was also the league's first Black referee. Williams would continue to play professional football outside the NFL for several more years, but for years he simmered with resentment over the NFL's willful amnesia about its early Black stars.

Although Williams and his fellow Black footballers were disappeared from the NFL, his profile and impact had never been so high in the race records world. In just four years, Williams developed a large and remarkable catalog of artists at Paramount, including some whose styles were strikingly different from the Black Swan/Paramount catalog he inherited in 1923. In Paramount's original *Book of the Blues* (1924), there is no one like Papa Charlie Jackson, Blind Lemon Jefferson, or Blind Blake. Tom Dorsey saw that Paramount's success had created enormous opportunities for blues singers—both male and female:

> The blues came to its own about '23, '24, until 1940. If you wasn't a blues singer, you wasn't nobody—whether or not you could sing 'em, you had to know 'em. And that's when the record companies, our pickings were good pickings, in the late twenties. The records went like wildfire, all over the country. Everybody liked 'em. Ma Rainey used to tell a story: she went to some show at some house, singing. A newspaper reporter come down to cover it there. The man went and stayed a while, he went back and said, "There was a big 200-pound woman down there singing something she called the blues. I don't know what it is, I don't know what they call it, they don't know what it is. But whatever it is, it was good." And she skyrocketed. She was good.[27]

Ma Rainey spent most of 1926 on the road, playing the T.O.B.A. circuit. Though both the T.O.B.A. circuit and classic blues were in decline at that time, Ma Rainey—who recorded nineteen sides for Paramount in 1926—continued to be an anomaly, earning enough from shows to buy a forty-three-thousand-dollar Mack bus with an on-board electric plant to run lights for tent shows.[28] Mayo Williams was careful to look after Ma Rainey, even recruiting Thomas A. Dorsey to join her band on piano.

Williams was not consumed by the bitterness he felt toward the NFL. Nor was he content with his astounding success at Paramount. Instead, he looked for an opportunity to gamble on his own future—and he would find it in 1927.

CHAPTER 15

Black Patti

By 1927, Mayo and Aleta Williams were riding high. Both were college educated and well connected—Mayo in entertainment, Aleta in education—and a delight to Chicago society. Aleta was part of a close-knit group of Black socialites associated with the Delta Sigma Theta sorority; her parties were widely reported in Black newspapers in Chicago, Pittsburgh, and New York. In the summer of 1927, a pair of "Chicago Society" reports in the *Pittsburgh Courier* noted that Mrs. Mayo Williams—a prominent schoolteacher in Chicago—hosted a bridge party at her "palatial apartment" on Michigan Avenue. "Mrs. Williams," reported Edith Spurlock Sampson, "always has lovely affairs."[1] With distance and time, "Chicago Society" and other similar columns can initially read as documents of profound superficiality. But the column's author—Edith Spurlock Sampson—had opened her own law practice at age twenty-six on the South Side in 1924 and had served as a probation officer. She would go on to become an assistant state's attorney for Cook County, the first Black delegate to the United Nations, and the first Black woman elected judge in the city of Chicago. In "Chicago Society," she chronicled Black women who were equally smart, accomplished, and feisty. Knowing that Aleta Williams kept company with Edith Spurlock Sampson suggests that the topics that interested Sampson likely made their way into conversations between Aleta and Mayo. This couple was connected through music, law, politics, and education.

The very successes that had enabled the Williamses to afford a "palatial" apartment on Michigan Avenue seem to have come at a price; namely, that Art Laibly wanted this kind of money and power and was rapidly ascending the ranks at Paramount. Mayo Williams felt increasingly distanced from his employers and uneasy with Laibly's increased monitoring of his professional activity.[2] As Laibly found favor with management, Williams's power decreased.

When Richard Gennett, the owner of Gennett Records, approached Williams about starting up a new race record label, Williams jumped at the chance.

Gennett was the closest thing that Paramount had to a direct competitor. Gennett was not a major label like Columbia, Victor, or Okeh, but it did robust business in jazz, hillbilly, and race records. Also like Paramount, Gennett was a subsidiary of a larger company—the Starr Piano Company—situated in the rural Midwest. Gennett's base was Richmond, Indiana, about dead center on the Indiana–Ohio state line. This was an unlikely home for a record company whose foremost artists were the earliest luminaries of jazz, among them Louis Armstrong, King Oliver, Hoagy Carmichael, Jelly Roll Morton, and Bix Beiderbecke. While Gennett's calling card in the race record industry was jazz, its catalogue in hillbilly music included the ubiquitous and prolific Vernon Dalhart and Bradley Kincaid. Richard Gennett was familiar with Williams as a magnate for race record talent—Gennett had periodically scooped some of Paramount's jazz-oriented artists—and saw him as a key player in building a new label dedicated exclusively to race records. According to Gennett and Williams, Edward Barret—the disgruntled son-in-law of Paramount's founder, Otto Moeser—had approached Gennett about starting a competing venture. As Williams recalled, Barret wanted to stick it to his father-in-law:

> [Barret] thought himself gettin' even with Paramount. [laughs] And in doing it with Gennett, Fred Gennett was a big socializer [with houses] down in Palm Beach, Florida, and Newport, Rhode Island. . . . I'd visit him. He'd dropped all the money, I had the talent, and Barret had the, nothing but good connections with Paramount, which were very real.[3]

Williams did not think highly of Barret, once describing him as "kind of uncontrollable," but he was eager to segue out of Paramount. The three men (Gennett, Williams, and Barret) pooled thirty thousand dollars to start the Chicago Record Company (CRC). Most of the money was Gennett's. The new company was founded on March 11, 1927. A publishing branch of the CRC was also founded—the State Street Music Company. Williams provided the three thousand dollars needed to start the publishing company.[4] In the filing papers, Aleta Williams was listed as helping out with the office work; she also served as an officer of the Chicago Music Company. The attorney William H. Temple, who was Williams's best man at his wedding, was also an officer of the company along with Aleta and Mayo. Ink's brother Maurice—now out of the state penitentiary in Joliet—was to be a handyman. Even Millie Williams's name was on the paperwork, though she had no official role in company business. Williams had been so successful at insulating himself from the Paramount executives that in the final months of his tenure at Paramount, he was using the 3621 State Street office to handle the business for both Paramount and its new direct competitors. Williams's Paramount secretary, Aletha Dickerson, was also employed as the State Street Music Company secretary.⁵ Williams named the company's record label imprint Black Patti.

The muse of Black Swan Records was the nineteenth-century Black concert singer Elizabeth Taylor Greenfield (1824–1876), also known as the "Black Swan." Williams's inspiration—Black Patti—intentionally echoed the Black Swan title, only with a personal twist. When Williams first moved to Providence, he lived adjacent to the home of Sissieretta "Black Patti" Jones. Like the "Black Swan," the "Black Patti" was a rare bird herself: a Black opera singer whose popularity arose in the considerable shadow of the European soprano Adelina Patti. The life story of Sissieretta "Black Patti" Jones, dubbed "the greatest singer of her race," unfolds in an uncanny representation of what Du Bois and Pace had had in mind with the Black Swan endeavor.

Jeremiah Malachi Joyner and Henrietta B. Joyner gave birth to Matilda Sissieretta Joyner on January 5, 1869, in Portsmouth, Virginia. The Joyners, who had been born into slavery in the Carolinas, moved with their young daughter to Providence, Rhode Island in 1876. Sissieretta recalled that her father was the leader of a church choir, and that her mother—also a singer—"had a very sweet voice." The Joyners became members of the Congdon Street Baptist Church, just blocks from the campus of Brown University, where a fellow churchgoer recalled young Sissieretta singing in church concerts "wearing short dresses and scared, while her voice was sweet and clear as a bell."⁶ At age fifteen, the young singer enrolled at the Providence Academy of Music, where she studied piano and voice for three years before moving on to a different academy—widely believed to be the New England Conservatory of Music (NECM), though more probably the Boston Conservatory. Sissieretta Jones's press materials consistently refer to NECM, though in interviews she appeared purposely vague on the particulars, stating only that she studied at "eastern" schools. The NECM registrar's office holds no record of Jones's enrollment, and the Boston Conservatory does not have records prior to 1930.⁷

In 1883, Joyner married Richard Jones, a Providence newsdealer who was described in a derogatory manner by the Joyner family and friends as a "Baltimore race-horse and gambling man." Richard Jones was short—half Sissieretta's height—and became an irresponsible, free-spending manager of Sissieretta's business affairs. Some thirty years after her death, Sissieretta Jones's biographer claimed to have heard the Joyner family make frequent reference to Richard Jones's penchant for lighting his cigars with ten-dollar bills. By the turn of the century, the Joneses had divorced, and Richard Jones relocated to New York City.⁸

Sissieretta Jones began performing professionally just as Adelina Patti concluded a sensationally popular tour of the United States. Ms. Jones's professional debut came in August 1888 with a concert at Wallack's Theatre in New York City. It was at this concert that a New York theater paper—the *New York*

Clipper—dubbed Jones the "Black Patti." Sissieretta Jones deeply disliked the "Black Patti" label, but the name stuck. Despite an extensive and well-received tour of the Caribbean, Jones was expected to perform in the United States for reduced fees on account of her race.[9] By April 1892, Jones had earned a place on the bill at the African Jubilee concert at Madison Square Garden, where she was accompanied by Jules Levy ("The World's Greatest Cornetist") and his band. The pairing was successful, and Jones toured with Levy following the Jubilee, making a stop at the White House at the request of President Benjamin Harrison. In 1893, Jones appeared at the World's Columbian Exposition (the Chicago World's Fair) and the Pittsburgh Exposition of 1893. Her star was rising, and in 1894, she appeared with Antonín Dvořák at the National Conservatory of Music. (Dvořák was the director at the time.)[10] Despite her meteoric rise to success, Jones's career stalled on account of legal wrangles with her one-time agent and racial barriers at major opera houses. Thus, appearing at the Metropolitan Opera was not an option for Jones. By 1895, Sissieretta Jones felt compelled to part with her dreams of operatic fame and returned to Providence to regroup.[11]

Though Sissieretta Jones believed the nickname "Black Patti" was demeaning, she recognized that it also had significant drawing power. So, with some trepidation, she undertook a new engagement with a traveling minstrel/vaudevillian tent-style show called The Black Patti Troubadours, in which she sang light opera and spirituals. The Black Patti Troubadours crisscrossed the United States for nearly twenty years, evolving from a minstrel show capped by an "operatic kaleidoscope" to a unified musical comedy. The show became a musical training ground for an entire generation of Black musicians (the young Louis Jordan played with former members of the Black Patti Troubadours), and the troupe's performances influenced countless audience members—including a young Huddie Ledbetter.

Jones had recently retired to her home at 7 Wheaton Street in Providence when Mayo Williams enrolled for his freshman year at Brown University. Ms. Jones tended to her sick mother, lived with the companionship of a parrot she had bought in Argentina twenty-eight years earlier, and cared for two wards of the state. She lived off her wealth—when she needed money, she began selling her jewelry—and was active in church life at the Congdon Street Baptist Church, becoming a well-known member. When standing in front of Ink Williams's freshman-year boardinghouse at 72 Meeting Street, one can see directly behind it to the lot where 7 Wheaton Street once stood, just one block away. Standing on the front steps of 72 Meeting Street, one can see the nearby steeple of the Congdon Street Baptist Church. Ink Williams would have seen the striking "Black Patti" in passing, and if Williams didn't know her personally, he did know where to find her. Even though Williams's own family typically attended AME churches in Illinois, he probably attended

Congdon Street Baptist Church (if indeed he attended church at all in college), given the size and geography of Providence's Black community at that time.

When Williams arrived in Chicago in 1921, it is hard to imagine that he did not think of Black Patti immediately on hearing the political rhetoric behind the Black Swan Records project. In 1923, Williams had suggested the name "Black Patti" for a new hair-straightener product being developed by Paramount's executive M. A. Supper. Williams claimed he had personally cleared the name with the opera singer by phone.[12] His decision to make Ms. Jones the figurehead for his new record label in 1927—a beautiful portrait of her was used in advertisements—marks a curious return to the politics of racial "uplift." Why Williams didn't use the Black Patti endeavor as an opportunity to record Jones herself (she never recorded) remains an unfortunate mystery. It is probable that Jones was either past her prime or in poor health. A trip to a recording studio in New York (or Indiana or Illinois for that matter) was out of the question.

Williams sang Ms. Jones's praises in Black Patti's debut advertisement in the *Chicago Defender* on May 21, 1927:

> All the world knows Black Patti—Our Own Beloved Sissieretta Jones. The biggest and brightest star in the firmament of song, her lustrous career is a great chapter in the history of music. The crowned heads of Europe applauded her; people crowded to hear her. Her name means everything that is best in the musical art.
>
> Knowing that these new, wonderful records are the best that art can produce or money can buy, she not only says they are good, but puts her name on them to prove it. . . . When Black Patti, with her lifetime of experience in what will bring joy to the heart, says a record is fine, you know what that means. . . . Look for Black Patti's name on each one. It is your guarantee.[13]

The advertisement stands as a possible document of what Williams's long-term vision for the Black Patti label might have been, rather than what the catalog actually consisted of at the time of the first releases.

The initial run of Black Patti releases, which featured a beautiful black and gold peacock design on the label, was a jumbled mess of outtakes and castoffs from Gennett and Paramount, with some new recordings overseen by Williams mixed in. Williams arranged to have Black Patti artists record at the Gennett studios in Richmond, Indiana, or at various studios in Chicago. At the time, Gennett's average payment for race recordings was five to fifteen dollars per session, or a penny-per-sale royalty deal.[14] Artists received a flat fee for their recordings for Black Patti. Williams said that at this stage in the development of the music business, it would have been "very unusual" for artists to receive any royalties. "I don't know a single one that was on a royalty basis."[15] Williams made a series of trips with a portable recording unit up to Minnesota, down to Indiana, and throughout Chicago for Black Patti. Some of these recordings were released on Paramount and Gennett. As Williams recalled:

> There wasn't any trouble finding artists. By that time, so many had come up here from the South and other parts of the country, because this had become a recording center along with New York. They'd bum rides and hop trains to get up here, any way they could, to get somebody to make a record of them.[16]

Despite the fact that recording talent was readily available, Black Patti reissued some of Gennett's Electrobeam sides, including recordings by the hillbilly singer Vernon Dalhart, Ralph Waldo Emerson (WLS radio's staff organist), sermons by the Reverend J. M. Gates, and recordings by the blues singer Jaybird Coleman.[17]

Immediately on releasing its first batch of recordings, Black Patti found itself frozen out of retail accounts. These accounts likely were under pressure from Paramount not to carry Black Patti titles. Fred Gennett—who appears to have contributed the vast majority of money for the Black Patti venture—quickly grew impatient with the lack of sales. After only six months and fifty-five releases, he folded the Chicago Record Company and Black Patti in September 1927. Clayton Jackson, who worked as the assistant manager for the Gennett Record Division, was assigned by Fred Gennett to tell Williams in person of the Chicago Record Company's (and Black Patti's) demise. "I'll never forget the look on his face when I told him it was all over," said Jackson.[18]

The Gennett historian John Mackenzie speculated that Paramount (and Otto Moeser) angrily tried to stifle Edward Barret's rogue, upstart competitor. Black Patti had serious difficulty being accepted as a new line by distributors; most of its sales outlets came from Chicago. Indeed, Williams corroborated this when he told Jim O'Neal "[Paramount] tried to block every entry that we tried to make into their territory." Of his relationship with Gennett, Williams said, "We got along fine. We just didn't make any money! [Gennett] found [Black Patti] wasn't making the kind of money he thought it would make and he just dissolved it of his own volition."[19]

Black Patti had barely been given a chance. Whether or not Mayo Williams had a grand vision for Black Patti as a medium between the down-home sounds of Paramount and the genteel light opera and balladry of Black Swan will never be known. Of Black Patti's entire catalog, only Long Cleve Reed and Little Harvey Hull's "Original Stack O'Lee Blues" stands out as particularly noteworthy: it is the first known commercial recording by Black artists of one of the most prevalent and enduring Black folk songs/murder ballads. Otherwise, Black Patti stumbled and fell before it hit its stride. But the venture was not without its upside for Gennett: working with Ink Williams gave the Indiana company an opportunity to bring Tom Dorsey, Big Bill Broonzy, and other veterans of Williams's productions into its catalog. Dorsey recorded for Gennett in 1927, singing and playing piano on eight blues sides; he recorded for the label again in 1930 with Bill Broonzy and with Scrapper Blackwell.[20]

As the Black Patti experiment came to an inglorious end, Williams found himself at a professional crossroads in both music and sports. He was still working for Paramount, for which he had secured new hitmakers four years running; but the power dynamics were shifting out of his favor. And despite dominating sports headlines over the entirety of his six seasons in the NFL, the 1927 season found him frozen out of the league. Nevertheless, Williams was not ready to give up on either front.

In September 1927, Williams was playing on an all-Black professional team called the Colored Giants (sometimes called the Chicago American Colored Giants), which also featured Fritz Pollard, Williams, Dick "Super Six" Hudson, and—it was rumored—Paul Robeson. The Colored Giants were headquartered in Hammond, Indiana, along with another professional team that appears to have absorbed several former Hammond Pros. Both teams, along with others from Racine, Evanston, Roseland, La Grange, and Pullman had banded together to form the Mid-West league. The Colored Giants periodically played against NFL teams (including a mid-September tilt against the Chicago Cardinals), as well as reconstituted ex-NFL teams such as the Racine Regulars.[21]

History is fuzzy regarding Williams's experiences with the Colored Giants, but he also played that season for the Hammond Boosters—led by Williams's former Hammond Pros teammate, the fullback Harry Curzon. The Boosters played an exhibition against Red Grange's New York Yankees (NFL) team and a Thanksgiving Day game against the Whiting Friars, where Williams received a standing ovation from the Hammond faithful when he left the field late in a 14–0 victory.[22] Williams's being taken out of the game was something new and was an indicator that time catches up to even the most fleet-footed and durable athlete. When the Boosters played three days later against Mills at Mills Stadium in Chicago, Williams appeared only as a substitute player. The man who had played so many games without substitution since high school was starting to run out of gas at age thirty-three.

Mayo Williams had now been out of college for nearly seven years, and his professional life was in transition. In sports, even for the biggest stars, the end comes suddenly and often ungracefully. The music business can be equally cruel, though Williams would prove deft in—to borrow a football phrase—finding daylight when his charted path became blocked. Such was the case for Williams with Paramount and Black Patti. In an awkward exchange with Jim O'Neal and George Paulus that was laced with antisemitism, Williams said that Paramount's general manager, Maurice Supper, was responsible for blocking Black Patti Records's access to the market, and that such maneuvering was typical of Supper's business dealings:

> Now, the man who was responsible for my situation was named Supper. And Supper, everybody said he was a Jew, because Jews are supposed to be cunning in their dealings with—I'm not saying anything. I don't mean anything. You might be [Jewish]. Are you? You're not? I see, I see. . . . Anytime we'd get a hit in Chicago Music Company, Mister Supper would go to New York and sell it. Nice money. Five thousand, ten thousand maybe. . . . Then he'd organize a new company. [laughs] And in doing it that way, [Paramount] kept ahead of the game.[23]

Such maneuvering on Supper's part helped Paramount, but Supper did not seem inclined to protect Williams against Laibly. When Paramount's CEO, Otto Moeser, proposed putting Williams on straight salary and taking away his expense account, Williams called a meeting with Moeser:

> I got in tough with Mister Moeser [at Paramount] and he told me to come to Milwaukee. So I did and when I got there he asked me what the matter was. I said I needed the money. . . . You see, everybody thought the record business was on its way out because of the radio. So that was one reason I wanted to get out of it.[24]

By the summer of 1928, Williams was prepared to resign from his position at Paramount on the pretext that he was afraid the record industry would lose out to radio. In the fall, he sold his interest in the company's copyrights for five thousand dollars.[25]

Like many others in the music business at the time, Williams watched with trepidation as the industry changed. The T.O.B.A. circuit was declining, and Paramount was concerned that the market for classic blues was drying up despite Ma Rainey's continued success. Indeed, 1928 would wind up being Rainey's finest artistic and commercial year as she drew on the backing work of Dorsey, Papa Charlie Jackson, and even country blues and jug bands. This is a testament to Williams's creativity in mixing and matching styles to achieve new variations in sound. The year would ultimately close out with Ma Rainey & Her Paramount Flappers playing a month-long engagement at Chicago's Monogram Theater, setting attendance records with large crowds and long lines. Although Paramount would continue to release Ma Rainey's recordings until 1930, her contract was terminated at the end of 1928, with one executive surmising that "her down-home material had gone out of fashion."[26]

One of Williams's most affecting encounters in his waning months at Paramount in 1928 was with a performer known as Blind Joe Taggart. Williams had encountered Taggart performing on the street in Chicago, likely sometime in 1927. With a nasally voice, a fine suit, one glass eye, street corner sermons, and country blues–gospel accompaniment, Taggart seemed like an eccentric musical cousin to Blind Lemon Jefferson and Blind Blake. Indeed, these three men had one thing in common—the need for the services of a trustworthy companion who was not visually impaired and could collect and count the money earned at street performances. Back in Dallas, Lead Belly had played this role for Lemon Jefferson for two years, periodically dancing and almost always accompanying him on guitar and vocals. When Williams saw Taggart in Chicago, he was struck with pity at the sight of the singer's bedraggled companion—a young boy, just shy of fourteen, who danced with grace, played guitar with skill well beyond his charge's, and begged for money in rags that clearly were not a costume. The boy, who played guitar almost as well as Jefferson and Blake, was named Josh White.

Joshua White was born in 1914 in Greenville, South Carolina. When he was seven, White's father, a minister, got in an altercation with a white bill collector who had spat on the floor of the Whites' home. Reverend White threw the man out, only to have a posse return to beat him, tie him up, and drag him on the ground to the local jail. Reverend White sustained significant brain trauma and was subsequently institutionalized. Within a year, the family was destitute. The eight-year-old Joshua saw an opportunity to earn money for the family by leading an itinerant blind musician, John Henry "Big Man" Arnold, in his travels across the South and Midwest. White's mother agreed, as long as Arnold would send the family four dollars a week for the boy's services. White sang, played tambourine, begged, and learned to accompany Arnold on guitar, but Arnold treated him with great cruelty: Joshua was kept barefoot and typically slept outdoors even when the older man had lodging. For all the mistreatment, White was excellent at his job, and Big Man Arnold rented his services out to other blind musicians, including Arthur Blake, Lemon Jefferson, and Joe Taggart. By the time Williams saw White on the street for the first time with Taggart, the teenager's skill on guitar nearly matched that of Jefferson and Blake.

Williams invited Taggart to record for Paramount in January 1928, including "Goin' to Rest Where Jesus Is," with guitar and fiddle accompaniment. As he observed White and Taggart more closely, Williams became outraged by Taggart's treatment of the teenage White. He threatened to call the authorities if Taggart did not release White from his indentured servitude. Williams then provided White with lodging. Accounts vary, suggesting either that he stayed with Mayo and Aleta Williams at their home or in an apartment with Mayo's mother, Millie Williams, where Blind Blake also stayed on occasion. The Williams family was able to get White proper clothing and enrolled him in school, looking after him until he went to live with his cousin, Marie Huff, who had recently moved to Chicago. White did not entirely disassociate himself from Taggart. In October 1928 the duo, billed as Blind Joe Taggart & Joshua White, recorded "Scandalous and a Shame," making the fourteen-year-old White the youngest known person ever to record for Paramount. Over the next four years, White recorded as a sideman for several groups, both Black and white, earning enough money eventually to return to his family in Greenville.[27]

Whatever the Josh White encounter reveals about Williams's character and humanity, he remained a shrewd businessman with a keen sense of the human condition. And Williams put these skills to work in planning his departure from Paramount. Playing off Otto Moeser's concerns about the growing threat of radio to the vitality of the record industry, Williams sold his interests in order to make a clean break from the company, knowing he had a better job offer waiting in the wings from Jack Kapp at Brunswick/Vocalion. By September 1928, Williams had left his job at Paramount to coach football at Paul Quinn College, a small HBCU in Waco, Texas. Paramount promoted Aletha Dickerson to fill Williams's vacated position in September of 1928, which was a complete shock to Dickerson:

> Nothing was said to me to indicate that he was leaving Paramount to connect with Vocalion-Brunswick. I would have preferred to go with him and remain his secretary. He later explained that since he was aware the company intended to place me in charge of recording; he thought I'd want the position. Which all goes to show the "gap" between males and females. He was ambitious. *Ergo*, to his way of thinking, I was too. Well, I was not![28]

MAYO WILLIAMS,
"Ink."
Junior. Left End. Weight, 160. Height, 5-11.

At age seventeen in 1911, Mayo Williams already carried the nickname, height, weight, and position he would hold for the next seventeen years.

Monmouth High School junior class of 1911, with Williams (far right, second row) sitting on the periphery. Although musicians and journalists speculated for years about the origin of his nickname, Williams had already been dubbed "Ink"—a pejorative reference to his complexion—as a teenager in Monmouth, Illinois.

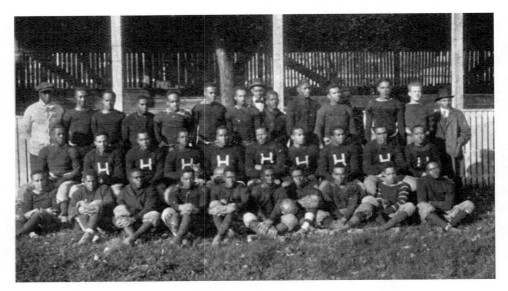

After graduating from Monmouth High, Williams appears to have spent three years considering where and when he would go to college. In 1915, he enrolled at Howard University in Washington, DC, where he starred in football (seated, far right) and track. (© Moorland-Spingarn Research Center, Howard University)

J. Mayo Williams, left end for Brown University's football team, circa 1919. (© Brown University Archives)

On December 10, 1918, Ink Williams and 22,499 other US Army officers and men pose for a photo at Fort Hancock's Machine Gun Training Center, where Williams served as a second lieutenant during World War I. (Library of Congress LC-USZ62-63709)

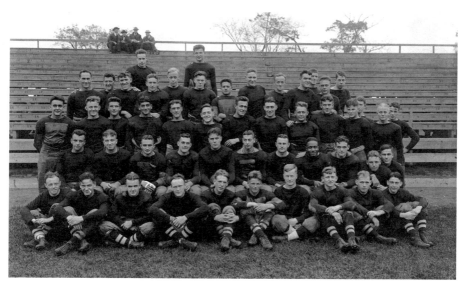

Boy soldiers: the 1919 Brown University football team strikes a cheerful pose at Andrews Field. Many of the players had been discharged from active military service only six months before. This was the year Williams (second row, fourth from right) excelled in the hostile Yale Bowl.
(© Brown University Archives)

Williams typically played football without a helmet—a trait that is on display in this 1920 image of Brown against the University of Maine. (© Brown University Archives)

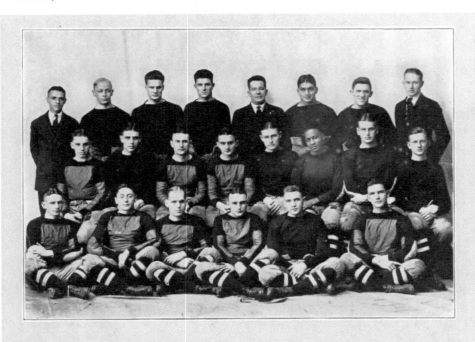

The 1920 Brown University Varsity Football Team: The Swedish-born Olof Gustave Hazard "Curly" Oden, seated far left in the middle row, remained lifelong friends with Williams (seated, third from right, middle row) and spent six years in the NFL with the Providence Steam Roller and the Boston Braves. (© Brown University Archives)

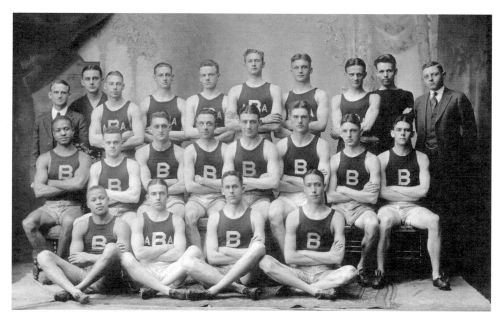

The 1921 Brown University track team: Coach Archie Hahn, the gold-medal Olympian who recruited Williams to Brown, stands in the back row, far left. Williams is seated directly in front of Hahn. Jimmy Murphy, Williams's vaudevillian co-star, is third from right, back row. The freshman J. F. S. Carter—one of the cofounders of the Providence chapter of Alpha Phi Alpha—is seated far left, front row. (© Brown University Archives)

Williams, as pictured in the 1921 Brown University yearbook, with the following caption:

Jay Mayo Williams, Monmouth, Ill.
"Ink" "Duke" "Speed"
Football: (2) (3) (4); Track: (2) (3) (4)

Introducing "Ink," the star end. We have seldom seen him miss a tackle, and have never seen him emerge from the scrimmage without that 5 inch grin. Not only does he excel in making his way thru interference, but also in executing end around plays. He has a wharhoop [sic] that defies description. This dusky warrior is as fast on the cinders as he is on the gridiron. In the dashes he shakes a fleet pair of heels. Au revoir, "Ink." (© Brown University Archives)

This 1922 *Akron Beacon Journal* advertisement for the Hammond Pros vs. Akron Pros game shows the tendency for print ads to promote Williams—"Famous Colored Star"—as the main draw for the event. Akron defeated Hammond, 22–0.

Williams (front, far left) stands with his fellow cofounders of the Xi Lambda chapter of Alpha Phi Alpha fraternity in Chicago in 1924. Also standing in the front row (fourth from left) is the legendary businessman Anthony Overton. He commissioned Bronzeville's Overton Hygienic Building, where Williams and Fritz Pollard had a business office. (Alpha Phi Alpha *Sphinx* Magazine)

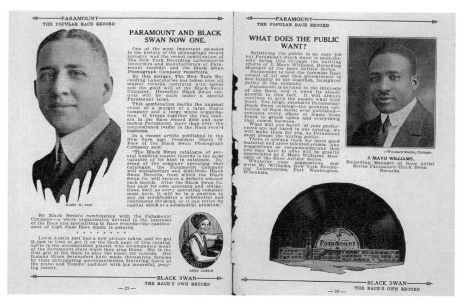

The 1924 Paramount Records Catalog announced the acquisition of Black Swan as "one of the most important episodes in the history of the phonograph industry" but signaled a more populist direction under the helm of its recording manager, J. Mayo Williams. The debonair thirty-year-old Williams says that "Paramount must please the buying public." (© Southern Folklife Collection Discographical Files [30014], Southern Folklife Collection at Wilson Special Collections Library, University of North Carolina at Chapel Hill)

Ragtag days: the 1928 Hammond football team, their first year after leaving the NFL, featured both Ink Williams (back row, second from left) and the forty-one-year-old Jim Thorpe (back row, fourth from left) in one game. This photo captures the former All-American, gold-medal Olympian, NFL and MLB star, pro basketball player, and inaugural NFL president, who was—along with Williams—at the very end of his professional career. (© Hammond Public Library/Suzanne G. Long Local History Room)

The singer Sissieretta Jones—known worldwide as the "Black Patti"—was the first Black singer to perform at Carnegie Hall (still called the "Music Hall" when she appeared there in 1892); performed with Antonín Dvořák at Madison Square Garden in 1894; gave concerts on six continents; sang for Presidents Harrison, Cleveland, McKinley, and (Theodore) Roosevelt; and founded the Black Patti Troubadours, whose tours of the Deep South were legendary. She was living in Providence, Rhode Island in relative obscurity just one block from J. Mayo Williams during his freshman year at Brown. She was the namesake of Williams's short-lived record label, Black Patti Records, in 1927.

Williams was 78 years old and still wearing a tie every day when Jim O'Neal visited his office in 1972. It was during this same visit that Little Brother Montgomery shared the tale of his incredulity at meeting Williams at Decca's Chicago office in 1930. (Photo by Jim O'Neal, BluEsoterica Archives, http://www.bluesoterica.com)

CHAPTER 16

Hokum

Black Patti Records had lasted only one year, from incorporation to dissolution. But Richard Gennett was not the only person in the race record industry who had noticed Williams's abilities. Jack Kapp understood that Williams was the catalyst for Paramount's success and offered him a job at the Brunswick-Balke-Collendar (BBC) Company. BBC was a manufacturing corporation specializing in billiard and bowling balls headquartered in Dubuque, Iowa. They had also been manufacturing phonographs since 1910 and like the Wisconsin Chair Company, manufactured records to be played on their phonographs. BBC's label, Brunswick, was based in Chicago and managed by Jack Kapp. In 1925, BBC acquired Vocalion Records, which had an underperforming race records series in need of some organization. Its blues musicians—primarily the songsters Henry "Ragtime Texas" Thomas, Furry Lewis, and Jim Jackson—typically were recorded in Chicago and were recommended by record dealers such as H. C. Speir of Jackson, Mississippi. Jack Kapp made it Williams's responsibility to put Vocalion's and Brunswick's race records house in order and actively to recruit talent for an expanded catalog.

Ink Williams had known Kapp since his first days at Black Swan in 1921. Jack had been a kid then, working in his father's Imperial Talking Machine Shop. In 1922, Jack and his brother, Dave, opened the Kapp Record Store in Chicago, where they continued their friendship with Williams while he grew the Paramount label. By 1926, Kapp was at BBC and in 1928 had caught wind of Williams's pending departure from Paramount. As Williams later recalled:

> Jack's family had a music store over on Halsted Street, over there in what we called "Jew Town." Jack was aware of my knowledge of the business. He had heard, by the grapevine I guess, that I had dropped out of Paramount records. You see, they always identified me with Paramount. The

label [Black Patti] didn't live long enough for me to get identified with Black Patti [chuckling]. But they always knew that I had been with Paramount and the NYRL.[1]

Jack Kapp, Williams recalled, "had been keeping in touch with me all of the time I was at Paramount. And I had no trouble getting in with him when he was the head of Brunswick and Vocalion."[2]

Kapp needed Williams to run the A&R Department for both Brunswick's and Vocalion's race records series so that he—Kapp—could focus greater energy on promoting the label's popular music stars, such as Bing Crosby. Although Williams appears to have formally left Paramount in the fall of 1928, he had clearly begun working on other projects (mainly Black Patti) unknown to Paramount in 1927. Though Williams was still working for Paramount through the early fall, he had begun recording artists for Vocalion in June 1928. On his arrival, Vocalion's race catalog consisted of jazz groups such as King Oliver's Dixie Syncopators and Jimmy Noone's Apex Jazz Band, as well as religious music—particularly the gospel songs and sermons of the Reverend A. W. Nix. Henry Thomas and Walter "Furry" Lewis were the only two blues artists who had made a significant number of records for Vocalion before Williams arrived. Looking to cement his relationship with the Kapps, Williams invited Jack and Dave Kapp on board at the State Street Music Company (SSMC), the publishing branch he had formed for the ill-fated Black Patti label.[3]

At BBC, Williams immediately employed the same managerial tactics that enabled his success at Paramount: imitating the army generals he saw during World War I, he surrounded himself with good lieutenants. Thomas A. Dorsey continued to help Williams identify and arrange talent, bringing a number of guitar-based artists to the label. In a significant move, Williams began leaning on the advice of two boogie-woogie piano players: Charles Edward "Cow Cow" Davenport and Sammy Price. Despite the enormous success of Dorsey and his groups, Davenport and Price opened the door for a new piano-based style of blues whose influence remains immeasurable. As he had with Papa Charlie Jackson, Blind Lemon Jefferson, and Blind Blake, Williams broke new ground by recording music that was at its heart dance music. This style of piano blues likely was evocative of what he had heard as kid back in Monmouth, Illinois and what his father would have heard in the lumber camps and riverboat towns of Arkansas and Tennessee.

Born in Anniston, Alabama in 1894, Charles Edward Davenport had a rebellious spirit, playing piano against the wishes of his father, who was a minister. Davenport's parents put him in Alabama Theological Seminary, only to see him expelled for playing ragtime. He soon fell into the kind of life his parents feared ragtime might lead to: playing in brothels in Atlanta's Black

Bottom district, doing barrelhouse gigs in Birmingham, and ultimately living the life of a carney, playing piano, dancing, and doing comedy for minstrel shows. In 1917, Davenport landed a gig at a vaudeville house in Augusta, Georgia with Ma Rainey and the very young Bessie Smith. There, Davenport paired up with the blues singer Dora Carr and toured the T.O.B.A. circuit as Davenport and Carr. By the time Davenport and Carr recorded for Ralph Peer at OKeh in 1925, they had already done a long stint with the Barkoot Carnival, managed by Syrian immigrant and entrepreneur Khalil G. Barkoot. Davenport, who wrote much of his own material, published songs in New York City with Clarence Williams and laid down the piano for a number of commercial player piano rolls. By this time, too, Davenport had become closely associated with his song "Cow Cow Blues." When he recorded for Williams at Paramount in 1927, he was known popularly as Cow Cow Davenport. By 1928, Davenport was growing weary of the itinerant road life. He mailed a letter to Mayo Williams inquiring about new opportunities. Williams encouraged Davenport to come to Chicago to record for Vocalion and to help advise him on new talent. Davenport didn't record for Vocalion until July 1928 but his role as "informal advisor" to Williams would help to shepherd in a new era of piano-driven blues.[4]

Williams's first act at Vocalion was Leroy Carr and Scrapper Blackwell, a blues duo from Indianapolis. Carr, who was born in Nashville, Tennessee in 1905, possessed a smooth but firm piano and vocal style. His musical partner, the guitarist Francis Hillman "Scrapper" Blackwell, was born in Syracuse, South Carolina in 1903, one of sixteen children in a Cherokee (or possibly Haliwa-Saponi) family who resettled in Indianapolis. Blackwell learned to play guitar on an instrument built from a mandolin neck and a cigar box. He was making a decent living selling bootleg liquor when he met Leroy Carr in early 1928. Blackwell's biting, single-note guitar style played a striking counterpoint to Carr's smooth and fluid right hand on piano, and the excited Leroy Carr wanted to get the duo on record. Blackwell was intrigued but had little interest in leaving Indianapolis, where his moonshine operation did a brisk business. Leroy told Scrapper that he had the connections to get someone from Chicago to bring a portable unit to Indianapolis to record them.[5] Perhaps he had met Williams when Ink was passing through Indianapolis during his NFL career or while Williams was visiting his Brown fraternity brother Russell Adrian Lane (who had become the principal of Crispus Attucks High School in Indianapolis in 1927), or on trips to Gennett's studio in nearby Richmond. (Williams recalled making recordings for Black Patti in Indianapolis on a portable device.) But it is more likely that Carr's connection to Williams was through Cow Cow Davenport. Williams arrived in Indianapolis with a portable unit to make the first recordings of Leroy Carr and Scrapper Blackwell on June 19, 1928.

The first session with the portable unit consisted of two solo performances by Scrapper Blackwell, his "Kokomo Blues," about the nearby Indiana town where Williams was threatened by the Klan a few years earlier with the Hammond Pros. ("Kokomo Blues" would become the blueprint eight years later for Robert Johnson's better-known "Sweet Home Chicago.") The portable recording unit took some getting used to, so Blackwell's single guitar and vocal would be a much easier place to start than a larger ensemble involving Carr's piano. With Blackwell's two records down, Blackwell and Carr recorded together on June 19, yielding "How Long, How Long Blues." Carr's song was based on "How Long Daddy, How Long," which Ida Cox and Papa Charlie Jackson had recorded for Williams at Paramount in 1925. "How Long, How Long Blues" became an enormous hit and an instant standard among blues, jazz, and country musicians. Williams also recorded two sides each by Lulu Jackson and Willie Jones before returning to Chicago. The subsequent release of Carr and Blackwell's "How Long, How Long Blues," and to a lesser degree Scrapper Blackwell's "Kokomo Blues," almost instantaneously launched the two men into the upper echelons of race-record fame. Blackwell recalled receiving significant and regular royalty checks from Vocalion, which was enough to convince him to make the trip to Chicago for their next Vocalion session in August.

Back in Chicago, Williams recorded Cow Cow Davenport in July, including the pianist's signature song, "Cow Cow Blues." The remainder of Williams's summer was busy, with Adam Rankin "Stovepipe" Johnson, Hound Head Henry, Leroy Carr and Scrapper Blackwell, and Lulu Jackson making records. When Williams officially vacated his position at Paramount in late August or early September, he left Chicago (temporarily) for Waco, Texas, to begin coaching football at Paul Quinn College. Williams made this work for him, once again planning his recording schedule around his fall football schedule. As the head of A&R for Brunswick and Vocalion, Williams could no longer afford to be the sedentary talent scout he was at Paramount. BBC expected Williams to scout talent beyond Chicago; he tried to make this dovetail with his southern-based coaching work as much as possible.[6] Williams traveled on an expense account, likely driving a car provided by the record company, frequently covering the over seven hundred miles between Waco and Chicago to oversee sessions for Vocalion. Williams recalled that he "went down to Carolina, New Orleans, Dallas" and elsewhere to find and record talent. He also periodically played football games for the Chicago Black Hawks—another all-Black pro team assembled by Fritz Pollard. The Black Hawks played exhibitions against all-white teams in Chicago and toured the West Coast during the winter months.[7]

Williams still maintained a presence in Chicago and continued his association with Thomas A. Dorsey. Born in rural Villa Rica, Georgia in 1899, Tom

Dorsey grew up in Atlanta and worked during his teenage years selling popcorn and at other concessions in a theater—the site of his first encounter with the music of Ma Rainey and Bessie Smith (and likely Cow Cow Davenport). The young Dorsey felt "all the action" was up in Chicago and moved there around 1915. There he met Mayo Williams (when Williams was working for Black Swan), worked as an arranger for Paramount, and assembled and led Ma Rainey's Wild Cats from 1925 until 1928. The breakneck pace of his life during these years caused Dorsey to have two nervous breakdowns, prompting long breaks from Rainey and her group. Dorsey eventually got off the road with Rainey's show when she seemed to lose her heart for the music following her arrest on trumped-up charges of jewelry theft in 1928.[8] Dorsey, who had married Nettie Harper (one of Ma Rainey's stagehands), was a working musician struggling to maintain a semblance of domestic life and spiritual purpose. This explains why he left Ma Rainey to work as Williams's arranger:

> Well, the money got short, times got hard, and she didn't fire me, and I didn't just run off and leave her. I gave the job to someone else, I forgot who it was now. After I left her, I didn't take any engagements too much—you know, regular show business. For I had something better to do. I was an arranger, a music arranger. I was working for Chicago Music Publishing Company, and I had an all-day job, and my nights at home. So that paid more anyway. And I could get out and do more gigs and make extra. And that took me off the road, too. I could stay home with my family. I made a pretty good living at that. Matter of fact, I had a office there on State Street where the Chicago Music Publishing Company [was located]. So, Ink Williams and Fritz Pollard, I think they ran the office there [Pollard maintained an adjacent office for his banking endeavors], in the thirty-sixth block on State Street. I think that was the Overton Building. There used to be a bank in that building.

Years later, Dorsey struggles to describe precisely what his job was with Vocalion:

> I don't know what they called it. Just hangin' around there, doing whatever come to happen. Making or arranging tunes. A guy'd come in with a song, and he'd sing it. He had nobody to arrange it, put it on paper. So, I put it on the paper. And see, and then the company would copyright it, see. Vocalion or Chicago Music Company—we were all mixed up in the Chicago Music Publishing Company under Ink Williams. I haven't seen a sheet of music they published yet![9]

Though in later years, Dorsey would speak critically of Williams, an element of friendship and collegiality seems to have existed between the two men.

Certainly, Dorsey's career path followed Williams's from his rounds as a Black Swan distributor to a Paramount song arranger and session musician to Ma Rainey's bandleader to a Vocalion songwriter, arranger, and recording artist. If Dorsey found Williams unsavory, he masterfully used their relationship to his advantage and achieved the rarest of feats for a songwriter: a family-friendly, middle-class existence.

By this time, Dorsey—who went by the stage name "Georgia Tom"—played in a casual pickup band called the Hokum Boys with Bobby Robinson, Williams's former Paramount secretary, Aletha Dickerson (who was married to Bobby Robinson), and a slide guitarist known as Tampa Red.

Tampa Red was born Hudson Woodbridge in Smithville, Georgia in 1904, and was raised by an aunt and grandmother in Tampa, Florida, taking their last name (Whittaker) after the death of his parents. Dorsey had met Tampa Red the same way he had met Williams—hanging around a Chicago record store—and the two became friends. Dorsey admired Tampa Red's vocal ability. Red's resonator slide guitar playing was both masterful and, at that time, unique in Chicago blues circles.

The Hokum Boys played blues and novelty songs that ranged from artful double-entendre to explicitly raunchy. Dorsey recalled that he and Tampa Red played only for Black audiences, never for whites:

> All black. See, we wasn't high powered enough. It's for other fellows who were up in the high music echelon. They got those jobs with the whites. For the money was bigger up there. We didn't have very much at that time.[10]

Sometime in the fall of 1928, in the vein of the Hokum Boys, Dorsey and Whittaker were inspired to write an off-color song called "It's Tight Like That." As Dorsey recalled years later:

> Tampa and, oh, it was a bunch of us, somewhere one night. And there used to be a phrase they used around town, you know, folks started saying, "Ah, it's tight like that! Tight like that!" So, we said, "Well, that oughta work." So, we picked out a song. Tampa and I got the guitar, sitting around the house one night, at the dinner table there after dinner, and J. Mayo Williams heard it, and he said, "Oh, man, we gonna record that! We gonna record that right away! Hold it right like that!"[11]

On November 6, Williams recorded Georgia Tom and Tampa Red's "It's Tight Like That," pairing it with Georgia Tom's "Grievin' Me Blues." The song was an instant, sensational hit that unleashed a torrent of what became known as "hokum blues" onto the race record market. As Dorsey remembered it, he and Whittaker actually earned revenues from the song for decades:

We made some money on that. And then the big bands started playing "Tight Like That," making arrangements of it for big bands, we made money on that. And that's the first thing that ever become countrywide, so far as a piece of music we had produced. And "Tight Like That," that's good yet. And we hold it in high esteem and keep the guard on it yet, can't ever tell when it'll bust loose somewhere and make some more money.[12]

The blues historian Jim O'Neal has noted that Dorsey's account of the genesis of "It's Tight Like That" in the film *The Rise of Gospel Blues* differs from his telling here. (In the film, Dorsey says Tampa Red brought him the lyrics and persuaded him to write music despite Dorsey's pledge to make only religious music.) Regardless of Dorsey's role in writing the music, his anecdote about the writing and recording of "It's Tight Like That" reflects that although the blues market had stepped up its "organic" or "down-home" (field-recording) recording practices, it was also moving increasingly closer to the point of artistic creation in a quest for instant "hits." Songs such as "It's Tight Like That" moved Dorsey from behind the arranging bench to stardom in his own right as Georgia Tom.

Dorsey recalled making four dollars a night gigging if the pay was good, two or three if they got ripped off. Many times, they were not paid at all. By that measure, he told Jim O'Neal, recording sessions paid fairly well:

DORSEY: Well, if you got 25 dollars, that was good. Most times you'd go and accompany somebody on a recording session, you'd sit there half the day and turn out with 10 or 15 dollars. Well, that was better than nothing. You could go out and get you a meal for 35 cents or 40 cents at the best, a good meal.

O'NEAL: How were the royalties then? Did you ever get royalties?

DORSEY: Oh, royalties were kinda late coming. You know, we had to kinda organize on these people to get the royalties, and we had a hard time. Course I've gotten mine, some of it with Paramount Records. 'Cause Williams course had that sewed up, and he got his. And if he got his, then we got ours. And if he didn't get his, then we didn't get ours.[13]

And Williams began to sew up quite a bit in the fall of 1928, producing follow-up sessions with Tampa Red and the Hokum Boys, Leroy Carr and Scrapper Blackwell, and Cow Cow Davenport. Williams was also on the road, recording sessions of sacred music in Birmingham (the Golden Leaf Quartet, Reverend I. B. Ware, and the Bessemer Sunset Four, whose name was clearly derived from the city's steel and iron industry), Memphis (Keghouse's "Canned Heat Blues"), Dallas, Kansas City, and New Orleans.[14] The September trip to Memphis yielded a number of recordings with Bo Carter, including the first recording of "Corrine Corrina," with Carter and "Papa" Charlie McCoy. The song—which appears to be an original take on an amalgamation of similar songs (and subjects) in blues, hillbilly, and jazz—became a hit and leaped seemingly instantly into the repertoire of every genre of American vernacular music.

Charlie McCoy, born in 1909 in Jackson, Mississippi, was from a large musical family. He maintained a recording history with Williams from 1928 through the 1930s. Bo Chatmon (who also went by the stage name Bo Carter), was born Armenter Chatmon in Bolton, Mississippi, in 1893. Chatmon also was a member of a large family of musicians, several of whom—including Bo—formed a highly influential string band called the Mississippi Sheiks. The Sheiks were popular with both Black and white audiences, expertly tailoring their performances to suit the tastes of each particular audience. As is the case, too, for Chatmon's "Corrine Corrina" with its lilting harmonies, fiddle, and mandolin the Sheiks' music can sound either like country blues or hillbilly music, depending on the inclinations of the listener. In this respect, their sound is likely more indicative of the wide-ranging tastes of both Black and white audiences in the multiracial South. Genuine musical inclinations were far more fluid than the rigid and clumsily race-based Jim Crow–inspired marketing categories of "race" and "hillbilly" music (which continue to resonate today under different names). The Mississippi Sheiks eventually made noteworthy recordings for Victor and other labels, including their signature and genre-defying 1930 OKeh recording, "Sittin' on Top of the World." Chatmon and McCoy's "Corrine Corrina" is, without a doubt, the most stylistically singular recording that Williams had made up to this point, mixing guitar, mandolin, and fiddle against a swinging country blues backdrop with a smooth male vocal. Williams would be forever tied to "Corrine Corrina," in part because he claimed a songwriting credit.

Between recording sessions in Dallas in late October and the September New Orleans session that produced "Corrine Corrina," Williams played some football. He had signed on with the Hammond Semcos, the latest incarnation of the post-NFL Hammond Pros. The *Times* of Munster, Indiana excitedly announced that the Hammond Semcos had hired "Two of America's greatest football stars—'Ink' Williams, a negro, and Jim Thorpe, a full-blooded Indian" to take on the Hammond Boosters. The *Times* erroneously reported that Williams was a three-time Walter Camp All-American (he only received honorable mention once) and winked about Williams's age by referring to him as a "past master in the art of snaring passes."[15]

Just eight years earlier, Thorpe was the president of the NFL.

A Semcos-Boosters showdown was far from the glories of the NFL for both veterans. Adding salt to the wound, Williams, Thorpe, and the Semcos lost, 7–6.

In a coincidence, just four days earlier, the New York *Daily News* sportswriter (and future television impresario) Ed Sullivan wrote a syndicated column focusing on the realities facing Black football players in the college game. Sullivan's column was prompted by the pending appearance of the Colgate University football team at Yankee Stadium. Sullivan, who had been a multisport star athlete in high school and who was then a known advocate for racial equality, pointed out that Black athletes on integrated teams needed to be beyond excellent:

> So deep rooted was prejudice in the past that whenever a colored player made a college team you could rest assured that he was at least 25 percent better than the white man he beat out for the position. He had to be to get recognition for the fraternities control college politics and can make their influence felt.[16]

Sullivan cited Paul Robeson, Duke Slater, Fritz Pollard, and Ink Williams as examples, even mentioning that Williams worked his way through Brown as a tailor. In other words, it was openly understood that nonwhite players who starred in the college game were the most exceptional players in the game, hence the regular mention of the race of players such as Thorpe or Williams in pre-game analyses.

After the Semco-Boosters game, Williams headed to Marshall, Texas—roughly equidistant between New Orleans and Dallas—to serve as assistant coach with Paul Quinn College in their game against their HBCU archrivals, the Wildcats of Wiley College, on Armistice Day, November 11. The *Marshall News Messenger* was impressed with "Inky Williams," who "sustains quite a reputation as a football player as well as coach. He will uncork some of the tricks which he learned in the East, and it is expected that the Cats are going to have trouble."[17] Quite coincidentally, Marshall, Texas markets itself today as the "birthplace of boogie-woogie," where men like Lead Belly had performed. Although he would first have one more game to play for the Semcos against the Chicago Nehis in East Chicago on November 18, it was almost as if Williams's trip to Marshall foreshadowed his next major discovery a few weeks later.

This next big development in Williams's catalog—and in Black vernacular music—came in late December through a recommendation from Cow Cow Davenport, enshrining boogie-woogie piano as a formidable element in the evolution from blues to jazz to rhythm and blues. Davenport recommended an unknown musician named Clarence "Pine Top" Smith to Williams, who recorded "Pine Top's Boogie-Woogie" for Vocalion on December 29, 1928. Born in 1904, Smith was raised in Birmingham, Alabama, where his tree-climbing habits are said to have earned him the nickname "Pine Top." Like many of Williams's most successful artists, Pine Top had cut his teeth on the

T.O.B.A. circuit and had even accompanied Ma Rainey in concert on piano for a time before settling in Chicago. There he lived with his young family in the same boardinghouse as the pianists Meade "Lux" Lewis and Albert Ammons. (Lewis had recorded for Mayo Williams at Paramount in 1927, resulting in the classic boogie-woogie track "Honky Tonk Train Blues.")

Williams's connections to boogie-woogie were present from the moment its sounds first hit wax. In October 1926, Elzadie Robinson—backed by the pianist Will Ezell—recorded Ezell's song "Sawmill Blues" for Paramount. Also known as "Pitchin' Boogie," this tune had been floating around the southern lumber camps and barrelhouses where pianists such as Ezell regularly played. Ezell's version—on which Williams claimed a writer's credit—spawned other commercial knockoffs. They struck Little Brother Montgomery, who had known the tune years before while he was playing the same barrelhouses as Ezell, as ludicrous. In Williams's telling:

> "Yeah, busy bootin' and you can't come in." "They got a steady rolling, and you can't come in." They got it all kind of ways. Well, at any rate, Little Brother kids me all the time, says, "You got your name on all the steady rollin' or busy bootin'?" I said, "Well, I got Will Ezell's, too." I said, "Will Ezell wrote the music, and I wrote the lyrics." [laughter] He said, "Man, I played that song down south 50 years—[laughter] 50 years ago!"[18]

"Pine Top's Boogie-Woogie" soon proved a major success and established the name of a genre. Smith was invited back to the studio two weeks later to record more sides for Vocalion in January 1929. These two sessions would be the only documentation of Pine Top's remarkable and influential playing; he died on March 19, 1929, at age twenty-five when he was hit by a stray bullet at a party.

CHAPTER 17

Bumble Bee

Nineteen twenty-eight was a year of progress for Williams—moving from Paramount to Vocalion and Brunswick and rapidly arranging a stable of highly popular blues and jazz artists as well as some calypso. Nineteen twenty-nine increased the commercial success he had with the various incarnations of Georgia Tom, Tampa Red, and the Hokum Boys and expanded further on the field recording trips Williams first started in the fall of 1928. Jabbo Smith and His Rhythm Aces became a regular, solid act for Brunswick. Over on Vocalion, Jim Jackson, Leroy Carr and Scrapper Blackwell, Cow Cow Davenport, Tampa Red and Georgia Tom, and Jimmy Noone's Apex Club Orchestra, all recorded in Chicago, continued to make up the bulk of the label's offerings through the fall of 1929. In September, Williams returned to his coaching duties in Waco at Paul Quinn College and resumed Vocalion/Brunswick's remote field recording activities. Again, Williams traveled to Memphis, New Orleans, Kansas City, Atlanta, and Birmingham, making recordings of blues and sacred music.[1] In Kansas City, Williams set up shop at the WDAF radio station, an affiliate of the *Kansas City Star*. He was quoted saying that George E. Lee's jazz band (many of whose members eventually were absorbed into Bennie Moten's band) "was one of the best he had ever heard."[2] In Memphis, Williams reconnected with artists he had met over the past two years and who had recorded for Paramount, Vocalion, and Brunswick: the singer Jim Jackson, the jug band musician and slide banjo player Gus Cannon, who had recorded a few sides for Paramount in late 1927 under the name "Banjo Joe." Williams also met various members of the Mississippi Sheiks, recording them under names such as "Walter Vincent with the Chapmons." He also re-encountered Charlie McCoy and his brother Joe, who recorded under the name Joe Williams (no relation to either Big Joe Williams or the lead singer of Count Basie's group in later decades). Given that Mayo Williams met Charlie

McCoy in the fall of 1928, it is likely that Charlie introduced Mayo to his brother, Joe, and to two close associates who also recorded for Williams and Brunswick: Robert Wilkins and his reported protégé (and eventual spouse of Joe McCoy), Memphis Minnie.

The pattern for Williams's fieldwork appears to have been this: after arriving in town, he connected with easily located musicians familiar with him or with his "lieutenants" such as Thomas A. Dorsey, then asked those musicians to introduce him to other local talent. Neither Williams nor the musicians were preoccupied with whether or not the artists in question had recording contracts with other labels. Williams would then watch performances and invite some artists to attend a recording session. In Memphis, the studio was the basement of the Peabody Hotel, where Jim Jackson had been a house performer. Jackson likely had been brought to Vocalion in a roundabout way by the talent scout and record distributor H. C. Speir in late 1927. (Speir reportedly considered Jackson a "coke head" and sold his contract to Loren Watson, another talent scout in Memphis.) Jackson held some sway with Williams and others because he had scored a major hit in the fall of 1927 with "Jim Jackson's Kansas City Blues (parts 1 and 2)." When artists arrived at the recording location, they worked quickly, setting down a handful of songs on wax, and receiving a flat fee from Williams. If they were lucky and their song was selected for release and sold in decent numbers, and if Williams had the time, inclination, or ability to stay in touch with them, they received additional payments.

Such was the experience of the boogie-woogie pianist Rufus George Perryman, who recorded for Williams in Memphis in September 1929. Perryman, known as "Speckled Red" (a reference to his being Black and albino), hailed from Hampton, Georgia, and had spent some time playing in brothels in Detroit before settling in Memphis, where he became friendly with Jim Jackson. Speckled Red recalled it this way:

> Jim Jackson was already playin' for Brunswick. Oh, he had done made a hit with that piece he made called "I'm Goin' Move to Kansas City." He knew the people that I was playin' for there on Maeweather an' Pauline, an' he'd come out there an' pick his guitar. So. Mayo Williams come to Memphis. Well, he come out there an' heard me play. He liked the "Dirty Dozen" when I played it, an' he asked me could I make it on record. I told him I never played on no record. An' then he say, "Well, I want you to play on record. You'll get paid for it." An' I said, "Well, anything to make me some money!"
>
> So, I played it for him there, an' then he give me an assignment to play. I went down to the Peabody Hotel in the basement floor. We recorded down there. I made eight songs that day: "Dirty Dozen," and "Wilkins Street Stomp," and.... I can't think of the rest of them.

The session with Speckled Red is noteworthy for his recording of "Dirty Dozen," which was Red's original musical interpretation of the "dirty dozens," an improvisational Black competitive insult game that many consider to be the precursor to rap and hip-hop. Williams liked Red's "Dirty Dozen" and asked him to modify the language so that it could be sold on a record:

> You know how boys do be around and telling lots o' foolishness, calling different kind of names? One try to out-talk the other, and played it when one beat the other one he say, "Well, you put me in the dozen." So, I decided I'd make a song. Heh! 'Course, on record it's all right. But I made it bad! When he wanted me to, put it on record, well, I just changed the words. It all mean the same thing, but I just changed the words.

Indeed, in changing the words, Williams stepped in and assumed a partial writing credit for "Dirty Dozen." He paid Red one hundred twenty-five dollars for the session and sent him a follow-up payment of seventy-five dollars. Speckled Red never received any more money from Vocalion.[3]

Williams's successful field trip to Memphis was aided by Thomas A. Dorsey and Tampa Red, who were along as assistants. Their presence doubtless improved Williams's status with the artists he recruited. Ever resourceful, Williams booked Tampa Red and Georgia Tom in a T.O.B.A. theater in Memphis during this same field recording trip. Dorsey remembered:

> Tampa Red, now, "Ink" Williams used to handle him. And we felt that we wanted to go to Memphis and rent a hall or something and put on a blues show. And we did, in many places. And blues sold at the hall, so they booked us at the theater for a week. So it was kind of a spontaneous thing. You never knew where you was going, you never knew what you was gonna run into, you never knew what was gonna run into you.[4]

It was a busy week of performances, scouting, and recording for Dorsey and Tampa:

> We'd got down in Mississippi, down in those cottonfields, we lookin' for talent. Some of the fellows who could hoot down there in the field. I think they brought some of them up there and recorded them. The Peabody Hotel, that's where we recorded [Jim Jackson, Furry Lewis, Speckled Red, Robert Wilkins, Jenny Pope, Joe Williams, Jed Davenport, Garfield Akers, Joe Calicott, Kid Bailey, and Betty Perkins, all recorded at Peabody Hotel for Vocalion in October 1929].[5]

Williams echoed Dorsey's anecdote, suggesting their scouting wasn't limited to Memphis's nightclubs:

See, I've been down in fields out of Memphis, in the cotton fields, and bring them into Memphis *barefooted* right out of the cotton field and record them. And that's the way most of them, had the, that was all the music they had.⁶

It is unclear who Williams is referring to in this anecdote, though it is possible that it is simply a reference to Garfield Akers, who recorded two sides—"Cottonfield Blues" and "Cottonfield Blues Part 2"—for Williams in Memphis on September 23, 1929. This itinerary shows how often Williams was on the move during this time: he recorded "Jim Jackson's Jamboree" in Memphis on October 14, Jimmy Noone's Orchestra in Chicago on October 15, and then played a football game for the Sunlight Laundry Team (of Hammond, Indiana) in East Chicago against the Hegewisch Eleven on October 20.⁷ Judging by the caliber of team Williams was playing for, it is clear that work had become so very busy (and lucrative) that he was playing football for the fun of it, when and where he could fit it in.

Throughout these field trips—as well as back in Chicago—Williams continued to require his singers to use lyric sheets when singing in the studio, even claiming that he stood next to blind singers and whispered the words in their ear as they sang. Williams encountered a greater number of illiterate singers on his forays into the South and so tore a page out of Ma Rainey's book:

The music was made just like drawing a picture. . . . There's a song called "Milk Cow Blues." That's a hell of a blues. If they's gonna sing "Milk Cow Blues," you just make a picture of a cow the best you could, and set it up on a stand, and so forth and so on. That's how they knew what they were gonna say. [laughs] And the music could go *any* way, you see?⁸

Williams made two field trips to Dallas in 1929. For someone like Williams, who was outfitted with a car, the trip from Waco to Dallas was relatively short (by streetcar, it took some three hours). In September, he reconnected with the Dallas pianist Sammy Price, who had originally sent Paramount the test record of Blind Lemon Jefferson four years earlier. Price remembered, "It was while I was in Dallas that I made my first recordings . . . for J. Mayo Williams."⁹ Price had spent his young life preparing for this moment, touring the T.O.B.A. circuit throughout the South and Midwest during the 1920s, using Dallas as his home base. Growing up in Waco and Dallas, Price had learned piano from Booker T. Washington's daughter, Portia Pittman, and had also worked as a dancer in a Dallas T.O.B.A. theater where he met Ida Cox and other Black vaudeville stars. In Dallas, Price began playing boogie-woogie, though they called it walking bass, or "booger-rooger."¹⁰ Sammy Price's "Blue Rhythm Stomp" didn't sell enough copies to warrant another release from Vocalion, but his skillful playing and easygoing disposition made a lasting impression on Williams, and that would bear fruit in later years. Williams's second session in Dallas is less significant for the artists who were recorded (Eddie Fennell and Sugar Lou's Hotel Tyler Orchestra) than for the fact that it took place on October 24, 1929, the date of the Wall Street crash, which triggered the Great Depression.

Vocalion Brunswick released a combined one hundred forty blues and gospel records in 1929 and similar numbers again in 1930. The hit records of Leroy Carr and Scrapper Blackwell and Tampa Red and Georgia Tom Dorsey were partial causes for the company's increased output. The 1929 sides by Tampa Red and Georgia Tom were successful enough that they had more singles released that year than Blind Blake, Leroy Carr, Blind Lemon Jefferson, and Lonnie Johnson. The discographers Robert M. Dixon and John Godrich attribute Vocalion's rapid expansion to "intensive recording activity in the field."[11] Williams, of course, was behind the field recording program of BBC's two race series. These successes not only marked an evolution in his approach to the work but the impressive results showed that he was able to identify networks of artists who could, in turn, yield strong recordings on the road. Williams also increased the output and variety of BBC's race series by releasing dozens of recordings by the West Indian calypso composer and bandleader Lionel Belasco in August 1928 and again in August 1930. These recordings appear to have been made by other companies and perhaps reissued by BBC. This was not Williams's first encounter with Belasco's music. Shortly after he took charge at Paramount in 1923, the company issued six sides by Belasco's South American Orchestra. It is noteworthy that Williams would elect to release music by Belasco on three separate occasions and on two different labels; it suggests he was aware that Paramount's and Brunswick's catalogues could appeal to Black Americans of a wide variety of ethnicities and nationalities. Belasco, who was born in Venezuela and raised in Trinidad, is considered one of the most significant Trinidadian musicians and composers in the evolution and international rise of calypso.

At BBC, Williams worked closely with Jack and Dave Kapp, who were the driving forces behind the signing of the majority of popular jazz artists on Brunswick and Vocalion. But Williams worked with the Kapps on occasion with jazz groups, particularly in Kansas City. Dave Kapp had an association with the saxophonist Andy Kirk, who by 1929 was playing in Kansas City with his Clouds of Joy when Kapp and Williams recorded them in a Kansas City hotel. Vocalion released some of Kirk's records under the name Andy Kirk and His Twelve Clouds of Joy, and Brunswick released others as John Williams and His Memphis Stompers. This latter also marked the recording debut of the jazz pianist Mary Lou Williams (no relation to Ink) and featured several of her original compositions (including "Lotta Sax Appeal"). Williams and Dave Kapp also recorded Walter Page's Blue Devils in Kansas City in November 1929. Besides being noteworthy for documenting one of the first important jazz bands of the thriving Kansas City scene, this recording also marked the debut of Count Basie, Jimmie Rushing, and Oran Thaddeus "Hot Lips" Page. Williams and Kapp returned to Kansas City together a number of times over the next several years with even more significant results.

In early 1930, Williams continued making recordings in the field for Vocalion in Atlanta and Memphis. The Memphis session in February yielded Williams's first recordings of Memphis Minnie and Kansas Joe McCoy. Williams had heard the duo during his 1929 field visit to Memphis with Georgia Tom and Tampa Red; if he knew that they had recorded for Columbia in 1929, it did not stop him from recording them for Vocalion in February of 1930. Born Lizzie Douglas in Algiers, Louisiana in 1897, Minnie—whose family called her "Kid"—grew up in Walls, Mississippi. She developed enough skill as a guitarist, banjoist, and singer by adolescence that she ran away to Memphis at age thirteen, where she made a living busking on Beale Street and working part time as a prostitute. By the time Ink Williams encountered her, she had spent four years touring with a Ringling Brothers circus and had recently begun performing with the songwriter Joe McCoy (her second husband). Columbia had dubbed them "Memphis Minnie and Kansas Joe."[12] Undeterred by Minnie's history with Columbia, Williams recorded her and Kansas Joe on February 21, including "I'm Talking About You," and the iconic "Bumble Bee." The latter is a masterpiece of blues double entendre and marks the emergence of a female guitar-based blues musician who sang with the same sexual swagger as Ma Rainey. This song helped to launch Memphis Minnie's prolific recording career, spanning two decades of solid commercial success. It also began the longtime association of Williams with Joe McCoy.

With the recording of Memphis Minnie's "Bumble Bee," it appeared that Williams was ready to continue expanding the race record market at his usual torrid pace in 1930. Indeed, in only eighteen months, Williams had transformed BBC's race records division from a poorly organized set of labels to what the discographers Dixon and Godrich characterized as the "undisputed leader of the race market." However, the ripple effects of the Wall Street crash finally reached the Brunswick-Balke-Collander corporation. The BBC records division was sold to Warner Brothers, which changed the company name to Brunswick Radio Corporation (BRC) and moved the label's headquarters from Chicago to New York City. Bill Broonzy recorded for BRC, but his records were released under the name "Big Bill" on BRC's dime-store subsidiaries.[13] Williams's recording activity seems to have dropped off at this time, suggesting that his future at the label—or perhaps the future of the label itself—was in doubt. By the end of the summer of 1930, Aleta and Mayo Williams were no longer living at their palatial Michigan Avenue apartment; instead, they were renting a place at 608 Fifty-first Street, overlooking Washington Park. In October, Consolidated Film Industries bought BRC from Warner and discontinued the Brunswick race series, choosing instead to issue all of its race titles in the Vocalion 1000 series.

Amid the swirl of BBC's changing ownership, Ink Williams found some time to play football. Once again, Fritz Pollard had organized a professional barnstorming unit that planned a tour through the industrial heartland, including the swath of Ohio and Pennsylvania where the professional game and the NFL had first found their legs. The Fritz Pollard All-Stars featured Williams, Pollard, Butler, Slater, and a collection of names known in the collegiate ranks who never caught on with NFL teams. The All-Stars started their tour on November 2 in Chicago, eventually making their way to western Pennsylvania for back-to-back games in Pittsburgh. A highlight included a showdown between Pollard's team and a professional squad named the Majestic Radios, owned by the player-coach Art Rooney. Pollard's team lost 12–7, due to the stellar play of Art Rooney's brother, Jim, who scored two touchdowns for Pittsburgh. Ink Williams played the entire game at left end without substitution. Sol Butler wowed the crowd of sixty-five hundred at Bridgeville Speedway with a showcase in offense and defense, including an interception and a touchdown.[14] Art Rooney's team renamed itself the Pittsburgh Pirates in 1933 (and later, the Pittsburgh Steelers), the year it gained admission to the National Football League. The lineup included a Black player named Ray Kemp at tackle (the last season any Black player appeared in the NFL until 1946). Kemp, who grew up working in the coal mines of western Pennsylvania, starred at Duquesne University from 1926 to 1930, working there as a coach while getting his master's degree in 1931.

It is interesting that the box score for the game lists "Posey" in the role of umpire, which most likely means that the referee squad was integrated, with the legendary Cumberland "Cum" Posey, Jr. officiating. Both a basketball and baseball Hall of Famer, Posey was a major figure in Pittsburgh, where he was the owner of the Homestead Grays Negro Leagues baseball team and had played semi-pro football in Pittsburgh in the 1910s. Art Rooney's decision to play the Fritz Pollard All-Stars falls in line with his racially progressive legacy. His sons Art Jr. and Dan played significant roles in advocating for greater racial diversity in the head coaching ranks of the NFL.

The heartland tour of the Fritz Pollard All-Stars was supposed to come to a climactic finish on Thanksgiving Day in Columbus, Ohio, as part of the Wilberforce Homecoming events. Special train schedules had been arranged to accommodate visitors and a schedule stacked with contests between Wilberforce and West Virginia, as well as a match between Bluefield Colored Institute (now Bluefield State University) and Morehouse. The Fritz Pollard All-Stars were scheduled to play an all-star team of ex-Ohio State players, and proceeds were to benefit the Shriners.[15] Extreme cold caused the game to be postponed until December 4, when it was finally held in a driving rain. Turnout was very low, and the few who showed up to watch the teams slog through the mud were doubtless disappointed to find that Fritz Pollard and Duke Slater never bothered to suit up for the game, and instead coached from the sidelines in street clothes. Williams played the entire game, and Sol Butler proved the standout for Pollard's team, but the team was understood to be past its prime:

> The phantom-like ghosts of gridiron greats of yesteryears stalked through a sea of mud and mist here Sunday on Neil Park Stadium, only to be halted by a scrappy team of Ohio State All-Stars by a score of 12 to 0.[16]

The low turnout at the Columbus game, due to the bad weather also, likely had something to do with the collapsing economy, which was putting the squeeze on professional sports across the country.

The Great Depression also exacerbated several existing problems in the Black music market. For starters, Thomas A. Dorsey's relationship with Tampa Red deteriorated. The reasons are complex but are rooted partly in Tampa Red's increasingly erratic behavior (and its dissonance with Dorsey's growing religiosity), which came to a head during a field visit to Memphis. In Williams's recollection, Tampa's dalliance with an underage girl in Memphis brought his partnership with Dorsey to a sudden end:

> Dorsey was the brains of the outfit. I took both of them to Memphis and put them on stage there. And Tampa fell in love with a little girl, and he wouldn't even come back to Chicago with us. And that disgusted Dorsey, and from then on, they split up. They split up after that. And Dorsey went back then to his gospel shows.[17]

If Dorsey and Tampa parted ways after Memphis, it is not clear from the recording schedules of Vocalion. In fact, after the 1929 field trip to Memphis, the two recorded and released a number of singles, so perhaps this incident occurred in 1930 or some later time. Dorsey never mentioned his falling out with Tampa Red as a reason for stepping away from blues music. Instead, he diplomatically blamed his exit from the blues on his desire to be at home and on what he saw as the end of the blues as a viable means of moneymaking during the Depression:

> You know, I got tired of traveling, and Tampa, he continued to travel, see. I had a family, and I wanted to stay home. But the blues ran out. It collapsed, seemingly, or the blues singers, they had nothing to do. I don't know what happened to the blues, they seemed to drop it all at once, it just went *down*, and Mayo Williams and Jack Kapp, and Dave Kapp, used to be at Vocalion, and all the bigwigs there. They couldn't see what was happening, and the artists were falling out because they couldn't get work. Well, there was just a slump on the record business after two or three years. And I just

did get out before it happened. It just seemed like the whole thing changed around, and wasn't no work for anybody, and they began to lose contact with each other. The record companies, they started publicizing some other types of music, see.[18]

Although it would be impossible to pinpoint the beginning of the end of the blues market of the 1920s, Ma Rainey—who was known for paying her musicians well and who even bought their instruments for them—was unable to pay her band in early 1929; members began to drop out of her tour by April. By 1930, her band had completely disintegrated.[19]

The musical, cultural, and economic landscape of the blues had indeed shifted. Gone were the classic blues singers who had been so much a part of Williams's early career, such as Ma Rainey, Ida Cox, and Ethel Waters. In their place were some of the artists Williams had helped to usher in: Leroy Carr and Scrapper Blackwell, Tampa Red, various incarnations of the Hokum Boys and other "dirty blues" musicians. Gospel quartets had also begun to gather steam on Vocalion, Brunswick, and other race record labels. The popular music catalog of Brunswick and Vocalion included a substantial number of jazz and swing bands such as the Duke Ellington Orchestra, the Mills Brothers, and Cab Calloway and his band, alongside the label's biggest (white) star, Bing Crosby. Additionally, a more muscular, blues-based form of jazz, evolving in Kansas City, became a new force in jazz. However, it, too, was considered race music and in the purview of Ink Williams. (Ellington, the Mills Brothers, and Calloway were Black and performed historically Black styles of music, but those styles were not categorized as race music.) But a wave of relatively new names gained some prominence, still rooted in Memphis—particularly Memphis Minnie, whose guitar playing heralded a new incarnation of a strong female blueswoman, singing powerful critiques of men and making it plain that women were just as interested in nightlife as men were.

Notably absent from Vocalion as 1930 turned to 1931 was the music of Georgia Tom. By mid-1930, Dorsey's association with Tampa Red was finished, and his recording sessions became infrequent. Progressively over the 1920s, Dorsey had begun to focus greater effort on writing blues-influenced sacred music—the style of music we now know as gospel. At that time, combining blues music with sacred text and expression was shocking to many; Dorsey's experiments with gospel in the 1920s had met with mixed results. Yet by 1930, Dorsey had begun to make some headway in the religious music world, appearing that year at the National Baptist Convention. By 1931, he had taken a job directing the choir at Pilgrim Baptist Church in Chicago, and his role as an arranger for Williams had ended. In 1932, Dorsey's wife, Nettie Harper, died giving birth to the couple's son. Two days later, their newborn son died, too. Dorsey was overwhelmed with grief, which is said to have been the source of inspiration for his genre-defining gospel song, "Take My Hand, Precious Lord." He made his final bow as Georgia Tom with the prototypical gospel blues "How About You," which he recorded for Vocalion in 1932.

As one of Williams's "lieutenants" at Paramount, Brunswick, and Vocalion, Dorsey had an influence on the blues that was—and remains—immeasurable. To call Dorsey a skilled arranger, songwriter, and talent scout is a gross understatement; without Dorsey, Williams was like a general without a cavalry, suddenly without his eyes and ears in the field. The loss of Dorsey would—along with the shifting tides of the Depression and its impact on the record business—be a major test of Williams's ability to adapt and to find new lieutenants who could help him understand the evolving landscape of blues music in America. Williams returned to some of his old tactics from the early days at Paramount, resuming his practice of attending blues competitions and signing the runners-up. He also developed a working relationship with a St. Louis club owner named Charles Johnson. In interviews, Williams was tight-lipped about his vices, but he appeared to have a growing penchant for gambling and playing the horses. Johnson was a gambling buddy who ran a "recording club" in St. Louis:

> [Johnson] had a club in St. Louis, a recording club, and we used to hold contests in the theaters, and I would go to this club and say, "I'm gonna record some people" and go to a couple contests. Now, there will also be other recording companies at these contests. But I could take the runner-up and make a star out of her, easier than I could take the star or the winner of the contest.[20]

Johnson shopped talent to various record labels, likely including Williams's chief competitor in Chicago, Lester Melrose, who signed several artists out of St. Louis, such as Big Joe Williams, receiving a fee in return for his services. Johnson's recording club became an important new source of talent for Williams—in particular, William Bunch, better known as Peetie Wheatstraw. Wheatstraw's origins are murky—he was born in either Tennessee or Arkansas. He consciously cultivated his mysterious persona to great effect, winning a large and loyal following in St. Louis and East St. Louis. Equally murky is how Williams landed a contract with Wheatstraw. Though Williams had a working agreement with Johnson's recording club, Williams claimed to have "won" Peetie Wheatstraw in a gambling spree with Johnson. Wheatstraw would make his debut at Vocalion with a session in September 1930, beginning one of blues music's most prolific recording careers. As wild and demonic as Wheatstraw's public persona was, Williams remembered he "wouldn't bother anybody":

> Wouldn't step on a fly. Was as nice as he could be but drank like hell. Yeah. And in drinking, it proved his undoing, 'cause he got killed in an automobile

crash. And he was a natural comedian too. Yeah, and you asked why he was making up his name "Peetie Wheatstraw, the Devil's Son-in-Law, the High Sheriff," and I says, "Well, who are you?" He says, "I'm Peetie Wheatstraw, the Devil's Son-in-Law, the High Sheriff of Hell." And he says, "How the hell am I gonna get all that on a hit record?" That's what his name is.[21]

Of the 161 records Wheatstraw made for Vocalion, Decca, and Bluebird, 159 were credited either to "Peetie Wheatstraw—The Devil's Son-in-Law" or "Peetie Wheatstraw—The High Sheriff from Hell." Landing a contract with Wheatstraw was a win for Ink Williams, but the world that Williams had known and helped to build since his arrival in Chicago in 1921 continued to crumble around him.

In the fall of 1931, another cast of Black football greats—both past and present—were assembled for a barnstorming tour of the Colored All-Stars, beginning with a showdown in Burnham, Illinois with the Burnham Athletic Club. By this point, Williams was thirty-seven years old and playing only occasionally. Sol Butler was thirty-six, and Duke Slater was a relative youngster at thirty-three. The "owner" of the Colored All-Stars was Dr. A. C. Johnson of Howard University, who announced that he planned several exhibitions for the team on the East Coast.[22]

Quite the opposite proved true, however; on Thursday, December 17, the *Los Angeles Times* announced the arrival of the Colored All-Stars for a Sunday game against a team of West Coast all-stars at White Sox Park in Los Angeles. The Colored All-Stars included Fritz Pollard, Joe Lillard, Sol Butler, Ink Williams, Duke Slater, and Halley Harding.[23] Harding's presence reveals some interesting synergy around the early era of integrated NFL football, the reintegration of the league in 1946, and Ink Williams. Harding was a native of Rock Island, Illinois; born in 1905, he was fifteen the year the first-ever NFL game (by any team) was played in Rock Island. The team featured the former Minnesota All-American Bobby Marshall at end. Bobby Marshall and Fritz Pollard were the league's sole Black players in its inaugural season. Marshall, Duke Slater, and Sol Butler all starred for the Rock Island Independents between 1920 and 1926. The Independents had also tried to snare Ink Williams. Just three years prior to the arrival of the Colored All-Stars in Los Angeles, Halley Harding had encountered Ink Williams in Marshall, Texas. Williams was then an assistant coach at Paul Quinn College, and Harding was the star quarterback for the opposing Wiley Wildcats. The assistant coach at Wiley was an English professor, Melvin B. Tolsen, who famously coached the Wiley debate team. (Tolsen was later played by Denzel Washington in the film *The Great Debaters*.) Harding played a significant role in the reintegration of the NFL in 1946.

When the All-Stars set out for the West Coast, Harding expressed serious trepidation about the team's finances, predicting they would run out of money and be stranded out West.[24] He was not wrong. Arriving in California, the group discovered that the promoters had wired them back in Chicago to say the first game was canceled.

Coached by A. C. Johnson of Howard, the Colored All-Stars played three poorly attended games—one in Los Angeles, one in San Diego, and one in San Francisco—and each against all-star teams led by Californian collegiate stars such as USC's quarterback Marshall Duffield and the future Hall of Fame fullback Ernie Nevers, who had starred at Stanford and played against Ink Williams in the NFL.[25]

Ink Williams was not without personal contacts in Los Angeles. His sister-in-law, Pearl Stokes (Aleta's oldest sister), had married a local trombonist and jazz and theater musician named Harry Southard. Pearl had married Harry in 1926 when she was thirty and Southard was fifty-one. Pearl and Aleta's mother, Julia Stokes, had moved in with the Southards by the time the census came knocking in 1930. Though Harry Southard was by this time playing trombone in Los Angeles theaters, he had made a reputation for himself in the city's jazz circles in the 1910s and '20s as the leader of a five-piece band called the Black and Tan Jazz Orchestra, widely considered the best Black jazz band in the city. The arrival of the New Orleans trombonist and bandleader Edward "Kid" Ory marked a turning point in both Los Angeles jazz and Southard's fame. Southard's clarinetist and saxophonist, Paul Howard, went on to play with Jelly Roll Morton and King Oliver when both were working in Los Angeles.[26] According to Jelly Roll Morton, Southard's band played from sheet music, was baffled by Ory's improvisation, and struggled with the New Orleans style.

By 1931, when Williams was visiting Los Angeles, Kid Ory, Jelly Roll Morton, and King Oliver had long since relocated to Chicago, where they had recorded for Williams on Paramount. One has to think that a visit by Williams to the Southard home must have included conversation about these men. It is entirely possible—likely, even—that Southard and Stokes had encouraged Kid Ory, Jelly Roll Morton, and other West Coast jazz musicians to seek out Williams when they moved to Chicago. Southard must have been past his musical prime, was someone Williams thought wouldn't cut it on record, or wasn't motivated enough to make a trip to Chicago; whatever the reason, one of Los Angeles's leading early jazz musicians never capitalized on his brother-in-law's influential role at Vocalion to make commercial recordings. Though the Black and Tan Orchestra maintained a space in the collective memory of Los Angeles jazz circles late into the twentieth century, Southard never recorded. Not long after Williams's visit, he had quit music and opened up a barbershop, but he was known far and wide as a preeminent music teacher. When the young Horace Tapscott and his mother first moved to Los Angeles from Houston in the 1940s, they immediately went to Southard's barbershop to set up lessons for Horace.[27] Tapscott went on to join Lionel Hampton and played a significant role in the civil rights movement and the music industry in Los Angeles.

Although Williams had personal connections in Los Angeles, three games in nearly a month in California meant the trip was a bust. The team couldn't generate the funds to get home. Nearly a month after leaving Chicago for Los Angeles, the *Chicago Defender* was unimpressed when Mayo Williams and two of his teammates came back to Chicago without the rest of the team:

> Here were three gentlemen, Mayo "Ink" Williams, Nate Blueitt, and Elmer Brown, all smiles over their trip even though they knew well their fellow grid stars were still on the Coast and are likely to be there some few weeks yet unless something, accounted for to date, turns up to provide bus fare home.

Brown (the trip's primary funder) and Williams (one of the three managers of the team) told the *Defender* that it "was a fine trip." The *Defender* wondered "if their statement will meet with the approval of the other players who are still somewhere on the Coast."[28]

However, the ugly optics of the situation did not spell the end of Williams's friendship and association with Pollard, Slater, Butler, Harding, and Lillard. Instead, their collaborating forces within the professional and ex-collegiate ranks of white football stars in California helped forge a lasting alliance that ultimately changed the course of the game.

CHAPTER 18

Maroon Tiger

As the fortunes of so many musicians and Americans were paralyzed by growing economic turmoil and abject poverty, the Great Depression cast the fortunes of BBC in doubt. Once again, Mayo Williams turned to football. Nineteen thirty-two had been his quietest year in the game; he refereed in the Lincoln-Wilberforce game in Chicago in October.[1] He started his final significant chapter in football in 1933, finding refuge from the Depression within the walls of Atlanta's Morehouse College, where he worked with the school's football team from the fall of 1933 through the fall of 1934.

Morehouse College was founded in 1867 as a beacon of Black higher education in the wake of the Civil War. Originally named Atlanta Theological Institute, this all-Black college emerged by the twentieth century as one of the foremost centers of Black intellectual activity under the leadership of John Hope, the college's first Black president, who served from 1906 to 1936. Hope had graduated from Brown University in 1894, and he dedicated his presidency to fostering the same intellectual spirit at Morehouse that he recalled as a student at Brown.[2] Hope's relationship with W. E. B. Du Bois in the Niagara Movement and its successor, the NAACP, made him widely celebrated for his advocacy of higher learning. Hope's time at Brown overlapped with that of John D. Rockefeller Jr., and Hope maintained a relationship with the Rockefeller family after graduation. The Rockefellers, in turn, provided significant support to Morehouse, as well as its sister school, Atlanta Baptist Female Seminary, later renamed Spelman College in honor of Rockefeller's wife (and Atlanta Baptist Female Seminary benefactor), Laura Spelman.

President Hope also maintained his connection to Brown, regularly attending graduation ceremonies in order to recruit faculty from among the school's Black graduates. Ink Williams met Hope at Brown's 1921 graduation ceremonies, but Williams had declined the college president's job offer (coaching football at Morehouse) in order to work at Black Swan. However, Hope was successful in recruiting other Brown graduates to teach at Morehouse, including Louis Lorenzo Redding (Brown, class of '23), who had cofounded Providence's Alpha Phi Alpha chapter with Williams, and his younger brother, J. Saunders Redding (class of '28). Louis, who served as part of the NAACP legal team that argued *Brown v. Board of Education* in 1954, had moved on from Morehouse by the time Williams arrived in 1933. But J. Saunders Redding (who in time became the first Black faculty member at both Brown and Cornell) was still at Morehouse. Redding's recollection of that period of his life was rife with angst:

> When I came up for graduation [from Brown] in 1928, it still had not occurred to me to think of finding work to do that would turn my education to some account. My brother had been graduated from Harvard Law, and I thought randomly of earning money to follow him there. My credits were transferred. But I earned very little and I could discover in myself no absorbing interest, no recognition of a purpose. The summer blazed along to August. Then, out of the blue, John Hope offered me a job at Morehouse College in Atlanta. I took it. I was twenty-one in October of that fall, a lonely, random-brooding youth, uncertain, purposeless, lost, and yet so tightly wound that every day I lived big-eyed as death in sharp expectancy of a mortal blow or a vitalizing fulfillment of the unnamable aching emptiness within me.

Redding's sense of emptiness only deepened when he arrived at Morehouse College:

> But Morehouse College and the southern environment disappointed me. The college tottered with spiritual decay. Its students were unimaginative, predatory, pretentious. Theirs was a naked, metal-hard world, stripped of all but its material values, and these glittered like artificial gems in the sun of their ambition. An unwholesome proportion of the faculty was effete, innocuous, and pretentious also, with a flabby softness of intellectual and spiritual fiber and even a lack of personal force. They clustered together like sheared sheep in a storm. They were a sort of mass-man, conscious of no spiritual status even as men, much less as a people. They were a futile, hamstrung group, who took a liberal education (they despised mechanical and technical learning) to be a process of devitalization and to be significant in extrinsics only. They awarded a lot of medallions and watch charms. Try as I might, I could feel no kinship with them. Obviously my home was not among them.[3]

Redding's writings are harshest when he comments on people who share his Black middle-class background. The depiction of an intellectually and spiritually stagnant Morehouse College is particularly stinging when compared with Redding's far more favorable writings on life as a Black student at the mostly white Brown University.

Though Morehouse may have been a haven of stodginess, its football program was highly respected, and with good reason. As Ink Williams had written for the *Chicago Whip* in his preseason forecast for college football back in 1921:

> Morehouse, for years, has won the championship of the extreme south in which vicinity such schools as Tuskeegee, Atlanta, and Talladega stand supreme in athletics. The success of Morehouse is due to the spirit with which they play the game, and the large squad from which the coaches pick the eleven.[4]

On October 1, 1933, the *Atlanta Constitution* announced that Ink Williams had been hired at Morehouse as an assistant football coach and that he was expected to implement a new and more competitive system of play. Morehouse was then considered one of the "Big Seven" Black colleges of the Southern Intercollegiate Athletic Conference (along with Alabama Teachers College, Clark University, Fisk University, Knoxville, Morris Brown College, and the Tuskegee Institute). Between October 6 and November 30, Morehouse played home games in Atlanta against Benedict College, Paine College, Clark, and Morris Brown and traveled for games in Tallahassee (Florida A&M), Nashville (Fisk), and Alabama at Tuskegee and Talledega.[5]

It is unclear who recruited Ink Williams to coach at Morehouse, but he was there to learn the ropes for a year before assuming interim head coaching duties in 1934 while the head coach, Franklin Forbes, took a sabbatical to attend graduate school. A native Philadelphian, Forbes had played several seasons of professional baseball for Negro Leagues teams in New York and New Jersey, then studied at the YMCA academy in Springfield, Massachusetts prior to attending—and graduating from—Morehouse in 1928.

The Morehouse Maroon Tigers lost their opening game against Florida A&M but won their second at Ponce de Leon Field in Atlanta against Benedict. Following the Atlanta game, Williams worked with the Maroon Tigers to shore up their weak defensive line while head coach Franklin Forbes focused on offense.[6] By mid-November, the *Atlanta Constitution* called the defense "air tight."[7] Anticipation ran high for Morehouse's final home game against the Clark Panthers, and Williams's defensive line was now called "legendary." Two thousand turned out to see the Maroon Tigers play at Ponce de Leon Park, where they eliminated Clark from contention for Atlanta's Loving Cup, and the players carried Williams and Forbes off the field.[8]

The lush enclave of the Morehouse and Spelman campuses, and their close proximity to the urban life of Atlanta, was likely a familiar and comfortable space for Ink Williams to wait out the Great Depression. The Morehouse-Spelman campuses, though accessible to the city, were culturally removed from Atlanta's urban Black community. Thomas A. Dorsey remembered this as a kid growing up in Atlanta, and Harry Pace's experience with Atlanta University was similar. J. Saunders Redding found the class-based cultural disconnect toxic:

> We were all withdrawn from the heady, brawling, lusty stream of culture which had nourished us and which was the stream by whose turbid waters all of America fed. We were spiritually homeless, dying and alone, each on his separate hammock of memory and experience.[9]

This "brawling, lusty stream of culture" is where Redding could have—had he ventured beyond the class-constructed walls of Morehouse—found Willie McTell, the virtuosic, blind songster, master of the 12-string guitar, and prolific race recording artist for a multitude of labels. McTell, though a self-described "rambler" who ranged across the Southeast and up into Chicago and New York, was a fixture in Atlanta then and could be found playing regularly at venues like the Pig and Whistle in Atlanta, on street corners, at tent revivals and medicine shows, and on passenger trains. It is unknown in which of these locations Williams encountered McTell while working at Morehouse, but he recruited him to record for Vocalion in September 1933. This was also the time when W. E. B. Du Bois returned to Atlanta to be at Morehouse, and Williams doubtless encountered DuBois, Hope, Redding, and Fletcher Henderson's father (Fletcher Hamilton Henderson) at Alpha Phi Alpha fraternity meetings at Atlanta's alumni chapter house. Williams, of course, was adept at reading human nature and fitting into seemingly any social circumstance, and it is likely he enjoyed the high culture of these Morehouse men. But what did Du Bois and the others make of their fraternity brother's drinking, gambling, and music-recording activities? Williams was unusually well traveled for any man of his era, particularly for a Black man living in the Deep South. Between working in Colorado in high school, his wartime service, his collegiate and professional football travels, and his commercial field-recording trips, Williams had visited at least thirty-one states and the District of Columbia, and he must have seemed profoundly unique in this respect. Williams had a pattern of ingratiating himself among his peers, and he did have much in common with these other men. Du Bois, of course, had written powerfully about the cultural significance of Black spirituals and had been a backer of Harry Pace's Black Swan Records. Fletcher Hamilton Henderson was certainly well aware of his own son's prolific career, including his time as the house arranger for Black Swan. But what would Du Bois have thought of Blind Lemon's "Matchbox Blues" or Ma Rainey's "Black Bottom Stomp" or Speckled Red's "Dirty Dozen"? And for all of Redding's longing to be nourished by the "turbid waters" of raw, vernacular culture, why did he not ask his fraternity brother to take him along to see Bumble Bee Slim, just a few blocks away?

Perhaps the men just talked about a safe, comfortable common ground—like Morehouse football. If so, by 1933, these conversations inevitably must have turned to the professional game. Despite any generational or class-based misgivings that Ivy League men such as Du Bois and Hope may have had about the professional game, it is likely they saw the NFL's final detour into segregation with consternation. Ink Williams's old friend Duke Slater had continued playing in the league with the Chicago Cardinals until 1931. In 1932, the Cardinals had signed the University of Oregon's star player, Joe Lillard, a Black running back whose flashy style of play was matched only by his explosive temper on the field, two traits that did not sit well with segregationists in the league. In 1933, the NFL Pittsburgh Pirates (later named the Pittsburgh Steelers) signed the former Duquense star tackle Ray Kemp, who was cut from the team partway through the season by Coach Forrest "Jap" Douds, despite strong play and support from Pittsburg's fans. Lillard and Kemp were the last two Black players in the league in 1933; despite being in their athletic prime, neither found work in the league in 1934, and no Blacks played in the NFL again until 1946. It is impossible to imagine that this development did not come up in conversation at the Alpha Phi Alpha fraternity gatherings.

Williams, Slater, and other Black athletes from Chicago remained staunchly committed to drawing attention to the world-class accomplishments of Black athletes. Just before heading to Morehouse, Williams and Slater helped to officiate at an amateur track meet in the summer of 1933, which featured E. O. Gourdin, who won the silver medal in the broad jump at the 1924 Olympics, and sprinter Eddie Tolan, who won gold in both the 100- and 200-meter sprints at the 1932 Olympics. (The Chicago native Ralph Metcalfe won silver and bronze in both events.) The twelve-team meet featured a celebrity 75-yard sprint, with Bill "Bojangles" Robinson running backward against Tolan.[10]

The legendary tennis great and civil rights activist Arthur Ashe once wrote that "If sports indeed related something of the character of the country between 1919 and 1945, then football was a less than satisfactory commentary on American life."[11] Such was true about the sickening power of a minority of racist NFL franchise owners that had shoved Ink Williams, Fritz Pollard, and Sol Butler forever to the sidelines in 1927, and the growing financial power that enabled the league's ownership group to bar Blacks fully after 1933. The existence of this off-the-books agreement is still disputed today, though a satisfactory explanation of the absence of Black players in the NFL has never been offered. Some team owners and coaches at the time ludicrously claimed that Blacks were excluded for their own safety. Fritz Pollard angrily responded to such claims, saying:

> I played twenty years with white teams and against them, and was never hurt so I had to quit the game. . . . I weighed only 160 pounds or so, and they never made me or Inky Williams quit either. So I can't say that's the reason they're keeping us out of the game.[12]

The color bar robbed Black players of an important source of income at a time when all Americans needed any cash they could get. Pollard's banking venture and his Chicago Black Hawks team—the all-Black traveling football squad that played exhibitions against White teams—went bust on account of the Depression. He moved from Chicago to Harlem to get a fresh start.

The NFL's freezeout of Black players—ostensibly part of the league's workforce—mirrored the experience and frustration of Black workers who had historically voted Republican. President Hoover's administration had frustrated Black Republicans, and many—including Mayo Williams—shifted party affiliation to elect Franklin D. Roosevelt. In the summer of 1934, Williams and several other Black veterans of World War I organized a dinner at Chicago's Hotel Grand to honor and back Arthur W. Mitchell's historic run for Congress. Veterans who spoke at the event "insisted that a new day has dawned in Negro politics and that no longer is the Negro dominated by Republicanism or by bosses or so-called leaders seeking to make themselves whole and at the same time leaving the masses of the people to suffer."[13] Mitchell's defeat of the incumbent Republican congressman Oscar DePriest marked the first time a Black Democrat was elected to national office, signaling a sea change in Black electoral politics. Williams's support for Mitchell marked a split from his friend, fellow veteran officer, and fraternity brother, the attorney William H. Temple—as well as Temple's former law partner, Benjamin W. Clayton. Both lost badly in the Republican primary for Congress and Illinois state legislatures, respectively.[14]

The fall of 1934 was a time of continued transition. In September, Aleta Williams's mother, Julia Stokes, passed away and was buried in Cairo, Illinois. At Morehouse, Franklin Forbes—the head coach of the football team—went on sabbatical for the 1934–35 academic year to get a masters degree at Michigan State University. Ink Williams was put in charge as head coach for the 1934 season. He brought on an all-new corps of assistant coaches, including T. B. Ellis, a student/player/coach who would later become head coach at Jackson State University, and the esteemed Samuel Howard Archer. Archer was a former football star at Colgate, a friend of W. E. B. Du Bois, and a former professor and dean at Morehouse who had become the Morehouse College president in 1931 while John Hope served double duty as the Atlanta

University president. (Archer chose Morehouse's school colors of maroon and white, which also were the school colors at Colgate.)[15]

Morehouse opened the 1934 season at Ponce de Leon Park against Florida A&M. The top Black collegiate teams that season were expected to be Wilberforce and Tuskegee, which opened the season against one another and were expected to play a Thanksgiving tilt at Soldier Field in Chicago. New Orleans's Xavier University was also expected to be among the top teams. For his part, Williams transformed Morehouse into a team to be reckoned with. When Morehouse arrived in Montgomery to play the Alabama State Hornets in early November, the *Montgomery Advertiser* wrote that the "once famous" Ink Williams had made Morehouse a dangerous opponent.[16] Though the Hornets had crushed Morehouse two years earlier, the Montgomery press credited Williams's two years at Morehouse for turning the team around at "such a fast clip that they are a much feared aggregation."[17] By game time, the *Advertiser* was pushing Williams—the "famous negro All-American" (without specifying that Williams was actually a third-team All-American)—as a draw for fans.[18]

Williams led the team to four wins against three losses and two ties.[19] By all accounts, Williams's time as head coach of the Morehouse Tigers was a success, turning a mediocre squad into a formidable opponent. Despite the success, Morehouse's regular head coach, Franklin Forbes, was coming back to Morehouse from Michigan State University after completing his masters in physical education. Though the *New York Age* announced that President Archer was interested in retaining Williams as an assistant coach, Williams left Atlanta to rejoin the fray of the record business.[20] After just two years at Morehouse, a new landscape was awaiting Williams: Fritz Pollard was now in Harlem, and Thomas A. Dorsey was firmly ensconced in Chicago's Pilgrim Baptist Church. Williams's next moves would reflect his resiliency, resourcefulness, and musical vision.

CHAPTER 19

Sepia

It was spring in Georgia, a pleasant time of year to go for a long drive. Now forty years old and officially finished with football, Ink Williams still enjoyed a little adventure. And on this spring afternoon, adventure looked like a seven-hundred-mile drive from Atlanta to Chicago with four musicians: the pianist Georgia White; the rambling Piedmont blues master and songster Blind Willie McTell and his wife, Kate; and McTell's guitar-playing sideman, Curley Weaver. On Saturday, April 20, 1935, Williams loaded the musicians and their instruments into his car, pulled out of Atlanta at 5:00 p.m., and drove until he couldn't stay awake any longer. After stopping along the roadside for a quick nap, Williams resumed driving until the group cruised beneath the lights of Chicago's Lake Michigan Avenue to arrive at the musicians' hotel. Monday, Wednesday, and Friday were days off, but on Tuesday and Thursday they were booked for sessions at the Decca recording studio, giving them plenty of time to explore the city's rich musical nightlife. Under Williams's guidance, Kate and Willie mingled with dancers and musicians at mixed-race dance halls, jammed with white hillbilly musicians, and played at Jack Johnson's nightclub, where Willie met the now fifty-seven-year-old ex-heavyweight champion.[1] It was a whirlwind week, yielding eight crisp recordings, including "Ticket Agent Blues," "Dying Gambler," and "Hillbilly Willie's Blues." McTell's twelve-string guitar—whether accompanied by a second guitar, or piano, or solo—achieved the same dance-band effect that had drawn Williams to Papa Charlie Jackson and Blind Blake. Willie and Kate, like Williams, were educated, verbose, adventuresome, able to code-switch across races and classes and held some religious convictions without being entirely sober. It was a combination that Williams enjoyed—good music, good company, and a good car. At the end of their heady week in Chicago, he drove them all seven hundred miles back to Atlanta.

Despite the tumultuous changes at BBC, Ink Williams had never really left his position as race records director of Vocalion and Brunswick; instead, he simply had waited out the transition to new ownership. In 1934, the British company Decca Records decided to start a label in the United States, hiring Jack Kapp to run its race series. Kapp, in turn, supervised the buyout of Vocalion from Consolidated Film Industries and wasted no time in bringing Williams on board as his race records talent scout. The new company began recording in New York City and Chicago in August 1934. By the end of the year, Decca had released several dozen records, all priced at thirty-five cents, notably underselling the competition.[2] The work was plentiful, the job was secure, and Jack Kapp placed a great deal of trust and responsibility in Williams. Decca worked to centralize its operations, shutting down its permanent studio in Chicago, meaning that Mayo Williams would conduct only a handful of brief, intensive sessions a year in Chicago.[3] With the label centralized in New York, Decca offered to move Mayo and Aleta Williams there:

> They tried to get me to go to New York, Decca did. Decca had pretty good connections, and they were gonna get my wife a job and everything, but I still liked Chicago, and commuted from Chicago to New York.[4]

The relocation offer, plus Decca's willingness to allow Williams to refuse it and work remotely, shows that the Kapp brothers and Decca considered Williams a valuable, trustworthy, and essential part of a successful Decca organization. Such high regard was a kind of job security that had been unattainable during the height of the Depression. Williams knew a good thing when he saw it. After the 1934 season at Morehouse—despite Morehouse President Samuel Howard Archer's interest in his staying on as Franklin Forbes's assistant coach—Williams stopped his regular involvement in football and focused all of his attention on scouting talent and producing records.

Williams's arrival at Decca intersected with another major change in music—the growing prevalence of electronic, amplified jukeboxes. Williams had, of course, been involved in installing some early jukeboxes in Chicago in the late 1920s, but the popularity of jukeboxes—particularly in bars, clubs, and eating establishments that primarily served Black patrons ("jukebox" and "juke joint" have a common Black vernacular derivation)—had a significant impact on the orientation of the record business; Decca was particularly attuned to the jukebox market and used it to track the popularity of its singles.

At Decca, Williams immediately began recording the artists who had been reliable race record hitmakers for Vocalion and Brunswick, as well as a few he had first encountered at Paramount. Peetie Wheatstraw, James "Kokomo" Arnold, Memphis Minnie, Kansas Joe McCoy, Blind Joe Taggart, Georgia White, Johnny Temple, and Victoria Spivey were all familiar faces from his

Vocalion and Paramount days whom he brought to Decca. He also recorded several new groups for Decca during his first year—most notably Roosevelt "the Honey Dripper" Sykes, Bumble Bee Slim, Blind Willie McTell and Kate McTell, and Red Nelson. Several of these "new" acts were, in fact, veteran recording artists like McTell who had made noteworthy records for other labels but were free agents following the turmoil of the Depression. Williams even worked in a loosely managerial capacity for Amos "Bumble Bee Slim" Easton, Johnny Temple, and Peetie Wheatstraw.

Williams's old employers, the Wisconsin Chair Company, had stumbled badly through the Depression. After three years of inactivity, Paramount Records was closed for good in 1935. Williams suspected there was money to be made from the old Paramount masters and returned to Port Washington, only to learn that he had arrived too late:

> I jumped on the train again and went on up to Port Washington to get all of the masters. . . . Well, at any rate, John Steiner had the same idea in mind. . . . I got up there and they had *junked* all of the masters for copper . . . and there wasn't a thing. And I got a contract for *salvage* on anything I could get from the catalog.[5]

John Steiner was a native of Milwaukee and a professional chemist who had translated his love of early jazz and blues into an independent record label (S/D Records) specializing in historical reissues and earning him powerful friends such as the legendary talent scout and producer John Hammond. Steiner and Williams knew each other well—they both lived in Chicago and ran in the same circles. Williams claimed to hold a contract giving him rights to the Paramount masters but never filed a lawsuit to regain what he claimed was rightfully his. Although Williams's business practices were often nefarious, he rarely lied by commission or fabricated truths wholesale in interviews. But he deliberately left certain mysteries unexplained. There did not appear to be any animosity between Williams and Steiner—in fact, the only recorded interview involving Williams where he sounds at all relaxed was conducted by the jazz musician Bill Russell and John Steiner in Chicago in 1970. Williams and Steiner sound like old friends, not in the least bit litigious. Perhaps Williams developed a side hustle with Steiner, cutting Decca out of the mix. Most likely, Williams felt there wasn't enough money to be made from Paramount reissues to warrant a legal battle with Steiner. Whatever the true circumstances were, we do not know.

Williams also remained close to Maurice Supper, his closest ally among the executives at the Wisconsin Chair Company and Paramount. Williams had been advising Supper as early as 1923 on entrepreneurial matters, such as the "Black Patti" brand hair straightener marketed to Black women. In

1936 Williams became the spokesman and vice president for Supper's Mello Brown Company, a line of cosmetics for Black men and women. As incongruous as this may appear with Williams's work in sports and music, Ink and Aleta had traveled to St. Louis in March 1935 to attend an event at Poro College, the iconic Black cosmetology school and hive of industry founded by the entrepreneur Annie Turnbo Malone. Judge Sidney Jones—an Alpha Phi Alpha brother of Williams's and a friend of Paul Robeson's—had helped to organize the event. John Hope, the president of Atlanta University, spoke at a fundraising dinner, with Harry Pace as master of ceremonies.[6]

But Maurice Supper was no Annie Turnbo Malone, and Mello Brown would not become the economic powerhouse that Poro College was. Advertisements featuring Williams's name and face in the *Pittsburgh Courier* claimed that working as a sales rep for Mello Brown cosmetic products was a way to "MAKE BIG MONEY":

> Mr. Williams Offers: To Send You Everything You Need To MAKE Up To $45 A WEEK. Send no money. JUST HELP ME—I TRUST YOU—YOU TAKE NO RISK. I guarantee you'll MAKE MONEY AT ONCE. I offer men and women of our own an easy way to make the money they need. . . . Just show my MELLO BROWN Hair Preparations, Cosmetics, Medicines . . . 150 popular products to your friends and neighbors. No experience required.

Interested parties only needed to clip and send a coupon from the *Pittsburgh Courier* to get started on making "BIG MONEY" from the Port Washington, Wisconsin–based company.[7] How brief Mello Brown's lifespan was is unclear—but Williams's dramatic advertisements vanished from newspapers shortly afterwards. Nevertheless, the venture shows quite plainly that he—like any good businessman of his day—maintained his professional network and never passed up a good opportunity for quick money. In the few interviews Williams ever gave, he never mentioned his ongoing relationship with interests in Wisconsin. Perhaps Williams didn't foresee the intense commercial interest that would arise in the old Paramount records; for a man as focused on living in the moment as Williams was, this would have been understandable. Not only were the Paramount sides mostly obscure in comparison to his commercial successes at Decca, Vocalion, and Brunswick but sound-recording technology had changed so substantially that the Paramount sides sound as though they come from a different century, when in fact he had been gone from the company fewer than nine years. One has to wonder if Paramount's artists would have receded so far from public memory had the catalog been reissued as part of Williams's portfolio at Decca.

At Decca, Williams was part of a large operation. His years at BBC (Vocalion and Brunswick) had been a step up from Paramount, with robust pop, jazz, hillbilly, and ethnic imprints alongside the race records catalog; but Decca was the American branch of an international corporation, with deep pockets, hundreds of releases, and many high-profile artists who reached an international market. Williams became a talent scout for Decca's race records imprints. "Race" as a marketing category had changed since his years at Paramount, where it had been a wholesale form of musical segregation—placing all Black artists of all genres into the monolithic category of "race records." At BBC, Brunswick and Vocalion had slightly more porous categorizations for Black artists—popular Black jazz and swing artists (such as Duke Ellington or the Mills Brothers) were marketed as jazz and popular music. On Decca, marketing based on race, class, and ethnicity was slightly more nuanced, with imprints for Scottish, Mexican, East Indian, South American, and other recordings. Black American artists on the label were not placed simply under "race": the Louisiana Creole music of the Black accordionist Amédé Ardoin landed in Decca's Cajun/creole series; calypso artists were marketed in the Caribbean series; and Duke Ellington, Cab Calloway, and other Black swing artists were to be found in the popular/jazz series. At Decca, then, "race" (sometimes titled the "Sepia Series") became increasingly synonymous with blues, gospel, and a newly evolving sound that would eventually become known as "rhythm and blues" or R&B, whose audience prior to the 1950s consisted of urban working-class and rural Blacks.

Though Decca used Williams strategically to help sign some significant Black artists to various Decca catalogs, his main responsibility was the race records catalog. And at Decca, all of these artists—regardless of race, class, or ethnicity—were running into one another at the studio. Decca's studios in Chicago and New York became places of racial, ethnic, and class mixing, and Williams regularly brushed up against international stars such as Bing Crosby and Cab Calloway. This new environment magnified awareness of class differences between "race" artists and others on Decca, and Williams caught flak from friends and colleagues who derided him as the "Dog Catcher." "They'd say, 'Here comes Williams the Dog Catcher.'"[8]

The paradox of Ink Williams was that he at once championed these "dogs" in front of wealthy and famous elites—to the detriment of his own social standing—while continuing to dole out poor financial treatment to the musicians he signed and recorded for the label. The harmonica player Hammie Nixon colorfully recalled playing for change with his partner, Sleepy John Estes, the day Williams saw them on a Chicago sidewalk:

> Chicago was full of soup lines. Somehow or another, those guys would get money from somewhere. We had a jug then, you know. I carried that gallon jug back then, had it full of money. Really, when . . . Mayo Williams, run in on us, we had almost a jug of money that day. We just set it down and

people would put money into it, must have around 500 people around us that day. We were there at around Calumet, and Forty-seventh and Calumet. He told us that we were too good to be on the streets like that. He said, "I can put you all making records, you know."

Williams told Estes and Nixon to come down to the Decca studio on July 9, 1935. The day before the session, the two bluesmen scrambled to borrow a guitar. Estes, who was blind in one eye (hence the nickname, "Sleepy"), got a guitar, got drunk, and nearly derailed the whole project:

> Shoot, I and John, we slicked around so much; I remember one time me and John were walking down the street, we were supposed to be making records the next day. A man had lent us a guitar. John got drunk, went to take a step, down a step, went down three or four! Man, I thought he was dead, the guitar was all around his neck. We had to make records the next day at 10 o'clock.

According to Nixon, Decca never paid the duo any royalties for their recordings, instead providing them with a car:

> See, most of the time the company furnished me with a car, a brand-new car. . . . We never did get any royalties. They tell you they gonna give you royalties, but we never got paid for them. They always promised that, but I have never gotten no kind of royalties.

Nixon also claimed Decca never paid him for playing on a 1934 session when he accompanied Abraham John "Son" Bonds on two sides, singing and playing harmonica (credited to Brother Son Bonds, Brownsville Son Bonds, or Hammie and Son). "Williams," said Nixon, "done messed so many guys up with them records." Such appears to have been the case for their July 1935 session, which yielded the iconic "Someday Baby Blues." This blues joined an astonishing line of songs—"See See Rider," "Shake That Thing," "Matchbox Blues," "How Long Blues," "Kokomo Blues," "Tight Like That," "Corinne, Corinna"—that, once recorded and released by Williams, almost instantly became part of the national vernacular repertoire. Estes echoed Nixon's assessment of working with Williams:

> That's right. "Someday Baby" ruined me. I never did get nothin' out of that. It sold half a million dollars' worth in Arkansas and Shelby County [Tennessee]. We made it two times. That last time was "Someday Baby You Ain't Gonna Trouble My Mind No More"—in '38 ["New Someday Baby"].[9]

Theirs is a familiar tale of street survival, coupled with the crippling alcoholism that plagued the blues community even after the end of Prohibition—a self-destructive streak that caused many like Nixon and Estes to lose the few material benefits that came from their blues recordings. The Great Depression had claimed the lives of many of the great early blues artists who had recorded for Williams: Blind Blake, Papa Charlie Jackson, Blind Lemon Jefferson, and Ma Rainey, to name a few. Estes and Nixon remembered that the Depression forced many of Chicago's blues singers to live in cardboard boxes. Under such circumstances, street performances were a much-needed source of income. Still, Williams admittedly used blues singers' need for cash up front as leverage to sign them to inherently disadvantageous deals. Estes and others were well aware of the fact that the money that the record companies awarded them was vastly disproportionate to what was—under a fair contract—rightfully owed to them. Complicating the situation was a new set of agreements between record labels and the American Federation of Musicians (the AFM is often referred to as the "musicians' union"), which stipulated that artists who signed a record deal had to join the AFM. The AFM, in turn, told its members that they could no longer perform on the street, denying them a valuable source of income.[10]

Williams did develop genuine friendships with some of the performers he recorded over the years, such as Scrapper Blackwell and Leroy Carr, with whom Williams periodically went joyriding:

> Now, [Scrapper Blackwell and Leroy Carr] . . . they were *very* good. They got a song "Even When the Sun Goes Down." It's great. And they came from Indianapolis. And they used to drive to New York with me. I recorded them in New York. And the funny thing, and this poor boy, one of them never been on a train in his life. And drive a car? He went all the way to New York barefooted. I did most of the driving, naturally. Never been on a train. [laughs]

Blackwell and Carr were well-heeled, urban Black men. On one Vocalion session in New York, Williams brought the young Josh White to accompany Carr and Blackwell. It is possible White was the "poor boy" Williams is referring to in the story. Either on this trip or a different excursion, Williams, Blackwell, and Carr went sightseeing in New England:

> I took them to Boston one day, to show them where Crispus Attucks fought the battle in the Revolution. And they just got out and wallowed in it, and had their photo on the site around this monument of Crispus Attucks. They were a funny combination.[11]

Crispus Attucks, the Black-Wampanoag sailor who died in the Boston Massacre on Milk Street in Boston, was the most famous Black man involved in the American Revolution. In the pre-interstate-highway days of the late

1930s, the trek from New York City to Boston was not a quick one. And although there were plenty of well-paved roads and fast trains that enabled a relatively comfortable journey between the two cities, Williams likely would not have undertaken such a trip with Blackwell and Carr had the three not gotten along well.

Though Williams would still occasionally bring artists in to Chicago, he made regular trips to New York City to work out of Decca's recording headquarters, where he blocked out a week to ten days of recording sessions. In July 1935, Williams brought Blind Boy Fuller (born Fulton Allen) to New York to record for Decca, and the recording career of yet another successful country blues "discovery" was underway. Later that summer, on August 9, Williams's younger brother, Maurice, succumbed to tuberculosis. Mayo—who was now the last survivor of Millie and John Williams's five children—paid for Sam's funeral back in Monmouth.

Until this point in his career, Williams had largely avoided conflict with other record executives. His friction with Art Laibly, which had resulted in his departure from Paramount Records, was a quiet power struggle that never broke out into open conflict. Even his rivalries with other Chicago race record talent scouts and A&R men—people like Lester Melrose and Clarence Williams—appear to have been fairly congenial. But now that Williams was at an economically powerful label with high-profile artists, and now that the rise of swing bands—and a growing group of record collectors—had generated a significant body of history, scholarship, and artistic critique, his work was now in the public view. He was seen as competition and as a scout whose artistic compass pointed in the direction of what the public (not critics) wanted to hear. John Hammond, the legendary talent scout and wealthy scion of the Vanderbilt family, was the first influential figure in American music to take a dislike to Mayo Williams. The flash point for this was Williams's role in Decca's signing of William James "Count" Basie in 1936. The Basie band was playing a house gig at the Reno Club in Kansas City, which was broadcast live on W9XBY. John Hammond heard the broadcast in his car—a Terraplane outfitted with a high-quality AM radio antenna that enabled him to tune in from New York City—in what the journalist Leonard Feather would dramatically refer to as the "most momentous chance audition in jazz history."[12] Hammond traveled to Kansas City to see the Count Basie Orchestra, was duly impressed, raved about them in *DownBeat* magazine, developed a trusting rapport with the band by sharing a mutual love for many of the same jazz and blues artists, and set to work on getting them a record deal.

Hammond had succeeded in lining up a tentative deal for the band at Brunswick, which was by then a competitor of Decca (BRC had sold Vocalion to Decca but had retained the Brunswick label). Hammond left for Kansas

City to tell the group the good news. But as Count Basie recalled, things did not go according to Hammond's plan:

> But before [Hammond] got back that second time, Dave Kapp from Decca Records came out there and told me that he was a friend of John's and said that John had been telling him all about us and so he had come out to hear us, and he offered me a contract to make twenty-four sides a year for three years.[13]

Dave Kapp had not traveled solo to Kansas City; along for the ride was Mayo Williams. Mayo Williams had kept in touch with the pianist Sam Price—the same pianist who had tipped him off to Blind Lemon Jefferson in 1925 and who had recorded for Williams (and Kapp) on Brunswick in 1929. Price had lived and performed in Kansas City from 1930 until 1934, where he got to know Basie, Pete Johnson, and other jazz and boogie-woogie musicians in town. (One has to wonder if Price was already in Kansas City by the time Williams and Kapp recorded Walter Page, Mary Lou Williams, and Andy Kirk there in 1929.) In 1934, he lived for a time in Chicago, where he played a house gig at the Derby Cafe.[14] However, with their urgency to sign Basie, the Kapps and Williams were under the impression that Hammond had sources on the inside at Decca who had already helped him scoop Decca-scouted artists such as Albert Ammons and Meade "Lux Lewis." Decca's desire to sign Basie was as much about retaliation against Hammond as it was an acknowledgment of the Basie band's enormous talent. According to Williams, when Jack Kapp told him, "Well, you go ahead to Kansas City and get Count Basie," he and Dave Kapp wasted no time:

> Well, now, John Hammond left New York at the same time I did on a train. I had a car, and a friend of mine [probably Dave Kapp] was driving. And I beat John Hammond into Kansas City, and got Count Basie, and brought him back here.[15]

Kapp and Williams signed Basie to a three-year deal that required Basie to deliver twelve records a year (that is, twenty-four sides). In return, Basie's band would receive seven hundred fifty dollars a year and transportation to the recording studio from Kansas City. Neither Basie nor the band would ever receive a cent of royalties for any of the recordings they made for Decca, as the contract called for no royalties ever to be paid them. At the time, the deal struck Basie as the greatest he had ever heard of:

> That was how I came to sign my first recording contract, and I really made a very big mistake on that one. [Dave Kapp] said something about how Decca was going to provide us with transportation for the band to go to Chicago

to record, and at that time that sounded like the biggest deal I'd ever heard of, and I asked him again, and he said, "Oh, yes." And I was ready to go. So I told the guys the good news, and the part about transportation made a big impression on most of them too.[16]

The magnitude of Basie's error began to resonate once the group was well into its deal with Decca. When Basie wrote his memoirs nearly fifty years later, he recognized that the deal—which encompassed such Basie standards as "One O'clock Jump," "Topsy," "Sent for You Yesterday," "Jumpin' at the Woodside," "Jive at Five," and "Blue and Sentimental"—continued to grow worse as each year brought greater rewards for the owners of the masters and none for him.[17]

After John Hammond's train pulled into Kansas City, the talent scout arrived at the Reno Club prepared to tell Basie and his band about the deal he had lined up for them at Brunswick. Basie remembered that Hammond was incredulous:

> When John came back out there a short time later and saw that contract, he hit the ceiling. Without realizing what I was doing, I had agreed to record twelve records a year for $750 a year outright, no royalties! I didn't know anything about royalties. John couldn't believe it. He couldn't get us out of that contract, but he was able to get Decca to raise the musicians' pay up to minimum scale. I don't think I had ever heard of minimum scale before that, and if I had, I had never paid any attention to it. I guess I just had to learn some things the hard way.[18]

As Basie tells in his memoirs, Hammond continued to advocate on the group's behalf, improving their recording fees, promoting their work, and assisting in getting them a better record deal after the Decca contract expired. Hammond would not forget his disdain for Williams or the Kapps.

Thus far at Decca, Williams had relied on several "lieutenants" to help him scout talent and arrange bands for recording sessions, though none with the same acumen as Thomas A. Dorsey or Lovie Austin. Aletha Dickerson rejoined his staff, maintaining her aloof posture with musicians who visited Williams's Chicago office and assisting in arranging some of the groups' songs. James Burke "St. Louis Jimmy" Oden helped Williams scout talent and recorded a number of sides for Decca. In 1936, Williams signed the Ink Spots to Decca. Although the group had recorded four sides for Victor in 1935, they had not yet begun working with the legendary tenor Bill Kenny and were without the signature sound that ultimately made them one of the defining vocal groups of the era. Though their Victor sides name them as the Ink Spots, the Chicago session guitarist Lefty Bates credited Williams with suggesting the Ink Spots's name and with launching the group's career.[19] Whatever the true story is,

Williams's signing of the Ink Spots was prescient, ushering in a relationship between Decca and the Ink Spots that resulted in millions of dollars of profits and hundreds of recordings from 1936 to 1950.

In 1937, Williams was signing and selecting arrangements for artists like Delores Jackson, a Pittsburgh singer he signed after a performance in Detroit with a symphony accompaniment that won praise from Noble Sissle.[20] He again ran into his old acquaintance Sammy Price while Price was playing piano in a Detroit club called the Tuxedo. Williams had the wherewithal to realize that Price, the diminutive boogie-woogie pianist from Waco, was the lieutenant that he had been looking for since Georgia Tom's retirement from secular music. Williams convinced Price to relocate to New York in 1937, offering him a recording contract just as the boogie-woogie craze was about to take off.[21] Though newspaper accounts of the day pinpoint Detroit as the place where Williams's and Price's paths crossed in 1937, Price would recall things slightly differently—that he moved to New York, where he ran into Williams. Whatever the circumstances, his timing was fortuitous:

> It was shortly after I arrived in New York that I met Mayo Williams again. I was in the Woodside Hotel and I saw Count Basie's valet Jack, who said that Mayo Williams was in town looking for somebody to play for Cow Cow Davenport. So I went and met Mayo and we renewed our acquaintance. He had told me that if I ever came to New York I should look him up. He said that Cow Cow Davenport had arthritis and couldn't play and that he was trying to find somebody that could play the blues. So I went up to see Cow Cow and he said, "Sam Price! Hey, Mayo, I got it! This kid beat me playing the piano in Norfolk, Virginia, and I liked him. I taught him 'The Cow Cow Blues.'" Anyway, we made "Railroad Blues," "That'll Get It" and other things. Most guys around New York wouldn't play a lot of those numbers, they'd only play [James P. Johnson's] "Carolina Shout" and all that. So after we recorded those things for Davenport Mayo said, "Listen, I'm going out to Chicago to get Roosevelt Sykes. You wanna ride with me?" And from that day on I was with Decca as house pianist and recording supervisor.[22]

Williams and Price returned from Chicago with Jimmie Gordon; Price played piano on Gordon's Decca recordings. Price took a liking to being in the same city as Count Basie and Duke Ellington and was proud to be on the same label as Basie, Guy Lombardo, and Bing Crosby. Plus, the previously down-and-out Price (he had once slept on doorsteps in Pittsburgh with his then-wife) was making one hundred dollars for a day's work:

> I had a car, a whole lot of money, and to earn it I did all kinds of things for Decca. Mayo used to call me up and say, "Come on down here. I want you

Sepia

to listen to this singer." You wouldn't believe how many lousy singers he'd have me sit and listen to. Decca used to get them out of the woodwork. One time they called me and said, "Guy Lombardo thinks his piano is out of tune. Would you look at it?"

I said, "Sure," and checked it out. I really didn't find anything wrong with it, but I didn't want to get on Guy's bad side by saying that, so I said, "Well, this key here is a little off," and everybody was happy.[23]

Sammy Price was successful at making sure everybody was happy and kept his job at Decca until the mid 1950s. Price's schedule at Decca is worth noting, as it likely bears a resemblance to Ink Williams's:

This would be my schedule. If I had a recording date it would be from 9 a.m. to 12. Then I'd go back home, eat breakfast and go back to bed. I'd wake up at six and go out to Mrs. Frazier's restaurant and eat, then maybe go down Broadway to a show or go to a play, and after that go to work at, say, ten o'clock.[24]

Price played on a great number of Decca recordings on Williams's watch, backing up the likes of Trixie Smith, Coot Grant and Wesley "Kid" Wilson, Louisa "Blue Lu" Barker, Johnnie Temple, Peetie Wheatstraw, Sister Rosetta Tharpe, Sidney Bechet, and Cow Cow Davenport. Price recalled a situation similar to that of Dorsey and Lovie Austin at Paramount: "I was the contractor all the time, so I booked the musicians. I'd get the best musicians available, like Chu Berry, Lester Young—any guy like that."[25] Price spoke fondly of his time with Jack and Dave Kapp and Mayo Williams, making a point of thanking the three of them first in his autobiography in 1990. Of his days at Decca, Price said:

But at Decca they let me do it my way; I got it right. And they made a lot of money, and I made a lot of money. . . . But the thing I liked about Decca was that they were nice to me; I was on the staff, and I had an office and all that.[26]

With the hiring of Sammy Price at Decca, Williams had again secured his generalship by finding the right lieutenant.

Sam Price was not always so fond of the talent—particularly Sister Rosetta Tharpe. Born in Cotton Plant, Arkansas in 1915, Tharpe had worked as a traveling evangelical singer and guitarist before settling in Chicago in the 1920s, where she became affiliated with the Church of God in Christ. By 1938 she began recording for Decca with the gospel song "Rock Me," which—on account of Tharpe's gritty electric guitar and belting vocal style—many see as a forerunner of rock and roll. But Tharpe—who followed her own sense of tempo and changed chords sometimes when she was inspired (rather than at the beginning of a measure)—had an unconventionality that the more sophisticated Sammy Price found frustrating to work with:

> So one day [the record producer] Milt Gabler asked Mayo to have me come down to see him. A guy had written a song called "Two Little Fishes and Five Loaves of Bread." It wasn't really a gospel song, but it was about the Lord taking the fishes and what he did with them and all. So he asked me, would I consider recording with Rosetta Tharpe. Well, you know Rosetta Tharpe tuned her guitar funny and sang in the wrong key, and the meter sometimes wasn't exact. She could sing and all that, but then she was a folksinger, more or less. So I told Mayo I'd have to think about it.

This is, of course, the same Sam Price who had enthusiastically sold Paramount on Blind Lemon Jefferson—another performer notorious for inexact meters, vernacular tunings, and folk stylings. Whatever his misgivings were, Williams and the Kapp brothers did not want Price to "think about it," and they surprised Price with a visit from Tharpe's mother:

> And they sent Rosetta Tharpe's mother to see me and to explain to me that if, when a song was played, the thinking behind it was right, then there was nothing wrong with it. I knew I wasn't going to play anything but the blues, anyway—blues, boogie-woogie, mix it up and play jazz—but in a religious vein. I was reluctant, but money will change your mind, and finally I said, "OK, let's try."

Williams sensed Tharpe's talent but seemed baffled at how to make successful records with her and hoped Price could help. Price's observations about the situation reveal how crucial a musical liaison could be between Williams and his artists:

> Jack and Dave Kapp and Mayo and me, we had this big conference, because they were wondering what to do with [Tharpe], and Jack, the president of Decca, asked me, "Sam, what can we do with her?" They used to ask me about artists, how to feature them, because they weren't trained musicians. I knew more about their music and how to present it because, although I wasn't trained, I'd had more practice; I could play with them. So I would tell them what to do.[27]

Price's bravado here underestimates Tharpe's creative power and energy, which is evident from her first recording (sans Price) in 1938, through Williams's early efforts to cover her rough edges with strings. Indeed, the combination of Tharpe and Price is truly inspired on songs like "Strange Things Happen Every Day," which remains one of the enduring recordings in the canon of American vernacular music. In Tharpe's music, we can hear the cycles of Williams's career at play—while she was accompanied by Williams's new lieutenant (Price), she was recording songs like "Take My Hand, Precious Lord," written by his old one (Dorsey). Like the Ink Spots, Sister Rosetta Tharpe would outlast Williams at Decca, remaining a moneymaker for the label until 1956.

In Tharpe's musical journey, we can hear recording technology evolve, as well as record production technique. Williams leaned on Price to help him keep up with the changes. No longer were producers simply trying to give the listener the best seat in the house at a live show. Instead, as recording equipment improved along with the high fidelity of record players and the speakers consumers had at home, producers were building a more intimate acoustic experience. These improvements drew producers further into the creative process as they tinkered with arrangements and instrumentation. Occasionally this produced spectacular results but it also sometimes blinded producers to the inherent strengths of performers such as Tharpe, whose gifts were on brilliant display through raw solo performances (performances that misguided producers sometimes obscured with smooth arrangements). Tharpe would not be Williams's only "miss" on a major talent whose musical approach he simply didn't understand; or perhaps he no longer trusted the instincts that had led him to record many raw, vernacular artists for Paramount and Vocalion. In May 1937, Williams recorded the first four sides by Mahalia Jackson but either failed to see her talent or failed to convince Decca's leadership that her records would sell. To Williams, Jackson's debut commercial recordings were made memorable because of her magnanimous personality. Williams chuckled about this oversight in later years, recalling, "Mahalia was so glad to *get* to record that she paid me. And you know what she paid me? A box of cigars and a pint of whiskey."[28]

Williams also failed—as a producer and as an advocate within Decca—to harness the enormous commercial potential of the Coles Brothers. The Coles brothers—Eddie, Freddy, and Nat (later known as Nat "King" Cole)—called themselves the Solid Swingsters and played a variety of jazz that owed a large stylistic debt to Earl "Fatha" Hines. Born in Birmingham, Alabama, and raised in Chicago's Bronzeville neighborhood, the Solid Swingsters were engaged in a six-month residency at Club Panama in Chicago when Eddie Coles lined up a recording deal with Mayo Williams on Decca's new Sepia Series. Eddie had played on several records made by the musician and playwright Noble Sissle in the early 1930s; Sissle had introduced Eddie Coles to Jack Kapp, who connected the group to Williams. According to Nat King Cole's various biographies, Eddie Coles got Jack Kapp to sign the Solid Swingsters to a record deal, and they recorded for Decca on July 28, 1936. The Solid Swingsters recorded four tunes, including "Honey Hush," which were released in September of same year.[29] Cole's biographers blame the Solid Swingsters' unoriginal sound for the failure of the Decca sides. According to Williams, Jack Kapp asked him to intentionally kill the group's contract:

> We had given him a contract. Decca told me to take him [Nat and his two brothers] in the studio and record him and get rid of his contract. I took him in the studio, helped him arrange that song "Straighten Up and Fly Right" 'til it made sense. But they didn't put ["Straighten Up and Fly Right"] out and when his contract ran out, he went on to California, got with a coupla small concerns, and then finally got with Capitol.[30]

Although Nat King Cole's enormous popular success on Capitol is widely credited with building that label's economic power, his path to success was indirect. The Coles brothers recalled going out to buy their Decca 78s in September of 1936 but knew within a month that the records were not taking off. In October, Eddie, Freddy, and Nat Coles joined the orchestra that was touring with the Noble Sissle musical *Shuffle Along*. When Sissle's payroll was stolen in Los Angeles a few months later, the show went bankrupt. The Coles brothers were stranded in California, where they settled down and decided to drop the "s" from their last name.[31] Nat King Cole's eventual success on Capitol Records was the source of later frustration for Ink Williams, who resented what he perceived as Cole's aloofness:

> Now, here's another funny thing. To show you how *disloyal* some of the artists are; *I go back after* [Nat King Cole is] *big*, down in Hotel Teresa down there in Harlem, and they're giving a party for Nat King Cole up in the penthouse tavern, and so on. And, you know, Nat King Cole accepted an introduction to me, after I had taken him to, from Chicago to New York, and *made him*, practically, and he says [imitates Nat King Cole] "How do you do, Mister Williams?" And so forth. And that's just how gratitude works in some people.[32]

Ink Williams may have felt entitled to gratitude from some artists he worked with along the way, but Cole's snubbing of Williams is perfectly understandable. Williams had by no means "made" him. Quite to the contrary, Williams was complicit in Jack Kapp's plan to "get rid of" the Solid Swingsters' contract. And although he claimed to have helped with the arrangement of the eventual smash hit for Capitol Records, "Straighten Up and Fly Right," he clearly did not try to convince the Kapp brothers to stick with the Coleses. In Williams's eyes, Cole's cool treatment of him boiled down to money:

> Money changes them.... My office in New York was right over the [Decca] studio. I could look down over the studio there on Eleventh Street.... Bing Crosby and all of those artists, they were coming in. And Burl Ives and all of them. And Walt Disney and all of them. I met them all, you see. And in

meeting them all, they were so different from the average artist that *hadn't* made it. And they were different! [laughs][33]

As 1938 drew to a close, the art music world of jazz criticism came crashing into Williams's down-home stable of artists. The ambitious and well-connected John Hammond had organized a first-of-its-kind racially integrated showcase of jazz, blues, and sacred music at New York's Carnegie Hall, titled "From Spirituals to Swing." The concert was the realization of Hammond's musical interests as well as his progressive, integrationist civil rights vision. The "From Spirituals to Swing" concert, held on December 23, 1938, is considered the first integrated concert at Carnegie Hall. The success of this concert led to a second show a year later, on Christmas Eve 1939. The vast majority of the acts featured over the two shows had a history with Ink Williams (including Count Basie, Meade "Lux" Lewis, Sidney Bechet, Sonny Terry, Fletcher Henderson, Joe Turner, Bill Broonzy, and Ida Cox), and presented them alongside major stars such as Benny Goodman and the gospel-singing Golden Gate Quartet. The language in the program notes and in the liner notes to the live recordings of the two concerts—written by Hammond himself—resembles the racial uplift message of Black Swan Records, as well as Williams's message of uplifting the perception of Black vernacular music. John Hammond, who was an active member of the American Civil Liberties Union (ACLU), writes forcefully of the "dignity" of blues, gospel, and jazz. Yet Hammond's essay (on page three of the program) is titled "The Music Nobody Knows." Although possibly true for many white Americans of the time, this title unintentionally implies that the large numbers of Blacks who had been listening to Sonny Terry, Bill Broonzy, Ida Cox, Count Basie, and Sidney Bechet all along were "nobody."

The "From Spirituals to Swing" concerts became a significant origin point for the widespread historical narrative that places Bessie Smith and Robert Johnson as the two "greats" of prewar blues. (The concert was dedicated to the late Bessie Smith, and Hammond had booked the relatively obscure Johnson, who died unexpectedly prior to the performance; Broonzy was his substitute.) A closer look at Mayo Williams's career suggests that Blind Lemon Jefferson certainly eclipsed Robert Johnson in both popularity and impact (musically and socially) within the Black blues community. Both Bessie Smith and Ida Cox were deeply influenced by Ma Rainey. Robert Johnson had been greatly influenced by Peetie Wheatstraw and Leroy Carr, both of whom were largely ignored by blues revivalists and rock musicians of the 1960s.[34] The program and liner notes to Hammond's concerts also advocate a history of the blues that boosts the prominence of Hammond's Columbia-based catalog. This is not to say that Hammond had a malicious interest in promoting Smith and Johnson above other performers, or that he was trying to promote himself as some kind of white savior of Black music (though some have accused him of doing so). However, it is curious that Hammond's concerts realigned the perception of American popular-music history in a way that implies "nobody" knew this music prior to his intervention, and that many of the acts that Ink Williams "discovered" (and which had been discovered by hundreds of thousands—if not millions—of Black record buyers) seemingly had been "discovered" by Hammond instead.[35] Many decades later, Williams—who never seemed terribly interested in receiving accolades for his work but who had an interest in getting the facts right—was rankled that many blues and jazz fans and historians had a skewed understanding of blues history and his (and his most successful and prolific artists') place in it.

No more did this seem to bother Williams than in the association of boogie-woogie piano with Hammond and the "From Spirituals to Swing" concerts. Although Williams does not appear to have interacted with Pete Johnson, the other two boogie-woogie pianists in Hammond's concert were Meade "Lux" Lewis and Albert Ammons, whom Williams knew from Chicago. Lewis had recorded for Paramount, and both Lewis and Ammons knew Clarence "Pine Top" Smith. Williams had recorded "Pine Top's Boogie Woogie" and seven other sides by Smith in a one-month stretch prior to Smith's untimely death on March 14, 1929.[36] Ammons, Lewis, and Smith lived in the same building and had gathered regularly at Ammons's apartment (he was reportedly the only one with a piano) for "cutting" sessions, where Pine Top taught Ammons his boogie-woogie style. According to Williams, Ammons and Lewis—both of whom worked as cab drivers in Chicago—"pinched the boogie-woogie" from Smith.[37] John Hammond, who made a practice of visiting Chicago, kept tabs on what was happening in jazz and blues circles through a wide network of promoters, performers, and A&R men. Hammond then "pinched" Ammons and Lewis when he signed them to Blue Note in 1938. Hammond had a notorious disregard for gatekeepers in the record business and showed little concern for Williams's feelings that he was encroaching on his Chicago-based territory. Williams developed the paranoid belief that "John Hammond had access to everything we had in our files, because he was a wealthy boy, and the company befriended him."[38]

Williams would later recall with obvious resignation, "Yeah, Albert Ammons was taken to New York for John Hammond." Ammons's subsequent stardom led Williams to feel oddly vindicated by the attention it brought to Pine Top Smith's legacy:

> John Hammond came out and got [Albert Ammons, Meade "Lux" Lewis, and Pete Johnson from Chicago]. Took 'em to New York. . . . And he brought these three boys into New York and recorded 'em and put 'em in his café uptown and downtown. Then, when the truth came out, everybody wanted a picture of *Pine Top*.[39]

Williams was interested in seeing Pine Top Smith get credit for being the early great of boogie-woogie, partly because he seemed to have a genuine affection for the late pianist and in part because he had a financial interest at stake: Williams owned the rights to Pine Top's music. In the few interviews he granted and in correspondence with blues scholars, Williams rarely sought credit or acclaim for his work in the field. His feelings about Pine Top Smith are a notable exception:

> Now then I had to bury Pine Top. Now I take over Pine Top's songs, all of his songs, buried him, and put him away. And then in doing that, Pine Top became very, very, I mean, boogie-woogie became very popular, and everyone had to boogie-woogie. You could have one. Everybody that could had a boogie-woogie song. . . . And this [Lester] Melrose had a publishing company over here, and nobody could arrange [boogie-woogie for sheet music]. Now, Fletcher Henderson comes into the picture again. . . . and Fletcher Henderson is the *only one* could arrange that boogie-woogie beat. Well he arranged it and put it in for me. And I sold that to this Melrose over there on the side for five thousand dollars. 'Cause I had *originated* it. It started out with Pine Top Smith, and everybody picked it up.[40]

Sadly, Williams never seemed to reflect on the very real contributions he had made to the awareness and popularity of boogie-woogie in a variety of incarnations, from the prototypical piano boogie of Jimmy Blythe's 1924 Paramount recording of "Chicago Stomp" to the "booger-rooger" of Blind Lemon Jefferson to the piano blues of Cow Cow Davenport, Speckled Red, Leroy Carr, or Peetie Wheatstraw. Perhaps this was due to the narrative that evolved out of the "From Spirituals to Swing" concerts, which created the erroneous impression that boogie-woogie had started with Pine Top, Ammons, and Lewis. This idea was already being formalized by 1939 with the publication of Frederic Ramsey and Charles Edward Smith's compilation of essays on jazz history, *Jazzmen*, which noted:

> Poor Pine Top never lived to see Boogie Woogie make its Carnegie Hall debut. Several years ago, he was shot down in a brawl over "some ol' gal in a cheap West Side dance hall," according to Mayo Williams. And Pine Top died as he had lived.

According to *Jazzmen*, Ammons's version of "Pine Top's Boogie Woogie" is without peer, superior even to the original.[41] *Jazzmen*, which is likely the first time Williams's name appears in any published account of Black music, reflects the sense at the time that the Carnegie Hall concerts were the apex of Black musical accomplishment to date—an impression that would not have sat well with Williams.

In early 1939, John Hammond decided that the best way to beat gatekeepers in the music business was to join them. The *Chicago Defender* announced that CBS (Columbia Broadcasting System) had acquired Vocalion and had hired the "rich swing enthusiast" John Hammond to manage the Columbia and Vocalion Race records division. The *Defender* speculated that Hammond's arrival might generate a departure of Decca talent for Columbia and the "possibilities of a personal 'battle' between Williams and Hammond."[42]

However influential Hammond was in shaping the grand narrative of Black music in America, Williams was not entirely uninvolved in assembling what would become the critical canon of commercial blues recordings. From 1939 to 1942, the folklorist Alan Lomax—the Assistant in Charge of the Archive of American Folk Song at the Library of Congress—corresponded with the Decca executives Dave and Jack Kapp and Frank Luther, as well as the producer Milt Gabler and possibly Mayo Williams. Lomax was working to assemble his now iconic 1942 "List of American Folk Songs On Commercial Records" report for the Division of Music at the Library of Congress. The list, which consists of hillbilly and race records, includes recordings by many of the artists that Williams produced: Kokomo Arnold, Blind Boy Fuller, Cow Cow Davenport, Texas Alexander, John Estes, the Golden Eagles Gospel Singers, Bo Carter, Tampa Red and Georgia Tom, Blind Joe Taggart, Buell Kazee, Memphis Minnie, Josh White, the Reverend Nathan Smith, Big Bill Broonzy, Jesse James, and Marc Williams. Lomax's letters to Decca consist mainly of requests for master recordings or clean archival copies of records. They also refer to Lomax's work with an eclectic group of record collectors and folk song enthusiasts such as the painter Thomas Hart Benton. Lomax, who was notoriously testy, showed some of his signature vinegar to Milt Gabler:

> Dear Milt,
>   You are a very poor correspondent, I am sorry to say. Would you be so kind as to send along the two dubbings that I asked for in my last letter; that is, "Things About Comin' My Way" by Tampa Red, and "Kansas City Blues" by Jim Jackson. I discovered that Tom Benton has a good copy of "Pretty Polly" by Doc Boggs. He has sent it to Frank Luther, and I hope you will dub it and sent [sic] it to me immediately so that I can include it in my album of ballads. Please hurry so that I can get the albums finished in the next week.[43]

Lomax thanks Mayo ("Mayor") Williams in the notes to the report, though there is no record of their corresponding with one another. Needless to say, Lomax's ability to work with Decca—and to gain access to their archives of Brunswick and Vocalion masters (essentially two decades of recordings produced by Mayo Williams)—had a considerable effect on Lomax's efforts to build a canonical list of blues and hillbilly commercial recordings. Williams's stamp on this list is indelible. Williams never spoke on the record about Alan Lomax, but he certainly was perturbed by John Hammond's encroachment on his turf. He did not stand flat-footed, nor was he lured into the Hammond crowd's debates about racial, cultural, and aesthetic authenticity in Black music. His next several moves at Decca would illuminate just how different his vision was from Hammond's.

CHAPTER 20

Outskirts

Back in Chicago, Williams pieced together a studio band called the Harlem Hamfats to back Decca's Chicago-based Sepia Series artists, such as Johnny Temple, Rosetta Howard, and Frankie "Half Pint" Jaxon.[1] The core of the group was formed around the brothers Charlie and Joe McCoy, who had recorded prolifically in various musical formations with Williams on Vocalion, beginning when Joe McCoy was still Memphis Minnie's guitarist and husband. The Harlem Hamfats had several successful radio hits—most notably "Oh Red!" in 1936—which featured a strong country backbeat that hints at such future rhythm and blues and rock and roll hits as Chuck Berry's "Maybelline" or the Coasters' "Yakkity Yak." In their songs, the Harlem Hamfats were an extension of the hokum blues that had proved so popular through the 1930s despite (or perhaps because of) their dirty lyrics. The McCoys wrote and performed a good amount of hokum, and the Harlem Hamfats made a name for themselves with songs like "Let's Get Drunk and Truck." Though the Harlem Hamfats never officially played any live shows, their sound provided the musical foundation for Decca's successful Sepia Series and were a precursor to Ink Williams's last great find, Louis Jordan.

Born in Brinkley, Arkansas in 1908, Louis Jordan followed in the footsteps of his father, who was a minstrel musician. By the time he was seventeen, Jordan was playing saxophone, singing, and dancing with such notable southern Black minstrel shows as the Rabbit Foot Minstrels, the Dixie Melody Syncopaters, and Silas Green from New Orleans. With these groups, Jordan worked his way across the South, playing tent shows and clubs in places like El Dorado and Hot Springs, Arkansas.[2] He gradually made his way north, joining up with a traveling medicine show that settled west of Philadelphia, Pennsylvania. In early 1934, Jordan started playing tenor sax with the jazz trumpeter and bandleader Charlie Gaines. Clarence Williams hired them to record Gaines's

"I Can't Dance I've Got Ants in My Pants" for Vocalion. The session marked Jordan's recording debut and punctuated his arrival in New York City. Soon after, Jordan landed a major gig playing tenor sax in Chick Webb's band, the house band at the Savoy Ballroom—the most popular Black swing dance club in New York City. Webb, a diminutive drummer from Baltimore, was emerging at the time of Jordan's arrival as one of the most electrifying bandleaders in swing. Webb's band featured the young Ella Fitzgerald on vocals. Webb landed a record deal with Decca in 1936, and by 1937, he was featuring Jordan's vocals on an ever-increasing number of singles.[3]

Webb's popularity arose from his furious and explosive drum solos (Gene Krupa acknowledged Webb as his primary influence), tight arrangements, and compelling vocals from Fitzgerald and Jordan. Webb, Fitzgerald, and Jordan each displayed a crowd-pleasing flair, for which John Hammond blasted them in a November 1937 issue of *DownBeat*:

> Instead of giving the public the Swing it desires and the kind of stuff he can do best [Webb] bores them with the sweet genteel work of a saccharine male vocalist, elaborate badly scored "white" arrangements, a "comedian" saxophonist and an athletic director who jumps around but contributes not a whit to the musical proceedings.[4]

It is possible that Hammond was still smarting from Decca's signing of Count Basie and that Webb's band bore the brunt of Hammond's vitriol toward the label. But his racialized critique of "white" arrangements (by an all-Black band that was the popular house band at New York's majority Black Savoy Ballroom) was a kind of social and aesthetic critique that was only then emerging as a defining aspect of jazz and swing criticism. White critics and promoters levied such charges of "whiteness" as a marker of inauthenticity—a critical debate that appears to have been contested mainly by white patrons, critics, and enthusiasts of Black music. The racialized marketing categories of American music that were hammered out in the forge of segregationist Jim Crow America spawned perversions of the idea that Blacks should remain in their place (or that racial groups even had—or should have—a "place"). Louis Jordan and many of the other race recording artists were saddled with such critiques as their popularity grew in mainstream mid-twentieth-century America.

Louis Jordan's career took an unexpected turn during an extended house gig in Boston in 1938, while Chick Webb—who, from birth, suffered from tuberculosis of the spine—was acutely ill back in New York. Webb could be difficult to work for; in his absence, Jordan solicited band members—including Ella Fitzgerald—to join him in a new group. When Webb returned to Boston, he discovered Jordan's plan to make off with the core of the band and fired him on the spot. Jordan returned to New York to form his own group. In the summer of 1938, Louis Jordan and the Tympany Four made their live debut as the house band at the Elks Rendezvous in Harlem. (Webb died the next year of complications from surgery—he was only thirty-four.)[5] Dan Burley, a reporter for the *Amsterdam News*, heard Jordan's new band and recommended them to Mayo Williams, as did Coot Grant and Sox Wilson, two Decca musicians based in Harlem. Williams went to the Elks to hear Jordan but felt that a string bass and tenor sax needed to be added before the group would be ready to record.

Decca already had a contract with another Elks Rendezvous act—the singer Rodney Sturgis—so Williams invited Jordan's group in to the studio as Sturgis's backup, augmenting the group with the two suggested pieces (tenor sax and string bass). Williams was actively making a number of recordings with the Harlem Hamfats at the time and had adopted a more interactive, hands-on production role. Williams drew on that experience to help Louis Jordan craft a new sound, cleverly using the session with Sturgis to give Jordan's group a chance to hear itself as Williams imagined them with an additional horn in the group. On December 29, 1938, the "Louie Jordan Elks Rendezvous Band" debuted on wax, first backing Sturgis on "Toodle-Loo On Down," and on two tunes without Sturgis, including the raunchy folk song "Barnacle Bill the Sailor," and the band's theme song, "Honey in the Bee Ball." The latter was released in the Sepia Series in early 1939 to fair results. The experiment was successful enough that Williams invited Jordan to record for Decca on the condition that a fifth member—a tenor sax player—be added, making the group the Tympany Five. Jordan rehearsed this new group relentlessly and agreed to Williams's terms. Jack Kapp gave Williams permission to book a follow-up session for Jordan's group in March, without Sturgis behind the microphone. On March 29, 1939, Louis Jordan and his Tympany Five made their official recording debut with "Keep A-Knockin,'" which became a modest hit.[6]

Augmenting his sound in order to please the audience was something Jordan felt comfortable with. His outlook on a life in music was remarkably compatible with Williams's idea of giving the people what they want:

> See, before I got a band I knew what I wanted to do with it. I wanted to give my whole life to making people enjoy my music. Make them laugh and smile. So I didn't stick to what you'd call jazz. I have always stuck to entertainment.[7]

Jordan proved to be a stylistic jack of all trades, saying "Generally a black artist at that time would either stick to the blues or do pop. I did everything."[8] Whereas the jazz critics in John Hammond's circle preferred stylistic orthodoxy, Jordan's all-encompassing taste and repertoire was something Williams had always longed to be able to produce from his earliest days at Paramount.

Williams was not working exclusively with Jordan; he was also recording the emergent gospel quartets such as the Selah Jubilee Singers and the Dixie Hummingbirds. Unlike Jordan, whose records had the potential for mass appeal, groups such as the Dixie Hummingbirds had a modest but very real commercial potential. The label might make some money, but the actual record sales were not likely to make the artists rich; as the Dixie Hummingbirds' James Davis recalled, "We did those records because they legitimized us, and they helped us make money on our [live] programs." Though the group likely received a flat fee for recording, Barney Parks, another singer in the group, could not recall seeing any money, declaring, "It wasn't about money anyway. Just wanting to record." Not all groups were so generous in their assessment: the Selah Jubilee Singers—who were initially impressed with Williams and the Decca studio in New York where Louis Jordan and Andy Kirk had recorded—felt ripped off. "Mayo Williams took our money," is how Thermon Ruth remembered it. "They gave me $12.50 a side. Never did see any of it. Never did get royalties."[9]

Williams's predatory practices finally caught up with him the year that the Dixie Hummingbirds recorded for Decca. On March 2, 1939, the *Pittsburgh Courier* reported that the American Federation of Musicians (AFM) called for the firing of J. Mayo Williams and threatened to revoke the recording licenses of Decca and Victor records on account of his swindling of artists:

> NEW YORK CITY, March 2—The age-old practice of seeking out talented but unwise colored artists from the South and other parts of the States where education is lacking and using them to make records of all kinds which have a good sales market, was brought to a halt here last week by the American Federation of Musicians, when it was discovered that these same performers were being paid under scale, without knowing what was happening.

The AFM had both Victor and Decca in its sights on account of their significant portion in the general record market and because they controlled the bulk of the race record market. The AFM was after two things—better pay for musicians, yes, but also an arrangement that would allow Decca and Victor to record only union artists. Of course, most vernacular musicians in the race and hillbilly records market were not union members, which required the ability to read sheet music. The AFM's proposal would have boxed a stunning number of vernacular musicians out of the record market entirely. Williams did prey on the vulnerability of nonunion Black musicians, but he was also the rare record executive who believed that such music should be recorded and delivered to the public on its own aesthetic and cultural terms. But over fifteen years of high-profile predatory practice made Williams the very visible target of the AFM's ire:

During the first heated round of controversy, the name of Mayo Williams was discussed by both the union and the record companies. In a letter to Decca, the Chicago union asked that Williams be fired, as it was he who imported non-union Negro musicians for their benefit. Going further, the union charges that the pay-off of most of these performers was done in the dark and much petty chiseling went on between intermediaries who did the contacting for race records.[10]

Decca did not fire Williams, but perhaps it was partly due to this new scrutiny that his work at this time focused almost exclusively on Louis Jordan. Jordan's sales figures gradually increased, and in 1940, Williams stepped up the Tympany Five's recording schedule with sessions in January, March, and April. Williams took a more significant role in Jordan's sessions than with any other artist he had worked with before. After insisting Jordan expand his group, Williams occasionally brought in different singers for Jordan to work with, such as Yack Taylor ("Hard Lovin' Blues"), Daisy Winchester, and Mabel Robinson. As Jordan and Williams sought to find a hit formula for the band, Jordan's catalog came to reflect an ever-widening range of styles. But the busy recording schedule began to affect the freshness of Jordan's recordings, and Decca did not schedule another session for five months (from April to September) while he woodshedded at the Elks Rendezvous in search of a new, more hit-making sound.[11]

Louis Jordan's biographer, John Chilton, credits Williams for what he calls the Blues Renaissance, which sprang from the Harlem Renaissance in the 1930s, calling him the "key figure in this movement."[12] Chilton's characterization is unusually generous but worth examining, because Williams did have connections to leading lights in the Harlem Renaissance. Williams and Paul Robeson maintained a close friendship throughout their adult lives, despite Williams's apparent antipathy for leftist politics, even as many of Robeson's closest friends and professional colleagues—including many who sympathized with him politically—publicly abandoned him. Williams worked with Luther and Fritz Pollard at Suntan Studios, which provided rehearsal space for Harlem-based jazz and R&B musicians; he also produced "soundies" (film-based precursors to music videos). The *New York Age* regarded Williams as a man-about-town; the paper reported on one occasion that Williams was driving the jazz pianist Lil Hardin Armstrong, the long-distance runner John Borican, and the tenor and orator J. Oliver Wilson from New York to Chicago in his Lincoln Zephyr.[13] On another occasion, the *New York Age* dubiously referred to Williams as a "lion" and that "all of the females seek his company."[14] This kind of report in the society pages either drew the ire—or the eye roll—of Aleta Williams (and her sister, Stella, who had moved in with Mayo and Aleta in 1940, along with her husband Eugene Sykes).

Aleta, too, also found her name in the society pages periodically. She used her modest celebrity to promote an "artists-models' ball"—an art exhibition, concert, and beauty pageant rolled into one—at Chicago's South Side Community Art Center (which had been dedicated by Eleanor Roosevelt in 1940).[15] Mayo Williams kept high-profile company—he was spotted at Harlem's Cavalcade with Fritz Pollard and the jazz musician Don Redman.[16] Rudolph Fischer, who—along with Williams and Pollard—was one of three Black students enrolled at Brown when Williams arrived in Providence in 1916, had been one of the leading literary figures of the Harlem Renaissance during the mid-1920s was now a pioneering radiologist. Fischer was a close friend of Langston Hughes and E. Franklin Frazier; he published literary fiction such as *The Walls of Jericho* as well as a number of mystery novels before his untimely death in 1937. Langston Hughes once called Fischer the "wittiest of these New Negroes of Harlem."[17]

Musical luminaries of the Harlem Renaissance, such as Ellington and Calloway, would have known Williams from Decca. And Williams's influence as a talent scout can be read into the later works of Ralph Ellison, whose *Invisible Man* includes a character named Peter Wheatstraw. Williams, in the few lengthy interviews he gave, never touched on the larger social and cultural scene of the Harlem Renaissance. Nevertheless, Sammy Price described Williams as a "genius, the man who changed the world's conception of blues music."[18] Chilton wrote that "Williams certainly played a big part in the selection of material that Louis Jordan recorded," and suggests that Williams's success with Jordan was rooted in an ear for melodies and lyrics as well as a knack for making important alterations to arrangements. Williams also appears to have genuinely liked Jordan and his music, putting him on a very short list of favorite blues artists (along with Ma Rainey, Bessie Smith, and Charlie Jackson). Unfortunately, and in contrast with his teetotaling early days at Paramount, Chilton notes Williams developed a reputation for drinking and playing the horses during his years with Louis Jordan.[19]

In interviews, Williams would allude to gambling, but never discussed it in depth. Doc Young—the owner of the Hammond Pros—was known to be a gambler, and Williams spent time with the Youngs at the racetrack. And although Williams discussed his efforts to avoid drinking with blues musicians while producing records at Paramount, we know that he made and sold bathtub gin during Prohibition and admitted to going on periodic benders (recall his lost weekend in Algiers with Papa Charlie Jackson). None of this means Williams was a drunk, of course, but he does audibly drink to excess in two of the recorded interviews he gave late in life, slurring his words by the end of the interviews while asking for more beer. For a proud man like Williams—who made a practice of carefully presenting himself to the public, particularly to a white public—these interviews imply that Williams had developed a drinking problem by middle age. Chilton suggests it was negatively affecting his work at Decca.

When Jordan returned to the studio in September of 1940, the Tympany Five incorporated a new "shuffle beat." Jordan's music was increasingly associated with the style known as "jump blues," and showed marked improvement in sales figures (sixty-two thousand copies), enough to encourage Kapp and Williams to book more sessions with the group. As Jordan's popularity increased, so did the complaints of critics such as Dan Burley, the editor of the *New Amsterdam News*, who encouraged Jordan to stick to "Black" material. Burley, like John Hammond, was extremely knowledgeable about regional Black vernacular music, particularly blues, and wanted Jordan's music to be "authentically black."[20]

Jordan's personal earnings skyrocketed as his sound and audience evolved, causing Mayo Williams to wonder if he should have gotten into the business of being Jordan's manager and booking agent:

> Louis Jordan, I got him up there in Harlem, making twenty-five dollars a week, and he end up making two thousand five hundred a week. Now, if I had one tenth of one percent of all the artists that I had signed that turned out big, I could just kick back. No, we never fooled with that personal representation.[21]

Jordan started to feel that his popularity in Harlem had reached a ceiling, so the group began a residency in Chicago at the Capitol Lounge, playing for a mostly white audience. With this booking, Jordan's sales grew even more. In 1941, he renegotiated his contract with Decca. At Jordan's next session in November 1941, Williams wrote and cowrote several songs, including "Mama Mama Blues"—a Williams composition culled together from old standard blues stanzas.[22] Williams also collaborated with Stovepipe Johnson on an arrangement of "The Green Grass Grows All Around." It was during this session that Jordan recorded "I'm Gonna Move to the Outskirts of Town," a song that launched him as a major popular recording star. In the aftermath of the song's success, many tried to claim responsibility for Jordan's hit formula and song choice, including Mayo Williams, Lester Melrose, and Jordan himself, who claimed to have heard the song years before.[23] This was Mayo Williams's second encounter with the song, which had originated with William "Casey Bill" Weldon as "We Gonna Move to the Outskirts of Town," a recording that Williams had produced for Vocalion in 1936. Weldon was a regular accompanist of artists produced by Williams—a supremely gifted slide guitarist sometimes known as the "Hawaiian Guitar Wizard." Like Williams, Weldon was born in Pine Bluff, Arkansas, though nine years after Mayo's family moved to Monmouth, Illinois.

Three weeks after Jordan's recording of "I'm Gonna Move to the Outskirts of Town," the Japanese bombed Pearl Harbor, the United States entered World War II, and Jordan volunteered his group for USO tours. His popularity—with both Black and white audiences—continued to skyrocket. By the middle of 1942, a survey of Harlem jukeboxes found Jordan in the top ten. "Knock Me a Kiss" had sold upward of three hundred thousand copies, and "Mama Mama Blues" had sales upwards of two hundred thousand copies.[24] It appeared as though Williams and Jordan—both originally from Arkansas with tastes rooted in dance music and a predilection for giving audiences what they wanted—made a successful combination. But when Jordan entered the Decca studios the following summer, J. Mayo Williams had been replaced by Milt Gabler.

Born on May 20, 1911, in Harlem to Jewish immigrants from eastern Europe, Milton Gabler was said to be a musician's A&R man. Not unlike the Kapp brothers, Gabler grew up in his father's radio shop (the Commodore Radio Corporation) and developed a jazz record dealership—old and new recordings issued on his own labels. By the late 1930s, Gabler was a widely respected connoisseur of jazz who helped a number of aspirational jazz artists. Billie Holiday recorded and released the song "Strange Fruit" on Gabler's Commodore Records because the major labels were too uncomfortable with the subject matter. Gabler was recruited by Decca the same year he began working with Louis Jordan, who later gave him a great deal of credit. Though the group recorded one J. Mayo Williams collaboration ("That'll Just 'Bout Knock Me Out") under Gabler, it can be presumed that the band was now successful enough to choose a more respected name in the business to oversee their recordings. It is also possible that Williams's claim for Jordan's success had rankled the notoriously proud and difficult bandleader and that Williams's worsening drinking and gambling had become problematic. At this first session with Gabler, the group recorded Jordan's first smash hit, "Five Guys Named Moe," released just prior to the 1942 recording ban imposed by the striking American Federation of Musicians. When the ban ended, Jordan was more popular than ever, releasing "Is You Is Or Is You Ain't My Baby" in late 1943, after Decca had settled with the AFM. This song also marked his film debut.

Shortly after World War II, Jordan became the king of the soundies, which Fritz Pollard had had a hand in creating.[25] In 1938, Pollard had joined together with the ballet and dance-revue choreographer Leonard Harper to form Suntan Studios. Suntan Studios was close to the Apollo Theater and became a rehearsal space for such Harlem-based performers as Cab Calloway, Duke Ellington, and Nat King Cole. Pollard claimed that in 1935 he had begun booking shows for Black artists; over time, his roster included Billie Holiday, Count Basie, Louis Jordan, Fats Waller, Andy Kirk, Redd Foxx, and Dizzy Gillespie. Pollard's relationship with both Joe Glaser and Ink Williams certainly makes it plausible that Pollard could have developed enough contacts within the industry to boast of such a star-studded portfolio of artists.[26] After Leonard Harper died in 1942, Pollard shifted the focus of Suntan Studios to the production of soundies for Gordon Mills's Soundies Distributing Corporation of America. With William Crouch and John Dorn—friends Pollard made in 1933 during the production of Paul Robeson's film *The Emperor Jones*—and with some help from Mayo Williams at Decca, Pollard produced soundies for Dorothy Dandridge, Duke Ellington, Louis Jordan, Cab Calloway, and others.[27]

Louis Jordan's popular success ushered in Decca's post-blues boom years. Gabler's success with Jordan and Bill Haley and His Comets marked a turning point in American music history. By this time, Decca no longer had any big-name blues singers on its roster. As a result of the major labels' neglect of blues, many new, small labels—some under Black ownership—began to crop up. Ink Williams was becoming expendable at Decca. Decca's 1942 announcement that Sam Price had been hired as the Decca Sepia Series's house pianist hinted that Williams's days at Decca were numbered.[28] In working so closely with Jordan, Williams had effectively put all of his eggs into one basket for the first and only time in his career. While Jordan reaped the benefits, Price's formal role as an arranger of the Sepia Series expanded, and Williams was left adrift without much of substance to occupy his attention.[29]

Williams directed some of his time and attention to philanthropy, including the "Keep 'em Smoking" campaign, which made cigarettes and cigars cheaply available to servicemen. This campaign brought him to Pittsburgh in February 1943 with the bandleader (and former Fisk University football star) Jimmy Lunceford, who had recently cut his own version of "I'm Gonna Move to the Outskirts of Town." (The *Pittsburgh Courier* columnist "Melancholy" Jones penned the rare article that linked both Lunceford's and Williams's football exploits and musical accomplishments in the same piece.)[30] Coverage of Williams's activities in the *Courier* during World War II also included a clearly staged photo of a laughing and heavier Mayo Williams reviewing musical arrangements at the Elks Rendezvous Lounge with the Tab Smith Orchestra in 1944.[31] The journey of an A&R director from an ascendant Louis Jordan to the obscure Tab Smith Orchestra had to have been a humbling one for Williams, and he must have known the end of his days at Decca were close.

In 1946, Decca Records released Mayo Williams from his A&R contract, with a two-year noncompete clause. As Williams recalled:

> [Decca] give me a consultation contract for two years, to keep anybody else from gettin' me, at a hundred and a quarter a week! [laughs] They didn't have any further use, you see [laughing], but they didn't want anybody else to get me. Let me see, a hundred-and-a-quarter a week for two years? Somethin' like ten, eleven thousand, twelve-thousand dollars. So I was satisfied, and they were satisfied, see.[32]

But although the severance package Williams received was comfortable (adjusted for inflation, Williams was earning the modern equivalent of $85,000 annually *not* to work), his two years' leave from the business, coupled with the gap left by the union recording ban and World War II, had made him largely inactive for most of a decade. When he resumed his career, the business had changed so much that he was unable to find the top of his game again.

CHAPTER 21

Kingfish

In 1946, the National Football League was reintegrated after a thirteen-year winter of segregation. It was an act of bravery by the athletes and the result of almost two decades of work by Williams and his friends to change minds and hearts. Despite the passage of time, Williams had remained a person of significance on the sports pages of Black newspapers, where awareness of early Black contributions to the NFL had not been forgotten.

Back in 1935, the *Brooklyn Daily Eagle* had run an interview with Fritz Pollard and Joe Lillard addressing NFL segregation. Lillard had been dismissed by the Chicago Cardinals at the close of the 1933 season, ushering in the NFL's segregated era. In the plainest terms, Pollard and Lillard refuted the idea that Black players faced on-field beatings in the NFL. They insisted that white NFL players were professional and congenial, and that most race-based rivalries (such as the rumored one between Jim Thorpe and Fritz Pollard) were fabricated publicity stunts intended to draw crowds to the games. Pollard and Lillard made the case that Black players were tenacious and durable: "I weighed only 160 or so," said Pollard, "and they never made me or the other colored boys—Paul Robeson, Inky Williams, Duke Slater, and the rest—who followed in the pro league, quit either. So they needn't say that's the reason they're keeping us out of the league." Instead, Pollard told the *Daily Eagle* that George Halas was partly responsible for the exclusion of Black players, citing the final NFL game Pollard played in the Providence Steam Roller against Halas and the Chicago Bears. That game took place on December 9, 1925 in front of fifteen thousand at Braves Field in Boston. Pollard claimed he was paid three thousand dollars to play for the Steam Roller, but—at the insistence of Halas—he was kept off the field until the final two minutes of the fourth quarter. Pollard's frustration with Halas was only exacerbated by the fact that both men were from Chicago, and that so many people blamed white southerners for barring Black players from the league. Instead, Pollard told the paper, he counted white Alabamians and Georgians among his closest friends, while he traced Halas's animosity back to their very first NFL game against one another in 1920, "and he's Chicago bred."[1]

Halas's legacy on race in the NFL is mixed. Pollard did not mince words in 1935, so it is with some irony that in 1938, there was a much-publicized exhibition game between the Chicago Bears and the Negro All-Stars. The Negro All-Stars lineup included the enormous Morgan State fullback Thomas "Tank" Conrad and the legendary halfback Ozzie Simmons of the University of Iowa. The squad bore a significant resemblance to Fritz Pollard's Brown Bombers team, which had disbanded in 1937. Pollard, however, was not involved with the All-Stars, who instead were led by the player-coach Ray Kemp (one of the last Black NFL players from 1933). Assisting Kemp in his coaching duties were Duke Slater and Ink Williams.[2]

George Strickler, the *Chicago Tribune* scribe who is credited with coining the "Four Horsemen" nickname to describe Notre Dame's famed backfield under Knute Rockne, was merciless in his assessment of the mismatched teams. The Bears, who had been the best team in the NFL in 1937 (though they lost the championship to Washington), pounded the All-Stars in a landslide, 51–0:

> The outstanding colored football players in the United States, selected in a nation-wide poll, held the Chicago Bears to seven touchdowns, a field goal, and six extra points in Soldier Field last night. The final score was 51 to 0, and it was arrived at before a disappointing assemblage of approximately 6,000.[3]

The 51–0 loss did not sit well with the players, who had been promised various stipends and travel costs, laying the blame at Coach Ray Kemp's feet. They were bitter over the fact that the Bears had over a hundred players, coaches, and trainers involved, whereas the Black All-Stars fielded just over thirty, many of whom arrived without pads or other equipment. Adding to the acrimony, the players wanted an equal split of the profits—which did not come to pass.[4]

For Ray Kemp, Ink Williams, and Duke Slater, the drubbing and the ensuing bad feelings must have been a blow to their attempt to showcase the talent and durability of Black football players. The presence of Slater and Simmons together is significant. From 1934 to 1936, Ozzie Simmons and his brother, Don, had dazzled sports fans at the University of Iowa. Originally from Gainesville, Texas, the Simmons brothers walked on at Iowa, which had earned a reputation as a football program friendly to Black players: Duke Slater had starred at Iowa and recruited Black high schoolers to play there. An elusive halfback, Ozzie Simmons earned the nickname the "Ebony Eel" and became one of Iowa's all-time rushing leaders and one of the best offensive players in the Big Ten. Observers of the game knew that the only thing keeping Ozzie Simmons from joining the NFL on graduation was the owners' desire to keep

Black players out of the league. Though Simmons played on a number of all-Black all-star teams and played two years of professional ball for the Paterson (New Jersey) Panthers in the American Association (a regional pro football league), he never made it to the NFL.

Jerome "Brud" Holland, a Black football star at Cornell, was named an All-American after the 1937 and 1938 seasons, which induced much debate about segregation in the professional game, including a call by Ed Sullivan to reintegrate the NFL. As the nation moved toward the midcentury mark, there was an increasing interest in seeing interracial competitions in baseball, football, and basketball. Certainly, professional boxing and track and field played a role in blazing this trail; the incredible successes of athletes such as Joe Louis and Jesse Owens were impossible for the public to ignore. Furthermore, professional sport in the 1930s was far more informal than it is today, with major league baseball, NFL, and NBA players regularly barnstorming on days off or playing exhibitions for extra cash in the offseason. For example, the New York Giants baseball team traveled to Havana for a series of games against Cuban teams; the HBCUs faced off against all-white, all-star teams of ex-collegiate greats. Fritz Pollard and Ink Williams had participated in plenty of these kinds of exhibitions; the goal was to make money while making the case for equality. The refusal of some white players ever to compete against Black players while others gladly embraced the opportunity (whatever their motivation) is a reminder of individual agency during Jim Crow segregation.

Black sports pages from this era demonstrate just how much the question of equality and fair play across racial barriers dominated discussions of sports in the 1930s. Civil rights and professional sports were, in many ways, inextricable in conversations on sports pages; oftentimes columns were written by former athletes themselves. In February 1938, the former Negro League shortstop E. C. "Pop" Turner penned an article illuminating the history of interracial exhibitions between Major League and Negro League baseball, stating with conviction that integration would be achieved in short order. Toward the end of his article, Turner mentions having run into Ink Williams in New York, reminds readers that Williams was a collegiate and professional football star, and identifies him as a producer at Decca. It is another of the rare instances when Williams's athletic and music careers are mentioned in the same piece.[5]

The Negro League executive (and baseball Hall of Famer) Cumberland "Cum" Posey penned an article in 1940 for the *Pittsburgh Courier* calling out the NFL and its president, Carl Storck, for pretending that Black players were not barred from the league, likening this "gentlemen's agreement" to the color barrier in Major League Baseball. Posey, the former owner of the Homestead Grays (one of the Negro Leagues baseball teams on which Pop Turner had played), had refereed one of the interracial games of the Fritz Pollard All-Stars in Pittsburgh and used his article to outline the history of Black participation in the NFL. While highlighting the integrated origins of the league (citing Black and Native American participants) and naming Williams, Pollard, Robeson, and Slater as the most noteworthy figures, Posey clearly aimed at NFL ownership, reminding them that their fledgling league was "still in its infancy, and groping for patronage of all races."[6]

About the time Ozzie Simmons was graduating from Iowa, a young Black football player for UCLA named Kenny Washington became a sensation when he led the nation in virtually every offensive category. Washington, known as the "Kingfish"—a nickname derived from a character on the radio minstrel comedy show *Amos 'n' Andy*—starred at UCLA with Jackie Robinson and Woody Strode. He earned himself a spot on the integrated national College All-Stars, who faced off against the Chicago Bears in the fall of 1940. In September, rumors abounded that Washington might be signed by the Chicago Bears, the New York Giants, or the Brooklyn Dodgers (football team). The (New York) *Daily News* columnist Jimmy Powers lamented the fact that the American Association—the regional eastern league where Joe Lillard and Ozzie Simmons had played briefly—was also now barring Black players from its rosters. Powers encouraged the New York Giants' owner, Tim Mara, to sign Kenny Washington, reminding readers that this would be in the league's best interest; he cited the role of Williams, Pollard, Robeson, and Slater as drawing cards that built local and national interest in the professional game.[7] Following the College All-Stars game against the Chicago Bears, Kenny Washington said that George Halas asked him to stick around Chicago in the event he could find room for him on the Bears' roster. Halas never called, and Washington returned to Los Angeles.[8]

After the United States entered World War II, there was a severe shortage of players to fill out NFL rosters. In response, league owners lured retired (white) players—some in their forties—back to their old teams. Numerous young, talented Black football players—Kenny Washington, Joe Lillard, Woody Strode, Jackie Robinson, and Ozzie Simmons, to name but a few—were available and in their prime but never were invited. The sports world took notice. Joe Lillard, in an interview with the *Globe-Gazette* of Mason City, Iowa (his hometown), fingered the owners George Halas and Tim Mara, and Paul Schissler (the former Chicago Cardinals and Brooklyn Dodgers coach), as the foremost culprits in enforcing the league's color bar. Although Lillard might have been right that Halas, Mara, and Schissler were complicit in keeping Black players out of the NFL, he neglected to include the Washington team owner, George Preston Marshall, the league's loudest, proudest white supremacist owner, who openly embraced segregation in sports.

As the owner of one of the NFL's winningest franchises of the 1930s and '40s, Marshall held significant sway over league policy, and other owners either agreed with him or silently acquiesced. But outside of the insular circle of NFL team owners, fans of the game found segregation out of step with a democratic society, a contradiction that grew increasingly glaring as the nation fought Germany's fascist, racist regime. As the *Globe-Gazette* saw it, integration of professional sports was part of the larger war effort:

> Let's give the Negro an equal share in the democracy he's fighting to preserve, and tell people like Adolph Hitler to go to hell when they point to the south and tell us to mind our own business and clear up our own problems 1st [*sic*].

The *Globe-Gazette* hoped that professional sports would follow the lead of New York City's boxing laws, noting that Mayor Fiorello La Guardia had just hired the first Black city boxing commissioner.[9]

A known hothead on the field, Joe Lillard had an ignominious role as the face of NFL segregation. Men such as Paul Schissler cited Lillard's temper as an excuse for segregation. Yet in 1933, Lillard, a tailback, had led the Chicago Cardinals in both rushing yardage (373) and passing yardage (269) as well as total points: between rushing touchdowns, a punt returned for a touchdown, kicking an extra point, and two field goals, Lillard scored nineteen of the team's fifty-four points for the entire season; he also passed for two touchdowns. In other words, Lillard—known as the "Midnight Express"—*was* the Chicago Cardinals offense, and his banishment from the league at only age twenty-eight remains indefensible.

Lillard was involved in on-field fistfights that led to two ejections during the 1933 season. This, plus owners' claims that southern white players sought to injure Black players—were touted as reasons to keep Black players off the field of play. Lillard was both the flashpoint of league segregation and the connective tissue between the first generation of Black NFL stars and the players who reintegrated the league in 1946. Lillard was a significant drawing card for the barnstorming all-Black Brown Bombers and the Fritz Pollard All-Stars, and as such had spent time traveling and playing with such early NFL luminaries as Williams, Pollard, Slater, and Butler, as well as with such Black collegiate stars as Ozzie Simmons who were denied entrance to the league. By the end of World War II, Lillard had also played five seasons of Negro Major League Baseball, including three seasons with the Chicago American Giants (1932–34, 1937), where he was a teammate of Pop Turner. There the drumbeat of integration of baseball was incessant.

It is interesting to look at the long-term impact that these barnstorming Black all-star football teams had on the future of the sport. In the short term, of course, their games were fought in the mud of obscurity in front of a few thousand curious fans. But these teams built significant synergy among mostly college-educated men of multiple generations, developed important allies across racial lines, and kept alive the bright memory of the NFL's integrated past. The all-star teams built very real human relationships among the storied players of the past, the spurned players of the present, and the athletes-turned-sportswriters and civil rights activists of the future.

William Claire Halley Harding's involvement with the Negro All-Stars shows this synergy—and shows Ink Williams's dynamic place in it. Williams's sideline gig as the assistant coach at Paul Quinn College had introduced him to Harding, who was the star of the opposing Wiley Wildcats in 1928. Harding joined Williams on the barnstorming Negro All-Stars a few years later in California. Harding would become the player who successfully pushed for reintegration of the NFL.

By 1945, Harding's résumé looked as if he was made for this work: tutelage in debate at Wiley with Melvin B. Tolsen; a storied collegiate football career at Wiley, Wilberforce, and Fisk; a long stint in Negro Leagues baseball (with Detroit, Kansas City, Chicago, and Baltimore); a personal connection with Williams, Pollard, Slater, Lillard, and Butler; and a belief that the segregation of the NFL was a great injustice. This set of experiences and perspectives made Harding a fierce and effective advocate for the reintegration of the league. When the opportunity presented itself in 1945, he was ready for it.

On a December day in 1945, with thermometers reading eight below zero, the Cleveland Rams won the NFL championship in front of 32,178 hometown fans. Despite consistently fielding excellent teams, the Rams struggled to attract enough fans to games. The Rams' owner, Dan Reeves, was sick of the cold and sick of losing money. The NFL was eager to expand to California, and Reeves wanted to take them there. A month after winning the league championship, Reeves prepared to move the team to Los Angeles, where they would play their games at the Los Angeles Memorial Coliseum. The Coliseum was city property, so the move needed to be approved by the Los Angeles Coliseum Commission, whose meetings were open to the public. Halley Harding, then the sports editor of the *Los Angeles Tribune*, saw his moment.

At the public hearing before the Coliseum Commission, Rams ownership—as well as actor Don Ameche, the owner of the Los Angeles Dons football team in the upstart, rival American Football League (AFL)—petitioned to have their teams play in the stadium. Seizing the moment, Harding stood up, eloquently educated the commission on the integrated early history of the NFL, making the case that any home team playing in the Coliseum could not legally be segregated. Harding succeeded in getting the Rams' ownership to commit—publicly and on the record—to giving Kenny Washington a tryout. Harding knew that Washington's standing in Los Angeles—and statewide—was so high that the city would reject any team that rejected Washington. History typically credits the Rams' owner, Dan Reeves, and the Coliseum Commission with forcing the NFL to reintegrate, but it was Harding's eloquence that made the difference.[10]

The Rams agreed to sign Kenny Washington and Woody Strode—and Black players were back in the league after thirteen years of exclusion.[11] Perhaps nobody else was made for the moment quite like Halley Harding, whose argument for equality had been built over a remarkable lifetime. When the opportunity arose, Harding did not fail.

On March 22, 1946, the news broke that the Los Angeles Rams had signed Washington and Strode, ending the league's embarrassing period of segregation. The *Oakland Tribune* noted that the NFL had, of course, formerly employed African American players, citing Pollard, Williams, and Slater as examples. They also noted that Kenny Washington had been Jackie Robinson's teammate at UCLA, and that Robinson was—at press time—on the Brooklyn Dodgers' minor-league affiliate, the Montreal Royals.[12] Everybody knew that integration was coming to Major League Baseball, but its pathway was blazed firmly in football. Branch Rickey, the Dodgers' general manager, had played with professional football's first African American player, Charles Follis, in 1906. Like Halley Harding, Rickey had been preparing over a lifetime for the moment to integrate baseball. It is nothing short of extraordinary that Kenny Washington and Jackie Robinson were college football teammates, roommates, and friends, and that their stories are—without question—intertwined with that of Ink Williams.

Kenny Washington and Woody Strode were both twenty-seven by the time they were signed to play for the Rams. At the time, Washington was making a living as an officer in the Los Angeles Police Department. Strode, Washington, and Robinson had played professional football together for the Hollywood Bears of the Pacific Coast League. Strode and Robinson were both members of Alpha Phi Alpha at UCLA. Kenny Washington's father, Blue Washington, was a former Negro League baseball player turned Hollywood actor who had played a bit part in the film *The Birth of a Nation*. Kenny's mother was from Jamaica, and he had been raised in a mostly Italian American neighborhood. Strode's grandparents included a Black Cherokee grandmother and a Black Creek grandfather; his wife (Luukialuana Kalaeloa) was Native Hawaiian. With the Rams, Washington and Strode roomed together and learned quickly that the racial climate of California was far more progressive than what they encountered on the road in the NFL in 1946. Strode later told *Sports Illustrated*, "If I have to integrate heaven, I don't want to go."[13]

CHAPTER 22

Ebony

Back in Chicago and trusting his supposedly golden parachute from Decca, Mayo Williams landed with a thud. He had returned from a ten-year engagement with jump blues to find that the whole world of music had changed without him: recording technology, popular music tastes, Black vernacular music in Chicago, the rise of small record labels, and the postagrarian urban culture of a new Black Chicago. In the past, Williams could always find lieutenants to help him navigate the shifting landscapes of Black music, but once released from Decca, he almost willfully ignored these new developments. Instead he sought to catch lightning in a bottle with an endless number of unknown performers, produced over the next two decades on his own small imprints. Fifty-two years old in 1946, Williams mistakenly presumed he could return to the sedentary scouting practices out of the same South Side Chicago office that he had occupied during his tenure at Decca. With the help of old friends such as "St. Louis Jimmy" Oden, Lee Brown, Little Brother Montgomery, and others, Williams located aspiring blues musicians, paired them with a backing band, and recorded songs that he then shopped to the major labels of the day. In the event that major labels were not interested, Williams released records on his own labels.

At the time, Chicago was becoming a hot spot for new and powerful independent record labels. Mercury Records was born in Chicago in 1945 and found significant success in pop music with acts such as Patti Page. The emergence of Chess Records was still a few years in the future; for a moment, Williams was almost the only game in Chicago for unknown Black musicians. Aspiring blues artists had only two such freelance producers to choose from in Chicago; as Muddy Waters recalled it, "There was a black one and a white one: [Lester] Melrose was the white one, and Mayo was the black."[1] Williams missed the moment.

Sensing his pending severance from Decca, Williams had started dabbling in recording music for his own independent labels—Southern, Chicago, and Harlem—in 1945 while still in New York at Decca. These sides include several recordings that are more interesting for their historical content—namely, Big Joe Williams's "His Spirit Lives On" (an ode to the late Franklin D. Roosevelt), Ann Sorter McCoy's "Tell It to the O.P.A," and James McCain's "Good Mr. Roosevelt." But other releases seem to have been sides that Decca had turned down, or demo tracks that were recorded illegally during the AFM recording ban. One noteworthy exception is Lee Brown's "Bobbie Town Boogie," recorded and released in 1945. Brown was a well-known figure in Chicago's evolving urban blues scene whose association with Williams caught the attention of a truck driver from Clarksdale, Mississippi named McKinley Morganfield. After moving to Chicago in 1945, Morganfield was performing in city clubs under the name Muddy Waters.

Born near Clarksdale, Mississippi in 1913, McKinley Morganfield was raised by his grandmother in a cabin on the Stovall Plantation, learning to play harmonica and guitar in the Delta blues style of Son House. In 1941 and 1942, Morganfield was becoming known in the Clarksdale area as Muddy Waters and was visited by the folklorists John Work III and Alan Lomax. Work and Lomax made field recordings of Waters for the Library of Congress. Although those recordings reveal Waters to be a singer with a strong voice and great confidence, he had not yet undergone the musical transformation that defined his later style, known as Chicago blues. Instead, Muddy's Mississippi field recordings demonstrate the decidedly rural dance string-band music favored at the time by local sharecroppers, built around guitar, vocals, and fiddle. The Library of Congress eventually released those recordings, but Muddy Waters had never made a commercial studio recording prior to arriving in Chicago in 1945.

In Chicago, Waters started playing guitar in Lee Brown's band and performing his own shows as an opener for Big Bill Broonzy. Muddy recalled that "Lee Brown and them had been recording for [Mayo Williams] a long time." Brown played a style of blues that tended toward the horn-driven jump blues of the Harlem Hamfats. One of Brown's songs—"Barber Town Boogie"—had been released on Williams's Southern label (mistitled "Bobbie Town Boogie") just after Waters joined Brown's band; the group played the song four times a night.[2]

Understanding that his guitarist had aspirations of his own, Lee Brown set up a session for Muddy with Mayo Williams. Muddy would later say that the scene at the studio was typical of one of Ink Williams's wholesale recording sessions, with a single studio band backing up multiple singers:

> Now I can't get in my mind, the guys on sessions, the back of my head, who the hell was it that day. We all did like a song or two. . . . There was

a bunch of us there, as I say. They just got a bunch of musicians, went in there, and did a session with probably one song. . . . One song or two songs by this and that, and they did a whole line of session, paid 'em sidemen [union-scale sidemen's fees], which was—we didn't get it, we got half sideman. We didn't get forty-one twenty-five. Forty-one twenty-five was with the sidemens then, you know. Eighty-two-fifty was the leader. I musta got twenty-something dollars out of it.[3]

Muddy sang one song that day—"Mean Red Spider"—and played guitar on another ("Let Me Be Your Coal Man," with an unknown singer). Ink Williams had difficulty pressing the recordings on account of a flawed master. When the record finally came out in 1947 on the Philadelphia-based 20th Century label (Williams had leased it to the label), Muddy was already recording for Chess, so it was issued under the name James "Sweet Lucy" Carter.[4] Waters didn't hear the recording until the 1970s, and he never worked with Williams again:

> No, that's the onliest thing, the only thing I did for him. I cut about a side or two, and he never did do anything with it. The onliest thing I did with Mayo Williams, the only thing. Those two things. But I thought that was buried under the ground somewhere! I never knew it was put out on records, man.[5]

Years later, Williams would recall that "Muddy Waters was glad to record," yet he totally missed an opportunity to sign the architect of Chicago blues. "Mean Red Spider" contains the blueprint of the sound that made Muddy a global musical influence at Chess Records. "I made a whole lot of mistakes in this period, too," Williams admitted, "but money was coming so . . . I just figured, 'I missed that, I'll get something else.'"[6] Lester Melrose also recorded Waters for Columbia in 1946 and made the same mistake of burying Muddy's talents in predictable contemporary blues arrangements. The Columbia sides went unreleased. Waters recorded in 1947 for the Aristocrat label, later renamed Chess Records. In 1948, he began to redefine the Chicago blues sound with his hit recordings of "Feel Like Going Home," "Can't Be Satisfied," and "Rolling Stone." Williams's inability to recognize Muddy Waters as a new, genre-defining artist—as he also had with Mahalia Jackson and Nat King Cole—would go down as his biggest failure.

Williams had lost his place of importance in Chicago's Black music community; this affected his ability to sell artists to the new Chicago-based record labels. Mercury Records' founder, Irving Green, was a friendly associate of Williams's before Mercury took off, but Williams felt that Green had no interest in supporting Williams's artists. Likewise, Leonard Chess rebuffed Williams in a manner that Ink felt was disrespectful:

> When Chess was just starting in the big time, see, I got in touch with him. He had been my distributor over here at Fifty-first Street. I got in touch

with him. Then he begin to make money, and got too big for *me*. Yeah. And I got in touch with him. . . . He tells me that he will send a couple of his lieutenants out to see me. And I told him about having these records, you see? He's gonna send a couple of lieutenants out to see me, and I just wouldn't see 'em. I want to talk to *Chess*. But he's too big for me.[7]

By the late 1940s, Williams was reportedly representing a number of musicians—Memphis Minnie, Sunnyland Slim, Jimmy Rodgers (the blues musician), Little Walter, "Baby-Face Leroy" Foster, and St. Louis Jimmy Oden.[8] Perhaps Williams intended to get started as an agent and manager around this time—he certainly voiced regret about not doing so with Louis Jordan—but his connection with most of these artists was tenuous.

That's not to say he had no success—in 1947, he recorded Stick McGhee and His Buddy singing "Drinkin' Wine Spo-Dee-O-Dee," which was released on Williams's Harlem label. Born Granville McGhee in Knoxville County, Tennessee in 1918, Granville earned the nickname "Stick" from his older brother, Walter, who used to push his younger brother around in a cart using a stick. Walter—better known as Brownie McGhee—made a name for himself as a Piedmont blues musician, having learned at the knee of Blind Boy Fuller (whom Williams had recorded for Decca in 1937) and playing with the harmonica virtuoso Sonny Terry. While serving in the US Army during World War II, Stick learned an off-color marching song, which he later cleaned up and turned into "Drinkin' Wine Spo-Dee-O-Dee." By the time Stick was discharged from the Army in 1946, Brownie McGhee and Sonny Terry had become firmly ensconced in the folk revival taking place in New York City. Stick moved to New York and was playing with his brother and Sonny Terry when Williams recorded his cleaned-up version of "Spo-Dee-O-Dee" in 1947. Though the song, on which Williams received a writing credit, later became a staple of early rhythm and blues and rockabilly, it languished in obscurity on the Harlem label.

Additionally, Williams released a number of gospel recordings that stand as important documents of that music's sound as it evolved into its second decade. Chicago had, in fact, become a center of gospel music by the late 1940s. Groups from as far away as Mississippi, California, and Michigan would regularly work their way through the city, performing at churches, cutting with other groups in impromptu concert battles, and generating gospel styles that were as vast and numerous as the many denominations of the city's churches. Such was the environment that produced Chicago-based gospel musicians such as Sam Cooke and the Staple Singers. Indeed, Williams released several sides by the era's most influential gospel group, the Soul Stirrers, under the name the Five Gospel Souls on his Harlem label. Williams also recorded noteworthy sides by the Dixieaires; the Famous Blue Jay Singers of Birmingham, Alabama; and Brother John Sellers with Melba Pope and Her Gospel Trio. Many of these records were leased to Syd Nathan, whose burgeoning label, King, out of Cincinnati, re-released them on King's subsidiary race label, Queen (and later on King, after Nathan discontinued Queen). But Williams's relationship with Nathan soured after one year—perhaps because Williams was unable to deliver the caliber of artists he had recorded over the previous three decades.

Unfortunately for Williams, Chicago was no longer the familiar friend it had been before his days with Louis Jordan. But despite his new struggles in the music business, Mayo Williams continued to find sustenance in Black fraternity life in Chicago, as well as in a number of athletic and philanthropic endeavors. He maintained his space as a mentor within athletic circles; in 1947 he served on the board of trustees for the South Side Boys Club and helped spearhead a fourteen-thousand-dollar campaign to raise their annual operating costs.[9] By the late 1940s, the Chicago-based Alpha Phi Alpha chapter house (Xi Lambda), which Williams had helped found in 1928, had become a center for discussion of Black ideas and ideals. Judge Sidney Jones, one of Ink Williams's fraternity brothers, remembered that Paul Robeson frequented the chapter house while he was playing Othello with Uta Hagen and Jose Ferrer in Chicago in 1945:

> We used to bring him out to the Alpha Phi Alpha fraternity house, of which he was a member . . . and he'd leave the performance and come out and stay until six-thirty, seven in the morning. He would come out to the fraternity house and sit around and talk to the fellows, just like one of the boys. And the point that Paul always made was, "Sure, I'm accepted, I've got it made. I'm in the best of circles." He said, "That doesn't satisfy me at all. That doesn't please me. If my people aren't accepted, if they accept me because I'm an artist, because I'm a performer, in the best of circles," he says, "that doesn't mean anything at all to me. I won't be satisfied until I can be accepted as an individual, as a human being, and because of what I am."[10]

By this time, Robeson was at the height of his stardom as an actor and public figure. His post–World War II political activities put him in the sights of Senator Joe McCarthy and the House Un-American Activities Committee (HUAC). After a personal meeting with President Harry Truman was cut short when Robeson demanded federal protection for Blacks under threat of lynching, Robeson's political tone became increasingly strident. With the encouragement of W. E. B. Du Bois, he founded the American Crusade Against Lynching (ACAL) in 1946. (Though Du Bois was by then in his late seventies, he had just served on the NAACP commission to the first United Nations meeting, and his calls for decolonization were growing in influence.) When called before the House Tenney Committee and the Senate Committee on the Judiciary, Robeson refused to disavow the Communist Party of America and later refused to disassociate himself from New York City Councilman

Benjamin Davis Jr. (Representing Harlem, Davis was the successor of Adam Clayton Powell Jr., who had recently been elected the first Black member of Congress in the twentieth century.) By 1948, Robeson was blacklisted; many longtime friends and trusted colleagues severed ties with him out of political conviction or under pressure from the FBI and the media. Somewhat surprisingly, Williams—a self-described political moderate—did not allow political pressure to sway his loyalty to Robeson, recalling in an interview with Studs Terkel how he visited Robeson at the New York headquarters of the Communist Party:

> I can remember one time, in coming back from New York, the Communist Party's Club was down near the Grand Central Station. And of course I had boarded the train, or was going to board the train from that station, so I thought I'd drop by to see Paul. And in doing so, I was followed from there ... to the Englewood Station at 63rd Street [in Chicago] by the FBI.[11]

The Department of Justice has acknowledged Freedom of Information Act (FOIA) requests for FBI files on Williams's interactions with Robeson but states that these files cannot be located.

Ink Williams held no sway in the growing ranks of new, powerful, independent R&B labels whose mostly Black artists experienced great success with white listeners. The case of Stick McGhee's "Drinkin' Wine Spo-Dee-O-Dee" demonstrates this. Though released in 1947 to no fanfare, the record began receiving significant spins by a radio disc jockey, or DJ (an emergent phenomenon that was rapidly displacing live music from the airwaves even as it empowered independent labels) in New Orleans in late 1948. The sudden demand for (hard-to-find) copies of the Harlem single caught the attention of Ahmet Ertegun, whose recently formed Atlantic Records was just then taking flight. Ertegun signed Stick McGhee to Atlantic and, in mid-1949, rerecorded "Drinkin' Wine Spo-Dee-O-Dee" to great success, this time with Stick backed by his brother, Brownie, on guitar and Wilbert Thirkield "Big Chief" Ellis on piano. The Atlantic version sold two hundred thousand copies within three months and helped establish the fledgling label as an important player in the R&B market.[12] Williams, scrambling to find an advantage, sold his Harlem masters of McGhee's recording to Decca, who reissued the Harlem version of the song on their label. In the end, Williams was left with neither the artist nor the original master and no significant buyout of McGhee's nonexistent contract with Harlem.[13]

By 1950, Ink Williams ceased operations with his Chicago, Harlem, and Southern labels and founded Ebony Records. For the first several years of its existence, Ebony had a licensing deal with Decca Records, "and I used to have two secretaries, two salesmen, and two in my staff. So I had about seven or eight people workin' at one time."[14] But Williams continued to struggle to find his footing in the larger, increasingly integrated landscape of American popular music, complaining to Jim O'Neal, "This record business has *changed* so much." Williams eventually felt swamped by R&B labels with far deeper pockets than Harlem could ever hope for:

> Then Mercury came into the picture. And they came in, and they had money. See? And King. I helped set up King Records down there in Cincinnati. Yeah. And in setting up King, there's King coming in, and there's Mercury coming in, and Capitol was just coming in at that time, see?[15]

In today's recording industry, Williams would have been well equipped to function as a high-level consultant, advising other labels (such as King, Chess, and Mercury) without having to keep his finger on the musical pulse of the city (or the nation) and without having to invest his own capital. In addition, he would not have had to try to keep up with the rapidly changing technology of *making* records or arranging hit songs, which was no longer an issue of putting a decent band behind a good singer with a great song. Williams had grown used to a system in which producers could record blues singers wholesale, with record sales showing what it was that the public wanted. Williams admitted that, to him, arranging songs "was 'just play the piano and guitar,' and I'd pick a little group, with a saxophone, drums, and a piano, and made hit records. You just can't do that no more."[16]

In an interesting twist, in 1949, just as Williams's profile as a producer and talent scout was taking a nosedive, the music writer Dan Burley (who had been so critical of the Louis Jordan records Williams produced) credited Williams with bringing the concept of race records to the mainstream music business, first by establishing the music's commercial value through the 1920s, then creating a framework (race records divisions) that enabled major labels such as Victor and Columbia (historically hesitant to integrate their catalogs) to enter the market. Burley traced the use of the term "race records" to Williams by way of Robert S. Abbott, publisher of the *Chicago Defender*. Abbott eschewed the use of "negro" and "colored," deeming "race" to be a neutral and enlightened term to apply to Black Americans. According to Burley, "Williams sold the record companies on the idea of setting up 'Race Divisions' to take care of Negro musicians and singers and keep them separated from the white artists." Although Burley saw this as a victory for Black entrepreneurship, he felt the aesthetic results were mixed. The kinds of race records peddled by the major labels were, in Burley's opinion, overproduced. Burley identified the music recorded by J. Mayo Williams, Clarence Williams, and others at Black Swan, Gennett, Vocalion, and OKeh as being "live, virile, pungent, down-to-earth stuff that had the widest appeal."[17] Burley, a Black tastemaker of significant clout in the mid-twentieth century, is the only journalist to give credit to Williams for knowing what he was doing.

Similarly, the Black sports media maintained an important place for Williams as a trailblazer for race relations and integration. In a sprawling overview of the integration of sports in 1950, the *New York Age* highlighted the contributions of Williams, Pollard, Drew, Butler, Slater, and others as being people with significant athletic ability and personal fortitude—using their track and field skills to broaden the minds of their white teammates and competitors and using their football skills to show their remarkable durability and mental toughness. As the world was celebrating the accomplishments of such men as Jackie Robinson, Kenny Washington, and Marion Motley, the *Age* wanted readers to be mindful of their predecessors: "They suffered insults to manhood and the searing effects of discrimination and segregation, but they carried on to pass the baton to their successors."[18] In other words, athletes of Williams's generation had been runners in the same relay race as Robinson.

Though Williams may have been a visionary in the music business and a trailblazer in sports, that all seemed to be in the past. Perhaps Williams's drinking was blunting the edge of his historically sharp social and organizational skills. This problem was prominently displayed in a 1950 column by the legendary sportswriter Fay Young. Considered the dean of Black sportswriters, Young was an organizer of two of the major baseball leagues (the Negro National League and the Negro American League), was a founder of Chicago's Lincoln Athletic Club (for which Williams may have played football after high school), and was a staple of the *Chicago Defender* sports pages as far back as the middle 1910s. He was a close friend and associate of seemingly every major (and minor) Black figure in professional sports. With humor, Young reported on an impromptu gathering at Horace Lomax's insurance office, where a boisterous Williams showed up. Young reported a lively conversation about football history, insisting that Williams's intake of "Scotch and soda got him sort of mixed up on dates." The more Williams drank, the louder and more "voiciferous" he got, arguing about dates and details of football history.[19] This was no longer the circumspect young Ivy League graduate who had navigated complex spaces of race, class, and entrepreneurship so expertly in the 1920s. Instead, Williams appears to be a buffoon.

Perhaps this is the reason that Ebony records—his new adventure—barely had a pulse. Williams would record and release some sides by Sunnyland Slim in 1953, but otherwise the output of Ebony plummeted into obscurity. Perhaps sensing that his fortunes were fading, Williams would report to the Brown University Alumni Office that, by 1953, he was also working as a "fund agent," though he left the specifics of that job unexplained. It is possible that Williams was exploring the interest in banking and finance that had brought him to Chicago in the first place in 1921; it is more likely that he was seeking to maintain the style of living he and Aleta had grown accustomed to during his time at Decca.[20] The Williamses had owned a vacation property in Benton

Harbor, Michigan, but defaulted on their mortgage in 1951. The house was seized in the summer of 1952 and put up for public auction.

By 1956, the Williamses had found some economic equilibrium, buying a new vacation property in Berrien, Michigan even as Williams's businesses were grinding to a halt. By the mid-1950s, Ebony Records was considered a failure. The label's association with Decca ceased by 1954—likely tied to the fact that the Kapp brothers were no longer at the label. (Jack Kapp died in 1949; Dave Kapp had left Decca to start his own label by 1954.) In September 1954, the *New York Age*, long a supporter of Williams in his music and athletic pursuits, ran a scathing article about the failure of Black athletes-turned-businessmen. Although Joe Louis bore the brunt of the *Age*'s ire, it cited Fritz Pollard as having achieved modest success (with soundies) but painted Williams as an entrepreneurial failure: "Ink Williams, who also starred at Brown, chose the recording field and rates as one of the pioneers in the field. Williams amassed a fortune as talent agent for several record houses but, as in the case of many others actual directing of the business was in the hand of others. Upon moving out for himself, he found things a little different."[21]

Outside of work, Williams maintained his ties and friendships in the athletic community. In 1956, Dick "Super Six" Hudson, Williams, Hallie Harding, Fritz Pollard, Duke Slater, Jesse Owens, and other prominent Black Chicago athletes organized the Varsity Club of Chicago.[22] The Varsity Club's first act was to throw a celebration to recognize the accomplishments of the basketball star Bill Russell, who had led University of San Francisco to the NCAA basketball title in 1955 and 1956, won a gold medal in 1956 as part of the US Olympic basketball team, and was poised to begin one of the all-time great NBA careers with the Boston Celtics. The Varsity Club was designed to "foster greater participation in organized athletics, both amateur and professional; to reward athletes for their endeavors, both on the sports field and in classes; and to encourage the social and civic betterment of the south side community." The organization, which also aimed at promoting the recognition of Black athletes, had a sponsoring committee that boasted such prominent figures as Jesse Owens, Ralph Metcalfe (a four-time Olympic medalist, who by 1955 had been elected a Chicago city alderman representing Chicago's South Side, and was later elected to Congress), Fritz Pollard Jr. (who won a bronze medal in the 1936 Olympics), Ink Williams, Ozzie Simmons, Duke Slater (who was a judge by this point), and Sam Peyton. Quite surprisingly, Williams's old employer from Black Swan and the *Chicago Whip*, Joe Bibb, was also on the committee; by now, Bibb had become the Illinois State Director of Public Safety. The Varsity Club of Chicago granted the William H. Lewis Award, an annual athletic scholarship named after the first Black player on Walter Camp's All-America football team. This was the same William H. Lewis who had served as assistant attorney general of the United States in

1910, and later—as the Massachusetts state attorney general—had sponsored Fritz Pollard's admission to both Harvard and Brown.[23] One of Williams's first responsibilities with the Varsity Club in 1956 was to track down Bobby Marshall so that the club could give him an award at its annual dinner. Williams also kept in contact with Brown alumni, even writing, narrating, and producing a campaign record for Otto Kerner (Brown class of 1930), who ran (successfully) for governor of Illinois in 1960.[24] In November 1960, both Williams and Duke Slater publicly endorsed Kerner for governor in a campaign advertisement in the *Chicago Tribune*.

By this time, Ebony was releasing records infrequently, and Williams was dancing with his past, issuing recordings of Little Brother Montgomery and Lil Hardin Armstrong. It is notable that Williams never made a strong attempt to harness the commercial power of the growing folk and blues revival that was drawing young people—particularly college students—to the sounds of so many of the artists he had recorded in the 1920s and '30s. At a time when white kids from the North were driving south to seek out the likes of Furry Lewis, Williams—who knew where to find so many older musicians still living in Chicago and elsewhere—never showed significant interest in the revival. Perhaps some of this came from his lifelong disinclination toward nostalgia, or perhaps it ran counter to his ingrained gut instincts about seeking contemporary music that resonated with working-class Black consumers. Perhaps Williams's relationships with artists such as Bill Broonzy, whose careers were reborn during the folk revival, were too caustic. The anti-Williams sentiment documented in the stories of early blues musicians was often mutual. Around 1960, Tampa Red—with whom Williams had enjoyed a long and prosperous commercial relationship—had a nervous breakdown exacerbated by alcoholism and the death of his wife. According to Williams, "Tampa lost his mind. They was lookin' for Tampa one day, and he was up on top of his roof gettin' ready to jump." And although the slide guitar great was considered a threat only to himself, Williams refused to let him into his South Side office on occasions when Tampa came to the door.[25]

By the early 1960s, Williams was spinning his wheels. Ironically, this happened at the very moment that the civil rights movement was reaching its zenith and prompting reflection on what the editors of Alpha Phi Alpha's membership magazine—the *Sphinx*—called "pace setters": men who had established themselves in different corners of professional life in the early twentieth century. In 1964, the *Sphinx* called Williams a pace setter "in the white collar class," noting that his success—particularly at Decca—had forged the way for Black professionals (and music) to be taken seriously.[26] But by then, Williams's business acumen had greatly diminished. As the folk and blues revival swirled around him, his only attempt to capitalize on it showed a complete lack of understanding of what the revivalists wanted: Williams took some old recordings and overdubbed contemporary arrangements on top of them, including Sleepy John Estes's 1938 Decca single "New Someday Baby"/"Brownsville Blues." Williams had Nixon, Estes, Jimmy Oden, and others record overdubs onto the original mixed track and slathered on reverb following Nixon and Estes's European tour in 1964. The revamped track was released on an Ebony 45rpm as "Someday Baby"/"Sleepy John's Blues," and credited to "The Original Sleepy John Estes with His 'Jug Buddy' Hammie Nix & 'Father Jazz' Booker T. Washington." It completely missed the mark with revivalists, who were interested in raw, stripped-down performances that adhered to the original recordings. Hammie Nixon and John Estes remembered the experience as a pain in the neck with no financial payoff:

> **NIXON**: Man, they took pictures for about three or four days. He said we had a whole lot of money or something, and he gonna get it for us, but we didn't get it.
> **ESTES**: No. I was sitting down waiting for a Coca-Cola and I didn't get a orange.
> **NIXON**: Shoot. [Williams] the one got it.[27]

The 45 apparently did well enough to warrant a repressing, which was recredited to "Sleepy John Estes with the Jimmy Odens Blues Soul Stirrers."[28]

If the early commercial blues musicians struck record collectors, folklorists, and folk revivalists as the authentic heart of "real" blues, early professional footballers seemed quaint, ancient, and relatively uninteresting by comparison. Periodically, a news article surfaced about the early NFL. In 1961, Hack Abbott, who had played college football against Ink Williams while at Syracuse and professional football as a member of the Dayton Triangles, told the *Lancaster Eagle Gazette* that Jim Thorpe was the greatest player he ever faced, but also listed Fritz Pollard, Ink Williams, Red Grange, Guy Chamberlain, and the six Nesser brothers as among the league's best. Abbott, who by 1961 was managing a filling station, chuckled about the attractiveness of modern-day professional football salaries, and—despite his thirty-year remove from the game—still felt that he could compete.[29] Like Williams, Abbott had graduated from college in 1921 and played seven years in the NFL. The look and profile of the game had changed enough that the baggy pants, leather helmets, and mud-caked fields of yore seemed impossibly ancient to contemporary fans of the game. Furthermore, to the predominantly counterculture record collectors, folklorists, and folk revivalists, Ink Williams's involvement in the seemingly square and conservative world of football was utterly uninteresting.

In the early 1960s, some of Williams's old press contacts tried to do him favors. The *Pittsburgh Courier* ran a story saying that the sudden popularity of Chubby Checker's "The Twist" had pushed Williams out of semiretirement and inspired him to promote the Ebony single "I Miss You So" by Bob Camp. Williams told the *Courier* that he knew the origins of the twist; within a few weeks' time, the *Courier* applauded Williams's enthusiasm for Camp's single, but showed little faith that it would be met with any success.[30] By the late 1960s, Williams's Ebony adventure ended much the way it had begun—without any fanfare. Even Williams found his Ebony recordings entirely unmemorable: when asked by interviewers about the Ebony catalog, he could not recall what the label's top sellers were, laughing and admitting that "strange as it may seem, I can't think of *any* of 'em."[31]

Mayo and Aleta Williams were now maintaining three places of residence—a primary residence on Drexel Boulevard in Chicago; a second home in Huntington, New York; and a vacation home in Michigan. Their Chicago home was just blocks from the Eighth Church of Christ, Scientist, where Aleta (and possibly Mayo) had become a member. Aleta Williams retired as a Chicago school teacher in 1967.[32] Aleta's health was in decline, and Ink placed her in the Robbins Convalescent Home, where she passed away in March 1968.[33] Now a widower and retired in practice, if not in name, Ink Williams traveled to Providence to attend the Brown University commencement in late spring 1968. He also had the time and crankiness to write letters to Brown's Alumni office asking for a copy of the commencement issue of the alumni newsletter. "To be certain," he wrote to the alumni office, "I am anxious to receive a copy as it was my first return to the commencement exercise at Brown in many years."[34]

Ink moved from the Drexel Boulevard home into 417 East 47th Street, Suite 340 on Chicago's South Side, the same building that had housed the original Ebony Records office. Williams began his slide into old age with an impatience to set the historical record straight. Again, Williams wrote to the Brown University Alumni Office to confirm some details of his football exploits, showing that he maintained contact with old teammates:

> Further, during my football days at Brown I was picked by Trainer McKinnon on his All Time team as the greatest end he had ever handled in his 50 years at Brown. This article appeared in in [sic] one of the Brown Alumni Monthlies a few years ago. Curley Oden who was a quarterback lives there in Providence. I suggest you contact him for verification.[35]

By the start of the new decade, Ebony Records was all but defunct, and its staff had vanished. Williams claimed it was because he simply wasn't interested in dealing with personnel issues, saying, "I just don't want to be responsible for anybody right now."[36] Williams kept a recording ledger for Ebony for a few years, and then discarded it. He estimated that Ebony and his other labels "must've put out maybe a hundred" records since 1950.[37]

CHAPTER 23

Pioneer

When Kenny Washington died in 1971 at the age of fifty-two, the news was reported nationwide. By this time, professional football—which benefited from a television broadcast–friendly format—had surpassed baseball as the nation's most popular professional sport. After a decade of competition between the NFL and the upstart American Football League (AFL), the first Super Bowl in 1967 was intended to facilitate the merger of the two leagues. By 1971, the Super Bowl had become a secular holiday. The media-savvy league marketed its origin story in a manner that simplified its relationship with segregation, aided by a growing emphasis on the Super Bowl era as the "modern era" of football. Kenny Washington was now, in the mind of the public, the man who had integrated football. Some people remembered the full story, however, and a wave of corrective articles washed across the nation in the wake of Washington's obituary—marking the last time that Ink Williams's name was mentioned repeatedly in the mainstream press. The *Honolulu Star* ran the most pointed correction, saying they found it curious that media reports characterized Kenny Washington and Dan Reeves's role in NFL history as being a corollary to Jackie Robinson and Branch Rickey in Major League Baseball. "History shows," wrote the sports editor Jim Hackleman, "there was no parallel in pro football," citing Fritz Pollard, Ink Williams, Duke Slater, Paul Robeson, and Bobby Marshall as examples.[1]

Coincidentally, the Los Angeles Rams' owner, Dan Reeves, had died shortly before Kenny Washington, which prompted a correction from the *Times*, the Munster, Indiana paper that had reported on the Hammond Pros' games five decades prior. A *Times* journalist asked Bill Kovacsy, a former Hammond Pros guard and now a local retired fuel dealer, what he thought of the suggestion that Reeves and Washington had broken the NFL's color barrier. Kovacsy's monosyllabic response was "Nuts." To Kovacsy's thinking, Doc Young had broken the barrier in the early 1920s when he hired Ink Williams, Fritz Pollard, and Sol Butler.[2] The *Times* was blinded on the integration issue by its own sense of local pride: technically, Ink Williams was the first Black player on the Hammond Pros (1921), but Fritz Pollard (Akron Pros) and Bobby Marshall (Rock Island Independents) were the first Black players in the first year of the NFL (1920), with Marshall starting in the first official league game of the season.

Awareness of the early days of the NFL was dwindling just as Williams's business dealings with Harlem records were dying. Ink Williams was agitated when he saw old peers continue to succeed while he was largely forgotten. When Williams took the train to his fiftieth class reunion at Brown in 1970 (though he graduated in 1921, he identified with the class of 1920), he found by chance that Thomas A. Dorsey—now an esteemed elder of gospel music—was on the same train. Though their lives had been so closely intertwined, with so many varied and shared experiences, both men seemed to look askance at each other. In the face of the sober father of gospel music—who was on his way to Boston to deliver a lecture—Williams laughed and said: "Dorsey, you are the eighth wonder of the world. You going to tell me you're going up there to give a lecture?" Dorsey answered in the affirmative, and Williams—who marveled that a man like Dorsey had risen to such great acclaim—angrily jabbed, "Listen, you ain't got enough hands on all your fingers to put in that many people's eyes."[3]

Just two weeks after Williams's encounter with Dorsey on the train, the Chicago social historian Studs Terkel invited Williams to participate in a group reminiscence marking the seventieth birthday of Paul Robeson. The panelists—all from Chicago—mainly answered questions specifically about Robeson. Judge Sidney Jones—Williams's Alpha Phi Alpha fraternity brother in Chicago's Xi Lambda chapter—remembered:

> And I think [Robeson] is one of the great men of this century. A man who literally threw away millions of dollars because of his convictions, his beliefs, his ideals, his desire to fight for the underdog and underprivileged. In these days of black power, and the young Turks and young rebels, they forget about a guy like Paul Robeson, who really talked about Black power, and Black pride, Black independence and things of that sort. And he really gave his fortune, his life, and everything he had for it.[4]

Williams, too, held a lifelong admiration for Paul Robeson, telling Terkel:

> I want to say that athletes as a rule are regarded as all brawn and no brains. And I will say that Paul Robeson disproved that. He was not only a great athlete in the football world, but he had more brains than most of the people saying that he didn't have any. As we all know, he was Phi Beta Kappa, a lawyer, doctor so to speak, and all that goes with it. And disproving this,

he went on to greater triumphs in so many phases of the artistic world that I just can't name them.[5]

Although Terkel's program was focused on Robeson, the radio host became distracted by Williams's discussion of his time playing against Robeson in the National Football League. Terkel and Williams engaged in an exchange that revealed how far the integration-segregation-reintegration history of the NFL had receded in Americans' popular consciousness:

TERKEL: Now, Mister Williams, you said something very revealing here. As you may know me, I follow sports, and how easy a man can become a nonperson. Robeson's one of the pioneers of pro football. Pro football?

WILLIAMS: *Pro* football.

TERKEL: I didn't know that.

WILLIAMS: [sounding frustrated] *N-F-L*. National professional Football League.

TERKEL: Yeah, wholly unaware of that.

WILLIAMS: Come by the office some day, and I'll show you a picture.

TERKEL: This is a very, very fascinating thing that you're saying. A new revelation to me, and I'm sure to many; certainly white football fans. I mean, none know of it, I would suggest.

WILLIAMS: Well, very few know of these things, you see. And coming here this evening, I said that Attorney Dickerson must be wanting me to bridge *several* generation gaps, because I knew [Robeson] in 1916, and from 1916 right straight through. And recently I was in New York, and he was in a very secluded position, and you couldn't see him at that particular time. But I always would see him whenever I could. And that's probably it, unless you want something else. [laughter]

TERKEL: Well, any anecdotes come to your mind? Any football anecdotes? Of [Robeson] on the field? These were the days when few Black football players, you know, in certainly the colleges, you know, up North.

WILLIAMS: Yeah. The four of us were the only Negroes in the football league at that time.

TERKEL: Fritz Pollard, you yourself, Mister Williams—

WILLIAMS: And Duke Slater.

TERKEL: Duke Slater, and Paul Robeson?

WILLIAMS: And Paul Robeson. And being one of the pioneers, I have been asked on several occasions about the beginning [of football]. Because in the present day, there are sixty Negroes in the National Professional League, and also the American Football League.

TERKEL: What was the relationship at the time? There were four black football players?

WILLIAMS: Four.[6]

Williams was noticeably irritated at Terkel's incredulity at the NFL's integrated beginnings. When discussing various racist slights he faced in pro football, Williams's irritation was compounded by the fact that Terkel appeared unprepared—in terms of history and practicality—during the round-table interview of Robeson. Williams admonished Terkel for, at one point, running out of tape mid-interview. Their conversation culminated in a feisty exchange that Williams finished off with crowd-pleasing panache:

> **WILLIAMS:** Well, I thought this program was to be on Paul Robeson?
> **TERKEL:** It is.
> **WILLIAMS:** Well, anything that you would like to ask me about *Paul Robeson*? Athletics I'll be glad to talk to you about.
> **TERKEL:** Sure. Any other memories you have about him? Either football, or off the field, his relationship to—
> **WILLIAMS:** Just this, I will say. We've often heard of that expression "A gentleman, a scholar, and a judge of good liquor." Now I'll say, [laughter] he was a gentleman and a scholar, but as to his being a judge of good liquor, I don't know. I don't think he ever tasted liquor.[7]

Despite Terkel's fascination with Williams's role in the early NFL, he never followed up with another interview. It is telling that Terkel—likely the preeminent popular historian of Chicago and a self-professed Chicago sports fan—was unaware of Williams's contributions—or, indeed, those of any Black Americans in professional football prior to Kenny Washington and Woody Strode's reintegration of the league in 1946.

Yet, to Williams's great surprise, he began receiving phone calls and letters from strangers, asking him questions about his career in early blues music. Steven Calt and Gayle Dean Wardlow, record collectors and blues researchers, sought Williams out by phone and mail in 1970. In November 1970, the record collector and chemist-turned-producer John Steiner (the man whose claim to the Paramount masters Mayo Williams never challenged) and the jazz historian Bill Russell visited Williams's office for a wide-ranging interview. Steiner, Russell, Calt, and Wardlow emerged from the subculture of record collecting. White collectors' preference for *rare* records over *popular* records that large numbers of Black customers actually purchased (and that had inspired subsequent generations of musicians and writers) struck Williams as bizarre. As early as the mid-1930s, record collectors—a quirky group of mainly white, northern intellectuals and misfits, lovingly documented by the music journalist Amanda Petrusich's *Do Not Sell At Any Price*—had begun to shape the narrative history of jazz. That narrative, in turn, informed the record industry's decisions about which historical recordings to keep in print through reissues. By the 1950s, record collectors' narrative of blues and country music often elevated the profiles of relatively obscure, regional artists like Moran Lee "Dock" Boggs and Robert Johnson and muted the importance of far more popular artists.

In 1951, the record collector Harry Smith curated and published a three-volume set of records called *The Anthology of American Folk Music* on Folkways Records.[8] With a total of eighty-four songs, the *Anthology* did what Ink Williams was unable to do, mixing race, hillbilly, and ethnic (e.g., Cajun, Kiowa) recordings. Smith had drawn all of the tracks from his personal collection of 78rpm records, which included a mixture of artists Williams recorded between 1927 and 1933 (Blind Lemon Jefferson, the Reverend J. M. Gates, Jim Jackson, Furry Lewis). Some of the artists on the *Anthology* had been popular in their day (the Carter Family), but it also included those who had certainly been forgotten (Mississippi John Hurt, Hoyt Ming and His Pep Steppers). Smith's *Anthology* became a bible of sorts for a growing folk revival.

In 1959, the record collector Sam Charters curated an LP for Folkways called *The Country Blues*, which he had culled from *his* collection of 78rpm records, and which mostly included artists connected with Williams: Big Bill Broonzy, Blind Lemon Jefferson, Blind Willie McTell, Leroy Carr, and Sleepy John Estes. Charters had also taken the then unusual step of doing fieldwork, seeking out the living artists and those who knew them personally, to document the history and context of these commercial sound recordings, which he published in a companion book to the LP, also called *The Country Blues*. The book places Williams in the story of the blues, though it paints him in the unflattering light that has dictated the way he has been remembered since. Although Smith's and Charters's collections both bear the influence of the whims and trends prevalent among collectors (including their interest in rarity), they also reflect the influence of Alan Lomax's 1942 Library of Congress report, "List of American Folk Songs on Commercial Records." Notably absent (or significantly downplayed, in the case of Lomax) in these versions of race records history are women. These collections virtually ignored the birth of commercial blues and the magnificent space in it that performers such as Ma Rainey and Bessie Smith occupied.

Two years after Charters's book was published, John Hammond—both a producer and a 78 collector—curated a reissue of Robert Johnson's music on a now famous LP called *King of the Delta Blues Singers*. Although Johnson, who had recorded for Vocalion in 1936 and 1937 (after Williams left Vocalion for Decca), was deeply influenced by several of Williams's most popular artists (particularly Peetie Wheatstraw and Leroy Carr and Scrapper Blackwell), his style was distinctively Delta blues, which was significantly less popular than its cultural cousins. But the influence of collectors, Hammond's power as a tastemaker, and the magnetism of Johnson's performances reconfigured the entire narrative of blues—certainly in the minds of white record buyers, and with musicians and consumers worldwide. The result stood the popular understanding of the blues on its head. No longer was the blues viewed through the lens of the Black musicians who commercially recorded it, the Black consumers who bought most of their original releases, and the Black communities who danced and listened to blues music at parties, juke joints, and theaters such as the Monogram. Instead, the broader world began to see blues through a romantic lens constructed around its most obscure, mysterious (and virtuosic) figures, such as Robert Johnson. Johnson, who had died in 1938 at age twenty-seven, only fourteen years before the Columbia reissue of *King of the Delta Blues Singers*, sounded to new listeners as if he came from another century. And although record collectors were, in many ways, responsible for preserving, protecting, and promoting the vast diversity of American vernacular music, they had also rendered its best-known practitioners obscure in the gaze of history. In turn, reissues like *King of the Delta Blues Singers*, *The Country Blues*, and *The Anthology of American Folk Music* ignited a folk and blues revival that shaped and dominated the popular music of the 1960s: groups as varied as the Rolling Stones, the honky-tonk singer Lefty Frizzell, the singer/songwriter Bob Dylan, the jazz singer Nina Simone, the R&B singer Lloyd Price, and the crooner Bing Crosby.

Major labels such as Columbia weren't the only ones involved in the reissue business, of course. In addition to the work of Folkways Records, a cottage industry of independent labels followed in Sam Charters's footsteps, complete with deep liner notes that illuminated the history and context of many hillbilly and race record artists. When Steven Calt first contacted Mayo Williams in 1970, he was connected with the blues reissue label Yazoo Records, which had worked closely with the record collector Gayle Dean Wardlow. Calt was researching a biography of the Delta blues singer Charlie Patton and wanted to know why recording directors such as Williams had favored the classic- or vaudeville-style blues singers such as Ma Rainey who had dominated the race record market from 1920 to 1926 over Delta blues guitarists such as Patton, whose late-starting recording careers were cut short by the Depression.

In Calt's assessment, only two race record executives had been interviewed by historians—Art Satherley, who focused on hillbilly music, and Art Laibly, who Calt said had "little inclination to discuss his role as Williams's successor at Paramount."[9] Calt was fairly certain that he was the first researcher to interview Williams, and he knew that the sparse existing literature—Bill Broonzy's 1957 autobiography *Big Bill Blues*, Samuel Charters's *Country Blues*, and a handful of *Downbeat* magazine articles by John Hammond—disparaged him. "These were the only references to Williams I was aware of," Calt remembered, and they "complemented a contemporary stereotype held by record collectors, which was that recording officials of the 1920s were crass, boorish figures who had no appreciation or understanding of blues." Calt believed that Williams had his own version of events, and "It turned out that the printed references to him were unreliable and irresponsible."[10]

Calt (who lived in New York) found Williams's address and phone number in a Chicago phone book at the New York Public Library. Concerned that a phone call might be off-putting, or that Williams might be in a bad mood and not want to talk, he began interviewing Williams by mail. These letters eventually led to phone conversations. "In our first phone conversation," Calt recalled, "he surprised me by asking, 'What is your ethnic background?'" In Calt, Williams saw an opportunity—to make some money from vintage records, to publish an autobiography, and to sell some Ebony 45s. Like so many of his blues revivalist peers, however, Calt was not terribly interested in doing any of that—something he regretted many years later:

> At the time I had no broad interest in him as a person, or as anything other than a former employee of Paramount (and later, Vocalion) Records. I was not even particularly interested in the work he had done for Decca in the 1930s, largely because it involved singers I was not enamored of.

Unknown to Calt, a blues and jazz researcher named John F. Mackenzie had also initiated a similar (though far less extensive) dialogue with Williams in 1970. Mackenzie had spent years researching the history of Gennett Records, which prompted him to contact Williams via phone for information about Black Patti Records. Mackenzie conducted two phone interviews with Williams from his home in Oregon in the summer of 1970 and spent the next several years preparing a manuscript on Gennett's history. Mackenzie died before the manuscript was completed, and his research was deposited in the Indiana State Historical Archives by his widow. Though the transcriptions of Mackenzie's phone interviews with Williams have proved invaluable, he never committed to paper any notes regarding his impressions of Williams.

Late in 1970, the New Orleans jazz historian (and musician/composer) William "Bill" Russell, accompanied by John Steiner, visited Williams and interviewed him extensively. Though their conversation drifted into a variety of topics, Russell was primarily interested in Williams's encounters with Jelly Roll Morton. Indeed, Mackenzie, Calt, and Russell were focused on particular labels or individuals, with Calt and Mackenzie being the most tightly focused on labels such as Gennett, Paramount, and Black Patti. They painstakingly reconstructed the history of the labels (from scouting artists to manufacturing plants and everything in between), including mapping out the history of recording dates and releases for labels (like Paramount) that did not leave ledger books behind. They also were interested in particular artists—especially those Delta bluesmen like Charley Patton, who had recorded for Paramount after Williams's departure from the label.

Seemingly all record collectors and blues revivalists were interested in Robert Johnson. Both Patton and Johnson occupy a significant place in Mississippi folklife, but neither were household names outside of that region during their recording days. Compared with the popular artists Williams recorded—Ma Rainey, Papa Charley Jackson, Leroy Carr, Tampa Red, Peetie Wheatstraw, Memphis Minnie, and Louis Jordan—Patton and Johnson were downright obscure. Williams was miffed by Calt and Mackenzie's palpable lack of interest in figures he deemed important. Calt was very much a product of his time and was utterly uninterested in Williams's popular accomplishments. Similarly, he had no interest in Williams's career in professional football or in the US Army. "I did not share my misgivings with Williams," Calt would write later, "for fear of turning off the spigot of reminiscence" instead entertaining Williams's ideas about an autobiography.

Eventually, Calt arranged to interview Williams in person in Chicago. In the summer of 1971, Calt, who was then twenty-six, headed from New York to Chicago to spend five days with the seventy-seven-year-old Williams. Calt was nervous that Williams would turn out to be an egomaniac but found him to be comfortable with his role in the history of blues music:

> I was astonished to discover that within a field populated by blowhards, Williams was genuinely modest. He never sought to credit himself with any historic accomplishment or brag about his achievements in the record business. Indeed, he never tried to present himself as an important personage on any level. He was completely indifferent to his reputation, be it positive or negative.

Calt was happily surprised by how well they got along, and—despite a tape recorder malfunction that caused Williams to grow temporarily irritated—the two settled into an easygoing relationship:

> The result was that I was exposed to a truly fascinating figure who was by far the most interesting and likeable of the fifty-odd persons I had interviewed over the preceding seven years as a self-anointed blues researcher. We had an easy, instant rapport: Williams said that I reminded him of Maurice Supper, the Paramount executive who had hired him and was (Williams said) considered the "brains" of the company.[11]

During the interviews, Calt found Williams to be honest even about his own dishonest practices, never varnishing the truth, to a degree that made him unusual:

> What was most surprising about Williams was his straightforwardness. He made no attempt to elevate the race recording business above the level of the swindle it basically was and gratuitously informed me of his own larcenies

within it. No one in the record business has ever similarly owned up to a single ethical shortcoming, at least in a public forum. Yet the business is rife with sharpies and crooks.[12]

Calt came away from the experience with the impression that Williams's candid remarks, his disinclination toward self-promotion, and his methodical approach to his work in the record industry came from a "spirit of objectivity," meaning, Williams just didn't care about the music in the same way its performers, consumers, and historians did. When Calt played him a copy of *Out Came the Blues*, a Decca compilation of historical blues recordings, Williams was utterly uninterested in listening. And when Calt played him a Yazoo LP reissue of Henry "Ragtime Texas" Thomas—whom Williams had recorded for Vocalion—"he had no memory of Thomas," despite the singer's memorable recordings of "Going Up the Country," and his unusual use of panpipes. Such recordings would have been relatively obscure during their original commercial lifetimes; Williams found white blues revivalists' preference for such obscure artists as Henry Thomas over popular artists like Leroy Carr annoying. "The impression Williams made," Calt would recall, "was that of a success-oriented figure who excelled at his position not because music or blues appealed to him on some deep level, but because he was determined to excel in life."[13] Calt's assessment of Williams as success oriented seems entirely accurate, but much of Williams's biography shows that he was personally interested and invested in blues music.

Calt also observed that Williams had no interest in representing himself as a racial pioneer. Williams refused to make observations within a racial context and seemed to show little interest in the kind of race consciousness that was ascendant in Black popular and intellectual circles in the early 1970s. "Without actually saying so," Calt reminisced, "Williams appeared to consider himself as an individual who happened to be Black."[14] Again, Calt's assessment was likely what Williams wanted him to think rather than what Williams himself believed. Based on Williams's writings for the *Chicago Whip*, his clear frustration with America's amnesia about the early integrated history of the NFL, and his lifelong commitment to Alpha Phi Alpha fraternity, it appears that what Calt experienced was Williams's supreme gift of intuitive code-switching, whereby he could navigate spaces of whiteness and racial integration in a way that caused race—or the kind of contentious race consciousness that Calt encountered on visiting the far more combative Fritz Pollard—to recede to the point of invisibility. Harry Young—the son of Williams's old Hammond Pros coach, Doc Young—wondered in later years if Ink Williams's congenial nature caused some to see him as an "Uncle Tom" compared with Fritz Pollard. Nevertheless, Williams's disposition achieved a remarkable feat in 1921: Young, the white son of a doctor from Indiana, openly hero-worshiped a Black man.[15]

Over the course of five days, Calt acquired a genuine appreciation of a man whom he had—admittedly—initially seen as only a treasure trove of information on Paramount Records:

> In the course of our conversations I developed great regard for him both as an individual and as a record executive. He struck me as an unaffected, unpretentious person who was the epitome of a gentleman. As a record executive, Williams gave positive evidence of brilliance in three instances. He signed Ma Rainey as a Paramount act despite the fact that she was not (as I later gleaned) even the headline act at the Monogram Theatre in Chicago, where Williams discovered her in 1923. In all likelihood, she had a small local reputation when Williams signed her. Even more impressive was his decision to record Papa Charlie Jackson, a banjo player who was a complete nonentity when Williams heard him perform on a street in 1924. His rationale for signing Jackson was that one could dance by the latter's music. Indeed, Jackson was the first black dance musician to reach the recording studio. Williams's ability to discern dance music was not only unique in the race record industry but is something that practically no blues specialist of today appears to possess. The plain fact is, most commentators who write about blues can't tell the difference between a dance tune and a street song. Finally, Williams's perceptiveness was illustrated by his comment that Blind Lemon Jefferson was a "soul singer, naturally." It so happens that Jefferson was the first vocalist to use devices associated with later "soul singers."[16]

Calt left Chicago with a commitment to assisting Williams in a variety of ways—selling some Decca test pressings for cash, trying to get him on a college lecture circuit (Yazoo and Adelphi Records were attempting to cocreate a booking agency together at this time), and the possibility of collaborating on an autobiography.[17]

Back in New York, Calt maintained a correspondence with Williams by mail. Williams began drafting an autobiography, which Calt remembered "consisted of a diatribe against then-contemporary black youths, whom, he felt, lacked a work ethic and expected things to be handed to them." Calt recoiled at this characterization and also had little interest in Williams's football exploits—which Williams showed considerably more pride in. Growing impatient with Calt's priorities, Williams granted the blues researcher permission to use the interviews in whatever form he pleased and forged ahead with two autobiographical projects: the first focused on football, the second a memoir of his work in music titled *There Will Always Be the Blues*.

The blues magazine editor, historian, and researcher Jim O'Neal interviewed Williams twice in 1972. On the first visit, he was accompanied by the record producer George Paulus, on the second by historian Paul Garon. Both visits took place at Williams's office; on the second they were joined by Little Brother

Montgomery and a fair amount of Heineken beer. As public interest in early blues (and Williams's role in it) was on the ascent, Williams continued to be frustrated by the increased whitewashing of early NFL history. The same annoyance Williams had with Studs Terkel in 1970 bubbled up again in his conversation with O'Neal and Paulus:

> **PAULUS:** It was an all-black team you were on, right?
> **WILLIAMS:** No, *no*. That's the *National Professional Football League*. The N-F-L. Yeah, no, they're not all Black by any means.[18]

When Williams said this to O'Neal and Paulus, it was only two months after the Dallas Cowboys' victory over the Miami Dolphins in Super Bowl VI, which was played in New Orleans. The NFL's prominence in the pantheon of professional sport—and in the popular culture of the country—was skyrocketing, as evidenced by the 56.6 million viewers who tuned in to watch the game on television (10 million more than the previous year). The halftime show was a tribute to Louis Armstrong and featured Ella Fitzgerald—the first Black woman to perform in the halftime show—as well as the Creole jazz banjoist-guitarist Danny Barker. Barker was a former sideman of Little Brother Montgomery, Cab Calloway, and his wife, Blue Lu Barker. Danny and Blue Lu recorded so-called dirty blues for Williams at Decca in 1939, with "Don't You Feel My Leg" and "Georgia Grind." A lifelong observer of the NFL, Williams doubtlessly noted that the Cowboys won the game largely on the legs of the star running back Duane Allen. A former standout at West Texas State University (an HBCU), Allen was a dazzling, high-profile Black athlete who is widely believed to have been denied the Super Bowl MVP because of his season-long refusal to speak to the press as a protest of his poor treatment by the Cowboys' ownership during contract negotiations.

With these intertwining threads of Williams's life playing out on television, it is difficult to imagine the frustration felt by Williams and other former Black football players that their presence and contributions to the league had been erased from the popular consciousness in only forty years' time. As a seasoned veteran of professional and collegiate football and a keen observer of human nature, Williams knew that the small numbers of Black men who played on integrated teams in the early twentieth century had superior athletic ability and great mental and emotional fortitude. Fritz Pollard adamantly believed that he, Paul Robeson, and Ink Williams should have been inducted into the Pro Football Hall of Fame in Canton, Ohio, which opened in 1963.[19] Many of Williams's comments suggest that he concurred with Pollard. (Pollard was inducted posthumously in 2005 and Duke Slater posthumously in 2020).

It also must have seemed a strange twist of fate to Williams that whereas the college-educated, popularly acclaimed Black football players who had once been the drawing cards of the early NFL had been forgotten, the blues artists—or "dogs," as Williams's Decca colleagues had derisively called them—he had recorded in the 1920s and '30s had attained a place of importance in the world of cultural politics and the popular imagination. Reminders of the blues artists of his past followed him throughout his life. In 1940 in Harlem, Williams was approached on the street by a girl with a guitar who claimed to be "Little Ma Rainey." And each time he heard the expression "It's your thing" in the late 1960s—the Isley Brothers' funk hit, "It's Your Thing," was released in early 1969—Papa Charlie Jackson came to mind:

> WILLIAMS: "Shake That Thing" was a raucous, bad song. Like shake your hips, shake your booty. All that shit. [quickly] All that stuff, pardon me. [pauses]
> PAULUS: That's all right. You can talk any way you like.
> WILLIAMS: Any time I hear, "He's only doing his thing," or "She's only doing her thing," I think of how "that thing" originated.[20]

During his conversation with O'Neal, Williams again demonstrates a greater interest in setting the record straight than in promoting his own importance in the history of the blues. Williams sensed Jim O'Neal's skepticism that he was the first to commercially record Muddy Waters, but Williams's disgust with Leonard Chess was enough to convince O'Neal that the 1945 Waters sessions were real.[21] Williams was still maintaining an office in 1972 when O'Neal visited; business was so slow that when O'Neal and Paulus asked Williams when he had quit recording, Williams emphatically responded, "I've *never* quit!" citing a forthcoming Ebony single, "Black Is Beautiful," as evidence.[22]

Williams was flummoxed by the interest of white collegiate folk and blues revivalists in his music career, but they were not the only people who remembered his contributions. In November 1973, the Chicago television journalist Vernon Jarrett published an article in the *Chicago Tribune* about a conversation he had with a local bandleader, Red Saunders. As the two men reminisced about the early blues and jazz greats who had played in Chicago, they realized that many of them were still living on Chicago's South Side, including two of Mayo Williams's associates, Little Brother Montgomery and Sunnyland Slim. Vernon Jarrett asked,

> What happened to Little Brother Montgomery and Sunnyland Slim, who started playing a unique piano blues during the era of Bessie Smith, Mamie Smith, and Ma Rainey? "They're right here and playing and playing the way it's 'sposed to."
> Red and I went down a list that included such names as Mayo "Ink" Williams, the famous Ivy League football star prior to World War I who helped launch the first Black recording company, and Eva Wheatley Edwards, who danced in Noble Sissle and [Eubie] Blake's landmark musical *Shuffle Along*.

I suggested to Red that we just had to do something big to salute these pioneers.

As soon as the men started to plan for a television extravaganza featuring Chicago's blues and jazz old-timers, some of them—such as the jazz violinist, trumpet player, and bandleader Charles Elgar—began to pass away. Williams himself was now pushing eighty years old. Jarrett and Saunders realized they needed to act now and planned to conduct oral histories with Black blues and jazz pioneers-turned-senior-citizens on Jarrett's *Black on Black* program on WLS-TV.[23]

Williams's health was in decline by 1974; in 1977 he finally listed himself as "retired" with the Brown University Alumni Office. By this time, Williams had taken up with a companion named Thelma Doyle Marshall, who became Williams's caretaker when the old athlete's health began to fail in the late 1970s. Doyle told *Living Blues* that during the last few years of Williams's life, "I kept him with me, because the poor child couldn't stand up without falling down." By the end of 1979, Williams was slipping in and out of consciousness. He fell into a coma around Christmas and passed away on January 2, 1980 in Chicago.[24] His death appears to have gone mostly unnoticed by the Chicago press, but his obituary in *Living Blues* noted that his longtime friend Little Brother Montgomery was present at the funeral.[25] The Chicago Board of Education notified Brown University of Williams's death, as did Dr. J. Herbert King, editor emeritus of Alpha Phi Alpha's *Sphinx* magazine, who requested Brown send photos, programs, and other memorabilia for a February memorial for Ink.[26]

With Mayo Williams's death, the family of John and Millie Williams, which had begun in Monmouth, Illinois one hundred years earlier, ceased to exist. Mayo was preceded in death by both of his parents, his sister, both of his brothers, and his wife. There would be nobody to carry on his legacy, to steward his memorabilia, or to maintain an awareness of his life and legacy. The autobiographies he was writing during his correspondences with Steven Calt in the early 1970s were never published, and the manuscripts have yet to be located. It was a quiet end to a life robustly lived.

Postscript
Indelible

The making of an LP requires fidelity to cohesive storytelling. The album's songs need to sound compatible—conceptually or aesthetically. In the pursuit of a cohesive narrative, much must be left out. The same is true of the writing of history. In this country, we are drawn to stories of progress that adhere to Dr. Martin Luther King Jr.'s vision of moral progressivism: "We shall overcome because the arc of the moral universe is long but it bends toward justice." In the writing and telling of American cultural history, much has been left out—particularly when it clouds a linear view of progress or neat categories of hero and villain. People such as Ink Williams are often removed from the story because their very presence causes cognitive dissonance; quite simply, they don't conform to what we think we know about our nation's story. Their presence means that progress happened only to be pushed backward. And, when people of color such as Frederick Douglass, Harriett Tubman, or Thurgood Marshall *are* allowed to remain in the landscape of history, it is only when they pass an impossibly high test of character. The Ink Williamses of history—people who have done heroic things, but whose personal character defies binary categorization of hero or villain—are usually erased.

However, without these complex characters on the historical landscape, we are left with a story that sounds good but that fails to explain how we have arrived in our current circumstances. For example, in the typical story of American popular music and its relationship to racial progress, the rise of Black-owned record labels such as Stax and Motown in the 1960s is seen as sign, symbol, and soundtrack of the march toward racial equity. In another arena, the integration of major league sports in the post–World War II era is often seen as ushering in the civil rights movement. Both are true, but what does it mean that advances like these—in music and sports—had been made once before in the 1920s, only to be shoved backward and erased from our collective memory?

August Wilson's exclusion of Ink Williams from his play *Ma Rainey's Black Bottom* (and the subsequent film adaptation) indicates just how faint the traces of Williams's life had become by the time the preeminent Black playwright published his monumental work in 1981. By then, Williams had already been dead for a year with nary a public notice. The small handful of people who remembered Williams's role in Ma Rainey's story (let alone the people who remembered Ma Rainey) mainly resided within a small, eclectic community of early record collectors and blues and jazz historians. Troy Maxson, the protagonist in Wilson's play *Fences*, is an example of how the playwright gravitated toward people like Ink Williams: men and women with extraordinary gifts grappling with—and traumatized by—the toxicity of a society that relegated them to punchlines and second-class status. Maxson is believed to have been inspired by Sam Bankhead, a Pittsburgh sanitation worker whose stellar twenty-year Negro Leagues baseball career (1930–50) suggests he would have been a Hall-of-Fame-caliber player in the Major Leagues, had he been allowed to play. (Sam's younger brother, the pitcher Dan Bankhead, joined Jackie Robinson in integrating the Brooklyn Dodgers in 1947.[1]) In other words, if August Wilson had known of Williams's existence, the storyline of *Ma Rainey's Black Bottom* would not only have been profoundly different but likely would have included Williams as a significant, complex character.

And yet, despite our willful, collective amnesia—a product of our nation's steadfast desire for a simple, smooth arc of historical and moral progress—Williams's mark on history has proven indelible. If we know how and where to look for him, he emerges seemingly everywhere in the primary-source materials that chronicle American music, sports, and society in the first half of the twentieth century.

Some historians love "great men" who heroically and (seemingly) single-handedly alter the course of history. Though he did great things, Mayo Williams was no "great man": he was often unethical, he likely dabbled in a fair number of illegal extracurriculars, and he certainly had his vices. American history allows for flawed "great men" to appear in its pages, but only when they have the privilege of being white. J. Mayo Williams was no hero, but he did heroic things, living a life of significant consequence in music, in athletics (often at great peril to himself), and in the advancement of civil rights.

Mayo Williams possessed a potent combination of intellect, resourcefulness, and instinct. He was the only one of five siblings who lived to old age: his father was murdered when Ink was only seven, his oldest brother died at birth, his only sister died before the age of ten, his brother Maurice died in his thirties of tuberculosis likely contracted during a long incarceration for a nonviolent crime, and his brother Luther died before the age of fifty. Ink

Williams emerged from a childhood framed by tragedy to become a student at Howard University, a graduate of Brown University, a second lieutenant in World War I, a record-setting sprinter and third team All-American football player, a major attraction during his six-year career in the NFL, the first Black man to referee an NFL game, and the most prominent and prolific Black record producer (and the most consequential producer of Black music) during the first half of the twentieth century. He lived a hearty life into old age.

In his college days, Ink Williams was measurably one of the fastest sprinters in the world. Sportswriters noted his tendency to hang back in the early heats, only to overwhelm the competition with a burst of speed at the end. Williams applied this explosive speed on the gridiron as well, stunning opponents with his ability to run to daylight on offense. Williams ran headlong, smiling, with no helmet, into the face of racist hostility, whooping as he was showered with vicious, hateful epithets from fans and competitors alike.

On multiple occasions, Williams starred for Brown University in football games against Yale University, one of the first schools to build a large football stadium. The Yale Bowl in New Haven, Connecticut was arguably the largest public venue of its kind in the United States. On the days that Williams played there, he was the only Black man on the field in front of forty thousand hostile fans, many of whom audibly chanted, "Kill that nigger!" After the game, he showered alongside admiring white opponents who had been instructed by their coach to injure him on the field. To survive such frightening circumstances is one thing, but to publicly excel in the face of them, as Williams did, is extraordinary, even heroic, and demonstrates remarkable focus and fortitude.

At his best, Ink Williams applied these abilities—to focus, to find and run to daylight, and to surprise and overwhelm his opponents—in all parts of his life, but particularly in the music business. Quite frankly, it is hard to imagine American vernacular music without the songs, styles, and artists that Williams ushered into the national canon of commercially recorded sound. These are the bedrock artists of classic blues, New Orleans and Kansas City jazz, gospel, boogie-woogie, R&B, and rockabilly: Ma Rainey, Thomas A. Dorsey, Blind Lemon Jefferson, Jelly Roll Morton, Joe "King" Oliver, Papa Charlie Jackson, Sister Rosetta Tharpe, Mahalia Jackson, Leroy Carr & Scrapper Blackwell, Memphis Minnie, Big Bill Broonzy, Pinetop Smith, Peetie Wheatstraw, Louis Jordan, Nat King Cole, Count Basie, and Muddy Waters—to name a few.

After spending years searching for Ink Williams's indelible mark on history, I find it harder to partition aspects of the American story that I previously had thought of as separate. If all the world is a stage, Williams's life—as an athlete, military officer, fraternity brother, and record producer—intersected with a far-ranging cast of characters: W. E. B. Du Bois, Jim Thorpe, Louis Armstrong, the Illinois governor Otto Kerner Jr., most members of the 1920 US Olympic Relay Team, Anthony Overton, Trixie Smith, John Hope, Alain

Locke, and Paul Robeson. As they are today, music, sports, politics, civil rights, and the old-boy network were intertwined—not just for Williams, but in the lives of many that he interacted with.

Yet for all of the places that Williams seems to turn up, searching for his story has felt like grasping at a ghost. Only five long-form interviews with him are known to exist, and all were conducted between 1970 and 1973. Three of the interviews focus almost exclusively on Williams's work with the Black Swan, Paramount, and Black Patti record labels (an eight-year span of time), and one focuses on Paul Robeson. Only two interviews—those by Jim O'Neal and Bill Russell—exist in complete high-fidelity form. Another (by Stephen Calt) exists only in parts: portions transcribed for a series of articles in *78 Quarterly* and one cassette tape that was recorded with a bad battery. One of the interviews (by John Mackenzie) exists only as a transcription. Studs Terkel's interview, in which Williams was part of a group of Chicagoans reminiscing about their late friend Paul Robeson, shares personal anecdotes about his professional football playing days. (The Russell interview does as well.) All of these interviews were conducted by white men.

Thus we have no recorded interviews that focus on Williams the person. How was he affected by the murder of his father? Did he have a strong religious faith? What did he experience on the field, in the locker room, on the bus? What was his rationale behind staying with the Hammond Pros when he was clearly one of the best players in the NFL and could have played for far more competitive teams? How did the segregation of sports square with the creolization of American music? What were his encounters like with W. E. B. Du Bois, or Alain Locke, or Harry Pace? Where did he see his work—in music and football—fit into theirs, if at all?

Without a personal account from Williams, another mystery looms large. Ink Williams was married to Aleta Stokes for nearly a half century, and yet we know little about her life, her career, and her personality. For this reason, it is hard to truly know the man who spent most of his life living with her. Both Mayo and Aleta were highly educated; both moved in the high circles of Chicago's Black society. They owned multiple homes. Williams was reluctant to move to New York City for Decca Records—even when Decca offered to relocate the couple and to find Aleta a comparable job—because Williams did not want to uproot Aleta from her life in Chicago. Both Mayo and Aleta were raised by parents who were born just at, or just before, the dawn of Emancipation, so it is extraordinary that they attended college and rose to the levels of society that they did. Yet they did not have children of their own, despite both being devoted to nurturing young lives in school and athletics.

We would know so very little about Williams (in his own voice) without the five recorded interviews we have. And although history owes a debt of gratitude to Williams's five interviewers, their interviews are also a product of their own time, demography, and culture. White collectors of blues and jazz records in the 1960s and '70s were notoriously fixated on the obscure and on the minutiae of discographical research. Thus their interest in the era's most popular blues artists—men such as Leroy Carr & Scrapper Blackwell, or women such as Memphis Minnie, whose music provided the soundtrack to so many Black lives—was minimal. Instead, collectors were drawn to artists whose hard-to-find releases made their surviving records rare and valuable. Further, the scarcity of their recordings made it easy for collectors to mythologize them. Artists such as Robert Johnson have become far better known over time than they were in their own time and better known than the popular artists who emulated their songs, sounds, and styles. As the folk blues guitarist and music historian Elijah Wald has pointed out, the popular history of Black music in the early twentieth century reflects more about the interests and aesthetic preferences of the white men who collected these records in the 1950s and '60s than it does about the interests and aesthetics of the Black audiences that consumed most race records, not to mention how J. Mayo Williams—the era's most prominent producer of Black music—saw and experienced it.[2] As a producer, Williams recorded artists who either became famous or remained obscure. He is audibly baffled—even annoyed—by his interviewers' obsessive interest in the obscure artists, as well as their deflection away from deep conversations focused on the most popular and influential musicians.

The same can be said of the interviewers' feelings about football: blues record collectors of the mid-twentieth century were a decidedly nonconformist bunch. The collectors Jim O'Neal and Stephen Calt both were ambivalent about a sport (football) associated with jocks, squares, and conservatives. They dodged Williams's attempts—on tape and in correspondence—to engage in conversations about the early NFL and about how these two worlds (music and sports) might have overlapped in Williams's life. Even on the occasions when interviewers did acknowledge Williams's efforts to talk football, he was clearly astonished by their unawareness (particularly Studs Terkel's) of the fact that the league Williams played in was the same NFL as the modern-day league. Only Russell and Steiner seemed happy to talk football with Williams—if only briefly and as it related to Chicago nightlife.

At times, I have wondered if Williams's life story should be told in separate streams: that of sports and that of music. I deliberately chose not to take this route, even though it means going against Williams's own plans to write two separate memoirs (football and blues), and even though it fits a problematic pattern of Black narratives framed by white men. My decision is rooted in the belief that a bifurcated narrative does not match the complex reality of Williams's lived experience—nor the lives of his contemporaries: the heavyweight boxer and jazz bassist Jack Johnson; the football, film, and singing star Paul Robeson; and the football star, entrepreneur, and media producer Fritz Pollard.

And I remain convinced that these two worlds were not so separate as we imagine them to be. In many ways, Williams, Johnson, Robeson, and Pollard were the forerunners of more recent athlete-entertainers such as the basketball, hip-hop, TV, and film star Shaquille O'Neal. J. Mayo "Ink" Williams was a man whose name regularly appeared—and was celebrated—nationwide, in both mainstream white newspapers and mainstream Black newspapers. Although many blues fans and musicians may have been illiterate, a great many were not. (After all, there is a reason that blues records were regularly advertised in print in Black newspapers.) Just as his fellow soldiers knew that J. Mayo "Ink" Williams was a celebrated athlete when he arrived at Officer Training School during World War I, readers of Black newspapers knew that the man whose name and face appeared in Paramount advertisements was the very same man who starred on the gridiron at Brown and in the NFL.

When we step back from the particular interests of record collectors, we can learn about stylistic evolution and continuity in Black music. If there is a through line in Williams's catalog as a producer, it is that he was drawn to—and had incredible commercial success with—dance music anchored in boogie-woogie, particularly on piano. Indeed, Williams's first major guitar-playing blues singer was Blind Lemon Jefferson, whose stylings on guitar most closely approximated the boogie-woogie piano rhythms that such itinerant musicians as Jefferson and Huddie Ledbetter encountered at brothels, work camps, and house parties. Williams's personal relationship with piano blues dates back to his childhood, when he heard the music of the river towns where his family lived and the lumber camps where his father worked. Although his major success as a producer of boogie-woogie on wax began with Jefferson, it continued through Cow Cow Davenport, Speckled Red, Pinetop Smith, Little Brother Montgomery, Sam Price, and Louis Jordan. This thread of blues tradition remains alive and well—in both the folk and pop continuum—in the music of the Black church and in rhythm and blues. Popular narrative histories of the blues that put Delta guitarists such as Robert Johnson at the forefront certainly illuminate a masterful player and a compelling regional tradition, but they also distort reality, hiding Mayo Williams "and his dogs" in the shadows and creating the confusing impression that the blues has nearly vanished.

Similarly, when we look at Williams's life story, we can see more clearly how sports and civil rights were interwoven. The movements that put Williams in the national spotlight—in sports and the military—were not simply precursors to midcentury civil rights progress but a deliberate and inextricable part of it. The high profile participation of men such as Ink Williams in college sports and in the US Army was part of a national strategy developed by NAACP leaders such as W. E. B. Du Bois and HBCU presidents such as John Hope. In the lives of the still famous Fritz Pollard, Paul Robeson, or Jim Thorpe,

Ink Williams is a sidebar at best. But although Pollard was the chief organizer of the barnstorming all-Black pro football squads in the 1920s and '30s (the Chicago Blackhawks, the Fritz Pollard All-Stars, and the Brown Bombers), it was Williams who brought Halley Harding into the mix. Though Harding was of a younger generation than Williams, his inclusion in the Pollard All-Stars brought Harding to California; gave him weeks on the road to soak up the stories of Williams, Pollard, Robeson, Butler, Slater, Lillard and other Black pro football pioneers; and motivated him—the athlete turned journalist—to successfully force the Los Angeles Rams to reintegrate the NFL in 1946.

The nickname that Williams carried with him throughout his life—"Ink"—forever hinted at his upbringing as a person of color living in a majority-white world, and—as Little Brother Montgomery so bluntly observes—at the Blackest and least privileged end of the spectrum in a color-conscious Black world. The context of his life can be read in the names of the first record label he worked for (Black Swan) as well as the first label he founded (Black Patti). Black leaders—in arts, humanities, and sciences—living and working in a white world were seen as shadows of their more famous white counterparts. The singer Elizabeth Taylor Greenfield (1820–1876) was the "Black Swan" as opposed to the Swedish soprano Jennie Lind, the "Swedish Nightingale" (1820–1877). Sissieretta Jones (1868–1933) was the "Black Patti" as opposed to the Italian soprano Adelina Patti (1843–1919). In the US Army, there were soldiers (white) and there were "Buffalo Soldiers" (Black). Sports certainly had its equivalents: Major League Baseball (white) had Babe Ruth, and Negro Leagues Baseball (Black) had the "Black Babe Ruth," Josh Gibson. I have made every effort to avoid the continuation of this tradition with regard to Williams the athlete and Williams the producer. His most comparable professional peers in sports were the Hall-of-Famers George Halas and Guy Chamberlain; in the world of record production it would be Ralph Peer. Yet characterizing Williams as the "Black Guy Chamberlain" or the "Black Ralph Peer" renders him a photo negative to the seemingly more authentic and pleasing originals, cheapens his legacy, and misses the entire point. Perhaps if the life and career of the legendary hillbilly and race record producer Ralph Peer were fused with that of the pro football Hall-of-Famer Guy Chamberlain, we would have something close to the "white Ink Williams." Williams was distinct. Aside from the occasions when he physically ran headlong into Halas or Chamberlain on the gridiron, or when he recorded a singer under a pseudonym who was under contract to Peer, a label would create the false impression that he was simply reacting to the ideas and actions of his celebrated white counterparts. Williams was gifted at navigating this space, but he was his own man.

The facts of J. Mayo "Ink" Williams's life are inconsistent and incomplete, and the unevenness of primary source material has many gaps that will prompt many questions. This may cause readers to feel frustrated with the author, but that is ultimately good: the more questions we ask about Williams, the more likely others will join the pursuit for details about this formative and significant person and time period in American cultural development. The more his name is drawn into discussions of American cultural life and history, the better. The giants who strode across the landscape of American cultural production during Williams's era—Alan Lomax, John Hammond, Ralph Peer, Milton Gabler—were white, knew Williams, and sometimes begrudged his existence. But the important work of those men also makes more sense when Williams stands beside them in the historical frame. The white men who loom so large on the early NFL landscape—George Halas, Ernie Nevers, Greasy Neale, and Curly Lambeau—crashed bodily into Williams, knew his toughness, and feared his quickness as he played for nearly every minute of every game, on both offense and defense, during his six-year NFL career. Ernie Nevers did not remain silent when George Preston Marshall successfully advocated for the segregation of the NFL. It is notable that Nevers was also the only one of those Hall of Fame players who was not by 1933 (the year the NFL became segregated) an owner or head coach of an NFL team. White owners shaped the narrative of the NFL, just as white cultural producers and collectors shaped the narrative of American vernacular music. So we are really meeting Williams just now, in a tale that is incomplete. It is my hope that my telling of his story marks the beginning, or a stepping stone, to a fuller tale in the future.

Speaking of tellers, the powerful conclusion of the Broadway musical *Hamilton* asks, "Who lives, who dies, who tells your story?" In the case of J. Mayo "Ink" Williams, I am conscious of my place as an imperfect teller of this particular tale. I am white and was raised in New Hampshire, which was—and remains—one of the least racially diverse states in the nation. I've competed in track and field and have watched countless hours of NFL games, but I have never played a single down of organized football. And although I've been a working rock musician, singer, songwriter, producer, and record-store clerk, the meanness I've encountered in the music business has been rooted in economics and aesthetics, not in the white supremacy of its Jim Crow origins and ongoing design. Unfortunately, like so many across the spectrum of race, class, and gender, I have inherited ideas about who can and should play various styles of music—a distortion born in Jim Crow and magnified by a century of race-based marketing. We are all the lesser for this. Each of us must work to unravel this knot in the fabric of our society.

My tenuous personal connection to J. Mayo Williams arises from the fact that both of us attended Brown University almost a century apart. I quit playing music for a living in 2003 and enrolled, at age thirty-one, in Brown's PhD program in ethnomusicology. During the first week of my first semester, in an independent study on the history of the hillbilly and race record industry, my advisor and professor, Jeff Todd Titon (author of the influential *Early*

Downhome Blues), gave me an old set of *78 Quarterly* magazines with articles about Paramount Records written by Stephen Calt. A footnote referred to the fact that Ink Williams had attended Brown on a football scholarship in the 1910s. I was dubious but intrigued and contacted the Brown alumni archives for verification. They confirmed that, yes, Williams had indeed enrolled at Brown in 1916 and had graduated in 1921; they showed me his senior yearbook and some football photos. This led me to reach out to Stephen Calt to see if he still had the tapes of his interview with Williams. I had been forewarned that Calt was famously prickly; he had published a notoriously caustic and controversial biography of Skip James (*I'd Rather Be the Devil*) just nine years earlier. But the infamous collector was so happily surprised to field an email about Ink Williams that he gave me his only existing cassette from the interview as well as all of his original correspondence with Williams. The more that I learned about Williams, the more incredulous I became that his story had gone untold (and, I believe, the more incredulous Calt became that he had turned down Williams's request to cowrite an autobiography with him). My journey with Ink Williams began twenty years ago as I write this. I have accepted the fact that I have become the person in the room who is the expert about J. Mayo "Ink" Williams while also decidedly *not* the expert about blues, football, or—least of all—what it was like to be a Black man living at the height of Jim Crow (or any era). I hope that a future teller will bring deep, meaningful insights and positionality to this story that I cannot. But ultimately, the world needs to know now about Williams's life—so my primary goal here has been to put the facts in order as best I can see them.

What is the cost of not knowing about Williams's life? Sowing the seeds of incomplete truth reaps a storm of confusion for future generations. Progress in America is always met with brutal reversals. Abolitionism was met with brutality and suppression; the Civil War, Emancipation, and Reconstruction were met with Jim Crow; the civil rights advances of the 1920s—as embodied in Williams's life in music and sports—were shoved backward during the Depression; the civil rights and Black power movements of the 1950s to the 1970s were countered by mass incarceration; the election of President Barack Obama was followed by the vitriol of a suddenly visible white supremacist movement and the ongoing deaths of Black men and women at the hands of police. Forgetting the very real existence of this racist/antiracist dynamic causes its reemergence to be stunning and disorienting. We need to know that violent opposition to progress is always coming.

Amnesia of the sort that caused Ink Williams to fade from the pages of history arises when we insist on telling ourselves simple stories of steady, undeterred progress. It also happens when we want only flawless protagonists. It is natural for human beings to want to know the truth. Yet it seems equally natural for human beings to avoid or deny the truth. Sometimes we want a story with an arc that bends toward justice, and we want all of the jagged reversals of justice to be ironed out for us. But when we soothe ourselves with smoothed-out tales of progress, inevitably we are confronted by ugly, confusing, and complicated realities. Some become so disoriented and disillusioned by historical reality that they resort to violence in order to maintain idealized versions of ourselves. Others become so disaffected by new truths that they distrust all information. But when we look at Williams's life, we see that progress—in music, in sports, in education, in economics, and as a whole society—is not unlike a football game: it can be ugly, and if you don't push forward, you will be pushed back. Sometimes you may get thrown for a loss, but you may gain a first down on the next play. Sometimes you may win the series, only to lose the game and yet still go on to win the championship. In this moment, it is hard to know where we are in the season of social progress in America. But what we do know—on meeting J. Mayo "Ink" Williams—is that for every generation that has successfully fought for progress, a preceding generation provided momentum, and a subsequent generation must protect those gains with utmost tenacity. Our greatest protagonists and our staunchest allies are always deeply imperfect. We must remember the lives of those who have helped to maintain society's progress—no matter how flawed the person, their tale, or their teller may be.

Notes

Introduction

1. This story is drawn from one told by Little Brother Montgomery—along with J. Mayo Williams—in an interview conducted by Jim O'Neal and Paul Garon in May 1972 in Chicago. Unpublished interview, personal archive of Jim O'Neal, BluEsoterica Archives, www.bluesoterica.com. All statements in quotations are direct quotes from Montgomery and Williams's telling of the story.

Chapter 1. Ink

1. "Tables Turned," *Pine Bluff Daily Graphic*, November 18, 1901, p. 1.
2. Ralph B. Eckley, "Resident Gives Picture of 'Ink,'" *Daily Review Atlas*, October 12, 1978, p. 38. Although J. Mayo Williams claimed in the 1930 census that his parents were born in Illinois, an 1887 birth certificate for an unnamed son of Daniel and Millie Williams shows the young parents claimed Tennessee as their birth state (Fort Donelson, specifically, for Millie McFall Williams).
3. Carl Moneyhon, "Delta Towns: Their Rise and Decline," in *The Arkansas Delta: Land of Paradox*, edited by Jeannie Whayne and Willard B. Gatewood (Fayetteville: University of Arkansas Press, 1993), p. 216; City of Pine Bluff, https://www.cityofpinebluff-ar.gov.
4. Haralson, who had represented Alabama's First Congressional District during Reconstruction, was sentenced to time in federal prison in 1894 on dubious charges of pension fraud, an event telling of growing tension between white Arkansans and Black civic leaders. Brian Lyman, "The Lost Congressman: What Happened to Jeremiah Haralson?," *Montgomery Advertiser*, March 20, 2020, https://www.montgomeryadvertiser.com/in-depth/news/2020/02/26/jeremiah-haralson-lost-congressman-alabama/2823015001/.
5. "Tables Turned"; "Killing in Cleveland County," *Arkansas Democrat*, November 18, 1901, p. 7; "Brief Mention," *Southern Standard*, November 21, 1901, p. 1.

6. Monmouth High School Yearbook, Monmouth, IL, 1908; personal correspondence with C. Bird Romano, district library media director and Monmouth High School technology contact, January 18, 2005.

7. Mary Huff, "Black Education in Monmouth," *Journal of Illinois History*, 45, no. 4 (January 1992): 73.

8. The 1909 Monmouth High School Yearbook's chronology of events jokingly notes in December 1908 that "'Ink' tries to write with a rubber pencil."

9. "Off to Colorado," *Monmouth Daily Atlas*, June 9, 1910, p. 1.

10. Monmouth High School Yearbook, 1910.

11. Jeff Holt, "Breaking the Color Barrier," *Daily Review Atlas*, 2002, p. 12.

12. Monmouth High School Yearbook, 1912.

13. J. Mayo Williams, interview by Jim O'Neal and George Paulus, March 17, 1972, Chicago, IL. Unpublished interview, personal archive of Jim O'Neal, BluEsoterica Archives, www.bluesoterica.com.

14. Williams, interview by O'Neal and Paulus, 1972.

15. "Monmouth Third in Big Eight Meet," *Monmouth Daily Atlas*, May 6, 1912, p. 6.

16. "Monmouth Third in Big Eight Meet."

17. Boys Track and Field Medalists, 1912, Illinois High School Association, https://www.ihsa.org/Sports-Activities/Boys-Track-Field/Records-History?url=/data/trb/records/index.htm.

18. Ralph B. Eckley, "Resident Gives Picture of 'Ink,'" *Daily Review Atlas*, October 12, 1978, p. 38.

19. Eckley, "Resident Gives Picture of 'Ink'"; J. Mayo Williams, transcripts, 1921, Brown University Alumni Archives, Providence, RI.

20. J. Mayo Williams, quoted by Stephen Calt in "Paramount—The Anatomy of a 'Race' Music Label," in *R&B—Rhythm and Business: The Political Economy of Black Music*, edited by Norman Kelly (Brooklyn, NY: Akashic, 2002), p. 89.

21. Williams, interview by O'Neal and Paulus.

Chapter 2. Howard

1. J. Mayo Williams, interview by William "Bill" Russell and John Steiner, November 20, 1970, Chicago, Historic New Orleans Collection, New Orleans.

2. Susan T. Hill, "The Traditional Black Institutions of Higher Education, 1860–1982," National Center for Education Statistics, US Department of Education, Washington, DC, p. 5, https://nces.ed.gov/pubs84/84308.pdf.

3. Robert Bruce Slater, "The Blacks Who First Entered the World of White Higher Education," *Journal of Blacks in Higher Education*, 4 (Summer 1994): 47–56.

4. John M. Carroll, *Fritz Pollard: Pioneer in Racial Advancement, Sport and Society* (Urbana: University of Illinois Press, 1992).

5. Williams, interview by Russell and Steiner.

6. Alonzo Morón, quoted in the *Providence Journal*, 1955, in Russell E. Malbrough, Alpha Gamma Chapter of Alpha Phi Alpha Fraternity, Inc. (independent

study project, Brown University, 1999), 2:21. Morón would receive a Phi Beta Kappa key on graduating from Brown in 1932.

7. J. Mayo Williams, transcripts, 1921, Brown University. Williams's high school transcripts reflect two years of English and algebra and one year each of geometry, elementary Latin, elementary German, Greek and Roman history, medieval and modern history, English history, chemistry, and physiography (physical geography).

Chapter 3. Brown

1. *Liber Brunensis*, 1917, p. 180.
2. Paul Robeson, quoted in Sheila Tully Boyle and Andrew Bunie, *Paul Robeson: The Years of Promise and Achievemen* (Amherst: University of Massachusetts Press, 2001), pp. 60–61.
3. Fritz Pollard, quoted in Boyle and Bunie, *Paul Robeson*, p. 60.
4. Boyle and Bunie, *Paul Robeson*, p. 52.
5. "'Varsity Squad in Stiff Scrimmage: Pollard's 86-Yard Run for Touchdown Features Strenuous Workout for Enlarged Squad," *Brown Daily Herald*, September 28, 1916, p. 1; "Brisk Scrimmage," *Brown Daily Herald*, September 29, 1916, p. 4.
6. "1920 Reception: Opening Gathering To-Night in Union at 7:30 for Whole College," *Brown Daily Herald*, September 28, 1916, p. 1; "Large Attendance at Annual Freshman Reception in Union: Speeches in Auditorium Well Received," *Brown Daily Herald*, September 29, 1916, p. 1.
7. J. Mayo Williams, transcripts, 1921, Brown University.
8. John M. Carroll, *Fritz Pollard: Pioneer in Racial Advancement, Sport and Society* (Urbana: University of Illinois Press, 1992), p. 93.
9. Carroll, *Fritz Pollard*, p. 67.
10. These works are John Carroll's excellent *Fritz Pollard*; Rosie Cheatham Mickey, "Russell Adrian Lane: Biography of an Urban Negro School Administrator" (PhD diss., University of Akron, 1983); and J. Saunders Redding's autobiographical *No Day of Triumph* (New York: Harper & Row, 1942).
11. "Annan '20 Features Football Work-Out," *Brown Daily Herald*, October 4, 1916, p. 1; "Long Scrimmage," *Brown Daily Herald*, October 5, 1916, p. 1; "Football Men Battle in Hard Scrimmage: Big Squad Reports," *Brown Daily Herald,* October 6, 1916, p. 1; "Varsity Plays Brilliant Game Against Trinity Team and Wins Decisive Victory," *Brown Daily Herald*, October 9, 1916, p. 1.
12. "Regulars Outclass Team B in Practice," *Brown Daily Herald*, October 12, 1916, p. 1.
13. "'Varsity Overwhelms Amherst in One-Sided Game by Score of 69–0," *Brown Daily Herald*, October 16, 1916, p. 1.
14. "Pollard Denies That He Will Speak for Wilson," *Brown Daily Herald*, October 19, 1916, p. 1.
15. A "smoker" was a social event where college men sat around and smoked. "1920 Gets Together—Over 200 Attend Year's Largest Smoker," *Brown Daily Herald*, October 19, 1916, p. 2.

16. "Open Track Meet," *Brown Daily Herald*, October 26, 1916, p. 3.

17. "Brown Meets Rutgers To-day in First Hard Test of Season," *Brown Daily Herald*, October 28, 1916, p. 1.

18. J. Mayo Williams, interview by Studs Terkel, "A Tribute to Paul Robeson," *Studs Terkel Program*, May 8, 1970, WFMT, Chicago. Studs Terkel Radio Archive, courtesy of Chicago History Museum and WFMT, https://studsterkel.wfmt.com/programs/gathering-friends-discussing-paul-robeson

19. Fritz Pollard, quoted in Boyle and Bunie, *Paul Robeson*, p. 60.

20. "'Varsity Overwhelms Rutgers 21–3 in Thrilling Contest," *Brown Daily Herald*, October 30, 1916, p. 1.

21. "Small Attendance at Mass Meeting," *Brown Daily Herald*, November 10, 1916, p. 1.

22. "Varsity Easily Outplays Vermont," "Seconds Lose Close Game To Worcester," *Brown Daily Herald*, November 6, 1916, p. 1.

23. William M. Ashby, "Black Yale, circa 1915," *Yale Alumni Magazine,* January, 1970, p. 26–28.

24. This seems to have been a popular chant among racist whites. Paul Robeson recalled hearing chants of "Kill that nigger!" when Rutgers played West Virginia. Boyle and Bunie, *Paul Robeson*, p. 64.

25. "Brown Humbles Old Eli 21–6," *Brown Daily Herald*, November 13, 1916, pp. 1–2.

26. "Football Practice," *Brown Daily Herald*, November 15, 1916, p. 1.

27. "Expert Sees Brown Team," *Brown Daily Herald*, November 15, 1916, p. 1.

28. "Football Men Have Vigorous Workout," *Brown Daily Herald*, November 16, 1916, p. 1.

29. "Seconds 0, Harvard 0—Wind-up Game of Season Devoid of Features," *Brown Daily Herald*, November 18, 1916, p. 1.

30. "Brown Humbles Harvard 21–0 in Great Contest," *Brown Daily Herald*, November 20, 1916, p. 1.

31. "Brown's Wizard Defeats Harvard," *Chicago Defender,* November 25, 1916, p. 1.

32. "Great Celebration of Harvard Victory," *Brown Daily Herald*, November 21, 1916, pp. 1–2.

33. "Scoreless Tie," *Brown Daily Herald*, December 4, 1916, p. 1; "Banquet Held For Football Team," *Brown Daily Herald*, December 6, 1916, p. 1; "Varsity B's," *Brown Daily Herald*, December 9, 1916, p. 1.

34. "Over 120 Men Compete on Lincoln Field in Opening Track Meet of Season," *Brown Daily Herald*, January 18, 1917, p. 1.

35. "Relay Team To Run," *Brown Daily Herald*, March 3, 1917, p. 1; "Williams '20, and White '19, Score Places at B. A. A. Games," *Brown Daily Herald*, March 5, 1917, p. 1.

36. "Williams '20, Wins 40-Yard Dash, Brown Loses Relay to M.I.T.," *Brown Daily Herald*, February 7, 1917, p. 4; "'Ink' Williams Wins Dash at Boston Meet," *Monmouth Daily Atlas*, February 5, 1917, p. 3.

37. "Annual Union Vaudeville Show Comes the 27th," *Brown Daily Herald*, March 19, 1917, p. 4.
38. "Vaudeville Show," *Brown Daily Herald*, March 20, 1917, p. 4.
39. "Change in Big Show," *Brown Daily Herald*, March 23, 1917, p. 4.
40. "Vaudeville Show," *Brown Daily Herald*, March 27, 1917, p. 1.
41. "Great Success," *Brown Daily Herald*, March 28, 1917, pp. 1–4.
42. "'Varsity to Play Game with Gras as Scheduled," *Brown Daily Herald*, April 13, 1917; "Meets Cancelled," *Brown Daily Herald*, April 16, 1917, p. 1.
43. "Drew to Try 'Comeback' Tonight," *Des Moines Register*, April 13, 1917, p. 8.
44. "Smart Set Meet Has Usual Success," *New York Age*, April 19, 1917, p. 6.
45. "Sol Butler Takes Broad Jump Event," *Chicago Defender*, May 5, 1917, p. 8.
46. "Many Men Leaving College to Take Up Farming," *Brown Daily Herald*, May 5, 1917, p. 1; "207 Have Been Excused to Take Up Outside Work," *Brown Daily Herald*, May 14, 1917, p. 1.
47. "Varsity Track Picture at 3:30 at Ye Rose Studio," "Freshman Cap Celebration To-Night," *Brown Daily Herald*, May 28, 1917, p. 1; "Freshman Cremation," *Brown Daily Herald*, May 29, 1917, p. 4.
48. "Pittsburg Independents Second in Press Meet," *Chicago Defender*, July 28, 1917, p. 10.
49. Advertisement for Pollard's Pressing Club Plan, *Brown Daily Herald*, September 27, 1917, p. 5.
50. The first was William H. Lewis of Harvard, who integrated college football at Amherst College in the late 1880s. After leaving Amherst for Harvard Law School, Lewis won All-American honors in 1892 and 1893. He went on to become the Massachusetts state attorney general and was instrumental in securing Fritz Pollard's admission to both Harvard and Brown.
51. "Brown Football Season at End," *Providence Journal*, November 26, 1917, p. 4; Carroll, *Fritz Pollard*, p. 111; Arthur R. Ashe Jr., *A Hard Road to Glory: A History of the African-American Athlete* (New York: Amistad, 1993), 1:100.
52. "President Faunce Urges Spirit of Service," *Brown Daily Herald*, September 26, 1917, p. 1.
53. Williams, transcripts, 1921, Brown University; "Brown Crushes Boston's High Hopes," *Brown Daily Herald*, October 23, 1917, p. 1.
54. "Colgate Succumbs to Brown Bear's Attack," *Brown Daily Herald*, October 30, 1917, p. 1.
55. "Colgate Succumbs to Brown Bear's Attack."
56. "Varsity Meets Colby in Last Home Game," *Brown Daily Herald*, November 17, 1917, pp. 1–4; "Newport Reserves Defeat Brown by Score of 35–0," *Brown Daily Herald*, November 13, 1917, pp. 1–3.
57. "Brown Defeats Dartmouth 13–0 in Sensational Game at Braves Field," *Brown Daily Herald*, November 27, 1917, p. 1.
58. "Three Brown Players on Football Honor Roll," *Brown Daily Herald*, December 4, 1917, p. 1; "Walter Camp Picks All-American Service Eleven and Also Names

Best College Players of Season. Weeks '19 on List," *Brown Daily Herald*, January 3, 1918, p. 6.

59. "List Continued of Last Year's Students Engaged in All Branches of Service," *Brown Daily Herald*, December 1, 1917, p. 1.

60. Pollard, quoted in Carroll, *Fritz Pollard*, p. 112.

61. Carroll, *Fritz Pollard*, pp. 112–16.

Chapter 4. Buffalo Soldier

1. Following the war, Wesley emerged as an important Black historian and served as the national president of Alpha Phi Alpha. James L. Conyers Jr., ed., *Charles H. Wesley: The Intellectual Tradition of a Black Historian* (New York: Taylor & Francis, 1997).

2. Carroll, *Fritz Pollard*, p. 121.

3. "Coach Hahn Expects Strong Track Team," *Brown Daily Herald*, December 6, 1917, p. 1; "Varsity Athletes in War Service," *Brown Daily Herald*, December 20, 1917, p. 1; "Track Prospects Exceptionally Bright," *Brown Daily Herald*, January 15, 1918, p. 5; "Relay Team Chosen for Triangular Meet," *Brown Daily Herald*, February 2, 1918, p. 1; "'Fritz' Pollard '19," *Brown Daily Herald*, February 16, 1918, p. 1.

4. Eckley, "Resident Gives Picture of 'Ink.'"

5. "Undergraduates in Service," Brown Commencement Program, 1918, p. 10; "Billy Sunday Speaks on Citizenship," *Brown Daily Herald*, October 18, 1918, p. 1.

6. "Thirteen Hits Young Man Hard," *Monmouth Daily Atlas*, July 14, 1917, p. 1.

7. "Colored Athletes Doing Their Part," *Los Angeles Times*, August 10, 1918, p. 6.

8. "A Report on the First Negro Signal Corps," *Camp Sherman News*, April 10, 1919, https://www.accessible-archives.com/2018/06/report-first-negro-signal-corps-1919/.

9. "Black Officers at Fort Des Moines in World War I," http://www.iowapbs.org/iowapathways/mypath/black-officers-fort-des-moines-ww-i/.

10. This appears to have been a standard path for students who went to OTC. Harvard University's publication on its students' contributions to World War I is more detailed than Brown's. Stanley Farrar Brewster, a 1913 Harvard graduate, went to Camp Sherman for OTC, then to Camp Hancock's Machine Gun Training Center before being detailed to France. Frederick S. Mead, *Harvard's Military Record in the World War* (Boston: Harvard Alumni Association, 1921), p. 116.

11. "Colonel Charles Young," biographical video, Charles Young Buffalo Soldier National Monument, https://www.nps.gov/chyo/index.htm

12. Oscar Price, "Camp Hancock, Georgia One of the Largest Cantonments in U. S.," *Xenia Evening Gazette*, November 12, 1918, p. 5. It is interesting to note the correspondence between Lieutenant Oscar Price (author of the news article) and Colonel Young, available at https://tinyurl.com/3m9pewmn.

13. "Personals," *Monmouth Daily Atlas*, February 21, 1919, p. 5.

14. "Wright & Ditson to Present Tablet to A. A.," *Brown Daily Herald*, December 7, 1918, p. 1.

Chapter 5. Williams vs. Yale

1. "With Malice toward None," *Hartford Courant*, January 28, 1949, p. 19.
2. 1919 Football File, Brown University Archives.
3. Williams, transcripts, 1921, Brown Univeresity.
4. "Bulldog Getting in Condition for Game with Brown," *Brown Daily Herald*, November 5, 1920, p. 1.
5. "Victory Wrested from Brown in Last Quarter of Game," *Brown Daily Herald*, November 8, 1920, p. 1.
6. "Record Crowd at B. A. A. Games," *Boston Globe*, February 8, 1920, p. 19.
7. "Brown Relayers Lose at B. A. A.," *Brown Daily Herald*, February 9, 1920, pp. 1–3; "Sporting Brevities," *Brown Daily Herald*, February 10, 1920, p. 4.
8. Charles Paddock, https://olympics.com/en/athletes/charles-paddock; Legendary USC Olympians: Charley Paddock, https://trojanswire.usatoday.com/2020/07/06/legendary-usc-olympians-charley-paddock/
9. "Track Artists Will Enter Boston Meet," *Brown Daily Herald*, February 20, 1920, p. 1; "Track Men Win in Boston," March 1, 1920, p. 1; "Live Tips and Topics," *Boston Globe*, March 11, 1920, p. 6.
10. "Yale Game to Be Reported in Union," *Brown Daily Herald*, November 7, 1919, p. 1; "Brunonian Eleven Yields to Yale in 14–0 Defeat," *Brown Daily Herald*, November 10, 1919, p. 1. "Brown's Football Standing Compared with Opponents," *Brown Daily Herald*, November 12, 1919, p. 1.
11. "With Malice toward None," *Hartford Courant*, January 28, 1949, p. 19.
12. "Yale's Offensive Strikes Its Stride against Brown," *Hartford Courant*, November 8, 1919, p. 42; Associated Press, "No Easy Task for Yale," *Baltimore Sun*, November 9, 1919, p. 12.
13. "Brown Battered to Defeat by Old Eli," *Boston Globe*, November 9, 1919, p. 15.
14. "Colored Boy Thrills Yale Bowl—Ink Williams, Brown University's Whirlwind End Plays Yale Bulldog Groggy," *Chicago Whip*, November 29, 1919, p. 7.
15. Jim Vance, "Williams and Slater—Stars in Gridiron Tournament," *Chicago Whip*, December 6, 1919, p. 5.
16. Calt, "Paramount, Part 2: The Mayo Williams Era," *78 Quarterly*, 1, no. 4 (1989), p. 13.
17. "Eastern Football Star Pays Visit to Whip," *Chicago Whip*, September 18, 1920, p. 5.
18. "Several Changes in Football Rules," *Brown Daily Herald*, September 25, 1920, p. 3.
19. "*Brown Herald* Picks All-American Team," *Brown Daily Herald*, November 29, 1920, p. 1; "*New York Times* Selects All-Americans," *Brown Daily Herald*, December 13, 1920, p. 1; "Camp Honors Six Players of 1920 'Varsity Eleven," December 21, 1920, p. 1.
20. "Post Selects All America," *Boston Post*, November 29, 1920, p. 15.
21. "Monmouth Boys Are Mentioned," *Monmouth Daily Atlas*, December 13, 1920, p. 3.

Chapter 6. Alpha

1. "Track Practice," *Brown Daily Herald*, December 17, 1920, pp. 1–4.
2. Inter-University Consortium for Political and Social Research. Study 00003: Historical Demographic, Economic, and Social Data: U.S., 1790–1970. Ann Arbor: ICPSR. http://fisher.lib.virginia.edu/, as quoted by Russell E. Malbrough, *Alpha Phi Alpha "Monster" Alpha Gamma Chapter History*, 2:11.
3. Charles Hamm, "The Last Minstrel Show?" In *Putting Popular Music in Its Place* (Cambridge: Cambridge University Press, 1995), pp. 354–66.
4. Charles H. Wesley, *The History of Alpha Phi Alpha: A Development in College Life* (Howard University Press, 1929), p. 139.
5. Malbrough, "Alpha Gamma Chapter of Alpha Phi Alpha Fraternity, Inc.," 2:18.
6. Alpha Phi Alpha Fraternity, Inc., https://apa1906.net
7. Mickey, "Russell Adrian Lane," p. 64; Malbrough, "Alpha Gamma Chapter of Alpha Phi Alpha Fraternity, Inc.," 2:17.
8. Ibid, p. 17.
9. Redding, *No Day of Triumph*, p. 41.
10. Ester Redding, telephone conversation with Rodney Robinson, November 1, 1989, quoted in *Alpha Phi Alpha "Monster" Alpha Gamma Chapter History*, 2:18.
11. Redding, *No Day of Triumph*, p. 39.
12. "Star-Vaudeville Features Freshman Talent at Mixer," *Brown Daily Herald*, October 26, 1920, p. 1.
13. "When 'Ink' Looked Over 'Bo,'" *Kansas City Times*, April 9, 1921, p. 32.
14. "His Idea About 'Bo,'" *Boston Globe*, April 12, 1921, p. 15.
15. "'Ink'" Wouldn't Pray If He Had Bo's Physique," *Dayton Daily News*, April 25, 1921, p. 14.
16. Lane, quoted in Mickey, "Russell Adrian Lane," p. 64.
17. Mickey, "Russell Adrian Lane," p. 66.
18. Louis L. Redding, quoted in Russell E. Malbrough, *Alpha Phi Alpha "Monster" Alpha Gamma Chapter History*, 2:41.
19. Malbrough, Alpha Gamma Chapter of Alpha Phi Alpha Fraternity, Inc., 2:18–19.
20. For an in-depth look at the accomplishments of Alpha Gamma's founders, see Russell E. Malbrough's *Alpha Phi Alpha "Monster" Alpha Gamma Chapter History*, vol. 2.
21. "Ex-Servicemen Notice!" *Brown Daily Herald*, March 22, 1921, p. 2; "Memorial Arch Is Dedicated with Most Impressive Ceremonies," *Brown Daily Herald*, April 7, 1921, p. 1.
22. Untitled *Providence Journal* clipping, April 7, 1921, Soldier's Gate File, Brown University Archives.
23. "New Track Coach Takes Charge," *Brown Daily Herald*, October 27, 1920, p. 1; "Haddleton Made New Track Coach," *Brown Daily Herald*, October 27, 1920, p. 3.

24. "Untried Track Men Will Meet Bowdoin in Meet Tomorrow," *Brown Daily Herald*, May 3, 1921, p. 1; "Track Men Defeat Bowdoin 64 2–3 to 61 1–3," *Brown Daily Herald*, May 5, 1921, p. 1.

25. "Brown Track Team Carries Off Second Honors in Three-Cornered Meet," *Brown Daily Herald*, March 16, 1921, pp. 1–3.

26. "Nation's Best Athletes in Annual Penn Relays," *Chicago Defender*, April 30, 1921, p. 10.

27. "Track Work Soon to Begin in Earnest at Andrews Field," *Brown Daily Herald*, April 2, 1921, p. 3; "'Varsity Track Squad Rapidly Working into Shape for Exceptionally Hard Schedule," *Brown Daily Herald Weekly Alumni Supplement*, April 22, 1921, p. 4; "Brown Places Fifth in Medley Sprint Relay Championship at Penn Carnival," *Brown Daily Herald*, May 2, 1921, p. 1.

28. "Brunonian Trackmen Face Strong Rivals at Intercollegiates," *Brown Daily Herald*, May 17, 1921, p. 1–2; "'Varsity Track Team Goes to N. E. I. Meet," *Brown Daily Herald*, May 20, 1921, p. 1; "'Varsity Track Team Qualifies Twelve Men in N. E. I. at Boston," *Brown Daily Herald*, May 21, 1921, p. 1; "Track Team Ties for Fifth Place in N. E. I. Meet," May 23, 1921, p. 1.

29. "Seniors and Juniors Cruise on Narragansett Bay, While Sophomores Dine at the Narragansett, and the Freshmen Burn Their Caps in Huge Bonfire on Lincoln Field Following Parade Through Downtown Streets," "'Varsity Awards in Track Made by A.A.," *Brown Daily Herald*, May 25, 1921, p. 1.

30. Williams, transcripts, 1921, Brown University.

31. *Liber Brunensis*, 1921, p. 163.

32. Lane eventually received a master's degree at Howard, then went to the University of Heidelberg for his PhD. When traveling to Germany, the Lanes had to pretend they were Cuban in order to gain passage on the steamship, which did not allow Blacks. Mickey, "Russell Adrian Lane," pp. 57–71.

33. *Liber Brunensis*, 1921, p. 161.

34. J. Mayo Williams to Stephen Calt, Summer 1971, Chicago.

Chapter 7. Sambo

1. "Williams Gets $200 Fine for Bootlegging," *Monmouth Daily Atlas*, September 6, 1916, p. 1.

2. "Have You Heard That," *Monmouth Daily Atlas*, June 4, 1919, p. 3.

3. "Two Men Are Now Facing Grand Jury," *Monmouth Daily Atlas*, March 29, 1920, p. 1, 8.

4. "Fingerprint Caused Arrest of Young Negro," *Monmouth Daily Atlas*, May 31, 1920, p. 1.

5. "Finds Williams Under New Name in Bridewell," *Monmouth Daily Atlas*, June 2, 1920, p. 1.

6. "Have You Heard That," *Monmouth Daily Atlas*, June 8, 1920, p. 3.

7. "Williams to Be Returned," *Monmouth Daily Atlas*, April 29, 1921, p. 1; "It's About Over, Says Williams," *Monmouth Daily Atlas*, April 30, 1921, p. 1.

8. "Roseville Man Named Head of Grand Jury," *Monmouth Daily Atlas*, May 2, 1921, p. 1.

9. "Williams Gets One to Twenty in State Pen," *Monmouth Daily Atlas*, May 3, 1921, p. 1; "Two More Men Sentenced to State Prisons," *Monmouth Daily Atlas*, May 5, 1921, p. 1.

Chapter 8. Black Swan

1. Williams, interview by O'Neal and Paulus; Williams to Calt, summer 1971.

2. Ted Vincent, "The Community That Gave Jazz to Chicago," *Black Music Research Journal*, 12, no. 1 (Spring 1992): 45, https://www.jstor.org/stable/779281?origin=crossref.

3. Vincent, "The Community That Gave Jazz to Chicago," 46–52.

4. Williams, interview by Stephen Calt, Chicago, summer 1971.

5. Matthew Bullock (1881–1972) of Everett, Massachusetts, graduated from Dartmouth in 1904, served as head coach of the University of Massachusetts football team in 1904, at Morehouse College 1909–11, and at Alabama Ag & Tech 1924–26. Joseph Edward Trigg (1894–1955) was the first Black oarsman for any crew team in the United States (1913–15) and was the first Black player on the Syracuse football team (1914–15). He served as a US army captain in World War I. He was an assistant football coach at Howard University while attending Howard Medical School, after which he became a prominent Washington, DC physician.

6. Ned Gourdin set a world record in the broad jump record in June 1921 and won silver at the 1924 Olympics.

7. J. Mayo Williams, "Football Prospects in the East: Ink Williams, Last Season's Brilliant Star Writing Exclusively for the *Whip*," *Chicago Whip*, August 27, 1921, p. 7.

8. W. C. (William Christopher) Handy wrote and published the song "Memphis Blues" in 1912. It is widely accepted as the opening commercial salvo of the blues and earned him the nickname "father of the blues."

9. Stephen Calt, "Paramount—The Anatomy of a 'Race' Music Label," in *R&B, Rhythm and Business: The Political Economy of Black Music*, edited by Norman Kelley (Brooklyn, NY: Akashic, 2002), p. 89.

10. Williams, interview by Russell and Steiner.

11. Williams, quoted in Calt, "Paramount, Part 2: The Mayo Williams Era," p. 13.

12. Williams, interview by O'Neal and Paulus.

13. David Suisman, "Co-workers in the Kingdom of Culture: Black Swan Records and the Political Economy of African American Music," *Journal of American History*, 90, no. 4 (2004): 1297.

14. *Chicago Whip*, 1919–22, Madison Historical Library, University of Wisconsin, Madison, WI, microfilm reel 1.

15. Black Swan advertisement, *Chicago Defender*, July 13, 1920, p. 4, quoted in Suisman, "Co-workers," 1302.

16. Suisman, "Co-workers," 1300.

17. W. E. B. Du Bois, *The Souls of Black Folk* (1903; New York: Modern Library, 2003), p. 3.
18. Suisman, "Co-workers," 1301.
19. "The Black Bourgeoisie," in *The Negro in New York: An Informal Social History 1626–1940*, edited by Roi Ottley and William J. Weatherby (New York: Praeger, 1967), p. 232.
20. W. E. B. Du Bois, "Phonograph Records," *Crisis*, 21 (Feb. 1921), p. 152, quoted in Suisman, "Co-workers," 1305.
21. Ted Vincent, *Keep Cool: The Black Activists Who Built the Jazz Age* (East Haven, CT: Pluto Press, 1995), pp. 92–95.
22. "The Black Bourgeoisie," pp. 232–33.
23. Suisman, "Co-workers," 1306–7.
24. Tony Langston, "Records Racial Melodies as Sung by Members of the Race," *Chicago Defender*, June 4, 1921, p. 7.
25. Suisman, "Co-workers," 1306–7.
26. Suisman, "Co-workers," 1307–8.
27. Suisman, "Co-workers," 1311.
28. Williams to Calt, summer 1971.

Chapter 9. Hammond Pro

1. "A Few Words to the Sporting Editor of the *Chicago American*," *Chicago Defender*, February 9, 1924, p. 10.
2. "Sport Squibs," *Chicago Defender*, December 10, 1921, p. 10.
3. Clair J. Purdy, quoted in Julie Des Jardins, *Walter Camp: Football and the Modern Man* (New York: Oxford University Press, 2015), p. 240.
4. Fritz Pollard, interviewer unknown, New Rochelle, New York, June 24, 1976, quoted in Chris Willis, *Old Leather: An Oral History of Early Pro Football in Ohio, 1920–1935* (Lanham, MD: Scarecrow Press, 2005), p. 14.
5. In 1941, the NFL amended its constitution and changed the title to "commissioner," which is what it is today. When Thorpe had the job, the title was "president."
6. Ocania Chalk, *Pioneers in Black Sport: The Early Days of the Black Professional Athlete in Baseball, Basketball, Boxing, and Football* (New York: Dodd, Mead, 1975), pp. 211–19.
7. Boyle and Bunie, *Paul Robeson*, p. 95.
8. Harry Young, interview by Bob Carroll, quoted in "Doc Young and the Hammond Pros," The Coffin Corner, https://profootballresearchers.org/archives/Website_Files/Coffin_Corner/17-01-596.pdf
9. John Carroll, notes from phone interview with Colonel Henry N. Young, December 2, 1988, author's files.
10. Bob Nash, quoted in Boyle and Bunie, *Paul Robeson*, p. 95.
11. Rickey later enjoyed a lengthy career as a professional baseball player and front-office executive for the St. Louis Browns and the Brooklyn Dodgers. Follis's example is said to have inspired Rickey to seek out a similarly stoic and intuitive

black athlete—Jackie Robinson—to integrate major-league baseball with the Brooklyn Dodgers in 1947. Ashe, *A Hard Road to Glory*, 1:98.

12. Young, interview by Carroll, quoted in "Doc Young and the Hammond Pros."

13. Williams's participation in the game isn't reflected in official league statistics but was documented in the *Pittsburgh Daily Post*, "Pollard's Blunder," October 24, 1921.

14. Williams, interview by Terkel.

15. "Now for Improving Game," *Akron Beacon Journal*, November 16, 1921, p. 14.

16. "'Ink' Williams Stars in Cardinal-Hammond Game," *Chicago Whip*, November 12, 1921, p. 5.

17. "Hammond to Play Canton Next Sunday," *Times* (Munster, IN), October 6, 1921, p. 11.

18. "Williams Shines in Hammond Defeat," *Chicago Whip*, October 8, 1921, p. 6.

19. Bob Osborn, quoted in "Williams Is Best of Pro Players: Osborn," *Chicago Whip*, December 17, 1921, p. 7.

20. "'Ink' Williams Stars in Cardinal-Hammond Game."

21. "'Ink' Williams" Was Official at Big Game," *Chicago Whip*, December 10, 1921, p. 7.

22. "Resume of Sport World for the Year," *Chicago Defender*, December 31, 1921, p. 10.

23. "Ink Williams Is Now Newspaper Man," *Macomb Daily By-stander*, February 17, 1922, p. 1.

24. John Shelburne, quoted in Chalk, *Pioneers of Black Sport*, p. 252.

25. "In Answer to Dr. Young," *Times* (Munster, IN), December 3, 1921, p. 10.

26. Williams, interview by Russell and Steiner.

27. "Pro Football," *Buffalo Morning Express*, September 24, 1922, p. 45.

28. "Toledo Wins from Hammond," *Pittsburgh Post-Gazette*, October 16, 1922, p. 12.

29. "'Inky' Williams," *News-Messenger*, October 17, 1922, p. 5.

30. Willis, *Old Leather*, pp. 25–27.

31. "Exciting Mitt Battles When Rivals Clash in Weekly Contests," *Dayton Herald*, October 23, 1922, p. 10.

32. "Hard Schedule for Pros Rest of This Season," *Akron Beacon Journal*, November 1, 1922, p. 18.

33. "Hammond Suffers Its Worst Defeat of Season in Akron," *Akron Beacon Journal*, November 6, 1922, p. 16.

34. "Lincoln Wins from Howard in 1922 Football Classic," *New York Age*, December 9, 1922, p. 6.

35. Williams and Robeson had played together on an exhibition team in the fall—the Dreamland Cabaret football team—fielded by Bill Bottoms in Chicago. Williams, interview by Terkel.

36. "Colored Stars Will Play Here," *Chicago Tribune*, December 8, 1922, p. 19.

37. Quoted in Neil Rozendaal, *Duke Slater: Pioneering Black NFL Player and Judge* (Jefferson, NC: McFarland, 2012), Kindle location 1574.

38. Rozendaal, *Duke Slater*, Kindle location 1574; Carroll, *Fritz Pollard*, p. 155.

39. Boyle and Bunie, *Paul Robeson*, p. 97.

Chapter 10. Paramount

1. David Suisman, "Black Swan Rising: The Brief Success of Harlem's Own Record Company," *Humanities*, 31, no. 6, (2010), pp. 1314–15.

2. Suisman, "Black Swan Rising."

3. Ottley and Weatherby, *The Negro in New York*, p. 234.

4. Suisman, "Black Swan Rising," p. 1320.

5. Vincent, *Keep Cool*, pp. 92–95; Eubie Blake, quoted by Calt in "Paramount, Part 1: The Anatomy of a 'Race' Label," p. 22.

6. Williams, interview by Calt.

7. Alex van der Tuuk, *Paramount's Rise and Fall: A History of the Wisconsin Chair Company and Its Recording Activities* (Denver: Mainspring, 2003), p. 89.

8. The quality of the composite materials NYRL used to make the physical records was notoriously bad, causing heavy surface noise even on mint-condition recordings. Otto E. Moeser, quoted by Calt, "Paramount, Part 1: The Anatomy of a 'Race' Label," p. 22.

9. Van der Tuuk, *Paramount's Rise and Fall*, p. 87–88.

10. Calt, "Paramount, Part 2: The Mayo Williams Era," p. 11.

11. Williams, quoted by Calt, "Paramount: Anatomy of a 'Race' Music Label," p. 90.

12. Suisman, David, "Black Swan Rising: The Brief Success of Harlem's Own Record Company," *Humanities*, November/December 2010, No. 6, https://www.neh.gov/humanities/2010/novemberdecember/feature/black-swan-rising.

13. Williams, quoted by Stephen Calt in "Paramount, Part 2: The Mayo Williams Era," p. 12.

14. Suisman, "Black Swan Rising," pp. 1319–22.

15. Williams, interview by O'Neal and Paulus.

16. Williams, interview by Stephen Calt, summer 1971, Chicago, transcribed by the author.

17. Calt, "Paramount—Anatomy of a 'Race' Music Label," p. 90.

18. Williams, interview by Russell and Steiner.

19. Williams, interview by O'Neal and Paulus.

20. Williams, interview by O'Neal and Paulus.

21. Calt, "Paramount—Anatomy of a 'Race' Music Label," p. 91–92.

22. Calt, "Paramount—Anatomy of a 'Race' Music Label," p. 91–92.

23. John K. Williams, telephone conversation with John Mackenzie, August 5, 1970, W. H. Smith Memorial Library, Indianapolis, IN.

24. Harold Barnett, Building Chicago—Sweet Home Chicago, Part 2: Building the Black Metropolis, January 4, 2017, https://buildingchicago.wordpress.com/2017/01/04/sweet-home-chicago-part-ii-building-the-black-metropolis/

25. Thomas A. Dorsey, interview by Jim O'Neal, in *The Voice of the Blues: Classic Interviews From* Living Blues *Magazine*, ed. Jim O'Neal and Amy van Singel (New York: Routledge, 2002), pp. 15–16.
26. Van der Tuuk, *Paramount's Rise and Fall*, p. 66.
27. Dorsey, interview by Jim O'Neal, in *The Voice of the Blues*, pp. 10–11.
28. Blake, quoted by Calt in "Paramount, Part 2: The Mayo Williams Era," p. 12.
29. Calt, "Paramount, Part 2," p. 16.

Chapter 11. Bronzeville

1. Williams, quoted by Calt in "Paramount, Part 2: The Mayo Williams Era." p. 19.
2. Williams, interview by Russell and Steiner.
3. Williams, quoted by Stephen Calt in liner notes to *Ma Rainey's Black Bottom*, Yazoo 1071, 1975, LP.
4. Quoted by Calt in "Paramount, Part 2."
5. Alex van der Tuuk, "Aletha Dickerson: Paramount's Reluctant Recording Manager," Vintage Jazz Mart, http://www.vjm.biz/new_page_18.htm.
6. Williams, interview by Russell and Steiner, 1970.
7. Calt, "Paramount, Part 2," p. 16.
8. Williams, quoted by Calt in "Paramount, Part 2, " p. 16.
9. Van der Tuuk, "Aletha Dickerson."
10. Van der Tuuk, "Aletha Dickerson."
11. Calt, "Paramount, Part 2," pp. 18–19.
12. Williams, interview by Russell and Steiner.
13. Karl Hagstrom Miller, *Segregating Sound: Inventing Folk and Pop Music in the Age of Jim Crow* (Durham, NC: Duke University Press, 2010).
14. Williams, quoted by Calt, "Paramount, Part 2," pp. 16, 30.
15. Calt, "Paramount, Part 2," pp. 16, 30.
16. Calt, "Paramount, Part 2," p. 13.
17. Williams, quoted by Calt, "Paramount, Part 2," p. 30.
18. Williams, interview by O'Neal and Paulus, 1972.
19. Calt, "Paramount, Part 2," p. 20.
20. Calt, "Paramount, Part 2," p. 20.
21. Williams, quote by Calt in, "Paramount, Part 2," p. 22.
22. Williams, quoted by Calt in "Paramount, Part 2," p. 22.
23. Williams, quoted by Calt in "Paramount—Anatomy of a 'Race' Label," p. 92.
24. Williams, quoted by Calt in "Paramount—Anatomy of a 'Race' Label," p. 96.
25. Van der Tuuk, *Paramount's Rise and Fall*, p. 96.
26. Williams, interview by Calt, 1971.
27. Eric R. Smith, "Brotherhood of Sleeping Car Porters," Encyclopedia of Chicago, http://www.encyclopedia.chicagohistory.org/pages/174.html.
28. Phil Pastras, *Dead Man Blues: Jelly Roll Morton Way Out West* (Berkeley: University of California Press, 2001), p. 130.

29. Jelly Roll Morton, quoted by Alan Lomax in *Mister Jelly Roll: The Fortunes of Jelly Roll Morton, New Orleans Creole and "Inventor of Jazz"* (New York: Pantheon, 1993), p. 360.

30. Morton, quoted by Lomax in *Mister Jelly Roll*, p. 361.

31. Frances M. Oliver, interview by William Russell, May 10, 1969, William Russell Oral History Collection Series, MSS530, William Russell Jazz Collection, Historic New Orleans Collection, New Orleans, LA.

32. Williams, interview by Russell and Steiner.

33. Williams, interview by O'Neal and Paulus.

34. Williams, interview by O'Neal and Paulus.

35. Chalk, *Pioneers of Black Sport*, p. 252; Dunc Annan, JT-SW.com, http://www.jt-sw.com/football/pro/players.nsf/ID/00140003.

36. Chalk, *Pioneers of Black Sport*, p. 252.

37. "'Pro' Champs Beat Hammond Team, 17–0," *Evening Review*, October 1, 1923, p. 14.

38. "Triangles Are Defeated in a Heart-Breaker," *Dayton Herald*, October 8, 1923, p. 13.

39. Rozendaal, *Duke Slater*, Kindle location 1739–1812.

40. "Cardinals Look for Stiff Game with Hammond," *Chicago Tribune*, November 7, 1923, p. 26.

41. Colonel H. N. Young, interview by John Carroll, notes from phone interview; Arthur R. Ashe Jr., *A Hard Road to Glory*, p. 100.

42. "Sol Butler Sold to Hammond Pro Football Team for $10,000," *Chicago Defender*, November 10, 1923, p. 6.

43. "A Few Words to the Sporting Editor of the Chicago American," *Chicago Defender*, February 9, 1924, p. 10.

44. "Bears Drill for Hammond Game," *Chicago Tribune*, November 20, 1923, p. 25.

45. "Cards Suffer 10–4 Trouncing from Racine Team; Bears Win Hot Tilt with Hammond, 14–7," *Rock Island Argus*, November 26, 1923, p. 16.

46. 1923 Hammond Pros, JT-SW.com, http://www.jt-sw.com/football/pro/results.nsf/Teams/1923-ham.

47. "Packers' Aerial Attack Buries Hammond 19 to 0," *Green Bay Press-Gazette*, November 30, 1923.

48. Young, interview by Carroll.

49. James H. Madison, *A Lynching in the Heartland: Race and Memory in America* (New York: Palgrave, 2001).

50. "Romney Only Local Star on Calhoun's Elevens," *Racine Journal-News*, December 21, 1923, p. 21.

51. "'Ink' Williams, Fastest End in Business, Probably Will Play with R. I. at Chicago," *Daily Times*, December 6, 1923, p. 19; "Kadesky Recalled for Go in Bears' Lair on Sunday," *Daily Times*, December 7, 1923, p. 30; "Kadesky Will Be Back at Independents' End Station in Bears Clash," *Rock Island Argus*, December 7, 1923, p. 37.

Chapter 12. Madame

1. John Wesley Work Jr., *American Negro Songs* (Mineola, NY: Dover, 1998), p. 33.
2. Jim O'Neal and Amy van Singel, *The Voice of the Blues*, pp. 12–13.
3. Calt, "Paramount—Anatomy of a 'Race' Music Label," pp. 103–4.
4. Calt, "Paramount—Anatomy of a 'Race' Music Label," pp. 103–4.
5. Williams to Steven Calt, ca. 1971.
6. Williams to Steven Calt, ca. 1971.
7. Paramount Records Catalog, 1924.
8. Paramount's *Book of Blues*.
9. Van der Tuuk, *Paramount's Rise and Fall*, p. 91.
10. Calt, "Paramount—Anatomy of a 'Race' Music Label," p. 105.
11. Williams, quoted by Calt in "Paramount, Part 2: The Mayo Williams Era," p. 24.
12. Williams, quoted by Calt in "Paramount, Part 2: The Mayo Williams Era," p. 24.
13. Williams, interview by Calt.
14. Williams, interview by O'Neal and Paulus.
15. Calt, "Paramount, Part 2: The Mayo Williams Era," pp. 21–24.
16. Williams, quoted by Calt, "Paramount, Part 2: The Mayo Williams Era," p. 24.
17. Calt, "Paramount, Part 2: The Mayo Williams Era," p. 26.
18. Calt, "Paramount, Part 2: The Mayo Williams Era," pp. 21–24.
19. Calt, "Paramount—The Anatomy of a 'Race' Music Label," p. 102.
20. Calt, "Paramount—The Anatomy of a 'Race' Music Label," p. 102; Dixon and Godrich, "Recording the Blues," pp. 264–70.
21. Both quotes in this paragraph are from Calt, "Paramount—The Anatomy of a 'Race' Music Label," p. 102.
22. Calt, "Paramount—Anatomy of a 'Race' Music Label," pp. 109–10.
23. "Theta Chapter," *Sphinx*, October 1924, p. 8.
24. United States Census, 1910, Danville (Vermilion County), IL.
25. "Teachers Attend Institute," *Chicago Defender*, April 21, 1917, p. 6.
26. "Theta Chapter, *Sphinx*, 10, no. 4 (October 1924), p. 22.
27. "Chicago Society," *Pittsburgh Courier*, December 10, 1927, p. 6.
28. "Weddings," *Chicago Defender*, June 21, 1924, p. 10.
29. "Around the Hub: Boston News," *Chicago Defender*, June 21, 1924, p. 15.
30. Williams, interview by Russell and Steiner.
31. Calt, "Paramount—Anatomy of a 'Race' Music Label," p. 97.
32. Frank C. Taylor and Gerald Cook, *Alberta Hunter: A Celebration in Blues* (New York: McGraw-Hill, 1986), p. 66; Van der Tuuk, *Paramount's Rise and Fall*, p. 64; Calt, "Paramount—Anatomy of a 'Race' Music Label," p. 98.
33. Calt, "Paramount—The Anatomy of a 'Race' Music Label," p. 98.
34. Williams, telephone conversation with Mackenzie, 1970.

35. William Broonzy and Yannick Bruynoghe, *Big Bill Blues: Big Bill Broonzy's Story as Told to Yannick Bruynoghe* (New York: Da Capo, 1992), pp. 46–48.
36. O'Neal and van Singel, *The Voice of the Blues*, pp. 10–11.
37. Williams to Calt, summer 1971.
38. Williams, interview by O'Neal and Garon.
39. O'Neal and van Singel, *Voice of the Blues*, pp. 16–17.
40. Williams, interview by O'Neal and Paulus.
41. Williams, interview by O'Neal and Paulus.
42. Dorsey to O'Neal, quoted in *Voice of the Blues*, pp. 15–16.
43. Williams, interview by O'Neal and Paulus; Paramount advertisement for "Ma Mystery Record," *Chicago Defender*, September 14, 1924.
44. Williams, interview by O'Neal and Paulus.
45. "Islanders Score at Will in Sabbath Contest with Hammond, Winning 26–0," *Daily Times*, October 13, 1924, p. 15.
46. "Sport Briefs," *Chicago Defender*, November 8, 1924, p. 9.
47. "Triangles Sign New Flanker for Cleveland Game," *Dayton Daily News*, November 2, 1924, p. 50.
48. 1924 Hammond Pros, jt-sw.com, http://www.jt-sw.com/football/pro/rosters.nsf/Annual/1924-ham.
49. "Independents Out to Wreck Kenosha Stars," *Rock Island Argus*, November 26, 1924, p. 11.
50. Police report, *Chicago Tribune*, November 23, 1924, p. 2.

Chapter 13. Bulldog

1. Calt, "Paramount—Anatomy of a 'Race' Music Label," p. 92.
2. Williams, interview by O'Neal and Paulus.
3. Williams, interview by O'Neal and Paulus.
4. Williams, interview by Terkel.
5. "All Stars Will Have Classy Squad; Ink Williams, Pollard and Other Stars In Line Up," *Green Bay Gazette*, Sept. 14, 1925.
6. "Packers and Hammond Open Pro Season on Sunday," *Green Bay Gazette*, September 19, 1925.
7. "Ex-W.&J. Stars on Hammond Squad," *Evening Review* (Liverpool, OH), October 2, 1925, p. 17.
8. "Bears Pile Up 28–7 Victory," *Chicago Tribune*, October 12, 1925, p. 31.
9. "National Pro Grid Notes," *Rock Island Argus*, October 30, 1925, p. 37.
10. J. Mayo Williams to Guy B. Johnson, October 26, 1925, Southern Folklife Collection, University of North Carolina, Chapel Hill.
11. "Panthers Keep Place in Lead," *Detroit Free Press*, November 2, 1925, pp. 16–17.
12. Williams, interview by Terkel.
13. Carroll, *Fritz Pollard*, p. 174; 1925 Cleveland Bulldogs, jt-sw.com, https://www.jt-sw.com/football/pro/rosters.nsf/Annual/1925-cle/.

14. It should be noted that both the Canton and Cleveland clubs were called the Bulldogs. Incidentally, the Cleveland Bulldogs did *not* become the Cleveland Browns, contrary to what Studs Terkel implies in his interview with Williams. The Cleveland Bulldogs franchise existed only during the 1923–25 seasons. The Canton Bulldogs franchise existed only during the 1920–26 seasons. The Cleveland Browns franchise of which Terkel speaks was founded in 1950.

15. The Maroons would become the 1925 NFL champions, only to have the title revoked and become barred from the league on account of playing an unsanctioned, late-season exhibition game in Philadelphia—technically the territory of the Yellow Jackets. (This was not the NFL's first disputed title—the Bears disputed Cleveland's claim to the 1924 title, but the league owners awarded the title to Cleveland.) The title was awarded instead to the Chicago Cardinals, who refused to accept the title on account of their championship game loss to the Maroons. The Pottsville issue contributed in a big way to the eventual restructuring of the NFL, which ended Hammond's status in the league and disenfranchised Black players going forward.

16. "Cleveland Eleven Jolts Shore Roses," *Philadelphia Inquirer*, November 29, 1925, p. 28.

17. 1925 Providence Steam Roller, jt-sw.com, https://www.jt-sw.com/football/pro/rosters.nsf/Annual/1925-prv/.

18. "Roller and Bull Dogs Battle to 7–7 Tie," *Providence Journal*, November 30, 1925.

19. Carroll, *Fritz Pollard*, p. 176.

20. Johnson and Seashore apparently made sound recordings of the singers and also used an oscillograph to trace (on a paper tape) the electrical frequency and magnitude of the singers' voices, thus creating a physical record. The whereabouts of these materials is unknown.

21. Guy B. Johnson to J. Mayo Williams, December 4, 1925.

22. Williams to Johnson, December 14, 1925.

23. Johnson to Williams, January 12, 1926.

Chapter 14. Blind Lemon

1. Charles Wolfe and Kip Lornell, *The Life and Legend of Leadbelly* (New York: HarperCollins, 1994), p. 37.

2. Ledbetter and Jefferson made for an unlikely pairing. Ledbetter has a hammering rhythm guitar style, whereas Jefferson is legendary for breaking time (erratic chord changes, slowing down and speeding up, playing guitar licks that were out of synch with the rhythm of the song). Perhaps when playing with Ledbetter, Jefferson did not break time. Ledbetter's vivid recollections of the duo playing for enthusiastic dancers suggests as much.

3. Sammy Price, *What Do They Want? A Jazz Autobiography* (Urbana: University of Illinois Press, 1990), p. 14.

4. Robert L. Uzzel, *Blind Lemon Jefferson: His Life, His Death, and His Legacy* (Austin: Eakin Press, 2002), pp. 29–30.

5. Williams, interview by O'Neal and Paulus.

6. Uzzel, *Blind Lemon Jefferson*, pp. 29–30.
7. Williams, interview by O'Neal and Paulus.
8. Williams, interview by O'Neal and Paulus.
9. Williams, interview by O'Neal and Paulus.
10. Van der Tuuk, *Paramount's Rise and Fall*, p. 124; Calt, "Paramount Part 2: The Mayo Williams Era," p. 28.
11. Stephen Calt and Woody Mann, liner notes to *Blind Blake—Ragtime Guitar's Foremost Fingerpicker*, Yazoo L-1068, 1989, 33 1/3 rpm.
12. Williams, interview by O'Neal and Paulus.
13. *Paramount Book of Blues* (1927), as reprinted in Calt and Mann, liner notes to *Blind Blake*.
14. Van der Tuuk, "Aletha Dickerson: Paramount's Reluctant Recording Manager."
15. Calt and Mann, liner notes to *Blind Blake*.
16. "Tornadoes Wallop Hammond," *Journal Times*, September 27, 1926, p. 9.
17. "Coach Asks Team to Improve," *Times*, September 28, 1926, p. 13.
18. "Pro Grid Fans Will Decide How Often Team Plays Here," *Akron Beacon Journal*, September 28, 1926, p. 26.
19. Colonel H. N. Young, interview by Carroll.
20. "Hammond Next for Maroons," *Pottsville Republican*, November 16, 1926, p. 11.
21. "The Sport X-Ray," *Pottsville Republican*, November 22, 1926, p. 20.
22. Paul Waggoner, "'Ad Astra per Aspera' Football," *Hutchinson News* (Kansas), January 28, 2016, https://www.hutchnews.com/story/opinion/columns/2016/01/29/ad-astra-per-aspera/21004568007/.
23. "Bulldogs Draw with N.Y. Giant Eleven, 7 to 7," *Daily News*, November 3, 1926, p. 44.
24. John Carroll, *Fritz Pollard*, pp. 178–79, 196–97.
25. Harry Young to Bob Carroll, quoted in "Doc Young and the Hammond Pros."
26. Williams, interview by Terkel.
27. Dorsey, quoted by O'Neal in *Voice of the Blues*, p. 4.
28. Sandra R. Lieb, *Mother of the Blues: A Study of Ma Rainey* (Amherst: University of Massachusetts Press, 1981), p. 39.

Chapter 15. Black Patti

1. "Chicago Society," *Pittsburgh Courier*, June 16, 1927, p. 6; "Chicago Society," *Pittsburgh Courier*, July 16, 1927, p. 6; "Chicago Society," *Pittsburgh Courier*, August 13, 1927, p. 7.
2. Van der Tuuk, *Paramount's Rise and Fall*, p. 128.
3. Williams, interview by Calt.
4. John Mackenzie Collection, W. H. Smith Memorial Library, Collection Number M0428, File B2, F13, Indiana Historical Society, Indianapolis.
5. Van der Tuuk, *Paramount's Rise and Fall*, p. 129.

6. Willia Estelle Daughtry, "Sissieretta Jones: A Study of the Negro's Contribution to Nineteenth Century American Concert and Theatrical Life" (PhD diss., Syracuse University, 1968), https://surface.syr.edu/crs_etd/32/, p. 1; Sissieretta Jones, personal correspondence, quoted in Daughtry, Sissieretta Jones, p. 10; Mrs. Richard Dudley to Willia Estelle Daughtry, June 11, 1966.

7. Daughtry, Sissieretta Jones, pp. 13–17.

8. Daughtry, Sissieretta Jones, pp. 17–19.

9. Daughtry, Sissieretta Jones, p. 20.

10. Daughtry, Sissieretta Jones, pp. 23–24.

11. Daughtry, Sissieretta Jones, p. 31.

12. Calt, "Paramount—The Anatomy of a 'Race' Music Label," p. 93.

13. Black Patti Records advertisement, *Chicago Defender*, May 21, 1927.

14. Rick Kennedy, *Jelly Roll, Bix, and Hoagy: Gennett Studios and the Birth of Recorded Jazz* (Bloomington: Indiana University Press, 1994), pp. 180–81.

15. Williams, telephone interview by John Mackenzie, August 5, 1970, John Mackenzie Collection.

16. Williams, telephone interview by Mackenzie.

17. Kennedy, *Jelly Roll, Bix, and Hoagy*, pp. 182–83.

18. Van der Tuuk, *Paramount's Rise and Fall*, p. 130; notes on Black Patti records, John Mackenzie Collection.

19. Williams, telephone interview by Mackenzie.

20. Kennedy, *Jelly Roll, Bix, and Hoagy*, p. 184.

21. "Regulars Drill for Clash with Hammond," *Journal Times*, September 21, 1927, p. 15.

22. "Red Peppers: Hot Sport Chatter for the Fans," *Times* (Munster, IN), November 25, 1927, p. 23.

23. Williams, interview by O'Neal and Paulus.

24. Williams, telephone interview by Mackenzie.

25. Van der Tuuk, *Paramount's Rise and Fall*, p. 131.

26. Lieb, *Mother of the Blues*, pp. 40–43.

27. Elijah Wald, *Josh White: Society Blues* (Amherst: University of Massachusetts Press, 2000), p. 24; Ellen Harold and Peter Stone, "Josh White," Association for Cultural Equity, n.d., https://www.culturalequity.org/alan-lomax/friends/white.

28. Van der Tuuk, "Aletha Dickerson."

Chapter 16. Hokum

1. Williams, telephone interview by Mackenzie.

2. Williams, interview by O'Neal and Paulus.

3. BBC eventually forced the Kapps out of the SSMC due to what they saw as a conflict of interest; Williams reorganized the operation, adding the word "Publishing" to State Street Music Publishing Company, or SSMPC. Williams, telephone interview by Mackenzie.

4. For an excellent overview of Cow Cow Davenport's life and the boogie-woogie piano scene in Chicago, see the "Chicago" chapter (ch. 4) of Peter Silvester's *The*

Story of Boogie Woogie: A Left Hand Like God (Lanham, MD: Scarecrow Press, 2009).

5. Scrapper Blackwell, interview by Theodore F. Watts, *Jazz Monthly*, July 1960, pp. 4–6.

6. Williams's alumni file at Brown shows that in 1928, he was employed as a football coach at Paul Quinn College in Waco, Texas. He does not list Brunswick/Vocalion as his employer.

7. Carroll, *Fritz Pollard*, pp. 182–83.

8. O'Neal and van Singel, *The Voice of the Blues*, pp. 7–13.

9. The Overton Hygienic Building, a historic landmark at 3619–3627 South State Street, once housed a number of Black-owned businesses. Dorsey to O'Neal, in O'Neal and van Singel, *The Voice of the Blues*, pp. 15–16.

10. Dorsey to O'Neal, in O'Neal and van Singel, *The Voice of the Blues*, p. 23.

11. Dorsey to O'Neal, in O'Neal and van Singel, *The Voice of the Blues*, p. 20.

12. Dorsey to O'Neal, in O'Neal and van Singel, *The Voice of the Blues*, p. 20.

13. Dorsey to O'Neal, in O'Neal and van Singel, *The Voice of the Blues*, p. 24.

14. Despite several conjectures, Keghouse's real name remains a mystery.

15. "All-Americans on Semco Team," *Times* (Munster, IN), November 2, 1928, p. 29.

16. "Ed Sullivan's Sports Whirl," *Daily News*, October 27, 1928, p. 3.

17. "Wiley to Meet Paul Quinn on Armistice Day," *Marshall News Messenger*, November 9, 1928.

18. Williams, interview by Russell and Steiner.

Chapter 17. Bumble Bee

1. The Knoxville sessions for Brunswick/Vocalion contributed some recordings to the race records catalog, most notably two sides by the Tennessee Chocolate Drops, supervised by the jazz pianist Richard Voynow.

2. "In Old Kaysee," *Chicago Defender*, November 23, 1929, p. 6.

3. Speckled Red, interview by Dave Mangurian, October 1959, *Jazz Journal*, June 1960.

4. Dorsey to O'Neal, *The Voice of the Blues*, pp. 10–11.

5. Dorsey to O'Neal, *The Voice of the Blues*, p. 23 (bracketed information supplied by O'Neal).

6. Williams, interview by Calt.

7. "Sunlight Grid Outfit Seeks First Win Sunday against Hegewisch 11," *Times* (Munster, IN), October 18, 1929.

8. Williams, interview by O'Neal and Paulus.

9. Price, *What Do They Want?*, pp. 38, 86–87.

10. Price claimed he had never heard the term "boogie-woogie" until Pine Top Smith's record "Pine Top's Boogie-Woogie." Price, *What Do They Want?*, pp. 16–30.

11. Dixon and Godrich, p. 292.

12. Paul and Beth Garon, *Woman with Guitar: Memphis Minnie's Blues* (New York: Da Capo, 1992).

13. Dixon and Godrich, "Recording the Blues," p. 301; Paul and Beth Garon, *Woman with Guitar*, pp. 26–27.
14. "Majestics Win over Pollards," *Pittsburgh Post-Gazette*, November 24, 1930, p. 15.
15. "Pollard, Butler & Co. to Meet All-Star Ohio 11 at Columbus Nov. 27," *Pittsburgh Courier*, November 8, 1930, p. 15.
16. "Ohio State Stars Beats Pollard 12–0 in Mud," *Pittsburgh Courier*, December 6, 1930, p. 15.
17. Williams, interview by O'Neal and Paulus.
18. Dorsey to O'Neal, *The Voice of the Blues*, p. 29.
19. Lieb, *Mother of the Blues*, p. 43.
20. Williams, interview by O'Neal and Paulus.
21. Williams, interview by O'Neal and Paulus.
22. "Burnham Team Battles Stars," *The Times*, November 7, 1931, p. 10.
23. "All-Star Team Arrives Today," *Los Angeles Times*, December 17, 1931, p. 26.
24. "Chicago Football Squad Off for Coast," *Chicago Defender*, December 19, 1931, p. 9.
25. "All-Star Team Arrives Today," *Los Angeles Times*, December 17, 1931, p. 26.
26. *Encyclopedia of African American Music*, ed. Tammy L. Kernodle, Horace Maxille, and Emmett George Price (Westport, CT: Greenwood), 2011, 1:562.
27. Peter Vacher, *Swingin' on Central Avenue: African American Jazz in Los Angeles* (Lanham, MD: Rowman & Littlefield, 2015), p. 218.
28. "All-Stars, Like Money Loaned Out, Return Home in Dribbles," *Chicago Defender*, January 16, 1932, p. 9.

Chapter 18. Maroon Tiger

1. "Chicago Awaits Wilberforce-Lincoln Battle," *Pittsburgh Courier*, October 22, 1932, p. 14.
2. Although Hope may not be a household name today, Buck Franklin was so impressed by his leadership that he named his son, the preeminent Black historian John Hope Franklin, after the educator. John Hope, New Georgia Encyclopedia, https://www.georgiaencyclopedia.org/articles/education/john-hope-1868–1936/.
3. Redding, *No Day of Triumph*, pp. 41–43.
4. "Ink Williams Forecasts Football Championship," *Chicago Whip*, October 1, 1921, p. 6.
5. "Colored Teams Open Season," *Atlanta Constitution*, October 1, 1933, p. 23.
6. "Morehouse Meets Paine on Sunday," *Atlanta Constitution*, October 17, 1933, p. 14.
7. "Morehouse to Play Last Game at Home," *Atlanta Constitution*, November 15, 1933, p. 9.
8. "Clark Beaten by Morehouse," *Atlanta Constitution*, November 19, 1933, p. 20.
9. Redding, *No Day of Triumph*, p. 41–43.
10. "Gordon, Olympic Ace, Jumps Here," *Chicago Defender*, August 5, 1933, p. 9.
11. Ashe, *Hard Road to Glory*, p. 92.

12. Fritz Pollard, quoted in *Hard Road to Glory*, p. 109.
13. "Ex-Service Men Entertain Atty. Arthur W. Mitchell," *Chicago Defender*, August 25, 1934, p. 13.
14. David W. Kellum, "Dawson Beats DePriest and Anderson," *Chicago Defender*, April 23, 1938, p. 1.
15. "Morehouse Opens Season on Friday," *Atlanta Constitution*, October 3, 1934, p. 9.
16. "Hornets Schedule Wilberforce Foe," *Montgomery Advertiser*, September 9, 1934, p. 13.
17. "Hornets Prepare for Veteran Team," *Montgomery Advertiser*, October 30, 1934, p. 8.
18. "Hornets to Battle Morehouse Tonight," *Montgomery Advertiser*, November 2, 1934, p. 8.
19. Correspondence with Henry Goodgame, Morehouse College Archives, in author's files.
20. "Two Faculty Members of Morehouse College Back," *New York Age*, August 24, 1935, p. 10.

Chapter 19. Sepia

1. Michael Gray, *Hand Me My Travelin' Shoes: In Search of Blind Willie McTell* (Chicago: Chicago Review Press, 2009), pp. 249–50.
2. Dixon and Godrich, "Recording the Blues," p. 307.
3. Dixon and Godrich, "Recording the Blues," p. 320.
4. Williams, interview by O'Neal and Paulus.
5. Williams, interview by O'Neal and Paulus.
6. "'To Lie Idle Is to Rot,' Dr. Hope Warns Race," *Chicago Defender*, March 9, 1935, p. 3.
7. Mello Brown Advertisement, *Pittsburgh Courier*, May 2, 1936, p. 5.
8. Williams, interview by O'Neal and Paulus.
9. Hammie Nixon and Sleepy John Estes, interview by Jim O'Neal, *The Voice of the Blues*, p. 55.
10. O'Neal and van Singel, *The Voice of the Blues*, pp. 58–59.
11. Williams, interview by O'Neal and Paulus.
12. Leonard Feather, quoted by Alun Morgan, *Count Basie* (New York: Hippocrene, 1984), p. 16.
13. Count Basie, *Good Morning Blues: The Autobiography of Count Basie, as Told to Albert Murray* (New York: Random House, 1985), p. 167.
14. Leonard Feather, "Sam Price—Pint Sized King of Boogie-Woogie," *Pittsburgh Courier*, June 7, 1941, p. 20.
15. Williams, interview by O'Neal and Paulus.
16. Basie, *Good Morning Blues*, p. 167.
17. Basie, *Good Morning Blues*, pp. 167–68.
18. Basie, *Good Morning Blues*, pp. 167–68.
19. "Ink Spots to Perform Here," *Cary-Grove Clarion*, September 27, 1985, p. 48.

20. "Decca Records Signs New Singing Sensation," *Pittsburgh Courier*, October 9, 1937, p. 21.

21. Feather, "Sam Price."

22. Price, *What Do They Want?* p. 48.

23. Price, *What Do They Want?* p. 49.

24. Price, *What Do They Want?* p. 49.

25. Price, *What Do They Want* p. 50.

26. Price, *What Do They Want?* pp. 53–54.

27. Price, *What Do They Want?* p. 52.

28. Williams, interview by O'Neal and Paulus.

29. Leslie Gourse, *Unforgettable: The Life and Mystique of Nat King Cole* (New York: St. Martin's, 1991), pp. 20–21; Daniel Mark Epstein, *Nat King Cole* (New York: Farrar, Straus and Giroux, 1999), pp. 57–58.

30. Williams, interview by O'Neal and Paulus.

31. Gene Lees, *You Can't Steal a Gift: Dizzy, Clark, Milt, and Nat* (New Haven: Yale University Press, 2001), p. 210.

32. Williams, interview by O'Neal and Paulus.

33. Williams, interview by O'Neal and Paulus.

34. "As if [Leroy Carr] was Pat Boone to [Robert] Johnson's Elvis" is how the musician, music historian, and Leroy Carr fan Elijah Wald characterized it in 2004 in the *New York Times*. Elijah Wald, "MUSIC: The Bluesman Who Behaved Too Well," *New York Times*, July 18, 2004, https://www.nytimes.com/2004/07/18/arts/music-the-bluesman-who-behaved-too-well.

35. James Dugan and John Hammond, program notes from "From Spirituals to Swing" Concert, December 23, 1938, Carnegie Hall, New York; reprint included in "From Spirituals to Swing" box set, Vanguard CD 3-169/71-2, 1996, three compact discs.

36. Dave E. Dexter Jr., liner notes to *Pine Top Smith: Boogie Woogie Piano*, p. 2, Brunswick Collectors Series B-1002, 1943, two ten-inch records.

37. Williams, interview by O'Neal and Paulus.

38. Williams, interview by O'Neal and Paulus.

39. Williams, interview by O'Neal and Paulus.

40. Williams, interview by O'Neal and Paulus.

41. William "Bill" Russell, "Boogie-Woogie," in *Jazzmen*, ed. Frederic Ramsey Jr. and Charles Edward Smith (New York: Harcourt, Brace & Co., 1939).

42. "Fight For Talent," *Chicago Defender*, February 18, 1939.

43. The correspondence of Alan Lomax, Milton Gabler, and the Kapp brothers can be found in the Alan Lomax collection at the American Folklife Center, Library of Congress, Washington, DC.

Chapter 20. Outskirts

1. Jim Powers, *Harlem Hamfats*, www.allmusic.com.

2. John Chilton, *Let the Good Times Roll: The Story of Louis Jordan and His Music* (Ann Arbor: University of Michigan Press, 1992), p. 22.

3. Chilton, *Let the Good Times Roll*, pp. 33–45.
4. Chilton, *Let the Good Times Roll*, p. 54.
5. Chilton, *Let the Good Times Roll*, p. 64.
6. Chilton, *Let the Good Times Roll*, p. 64–67.
7. Jordan, quoted in Chilton, *Let the Good Times Roll*, p. 65.
8. Jordan, quoted in Chilton, *Let the Good Times Roll*, p. 71.
9. Jerry Zolten, *Great God A'Mighty! The Dixie Hummingbirds: Celebrating the Rise of Soul Gospel Music* (New York: Oxford University Press, 2003), pp. 45–46.
10. "AFM Probe Brings New Set-Up for Race Records," *Pittsburgh Courier*, March 4, 1939, p. 20.
11. Chilton, *Let the Good Times Roll*, pp. 71–74.
12. Chilton, *Let the Good Times Roll*, p. 72.
13. "Harlem," *New York Age*, March 30, 1940, p. 5.
14. "Harlem," *New York Age*, January 27, 1940, p. 4.
15. "Annual Artists-Models' Ball the Smartest and Most Exciting Event in the Windy City," *Pittsburgh Courier*, October 18, 1941, p. 8.
16. "Harlem Night Life," *New York Age*, April 25, 1942, p. 10.
17. Langston Hughes, quoted in "Rudolph Fischer, '19, Physician and Literary Wit of the Harlem Renaissance," *News from Brown*, https://news.brown.edu/articles/2011/02/fisher/.
18. Price, quoted in *Let the Good Times Roll*, p. 73.
19. Chilton, *Let the Good Times Roll*, p. 73.
20. Chilton, *Let the Good Times Roll*, pp. 80–81.
21. Williams, interview by Calt.
22. Chilton, *Let the Good Times Roll*, pp. 86–87.
23. Chilton, *Let the Good Times Roll*, p. 88.
24. Chilton, *Let the Good Times Roll*, pp. 90–91.
25. Chilton, *Let the Good Times Roll*, p. 127.
26. Carroll, *Fritz Pollard*, p. 211.
27. Carroll, *Fritz Pollard*, p. 212.
28. "Theatrical Notes," *New York Age*, January 24, 1942, p. 10.
29. Dixon and Godrich, *Yonder Come the Blues*, p. 329.
30. "The Sports Roundup," *Pittsburgh Courier*, February 6, 1943, p. 19.
31. "Tab Smith's Orchestra to Entertain Patrons at Elks Rendezvous," *New York Age*, May 20, 1944.
32. Williams, interview by O'Neal and Paulus.

Chapter 21. Kingfish

1. "Louis Shuffle Grid Offense [sic] of Brown Bomber," *Brooklyn Daily Eagle*, November 15, 1935, pp. 26, 28.
2. "Ray Kemp to Do Double Duty Against Bears," *Chicago Tribune*, September 22, 1938, p. 23.
3. George Strickler, "Bears Roll Up 51 Points and Stars Get None," *Chicago Tribune*, September 24, 1938, p. 17.

4. "All Star Players Complain About Division of Money," *Chicago Defender*, October 1, 1938, p. 8.

5. "The Sports Parade," *New York Age*, February 5, 1938, p. 8.

6. "Posey's Points," *Pittsburgh Courier*, October 5, 1940, p. 16.

7. Jimmy Powers, "Powerhouse," *Daily News*, September 2, 1940, p. 312.

8. Alexander Wolff, "The NFL's Jackie Robinson," *Sports Illustrated*, October 12, 2009, https://vault.si.com/vault/2009/10/12/the-nfls-jackie-robinson.

9. Rosenblum, Roger, "Spotlight Sports," *Globe-Gazette*, September 21, 1943, p. 11.

10. For an exceptional, in-depth look at the UCLA players who reintegrated the NFL and integrated MLB (Washington, Robinson, and Strode), and to read more about Halley Harding's role in making the case to integrate the Rams, see Gretchen Atwood's *Lost Champions: Four Men, Two Teams, and the Breaking of Pro Football's Color Line* (New York: Bloomsbury USA, 2016).

11. Wolff, "The NFL's Jackie Robinson."

12. "Rams Sign Washington, Negro Star," *Oakland Tribune*, March 22, 1946, p. 12.

13. Wolff, "The NFL's Jackie Robinson."

Chapter 22. Ebony

1. Muddy Waters, quoted in O'Neal and van Singel, *The Voice of the Blues*, p. 181.

2. Muddy Waters, quoted in O'Neal and van Singel, *The Voice of the Blues*, p. 181.

3. Muddy Waters, quoted in O'Neal and van Singel, *The Voice of the Blues*, p. 181.

4. O'Neal and van Singel, *The Voice of the Blues*, p. 180.

5. Muddy Waters, quoted in O'Neal and van Singel, *The Voice of the Blues*, p. 180.

6. Williams, interview by O'Neal and Paulus.

7. Williams, interview by O'Neal and Paulus.

8. Al Leichter, "Rockin' All Nite Long," *News Leader* (Staunton, VA), March 25, 1994, p. 22.

9. "South Side Boys Club Will Open $14,000 Drive," *Chicago Tribune*, March 23, 1947, p. 6.

10. Sidney Jones, interview by Terkel, "A Tribute to Paul Robeson."

11. Williams, interview by Terkel.

12. Leichter, "Rockin' All Nite Long."

13. George Paulus, Robert Campbell, Robert Pruter, Dr. Robert Stallworth, Dave Sax, and Jim O'Neal, "Ebony, Chicago, Southern, and Harlem: The Mayo Williams Indies," http://campber.people.clemson.edu/ebony.html, revised October 29, 2022.

14. Williams, interview by O'Neal and Paulus.

15. Williams, interview by O'Neal and Paulus.

16. Williams, interview by O'Neal and Paulus.
17. Dan Burley, "Dan Burley's Back Door Stuff," *New York Age*, December 1, 1949, p. 18.
18. "Negro in Sports," *New York Age*, July 22, 1950, p. 30.
19. "Fay Says: Ink Williams and Pollard," *Chicago Defender*, August 26, 1950.
20. Alumni Information Card, May 22, 1953, J. Mayo Williams Brown University Alumni file.
21. "Stars in Business a Success? Scribe Has His Say on 'Subject,'" *New York Age*, September 25, 1954, p. 18.
22. "Stars of Past Fete Athletes Here, Jan. 25," *Chicago Defender*, January 21, 1963, p. 22A.
23. "Negro Athletes Organize to Boost Sportsmanship," *Chicago Tribune*, January 17, 1960, p. 12.
24. J. Mayo Williams Brown University Alumni File.
25. Williams, interview by O'Neal and Paulus.
26. *Sphinx*, 50, no. 2 (Spring/Summer 1964), p. 48.
27. Hammie Nixon and Sleepy John Estes, quoted in O'Neal and van Singel, *The Voice of the Blues*, p. 60.
28. *Voice of the Blues*, p. 60.
29. "Abbott Tells of Pro Football Heydays," *Lancaster Eagle Gazette*, January 14, 1961, p. 8.
30. Ted Watson, "Ted Watson—The Midnight Man In Chicago," *Pittsburgh Courier*, September 1, 1962, p. 14; "Ted Watson—The Midnight Man In Chicago," *Pittsburgh Courier*, September 22, 1962, p. 14.
31. Williams, interview by O'Neal and Paulus.
32. Clarence E. Mansfield to Brown University Alumni Office, April 13, 1967, copy in J. Mayo Williams Brown University Alumni File.
33. "Mrs. Aleta S. Williams, 69, Dies," *Chicago Defender*, March 26, 1968, p. 20.
34. Williams to Brown University Alumni Office, September 9, 1968, copy in J. Mayo Williams Alumni File.
35. Williams to Jay Barry, June 16, 1969, copy in J. Mayo Williams Brown University Alumni File.
36. Williams, interview by O'Neal and Paulus.
37. Williams, interview by O'Neal and Paulus.

Chapter 23. Pioneer

1. "The Hack Stand," *Honolulu Star-Bulletin*, June 28, 1971, p. 33.
2. "Earl Monroe Rates NBA Bonus," *The Times* (Munster, IN), April 21, 1972, p. 29.
3. Williams, interview by Russell and Steiner.
4. Sidney Jones, interview by Terkel, "A Tribute to Paul Robeson."
5. Williams, interview by Terkel.
6. Williams, interview by Terkel.

7. Williams, interview by Terkel.

8. Folkways was an independent record label, owned and operated by Moses Asch, from 1948 to 1987, when it was acquired (and is now operated) by the Smithsonian Institution.

9. Steven Calt, "Remembering Mayo Williams," unpublished memoir, email, March 15, 2005. Copy in author files.

10. Calt, "Remembering Mayo Williams."

11. Calt, "Remembering Mayo Williams."

12. Calt, "Remembering Mayo Williams."

13. Calt, "Remembering Mayo Williams."

14. Calt, "Remembering Mayo Williams."

15. Young, interview by Carroll.

16. Calt, "Remembering Mayo Williams."

17. Calt, "Remembering Mayo Williams."

18. Williams, interview by O'Neal and Paulus.

19. Carroll, *Fritz Pollard*, p. 81.

20. Williams, interview by O'Neal and Paulus.

21. O'Neal eventually got hold of the recordings and played them for Muddy Waters in 1974. It was the first time Muddy had heard the recordings since 1945.

22. Williams, interview by O'Neal and Paulus.

23. Vernon Jarrett, "Educational Value of Senior Citizens," *Chicago Tribune*, November 9, 1973, p. 16.

24. Thelma Doyle Marshall, quoted by Jim O'Neal, "J. Mayo Williams," *Living Blues*, no. 45/46, (Spring 1980), p. 94.

25. O'Neal, "J. Mayo Williams."

26. Handwritten note dated March 4, 1980; J. Herbert King to Jay Barry, January 22, 1980, both in J. Mayo Williams Brown University alumni file.

Postscript

1. Pete Peterson, "He Never Made It to the Promised Land: The Great Negro League Player Sam Bankhead," *Pittsburgh Post-Gazette*, February 24, 2018, https://www.post-gazette.com/opinion/Op-Ed/2018/02/25/Sam-Bankhead-one-of-the-greatest-Negro-League-ballplayers-still-is-not-in-the-National-Baseball-Hall-of-Fame/stories/201802250011.

2. Wald, "MUSIC: The Bluesmen Who Behaved Too Well."

References

In addition to the sources listed below, I have also drawn heavily on the following newspapers and other periodicals:

Afro-American (Baltimore, MD)
Akron Beacon Journal (Akron, OH)
Arkansas Democrat (Little Rock, AR)
Atlanta Constitution (Atlanta, GA)
Baltimore Sun (Baltimore, MD)
Boston Globe (Boston, MA)
Boston Post (Boston, MA)
Brooklyn Daily Eagle (Brooklyn, NY)
Brown Daily Herald (Providence, RI)
Buffalo Morning Express (Buffalo, NY)
Buffalo Times (Buffalo, NY)
Bureau County Tribune (Princeton, IL)
Bystander (Des Moines, IA)
Camp Sherman News (Chillicothe, OH)
Cary-Grove Clarion (Cary, IL)
Chicago Bee (Chicago, IL)
Chicago Defender (Chicago, IL)
Chicago Tribune (Chicago, IL)
Chicago Whip (Chicago, IL)
Courier-Journal (Louisville, KY)
Crisis (Baltimore, MD)
Daily Gate City (Keokuk, IA)
Daily News (Mount Carmel, PA)
Daily News (New York, NY)
Daily Review Atlas (Monmouth, IL)
Daily Times (Davenport, IA)

Daily Tribune (Wisconsin Rapids, WI)
Dayton Daily News (Dayton, OH)
Dayton Herald (Dayton, OH)
Decatur Daily Review (Decatur, IL)
Democrat and Chronicle (Rochester, NY)
Des Moines Register (Des Moines, IA)
Detroit Free Press (Detroit, MI)
Dispatch (Moline, IL)
Dixon Evening Telegraph (Dixon, IL)
Evening Gazette (Monmouth, IL)
Evening Gazette (Xenia, OH)
Evening Review (East Liverpool, OH)
Evening Star (Washington, DC)
Flora Hoosier Democrat (Flora, IN)
Gazette (Montréal, Quebec)
Globe-Gazette (Mason City, IA)
Green Bay Press-Gazette (Green Bay, WI)
Harrisburg Telegraph (Harrisburg, PA)
Hartford Courant (Hartford, CT)
Herald-Press (St. Joseph, MI)
Honolulu Star-Bulletin (Honolulu, HI)
Howard University Journal (Washington, DC)
Indianapolis Recorder (Indianapolis, IN)
Journal Times (Racine, WI)
Kansas City Sun (Kansas City, MO)
Kansas City Times (Kansas City, MO)
Lancaster Eagle-Gazette (Lancaster, OH)
Lansing State Journal (Lansing, MI)
Los Angeles Times (Los Angeles, CA)
Macomb Journal (Macomb, IL)
Macomb Daily By-Stander (Macomb, IL)
Marshall News Messenger (Marshall, TX)
Minneapolis Star (Minneapolis, MN)
Missoulan (Missoula, MT)
Monmouth Daily Atlas (Monmouth, IL)
Montgomery Advertiser (Montgomery, AL)
Nashua Telegraph (Nashua, NH)
New York Age (New York, NY)
New York Herald (New York, NY)
New York Times (New York, NY)
New York World (New York, NY)
News Leader (Staunton, VA)
News-Messenger (Fremont, OH)
News-Palladium (Benton Harbor, MI)
Oakland Tribune (Oakland, CA)

Oregon Daily Journal (Portland, OR)
Philadelphia Inquirer (Philadelphia, PA)
Pine Bluff Daily Graphic (Pine Bluff, AR)
Pittsburgh Courier (Pittsburgh, PA)
Pittsburgh Post-Gazette (Pittsburgh, PA)
Pottsville Republican (Pottsville, PA)
Providence Journal (Providence, RI)
Quad City Times (Davenport, IA)
Racine Journal-News (Racine, WI)
Record-Herald (Washington Court House, OH)
Republican-Atlas (Monmouth, IL)
Richmond Item (Richmond, IN)
Rock Island Argus (Rock Island, IL)
Southern Standard (Arkadelphia, AR)
The Sphinx (Atlanta, GA)
Tennessean (Nashville, TN)

Abbott, Lynn, and Doug Seroff. "'They Cert'ly Sound Good to Me': Sheet Music, Southern Vaudeville, and the Commercial Ascendancy of the Blues." *American Music* 14, no. 4 (1996): 402–54.

Abrams, Steven, and Tyrone Settlemier, eds. The Online Discographical Project. http://www.78discography.com.

Ashby, William M. 1970. "Black Yale, circa 1915." *Yale Alumni Magazine*, January 1970, pp. 26–28.

Ashe, Arthur. 1993. *A Hard Road to Glory: A History of the African-American Athlete*. 3 vols. New York: Amistad.

Associated Press. 1919. "No Easy Task for Yale." *Baltimore Sun*, November 9, 1919, p. 12.

Atwood, Gretchen. 2016. *Lost Champions: Four Men, Two Teams, and the Breaking of Pro Football's Color Line*. New York: Bloomsbury USA.

Baraka, Amiri. 2002. *Blues People: Negro Music in White America*. New York: Perennial.

Barnett, Harold. 2017. Building Chicago—Sweet Home Chicago, Part II: Building the Black Metropolis. January 4, 2017: https://buildingchicago.wordpress.com/2017/01/04/sweet-home-chicago-part-ii-building-the-black-metropolis/.

Basie, Count, 1985. *Good Morning Blues: The Autobiography of Count Basie, as Told to Albert Murray*. New York: Random House.

Black Officers at Fort Des Moines in World War I. N.d. Iowa PBS. http://www.iowapbs.org/iowapathways/mypath/black-officers-fort-des-moines-ww-i/.

Boyle, Sheila Tully, and Andrew Bunie. 2001. *Paul Robeson: The Years of Promise and Achievement*. Amherst: University of Massachusetts Press.

Brooks, Tim, and Richard K. Spottswood. 2005. *Lost Sounds: Blacks and the Birth of the Recording Industry, 1890–1919*. Urbana: University of Illinois Press.

Broonzy, Big Bill, and Yannick Bruynoghe. 1992. *Big Bill Blues: Big Bill Broonzy's Story as Told to Yannick Bruynoghe*. New York: Da Capo.

Calt, Stephen. 1994. *I'd Rather Be the Devil: Skip James and the Blues*. New York: Da Capo Press.

———. 1988. "Paramount, Part 1: The Anatomy of a 'Race' Label." *78 Quarterly*, 1, no. 3, pp. 9–23.

———. 1989. "Paramount, Part 2: The Mayo Williams Era." *78 Quarterly* 1, no. 4, pp. 9–30.

———. 1990. "Paramount, Part 4: The Advent of Arthur Laibly." *78 Quarterly* 1, no. , 8–26.

———. 2002. "Paramount—The Anatomy of a 'Race' Music Label." In *R&B, Rhythm and Business: The Political Economy of Black Music*, ed. Norman Kelley, 86–111. Brooklyn, NY: Akashic.

———. Liner notes to *Ma Rainey's Black Bottom*, Yazoo 1071, 1985, 33 1/3 rpm.

Calt, Stephen, and Woody Mann. Liner notes to *Blind Blake—Ragtime Guitar's Foremost Fingerpicker*, Yazoo L-1068, 1989, 33 1/3 rpm.

Calt, Stephen, and Gayle Dean Wardlow. 1990. "Paramount, Part 3: The Buying and Selling of Paramount." *78 Quarterly* 1, no. 5, pp. 7–24.

Carroll, Bob. 1995. "Doc Young and the Hammond Pros." *Coffin Corner* 17, no. 1, pp. 1–3.

Carroll, John M. 1992. *Fritz Pollard: Pioneer in Racial Advancement, Sport and Society*. Urbana: University of Illinois Press.

Chalk, Ocania. 1975. *Pioneers of Black Sport: The Early Days of the Black Professional Athlete in Baseball, Basketball, Boxing, and Football*. New York: Dodd, Mead.

Charters, Samuel B. 1975. *The Country Blues*. New York: Da Capo.

Chilton, John. 1992. *Let the Good Times Roll: The Story of Louis Jordan and His Music*. Ann Arbor: University of Michigan Press.

"Colonel Charles Young." N.d. Biographical video. Charles Young Buffalo Soldier National Monument. https://www.nps.gov/chyo/index.htm/.

Conyers, James L., Jr., ed. 1997. *Charles H. Wesley: The Intellectual Tradition of a Black Historian*. New York: Taylor & Francis.

The Country Blues. 1959. Blind Lemon Jefferson, Lonnie Johnson, Cannon's Jug Stompers, Peg Leg Howell, Blind Willie McTell, Memphis Jug Band, Blind Willie Johnson, Leroy Carr, Sleepy John Estes, Big Bill [Broonzy], Bukka White, Tommy McClennan, Robert Johnson, and Washboard Sam. Samuel Charters, producer. New York: RBF Records RF1, 33 1/3 rpm.

Daughtry, Willia Estelle. 1968. "Sissieretta Jones: A Study of the Negro's Contribution to Nineteenth-Century American Concert and Theatrical Life." PhD diss., Syracuse University. https://surface.syr.edu/crs_etd/32.

———. 2002. *Vision and Reality: The Story of "Black Patti" Matilda Sissieretta Joyner Jones*. Pittsburgh: Dorrance.

Dean Wardlow, Gayle. 1998. *Chasin' That Devil Music: Searching for the Blues*. Lanham, MD: Backbeat.

Des Jardins, Julie. 2015. *Walter Camp: Football and the Modern Man*. New York: Oxford University Press.

Dexter, Dave E., Jr. 1943. Liner notes to *Pine Top Smith: Boogie Woogie Piano*. Brunswick Collectors Series B-1002, two ten-inch records.

Dixon, Robert M. W., and John Godrich. 2001. "Recording the Blues," in *Yonder Come the Blues: Evolution of a Genre*, ed. Paul Oliver, Tony Russell, Robert M. W. Dixon, John Godrich, and Howard Rye. New York: Cambridge University Press.

Du Bois, W. E. B. 2003. *The Souls of Black Folk*. New York: Modern Library.

Dugan, James, and John Hammond. 1938. Program notes to "From Spirituals to Swing" Concert, December 23, 1938, Carnegie Hall, New York; reprint included in *From Spirituals to Swing*, Vanguard CD 3–169/71–2, 1996, three compact discs.

Eckley, Ralph B. 1978. "Resident Gives Picture of 'Ink,'" *Daily Review Atlas*, October 12, 1978, p. 38.

Epstein, Daniel Mark. 1999. *Nat King Cole*. New York: Farrar Straus Giroux.

Feather, Leonard. 1941. "Sam Price—Pint-Sized King of Boogie-Woogie," *Pittsburgh Courier*, June 7, 1941, p. 20.

Foreman, Ronald Clifford. 1969. "Jazz and Race Records, 1920–32: Their Origins and Their Significance for the Record Industry and Society." PhD diss., University of Illinois.

Garon, Paul. 1971. *The Devil's Son-in-Law: The Story of Peetie Wheatstraw and His Songs*. London: Studio Vista.

Garon, Paul, and Beth Garon. 1992. *Woman with Guitar: Memphis Minnie's Blues*. New York: Da Capo.

Gill, Bob, with Joe Cronin, Steve Brainerd, Steve Daniel, Roy Sye, Mark Wald, and Rupert Patrick, eds. Pro Football Archives. https://www.profootballarchives.com/.

Gourse, Leslie. 1991. *Unforgettable: The Life and Mystique of Nat King Cole*. New York: St. Martin's Press.

Gray, Michael. 2009. *Hand Me My Travelin' Shoes: In Search of Blind Willie McTell*. Chicago: Chicago Review Press.

Hamm, Charles. 1995. "The Last Minstrel Show?" In *Putting Popular Music in Its Place* (Cambridge: Cambridge University Press), pp. 354–66.

Harold, Ellen, and Peter Stone. N.d. "Josh White," Association for Cultural Equity. https://www.culturalequity.org/alan-lomax/friends/white.

Hill, Susan T. 1984. "The Traditional Black Institutions of Higher Education, 1860–1982." National Center for Education Statistics, US Department of Education, Washington, DC, p. 5, https://nces.ed.gov/pubs84/84308.pdf.

Huff, Mary. 1992. "Black Education in Monmouth." *Illinois History*, 45, No. 4 (January), p. 73.

Jenkins, Sally. 2007. *The Real All Americans: The Team That Changed a Game, a People, a Nation*. New York: Doubleday.

Kennedy, Rick. 1994. *Jelly Roll, Bix, and Hoagy: Gennett Studios and the Birth of Recorded Jazz*. Bloomington: Indiana University Press.

Kennedy, Rick, and Randy McNutt. 1999. *Little Labels—Big Sound: Small Record Companies and the Rise of American Music*. Bloomington: Indiana University Press.

Kernodle, Tammy L., Horace Maxille, and Emmett George Price, eds. 2011. *Encyclopedia of African American Music*. 3 vols. Santa Barbara: Greenwood.

Langston, Tony. 1921 "Records Racial Melodies as Sung by Members of the Race," *Chicago Defender*, June 4, 1921, p. 7.

Lees, Gene. 2001. *You Can't Steal a Gift: Dizzy, Clark, Milt, and Nat*. New Haven: Yale University Press.
Lieb, Sandra R. 1981. *Mother of the Blues: A Study of Ma Rainey*. Amherst: University of Massachusetts Press.
Lomax, Alan. 2002. *The Land Where the Blues Began*. New York: New Press.
———. 1993. *Mister Jelly Roll: The Fortunes of Jelly Roll Morton, New Orleans Creole and "Inventor of Jazz."* New York: Pantheon.
Lyman, Brian. 2020. "The Lost Congressman: What Happened to Jeremiah Haralson?" *Montgomery Advertiser*, March 20, 2020. https://www.montgomeryadvertiser.com/in-depth/news/2020/02/26/jeremiah-haralson-lost-congressman-alabama/2823015001/.
MacCambridge, Michael. 2004. *America's Game: The Epic Story of How Pro Football Captured a Nation*. New York: Random House.
Madison, James H. 2003. *A Lynching in the Heartland: Race and Memory in America*. New York: Palgrave.
Malbrough, Russell E. 1999. "Alpha Gamma Chapter of Alpha Phi Alpha Fraternity, Inc." Independent study project, Brown University.
Mazor, Barry. 2014. *Ralph Peer and the Making of Popular Roots Music*. Chicago: Chicago Review Press.
Mead, Frederick S. 1921. *Harvard's Military Record in the World War*. Boston: Harvard Alumni Association.
Mickey, Rosie Cheatham. 1983. "Russell Adrian Lane: Biography of an Urban Negro School Administrator." PhD diss., University of Akron.
Miller, Karl Hagstrom. 2010. *Segregating Sound: Inventing Folk and Pop Music in the Age of Jim Crow*. Durham, NC: Duke University Press.
Moneyhon, Carl H. 1993. "Delta Towns: Their Rise and Decline." In *The Arkansas Delta: Land of Paradox*, edited by Jeannie Whayne and Willard B. Gatewood. Fayetteville: University of Arkansas Press, pp. 208–37.
Morgan, Alun. 1984. *Count Basie*. New York: Hippocrene.
O'Neal, Jim. 1980. "J. Mayo 'Ink' Williams." *Living Blues*, no. 45/46, (Spring), p. 94.
O'Neal, Jim, and Amy van Singel, eds. 2002. *The Voice of the Blues: Classic Interviews from* Living Blues *Magazine*. New York: Routledge.
Oliver, Paul. 1988. *Blues Off the Record: Thirty Years of Blues Commentary*. New York: Da Capo.
Ottley, Roi, and William J. Weatherby. 1967. *The Negro in New York: An Informal Social History, 1626–1940*. New York: Praeger.
Palmer, Pete, Ken Pullis, and Gary Gillette, eds. Pro Football Reference. https://www.pro-football-reference.com.
Palmer, Robert. 1982. *Deep Blues: A Musical and Cultural History, from the Mississippi Delta to Chicago's South Side*. New York: Penguin Books.
Pastras, Philip. 2001. *Dead Man Blues: Jelly Roll Morton Way Out West*. Berkeley: University of California Press.
Paulus, George, with Robert Campbell, Robert Pruter, Dr. Robert Stallworth, Dave Sax, and Jim O'Neal. 2022. "Ebony, Chicago, Southern, and Harlem: The Mayo Williams Indies." http://campber.people.clemson.edu/ebony.html.

Peterson, Robert. 1997. *Pigskin: The Early Years of Pro Football*. New York: Oxford University Press.
Petrusich, Amanda. 2014. *Do Not Sell at Any Price: The Wild, Obsessive Hunt for the World's Rarest 78rpm Records*. New York: Scribner.
Prial, Dunstan. 2006. *The Producer: John Hammond and the Soul of American Music*. New York: Farrar, Straus and Giroux.
Price, Oscar. 1918. "Camp Hancock, Georgia One of the Largest Cantonments in U. S.," *Xenia Evening Gazette*, November 12, 1918, p. 5.
Price, Sammy, Bob Weir, and Caroline Richmond. 1990. *What Do They Want? A Jazz Autobiography*. Urbana: University of Illinois Press.
Ramsey, Frederic, and Charles Edward Smith. 1985. *Jazzmen*. New York: Harper & Row.
Redding, J. Saunders. 1942. *No Day of Triumph: A Negro Discovers America*. New York: Harper & Brothers.
Reed, Ishmael. 2017. *Mumbo Jumbo*. New York: Penguin.
"A Report on the First Negro Signal Corps." 1919. *Camp Sherman News*, April 10, 1919, https://www.accessible-archives.com/2018/06/report-first-negro-signal-corps-1919/.
Robeson, Paul. 1998. *Here I Stand*. Boston: Beacon Press.
Rozendaal, Neal. 2012. *Duke Slater: Pioneering Black NFL Player and Judge*. Jefferson, NC: McFarland.
Russell, William "Bill." 1939. "Boogie-Woogie." In *Jazzmen*, edited by Frederic Ramsey Jr. and Charles Edward Smith. New York: Harcourt, Brace & Co.
———. 1969. Interview by Frances M. Oliver. May 10. Oral History Collection Series MSS530. William Russell Jazz Collection, Historic New Orleans Collection, New Orleans.
Sanjek, David. 1997. "One Size Does Not Fit All: The Precarious Position of the African American Entrepreneur in Post–World War II American Popular Music." *American Music*, 15, no. 4: 535–62.
Silvester, Peter J. 2009. *The Story of Boogie-Woogie: A Left Hand Like God*. Lanham, MD: Scarecrow Press.
Slater, Robert Bruce. 1994. "The Blacks Who First Entered the World of White Higher Education." *Journal of Blacks in Higher Education*, no. 4: 47–56.
Smith, Eric R. 2004. "Brotherhood of Sleeping Car Porters," Encyclopedia of Chicago. http://www.encyclopedia.chicagohistory.org/pages/174.html.
Story, Rosalyn M. 1993. *And So I Sing: African-American Divas of Opera and Concert*. New York: Amistad.
Suisman, David. 2010. "Black Swan Rising: The Brief Success of Harlem's Own Record Company," *Humanities*, 31, no. 6, pp. 1314–15. https://www.neh.gov/humanities/2010/novemberdecember/feature/black-swan-rising.
———. "Co-Workers in the Kingdom of Culture: Black Swan Records and the Political Economy of African American Music." *Journal of American History*, 90, no. 4: 1295–1324.
Szwed, John F. 2010. *Alan Lomax: The Man Who Recorded the World*. New York: Penguin.

"Tables Turned." 1901. *Pine Bluff Daily Graphic*, November 18, 1901, p. 1.
Taylor, Frank C., and Gerald Cook. 1987. *Alberta Hunter: A Celebration in Blues*. New York: McGraw-Hill.
Terkel, Studs. 1970. "A Tribute to Paul Robeson." May 8, 1970. *Studs Terkel Program*. WFMT, Chicago. Studs Terkel Radio Archive, courtesy of Chicago History Museum and WFMT. https://studsterkel.wfmt.com/programs/gathering-friends-discussing-paul-robeson.
Titon, Jeff Todd. 1995. *Early Downhome Blues: A Musical and Cultural Analysis*. 2nd ed. Chapel Hill: University of North Carolina Press.
Uzzel, Robert L. 2002. *Blind Lemon Jefferson: His Life, His Death, and His Legacy*. Austin: Eakin Press.
Vacher, Peter. 2015. *Swingin' on Central Avenue: African American Jazz in Los Angeles*. Lanham, MD: Rowman & Littlefield.
van der Tuuk, Alex, comp. "Aletha Dickerson: Paramount's Reluctant Recording Manager." Vintage Jazz Mart, http://www.vjm.biz/new_page_18.htm.
———. 2003. *Paramount's Rise and Fall: A History of the Wisconsin Chair Company and Its Recording Activities*. Denver: Mainspring Press.
Vance, Jim. 1919. "Williams and Slater—Stars in Gridiron Tournament." *Chicago Whip*, December 6, 1919, p. 5.
Vincent, Ted. 1992. "The Community That Gave Jazz to Chicago." *Black Music Research Journal*, 12, no. 1: 43–55.
———. 1995. *Keep Cool: The Black Activists Who Built the Jazz Age*. East Haven, CT: Pluto Press.
Wald, Elijah. 2004. *Escaping the Delta: Robert Johnson and the Invention of the Blues*. New York: Amistad.
———. 2000. *Josh White: Society Blues*. Amherst: University of Massachusetts Press.
Wesley, Charles H. 1996. *The History of Alpha Phi Alpha: A Development in College Life*. Baltimore: Foundation Publishers.
Williams, J. Mayo. 1921. "Football Prospects in the East: Ink Williams, Last Season's Brilliant Star Writing Exclusively for the *Whip*." *Chicago Whip*, August 27, 1921, p. 7.
———. 1970a. Telephone conversation with John K. Mackenzie, July 28, 1970. John K. Mackenzie Gennett Record Company Collection, 1887–1976. Manuscript and Visual Collections Department, William Henry Smith Memorial Library, Indiana Historical Society, Indianapolis.
———. 1970b. Telephone conversation with John K. Mackenzie, August 5, 1970. John K. Mackenzie Gennett Record Company Collection, 1887–1976. Number M0428, File B2, F13, Indiana Historical Society Collection, Manuscript and Visual Collections Department, William Henry Smith Memorial Library, Indiana Historical Society Indianapolis.
———. 1970c. Interview by William "Bill" Russell and John Steiner, November 20, 1970, Chicago. Historic New Orleans Collection, New Orleans.
———. 1970d. Interview by Studs Terkel. "A Tribute to Paul Robeson." *Studs Terkel Program*, May 8, 1970, WFMT, Chicago. Studs Terkel Radio Archive,

courtesy of Chicago History Museum and WFMT. https://studsterkel.wfmt.com/programs/gathering-friends-discussing-paul-robeson

———. 1971. Interview by Stephen Calt, summer 1971, Chicago.

———. 1972. Interview by Jim O'Neal and George Paulus, March 17, 1972, Chicago. Unpublished interview. Jim O'Neal archive, Bluesoterica Archives, www.bluesoterica.com.

Williams, J. Mayo, and Little Brother Montgomery. 1972. Interview by Jim O'Neal and Paul Garon, May 1972, Chicago. Unpublished interview, Jim O'Neal archive, Bluesoterica Archives, www.bluesoterica.com.

Willis, Chris. 2005. *Old Leather: An Oral History of Early Pro Football in Ohio, 1920–1935*. Lanham, MD: Scarecrow Press.

Wolfe, Charles K., and Kip Lornell. 1992. *The Life and Legend of Leadbelly*. New York: HarperCollins.

Work, John Wesley. 1988. *American Negro Songs: 230 Folk Songs and Spirituals, Religious and Secular*. Mineola, NY: Dover.

Work, John W., III, Lewis Wade Jones, and Samuel C. Adams Jr. 2005. *Lost Delta Found: Rediscovering the Fisk University–Library of Congress Coahoma County Study, 1941–1942*. Edited by Robert Gordon and Bruce Nemerov. Nashville: Vanderbilt University Press.

Zolten, Jerry. 2003. *Great God A'Mighty! The Dixie Hummingbirds: Celebrating the Rise of Soul Gospel Music*. New York: Oxford University Press.

Index

Page numbers in italic indicate photos.

Abbott, Robert S., 232
African Americans: in Army in World War I, 37, 39–40, 41; athletes seen as point of pride, 48; in Atlanta, 185; *The Birth of a Nation*'s depiction of, 16; Black Swan Records as Black-owned, 66, 68, 88; at Brown University, 26, 30, 51–52, 184; class differences among, 98; color consciousness among, 257; cultural influence of, 68; in Danville, Illinois, 114; erased from history of NFL, 248; first arrival of slaves in America, 19; first Black football All-American, 15; first Black NFL official, 74; first commercial recording by Black musician, 13, 48; in football, 18, 79; fraternities and sororities, 15, 19, 25, 28, 51, 114; Great Migration, 1, 62; with Hammond Pros, 80; Harlem Renaissance, 213, 214; have to be disproportionately excellent, 44, 167; higher education for, 15; at Ivy League schools, 21; lynching, 41, 48, 50, 67, 105, 230; population in 1920, 50; products that de-emphasize Black features, 70; in Providence, Rhode Island, 24, 26, 50, 51; Republicans, 187; Sullivan on Black athletes, 167; vernacular cultural forms of, 17; in Washington, DC, 16. *See also* civil rights; integration; race records; racial progress; racism; segregation
Akers, Garfield, 171, 172
Albright, "Rats," 46, 47, 49
Alexander, Texas, 207
Allen, Duane, 248
Alpha Phi Alpha, 50–52; on Blacks in the Army, 37, 40; Brown University and, 26, 51–52, 183; founding of, 51; Frazier and Temple in, 115; at Howard University, 19; in intercollegiate social network, 28; memorial for Williams, 250; mission of, 55; Overton in, 92, *155*; on pace setters, 235; reception of 1922, 85; Robeson in, 51, 230; Jackie Robinson in, 225; Williams in, 50, 51, 52, 85, *156*, 185, 230, 239, 246
American Crusade Against Lynching, 230
American Federation of Musicians (AFM), 195, 212–13, 216, 218, 227
American Professional Football Association (APFL), 73, 75, 76, 79. *See also* NFL (National Football League)
Ammons, Albert, 168, 205, 206
Annan, Dunc: with Akron Pros, 123, 124; at Brown University, 26–27; with Hammond Pros, 102, 119, 120, 123, 135; indoor football league in Chicago developed by, 83

Anthology of American Folk Music, 242, 243
Archer, Samuel Howard, 187–88, 190
Ardoin, Amédé, 193
Armstrong, Lil Hardin, 97, 213, 236
Armstrong, Louis, 119, 142, 248, 253
Arnold, James "Kokomo," 190, 207
Arnold, John Henry "Big Man," 149
Ashby, William H., 28
Ashford, R. T., 129, 130, 133
Ashley, Clarence, 129
Atlantic Records, 231
Austin, Kid, 96
Austin, Lovie, 95, 108, 109, 110, 122
Ayler, Herbert, 64

Bailey, Kid, 171
Barker, Louise "Blue Lu," 200, 248
Barr, Johnny, 46
Barret, Edward, 142, 146
Basie, Count: Brunswick/Vocalion records, 174, 253; at "From Spirituals to Swing" concerts, 204; Pollard books, 216; signs with Decca, 196–98, 210; on T.O.B.A., 99
Bechet, Sidney, 118, 200, 204
Belasco, Lionel, 173
Bell, Bert, 49, 78
Berry, Chu, 200
Bibb, Joe: at Black Swan Records, 63, 71, 87; at *Chicago Whip,* 48, 63; embezzlement by, 72, 88–89, 91; meets Williams, 48, 50; offers Williams job on *Chicago Whip,* 57, 62–63; Pace as brother-in-law of, 66, 89; in Varsity Club of Chicago, 234
Bibb, Viola, 89
Birth of a Nation, The (film), 16, 17, 24, 225
"black and tan" clubs, 63–64
blackface, 32, 50, 53, 54, 128
Black Patti Records, 141–47; demise of, 146, 147, 159; finding artists for, 146; as hair-straightener name, 94, 145, 191; interest in Williams's time at, 254; Mackenzie seeks information on, 244; name's origin, 143, 257
Black Swan Records, 66–72; ad campaign addressed at Blacks, 87; bankruptcy, 89; Bibb embezzles from, 72, 88–89, 91; as Black-owned, 66, 68, 88; blues records, 71, 90; Burley on music of, 232; cash-flow problems, 71–72, 88; competition for, 87–88; context of establishment of, 66–67; cultural "uplift" as goal, 68, 100, 111, 143, 145, 204; disinclination to give people what they wanted, 92; Du Bois and, 69, 143, 185; first release, 70; Henderson at, 70, 71, 90, 93; name's origin, 69, 257; New York Recording Laboratory presses records, 70, 88; Olympic Records purchased by, 88; Paramount Records acquires catalog, 89, *157;* popular music on, 71; revenues, 71, 89; serious music emphasized, 70–71; Bessie Smith turned down by, 88; Swanola phonograph, 88; white-owned labels oppose, 69–70; wide spectrum of music on, 68, 71, 146; Williams at, 66, 71–72, 87–89, 119, 254
Blackwell, Scrapper, 161; "How Long, How Long Blues," 162; Robert Johnson influenced by, 242; "Kokomo Blues," 162; record collectors ignore, 255; records for Gennett, 147; Williams records Carr and, 161–62, 165, 169, 173, 177, 253; Williams's friendship with, 195–96
Blake, Blind: Depression affects, 195; musical style of, 189; Taggart compared with, 148–49; Tampa Red Georgia Tom have more releases than, 173; Williams produces, 133–35, 140
Blake, Eubie, 33, 85, 93, 249
Blueitt, Napoleon and Virgil, 85
blues: alcoholism among singers, 113, 132, 194–95, 235; beginning of end of market for, 177; Black artists restricted to, 98; on Black Swan records, 71, 90, 112; "blues craze" of 1920s, 68; Blues Renaissance, 213; in Chicago, 62, 63, 227, 228; classic, 107, 108, 131, 136, 140, 148, 177, 243, 253; country, 131–32, 133, 148; on Decca Records, 193; Delta, 131, 227, 242–43, 244, 256; Depression

affects singers, 195; Dickerson on, 97; Dorsey's influence on, 178; down-home, 146, 148, 165, 204; exploitative commercial relationships in, 116; female guitar-based musicians, 174; financial viability of, 93; first commercial recording by Black musician, 13, 48; gospel music and, 177; hokum, 164, 209; illiterate singers, 110, 172; jump, 215, 226, 227; in "List of American Folk Songs On Commercial Records," 207–8, 242; male artists, 112, 113; in Monmouth, Illinois, 12–13, 160; *Out Came the Blues* compilation, 246; on Paramount records, 112, 133, 140; piano-based, 12, 160, 161, 256; of Rainey, 108; record collectors shape narrative of, 236, 241–42, 243, 258; revival, 117, 118, 204, 235–36, 243, 244, 245, 246, 249; small labels for, 217; Bessie Smith's approach to, 88; Mamie Smith's "Crazy Blues," 48, 68; as unknown in Port Washington, Wisconsin, 90; as what the people wanted, 92; Williams as A&R man for, 92; Williams on, 98, 101–2, 246; Williams's favorite artists, 214; Williams sings at Brown show, 32, 101

Blythe, Jimmy, 136, 206

Bonds, Abraham John "Son," 194

boogie-woogie: craze, 199, 206; Davenport plays, 160; Hammond associated with, 205; "Honky Tonk Train Blues," 168; Jefferson and, 130, 206, 256; in Kansas City, 197; Montgomery plays, 2; "Pine Top's Boogie-Woogie," 167, 168, 205; Pine Top Smith and, 206, 256; Price plays, 160, 172, 199, 201, 256; Speckled Red plays, 170; Williams associated with, 168, 206, 253, 256

Bottoms, Bill, 63, 272n35

Bradford, Perry, 68

Brady, Bruce, 11, 61

Bronzeville (Chicago): Coles Brothers from, 203; Overton Hygienic Building, 92, 163; the Stroll, 95; Luther Williams lives in, 10; Williams robbed in, 120; Williams seeks artists in, 99, 122

Broonzy, Big Bill, 116–17; autobiography, 243; in blues revival, 235; Brunswick/Vocalion recordings, 174, 253; in Charters's *The Country Blues,* 242; at "From Spirituals to Swing" concerts, 204; Gennett records, 146–47; on "List of American Folk Songs On Commercial Records," 207; Muddy Waters opens for, 227

Brotherhood of Sleeping Car Porters, 100

Brown, Lee, 226, 227

Brown University, 23–36; Alpha Phi Alpha and, 26, 51–52; Black students at, 26, 30, 51–52, 184; in first Rose Bowl, 20, 74; football at, 24, 26–30, 35–36, 42–49; fraternity life at, 26; Hope as graduate of, 57, 182–83; integration at, 26, 50; military training at, 31; minstrelsy at, 32, 48, 50, 52–53; Pollard at, 20; racial and social characteristics at, 23–24; segregation at, 50; Soldier's Gate, 55; students leave for war, 33–34, 36; Union Vaudeville Show, 31–32; Williams attends 1968 commencement, 237; Williams transfers to, 21, 259

Brunswick-Balke-Collendar Company (BBC), 159, 174–75, 182, 190

Brunswick/Vocalion: Burley on music of, 232; CBS purchases Vocalion, 207; Dorsey at, 160, 163; gospel and popular music on, 177; Robert Johnson records for, 242; and "List of American Folk Songs On Commercial Records," 207; race records, 159, 160, 173, 174, 175, 193; as step up from Paramount, 192–93; Williams at, 150, 159–79, 190

Buffalo Divisions, 39–40, 257

Bullock, Matthew, 64, 270n5

Burley, Dan, 211, 215, 232

Butler, Solomon "Sol": with Canton Bulldogs, 137, 138; with Colored All-Stars, 179, 181; with Fritz Pollard's All-Stars, 85, 175, 176; with Hammond Pros, 80, 102, 103, 104, 105, 119, 120,

Butler, Solomon (*continued*) 123, 137, 239; Harding's connection with, 224; in integration of sports, 181, 233; Lillard and, 223; at Olympics of 1920, 46; out of NFL, 138, 186; at Penn Relays, 33; with Rock Island Independents, 106, 179

Calhoun, George, 105–6
Calicott, Joe, 171
Calloway, Cab: Barker as sideman of, 248; in Brunswick/Vocalion catalog, 177; Decca's marketing of, 193; in "soundie," 217; at Suntan Studios, 216; Williams known by, 214
Calt, Stephen, 91, 92, 94, 98, 241, 243–44, 250, 255, 259
calypso, 169, 173, 193
Camp, Bob, 237
Camp, Walter, 34, 36, 41, 49, 234
Cannon, Gus, 169
Canton Bulldogs, 75, 76, 80, 81, 84, 102, 125, 126, 137–38, 278n14
Carlisle Indian Industrial School, 18, 75, 79, 136
Carr, Dora, 161
Carr, Joseph, 138
Carr, Leroy, 161; boogie-woogie of, 206; in Charters's *The Country Blues,* 242; "How Long, How Long Blues," 162; Robert Johnson and, 204, 242, 245, 284n34; record collectors ignore, 246, 255; Tampa Red Georgia Tom have more releases than, 173; Williams records Blackwell and, 161–62, 165, 169, 173, 177, 253; Williams's friendship with, 195–96
Carter (Chatmon), Bo, 165–66
Carter, J. F. S., 45, 46, 55, 56, *154*
Casey, Alvro, 136
Centre College, 53
Chamberlain, Guy, 236, 257
Charters, Samuel, 131, 242, 243
Chess, Leonard, 228–29, 249
Chess Records, 226, 228, 232
Chicago: African Americans migrate to, 62; as Black Swan's primary market, 89; blues in, 62, 63, 227, 228; at dawn of Great Depression, 1–2; gospel music in, 229; independent record labels in, 226; jazz in, 62, 63, 67; Stokes family settles in, 114; Maurice Williams comes to, 60; Williams family migrates to, 57, 61; Williams moves to after graduation, 62. *See also* Bronzeville (Chicago)
Chicago Defender (newspaper): on Black athletes as point of pride, 48; on Black athletes of 1921, 82; Black Patti ad in, 145; on Black Swan Records, 69, 70; on Brown-Harvard game, 30; on CBS's purchase of Vocalion, 207; *Chicago Whip* modeled after, 63; on Colored All-Stars team, 181; on first Black NFL official, 75; on integration as economic issue, 104; on riots of 1919, 67; on Smith's OKeh recordings, 68; Young writes for, 233
Chicago Music Publishing Company: Bronzeville offices of, 95; dissolution of, 113; Dorsey at, 163; Moeser never visits, 133; as publishing arm of Paramount, 92–94; song rights purchased by, 116, 119; staff of, 96–97
Chicago Record Company (CRC), 142, 146
Chicago Whip (newspaper), 63; on Black Swan Records, 69; entertainment as emphasis of, 63; noble aims of, 63; as radical separatist paper, 63; on riots of 1919, 67; Williams mentioned in, 47–48, 49, 63; Williams offered job on, 62–63; on Williams with Hammond Pros, 81, 82; Williams writes for, 64–66, 83, 184, 246
civil rights: Army experiments in, 37, 41; athletes turned activists, 224; Hammond's vision of, 204; integration seen as economics not just, 104; NAACP in, 16; reversals of, 259; sports and, 221, 251–52, 254, 256; Tapscott's role in, 181; Williams in advancement of, 252; zenith of, 235
Cole, Nat "King," 202, 203, 216, 228, 253
Coles Brothers, 202–4
Columbia (record label): as competition for Black Swan, 87; as competition for

Paramount, 89; Hammond and, 204, 207; Robert Johnson reissued on, 243; Memphis Minnie and Kansas Joe record for, 174; race records division, 207, 232; records demeaning to Blacks of, 68; Muddy Waters records for, 228; Clarence Williams finds talent for, 122
Cook, Will Marion, 33
"coon songs," 67, 100
Country Blues, The (Charters), 131, 242, 243
Cox, Ida: classic blues of, 177; at "From Spirituals to Swing" concerts, 204; "How Long Daddy, How Long Blues," 162; Price meets, 172; Rainey influences, 204; "Sweet Mama Tree Top Tall," 128; Williams and, 99, 108, 113, 122
Crisis (journal), 14, 15, 16, 69
Crouch, William, 217
Curzon, Harry, 123, 135

Daley, George "Herbert," 29
Dalhart, Vernon, 142, 145
dance music: Blind Blake plays, 133; early Muddy Waters plays, 227; Papa Charlie Jackson plays, 112; Blind Lemon Jefferson plays, 130, 131; Monmouth blues as, 12–13, 160; Williams on, 92, 102, 216, 247, 256
Dandridge, Dorothy, 217
Davenport, Cow Cow, 160–61; boogie-woogie and, 256; "Cow Cow Blues," 161, 162, 199, 206; on "List of American Folk Songs On Commercial Records," 207; Price and, 199, 200; Pine Top Smith recommended by, 167; Williams produces, 161, 165, 169
Davenport, Jed, 171
Davis, Reverend Gary, 133
Decca Records: American Federation of Musicians and, 212, 213, 216; Basie signed by, 196–98; Ebony Records has deal with, 231, 234; Harlem Hamfats back artists of, 209; jukeboxes and marketing of, 190; Kapp at, 190; and "List of American Folk Songs On Commercial Records," 207; Montgomery and Scruggs seek deal with, 1–2; *Out Came the Blues* compilation, 246; post-blues boom, 217; race records, 1, 190, 193, 212; "Sepia Series," 193; as step up from Brunswick/Vocalion, 193; Wheatstraw records for, 179; Williams at, 190–204, 209–18, 254
Delta blues, 131, 227, 242–43, 244, 256
Depler, Jack, 78
De Priest, Oscar, 85, 187
Derr, Ben, 78
Dickerson, Aletha: at Chicago Music Company, 96, 98, 109, 110, 122, 134; at Decca, 198; in Hokum Boys, 164; at Paramount, 150; at State Street Record Company, 142–43
Dixie Hummingbirds, 212
Dorn, John, 217
Dorsey, Thomas A. (Georgia Tom), 162–63; on Atlanta's Black community, 185; at Brunswick/Vocalion, 160, 163, 170–71; gospel music of, 177–78, 239; in Hokum Boys, 164; "How About You," 178; "It's Tight Like That," 164–65; on "List of American Folk Songs On Commercial Records," 207; marriage of, 163; on a musicians' union, 119; nervous breakdowns of, 163; as Paramount arranger, 93, 96, 163; on Paramount creating opportunities for blues singers, 140; at Pilgrim Baptist Church, 177, 188; Rainey and, 108, 109, 140, 148, 163, 164; records for Gennett, 146–47; relationship with Williams, 163–64, 178, 239; on royalties, 165; "Take My Hand, Precious Lord," 202; and Tampa Red, 164, 173, 176; at T.O.B.A. theater in Memphis, 171; wife's death, 177–78; Williams produces, 98, 169, 253; on Williams's business practices, 117–18; withdraws from the blues, 176–77, 199
Douglass, Frederick, 16, 251
dozens, 171
Drew, Howard P., 19–20, 33, 43, 46, 233

Driscoll, Paddy: with Chicago Cardinals, 73, 76–77, 81, 103, 120, 123; as former collegiate star, 75, 105

Du Bois, W. E. B.: in Alpha Phi Alpha, 51, 85; American Crusade Against Lynching and, 230; Archer and, 187; on Black-owned businesses, 68; on Blacks in the Army, 37, 39; on Black Swan project, 69, 143, 185; on blues, 71; civil rights strategy of, 256; as *Crisis* editor, 14; Hope and, 182; *Moon Illustrated Weekly* newsletter of, 68–69; at Morehouse University, 185; as NAACP leader, 16; Pace and, 68–69; and segregation of professional football, 186; and Washington differ on strategy for racial progress, 17; Wesley and, 38; Williams and, 253; Young and, 41

Ebony Records, 231–32; "Black Is Beautiful," 249; Camp records for, 237; deal with Decca, 231, 234; infrequent releases, 235; Nixon and Estes record for, 236; output plummets into obscurity, 233; Williams on records of, 237; Williams tries to sell 45s to Calt, 244

Eckstein, Dolph, 126

Ellington, Duke: Cook as mentor to, 33; Decca's marketing of, 193; records for Brunswick/Vocalion, 177; as soda jerk, 16; in "soundie," 217; at Suntan Studios, 216; Williams known by, 214

Ellis, Big Chief, 231

Ertegun, Ahmet, 231

Estes, Sleepy John, 193–95, 207, 236, 242

Faunce, William H. P., 25, 35, 51

field recordings, 124–25, 145–46, 165, 169–75, 227

Fischer, Rudolph, 26, 214

Fitzgerald, Ella, 210, 248

folk revival: *Anthology of American Folk Music* and, 242; royalties and, 118; Terry and McGhee in, 229; Williams and, 235–36

Folkways Records, 242, 243

Follis, Charles W., 79, 225

football: African-American participation in, 18, 79; barnstorming Black all-star teams, 223–24; at Brown University, 24, 26–30, 35–36; Camp's role in, 34; college, 18, 20, 24; first Black All-American, 15; Grange changes game, 126–27; modern style of, 17–18, 48–49; transition to working-class game, 78–79; at Yale University, 18, 28, 40, 78, 253. *See also* NFL (National Football League)

Forbes, Franklin, 184, 187, 190

Frazier, E. Franklin, 17, 115, 214

"From Spirituals to Swing" concerts, 204–5, 206

Fuller, Blind Boy, 196, 207, 229

Gabler, Milt, 201, 207, 216, 217, 258

Gaines, Charlie, 209–10

Galvin, Bill, 42–43, 44, 47

Garvey, Marcus, 63, 68, 70

Gates, J. M., 136, 145, 242

Gennett, Fred, 146

Gennett, Richard, 142, 159

Gennett Records, 142, 145, 146–47, 232, 244

Georgia Tom. *See* Dorsey, Thomas A. (Georgia Tom)

Gillo, Hank, 78

Golden Gate Quartet, 204

Gordon, E. O., 186

gospel music: Dorsey and, 177–78, 239; race and, 193; Williams records for his labels, 229–30, 253; Williams records quartets for Decca, 212

Gourdin, E. O. (Ned), 56, 65, 82, 270n6

Grange, Red, 126–27, 138, 147, 236

Grant, Coot, 200, 211

Great Migration, 1, 62

Greenfield, Elizabeth Taylor, 69, 143, 257

Grimké, Archibald, 16–17

Gulian, Mike, 126

Hahn, Archie, 20–21, 55, *154*

Halas, George: with Chicago Bears, 76, 77, 104, 219–20; Driscoll meets, 76; in segregation of NFL, 104–5,

123–24, 139, 219, 222; Williams and, 257, 258
Haley, Bill, 217
Hammond, John: attempts to sign Basie for Brunswick, 196–98, 210; boogie-woogie associated with, 205; "From Spirituals to Swing" concerts of, 204–5; Robert Johnson LP released by, 242; on Jordan, 215; Steiner and, 191; on Webb's band, 210; Williams and, 196, 198, 205, 208, 243, 258
Hampton University, 18–19, 20, 55
Handy, W. C., 69, 70, 97, 270n8
Hardin (Armstrong), Lil, 97, 213, 235
Harding, Halley, 179; in integration of NFL, 179, 181, 225, 257; meets Williams, 179, 224; with Negro All-Stars, 224, 257; in Varsity Club of Chicago, 234
Harlem Hamfats, 209, 211, 227
Harlem Renaissance, 213, 214
Harper, Leonard, 216, 217
HBCUs (Historically Black Colleges and Universities): Army recruiting from, 38, 40; football at, 18, 79; as legacy of abolition, 15; Morehouse College, 57, 182–85, 187–88; Paul Quinn College, 150, 167; play all-white teams, 221; Spelman College, 182, 184–85. *See also* Howard University
Hegamin, Lucille, 89
Henderson, Fletcher: at Black Swan Records, 70, 71, 90, 93, 111, 185; boogie-woogie arranged by, 206; at "From Spirituals to Swing" concerts, 204; works with Williams, 119
Henderson, Fletcher Hamilton, 185
Henry, Hound Head, 162
Hess, Wally, 78, 83
Hilburn, J. H., 51
hokum blues, 164, 209
Hokum Boys, 164–65, 177
Hope, John, 182–83; in Alpha Phi Alpha, 185; as Atlanta University president, 187–88, 192; civil rights strategy of, 256; Franklin and, 282n2; and segregation of professional football, 186; Williams and, 57, 176, 253
House, Son, 227

Howard, Paul, 180
Howard, Rosetta, 209
Howard University, 14–22; Afrocentric worldview at, 15, 18; Commercial College, 15; establishment of, 16; football at, 17–19, 20; fraternities, 19; Frazier at, 17, 115; as HBCU, 15; NAACP chapter at, 16, 17; seeks to be officer training site, 40; Thanksgiving 1922 football game, 85; on vernacular Black cultural forms, 17; Williams rarely mentions, 21–22, 31
Hudson, Dick "Super Six": with Colored Giants, 147; with Fritz Pollard's All-Stars, 85; with Hammond Pros, 80, 123, 125, 136; out of football, 138; in Varsity Club of Chicago, 234
Hughes, Charles Evans, 24, 27–28
Hughes, Langston, 214
Hughes, Revella, 70
Hull, Little Harvey, 146
Hunter, Alberta: ballads known by, 98; Black Swan launches recording career, 90; Bottoms hires, 63; business relationship with Williams, 117; "Down Hearted Blues," 92, 95; as Paramount artist, 93; success of blues records of, 71, 88; Williams loathed by, 115
Hurt, Mississippi John, 242

Ink Spots, 198–99, 202
integration: "black and tan" clubs, 63–64; Black media call for re-integration of pro sports, 103–4; at Brown University, 26, 50; in college football, 43; Halas seen as positive force for, 105; Hammond and, 204; of Hammond Pros, 102; interracial socializing among athletes, 53–54; of NFL, 3, 179, 219, 221–25, 238–41, 246, 248, 257; of professional baseball, 3, 221, 223; of professional sports, 223, 233, 251; in track and field, 19; white football players and, 139

Jackson, Jim: in *Anthology of American Folk Music,* 242; Lomax requests record of, 207; on Vocalion, 159; Williams records, 169, 170, 171, 172, 253

Jackson, Lulu, 162
Jackson, Mahalia, 202, 228, 253
Jackson, Papa Charlie: classic blues of, 131; Depression affects, 195; "How Long Daddy, How Long," 162; Robert Johnson compared with, 245; musical style, 112, 133, 189; as Paramount staple, 122; Rainey backed by, 148; "Shake That Thing," 112, 194, 249; Williams produces, 112–13, 140, 247; among Williams's favorite artists, 214
James, Jesse, 207
Jarrett, Vernon, 249–50
Jaxon, Frankie "Half Pint," 209
jazz: Black artists restricted to, 98; on Black Swan records, 71, 90, 112; in Chicago, 62, 63, 67; criticism, 204, 210, 211; on Gennett Records, 142; in Kansas City, 169, 197, 253; Kapp brothers and, 173–74; in Los Angeles, 180; Morton and, 101; popularity among whites, 67–68; record collectors shape narrative of, 241; Williams as A&R man for, 92
Jefferson, Blind Lemon, 129–30; in *Anthology of American Folk Music*, 242; boogie-woogie and, 130, 206, 256; in Charters's *The Country Blues*, 242; death, 132; Depression affects, 195; discovery, 131; Robert Johnson compared with, 204; Lead Belly and, 129, 278n2; musical style, 133, 201; Price and, 130, 131, 201; as soul singer, 247; Taggart compared with, 148–49; Tampa Red Georgia Tom have more releases than, 173; Williams produces, 129, 130–33, 140, 242, 253
Jews: at Brown University, 21, 26, 51, 52, 75; Brown University bans Jewish fraternities, 51; Gabler as, 216; "Jew Town" in Chicago, 159; Williams on Supper as, 148; Williams's Jewish friends, 115
Jim Crow: addressing white males during, 116–17; individual agency in, 221; "race music" as artifact of, 98, 210; in record business's origins, 258; in the South, 14; Wilson's policies toward, 27. *See also* segregation

Johnson, A. C., 179, 180
Johnson, Guy B., 121–22, 124–25, 127–28
Johnson, Jack, 63, 99, 189, 255, 256
Johnson, James Weldon, 85
Johnson, Lonnie, 173
Johnson, Pete, 197, 205
Johnson, Robert, 162, 242–43, 245, 255, 256
Johnson, Stovepipe, 162, 215
Jones, Melancholy, 217
Jones, Sidney, 192, 230, 239
Jones, Sissieretta ("Black Patti"), 33, 130, 143–45, *158*, 257
Jones, Willie, 162
Jordan, Louis, 209–11; attitude toward music, 211, 216; and Black Patti Troubadours, 144; criticism of, 215; film career, 216, 217; "Five Guys Named Moe," 216; Gabler produces, 216; "Honey in the Bee Ball," 211; "I'm Gonna Move to the Outskirts of Town," 215–16; Robert Johnson compared with, 245; jump blues of, 215; "Mama Mama Blues," 215, 216; USO tours, 216; Williams produces, 211, 212, 213, 214, 215–16, 217, 232, 253
jukeboxes, 99, 130, 190, 216
jump blues, 215, 226, 227

Kapp, Dave: leaves Decca, 234; and "List of American Folk Songs On Commercial Records," 207; Price on, 200; in signing of Basie for Decca, 197, 198; at State Street Music Company, 160, 280n3; Tharpe and, 201; Williams works with, 173–74
Kapp, Jack: Coles Brothers and, 202, 203; death, 234; at Decca Records, 190; Louis Jordan and, 211, 215; and "List of American Folk Songs On Commercial Records," 207; Price on, 200; in signing of Basie for Decca, 197, 198; at State Street Music Company, 160, 280n3; Tharpe and, 201; Williams and, 150, 173–74
Kazee, Buell, 207
Kemp, Ray, 175, 186, 220
King, Dick "Rip," 78, 85

King Records, 230, 232
Kirk, Andy, 173, 197, 212, 216
Kovacsy, Bill, 238–39
Ku Klux Klan (KKK): in Detroit, 125; in Indiana, 80, 102, 105, 162; uprisings in Midwest, 48

Ladnier, Tommy, 108, 109, 110
Laibly, Art: Calt on, 243; claims to have discovered Jefferson, 131, 132; Williams undermined by, 120, 133, 141–42, 148, 196
Lambeau, Curly, 105, 258
Lane, Russell Adrian, 52, 55, 57, 161, 269n32
Lattimore, William W., 33, 65, 66
Lead Belly (Huddie Ledbetter): Black Patti Troubadours influence, 144; boogie-woogie and, 256; Jefferson and, 129–30, 149, 278n2; Marshall, Texas, and, 167
Lee, George F., 169
Lewis, Furry, 159, 160, 171, 235, 242
Lewis, Meade "Lux," 168, 204, 205
Lewis, William H., 64, 234–35, 265n50
Library of Congress, 96, 207, 227, 242
Lillard, Joe: with Chicago Cardinals, 186, 219; with Colored All-Stars, 179; in eastern regional league, 222; Harding and, 224, 257; as hothead, 223; in integration of NFL, 181, 223, 257
Linton, William, 63
"List of American Folk Songs On Commercial Records," 207–8, 242
Little Twig, Joe, 103, 135
Little Walter, 229
Locke, Alain, 16, 17, 68, 253–54
Lomax, Alan, 207–8, 227, 242, 258
Louis, Joe, 221, 234
Lunceford, Jimmy, 217
lynching, 41, 48, 50, 67, 105, 230

Mackenzie, John, 146, 244, 245
MacNeal, Arthur Clement, 63
Magruder, Miles (stepfather), 7–8
Malone, Annie Turbo, 192
Mara, Tim, 138, 139, 222

Ma Rainey's Black Bottom (Wilson), 2–3, 252
Marsh, Otto, 107, 109, 110
Marshall, Bobby, 106, 179, 235, 238, 239
Marshall, George Preston, 138, 139, 222–23, 258
Martin, Harry, 34
McCain, James, 227
McCombs, Nat, 136
McCoy, Ann Sorter, 227
McCoy, Charlie, 165, 169, 170, 209
McCoy, Kansas Joe, 174, 190, 209
McFall, Jennie (grandmother), 7, 12, 38, 60
McFall, John (grandfather), 7, 12
McGhee, Brownie, 229, 231
McGhee, Stick, 229, 231
McMahon (Horween), Ralph and Arnold, 73, 75, 80, 81
McMillan, Bo, 53–54
McTell, Blind Willie, 185, 189, 191, 242
McTell, Kate, 189, 191
Melrose, Lester: as congenial, 196; Charles Johnson shops talent to, 178; Louis Jordan and, 215; as music publisher, 93, 206; takes artists from Williams, 97; Muddy Waters recorded by, 228; as white freelance producer, 226
Memphis Minnie, 174; "Bumble Bee," 174; Robert Johnson compared with, 245; on "List of American Folk Songs On Commercial Records," 207; Kansas Joe McCoy and, 174, 209; record collectors ignore, 255; as strong female blueswoman, 177; Williams and, 170, 174, 190, 253, 229
Mercury Records, 226, 228, 232
Metcalfe, Ralph, 186, 234
Mills Brothers, 177, 193
Ming, Hoyt, 242
minstrelsy: Black Patti Troubadours and, 144; Black record buyers reject, 100; Brown University shows as, 32, 48, 52–53; "coon songs" in, 67; Papa Charlie Jackson influenced by, 112; in New England, 50; popularity in 1917, 68; Rabbit Foot Minstrels, 108, 209

Mississippi Sheiks, 165, 169
Moeser, Otto: Black Patti and, 142, 146, 148; on going to race records, 89; on radio and record business, 150; Williams and, 113, 133
Montgomery, Little Brother: background of, 1–2; Barker as sideman of, 248; Blake plays with, 135; boogie-woogie and, 256; on color consciousness, 257; Ebony releases recordings, 235; helps Williams locate artists, 226; Jarrett and Saunders program on, 249; meet Williams at Decca, 1–2; at Williams-O'Neal interview, 248; at Williams's funeral, 250
Moore, Spec, 59, 60
Morehouse College, 57, 182–85, 187–88
Morton, Jelly Roll: on Gennett Records, 142; Howard plays with, 180; label hopping by, 100–101; Ledbetter influenced by, 130; Montgomery influenced by, 2; Russell's interest in, 244; Williams produces, 100, 180, 253; "Wolverine Blues," 100
Motley, Marion, 3, 233
Murchison, Loren, 45, 46
Murphy, Jimmy, 31–32, *154*

NAACP (National Association for the Advancement of Colored People): on Blacks in the Army, 37, 40; Black Swan Records and, 66, 68, 69, 71, 90; *Brown v. Board of Education* legal team, 183; civil rights strategy of, 256; *Crisis* journal, 14; Grimké and, 16–17; Hope and, 182; at Howard University, 16, 17
Nash, Bob, 78
Nathan, Syd, 230
National Collegiate Athletic Association (NCAA), 18
National Council of Colored People, 16
Neale, Alfred Earl "Greasy," 120, 258
Negro and His Songs, The (Odum and Johnson), 121, 122, 124
Negro Workday Songs (Odum and Johnson), 121, 124
Nelson, Red, 191
Nevers, Ernie, 136, 180, 258

New York Recording Laboratory, 70, 88, 89
NFL (National Football League): article on early, 236; Black players erased from history of, 248; establishment of, 74–75, 79; first Black official, 74, 80–81, 139, 253; integration of, 3, 179, 219, 221–25, 238–41, 246, 248, 257; new standards for teams in, 83; prominence of, 248; reorganization of, 138; segregation in, 3, 80, 104–5, 135, 138–39, 186–87, 219–23, 258; Super Bowl, 238; transition to working-class game, 78–79; white owners shape narrative of, 258; Williams in, 3, 74, 139, 223, 238, 240, 253, 258
Nied, Frank, 135, 136
Nix, A. W., 160
Nixon, Hammie, 193–95, 236
Noone, Jimmy, 95, 160, 169, 172

O'Bryant, Jimmy, 108, 109, 110
Oden, Curly: on Brown University football team, 44, 45, 46, *154*, 237; with Providence Steam Rollers, 126
Oden, St. Louis Jimmy, 198, 226, 229, 236
Odum, Howard T., 121, 124, 125, 127
OKeh Records: Burney on music of, 232; as competition for Black Swan, 87; Davenport records for, 161; Mississippi Sheiks record for, 165; Morton records for, 101; Peer at, 93, 161; Scruggs records for, 1; Mamie Smith records for, 68; Clarence Williams finds talent for, 122
Oliver, Joe "King": at Dreamland Cafe, 63; Gennett records, 142; Howard plays with, 180; "Riverside Blues," 93; Scruggs and, 1; Williams produces, 180, 253; "Wolverine Blues," 100
O'Neal, Jim, 12, 93, 101, 132, 146, 147, 165, 232, 247–48, 249, 254, 255, 261n1
Ory, Edward "Kid," 1, 180
Osborn, Bob "Duke," 81–82
Overton, Anthony, 92, 253
Owens, Jesse, 221, 234

Pace, Harry, 68–69; at Alpha Phi Alpha reception, 85; and Atlanta University, 185; Bibb as brother-in-law of, 66, 89; at Black Swan Records, 66, 68, 69–72, 87–89, 143; Du Bois and, 68–69; musical taste, 69; at Pace & Handy, 66, 68, 69, 87; at Poro College event, 192; on radio and Black Swan, 87–88; in Rainey's "Mystery Record" competition, 119; Williams compared with, 112

Pace & Handy Music Publishing Company, 66, 67, 68, 69–70, 87, 93

Pace Recording Company, 69

Paddock, Charlie, 45, 46, 56

Page, Walter, 173–74, 197

Paramount Records: Black Swan catalog acquired by, 89, *157*; blues researchers' interest in, 244; commercial interest in old records of, 191; "de Mayo 1923" on labels, 133; folds, 135, 191; Gennett Records as competitor of, 142; headquarters of, 90; lost copyright revenues, 92; New York studio closed, 122; Patton records for, 244; physical condition of records, 273n8; race records as emphasis of, 89; royalty paid by, 97; Scruggs records for, 1; Williams at, 91–113, 115–22, 129–35, 140, 147–50, 254; Williams attempts to buy old masters, 191, 241; Williams leaves, 150, 160, 162, 196; Williams's deal with, 91–92; Williams visits headquarters of, 90–91

Parham, Tiny, 96

Parks, Barney, 212

Patti, Adelina, 143–44, 257

Patton, Charlie, 243, 244, 245

Peer, Ralph, 91, 93, 161, 257, 258

Perkins, Betty, 171

Pickens, William, 16, 85

Pollard, Fritz: with Akron Pros, 123–24, 239; as All-American, 20, 34, 36; at Alpha Phi Alpha reception, 85; in article on early NFL, 236; as Black athlete of 1921, 82; as Black athlete-turned-businessman, 234; on Blacks in NFL, 187, 219; Brown Bombers team, 220, 257; at Brown University, 20, 36, 265n50; on Brown University football team, 24–25, 27, 28–29, 30, 34–35, 43; with Chicago Black Hawks team, 162, 187, 257; clothes-pressing shop at Brown, 26, 27, 35, 36, 57; with Colored All-Stars, 179, 181; with Colored Giants, 147; as controversial figure, 122–23; friendship with Robeson, 27; Fritz Pollard's All-Stars, 85, 103, 175–76, 221, 223, 257; on Halas, 139, 219–20; with Hammond Pros, 102, 103, 122–24, 239; Harding's connection with, 224; at Harlem's Cavalcade with Williams, 214; indoor football league developed by, 83; as informal advisor to Williams, 100, 101; in integration of sports, 181, 233; Lewis as sponsor of, 235; as lifelong friend of Williams, 11; on Mara, 138; in minstrel shows at Brown, 31–32; moves to Chicago, 62; moves to Harlem, 187, 188; at Narragansett Pier during summer, 34; newspapers' racialized descriptions of, 52; in NFL, 73, 74, 75, 76, 80, 81, 82, 84, 139, 223, 238, 240; out of NFL, 138, 186; in Pro Football Hall of Fame, 248; with Providence Steam Rollers, 126, 127, 219; race consciousness of, 246; as race "pioneer," 48; recommends Williams to Brown University, 21; recruits Black men for officer training, 37, 38; rivalry with Thorpe, 219; rumor about Wilson and, 27; on segregation in NFL, 139, 219–20; shows booked by, 216–17; at Smart Set track meet, 33, 66; and "soundies," 216, 217, 234; sports and media of, 255, 256; Sullivan on, 167; Suntan Studios, 213, 216–17; as track star, 11–12; in Varsity Club of Chicago, 234; on white players and integration, 139; Williams as in shadow of, 44; Williams charged with covering, 26; Williams compared with, 256–57; Williams in *Chicago Whip* on, 64

Posey, Cumberland "Cum," 175, 221–23

Powell, Adam Clayton, Jr., 231

Powell, Adam Clayton, Sr., 85
Powers, Jimmy, 222
Preer, Frank, 63
Price, Sammy: in Basie signing with Decca, 197; boogie-woogie played by, 160, 172, 199, 201, 256; at Decca Records, 199–200, 217; on Jefferson, 130, 131, 201; on Tharpe, 200–202; Williams and, 160, 172, 214
Providence (Rhode Island), 23, 24, 26, 35, 50, 51–52, 126, 143, 144
Purdy, Clair J., 24, 74, 76

"Race Contacts and Inter-Racial Relations" (Locke), 17
race records: of Brunswick/Vocalion, 159, 160, 173, 174, 175, 193; Carr and Blackwell and, 162; of Columbia, 207, 232; of Decca, 1, 190, 193, 212; exploitation in industry, 115, 118; of Gennett, 142; genuine musical inclinations versus, 166; gospel and popular music on labels, 177; Paramount concentrates on, 89; racialized marketing of music, 98, 210; Speir's role in, 159; white collectors versus Black buyers, 255; Williams and, 66, 87, 91, 92, 100, 102, 135, 140, 174, 232; in Wilson's *Ma Rainey's Black Bottom*, 2–3
racial progress: Du Bois and Washington differ on strategy, 17; in Howard University discourse, 17; integration of professional sports and, 3; as not smooth arc, 251–52; reversals of, 258–59. *See also* civil rights
racism: of football owners, 139, 186; of football spectators, 80, 138; institutionalized, 14; on minorities' lack of impartiality, 82; in minstrelsy at Brown University, 53; racist/antiracist dynamic, 259; Maurice Williams affected by, 58; Williams's privilege opens him up to, 54; after World War I, 67; at Yale, 42
Rainey, Ma, 107–8; arrest of, 163; business relationship with Williams, 117; Calt questions Williams about, 243; Charters's *The Country Blues* and, 242; classic blues of, 131, 136, 177; Davenport plays with, 161; Depression affects, 177, 195; Dorsey and, 108, 109, 140, 148, 163, 164; Robert Johnson compared with, 245; Memphis Minnie compared with, 174; Monogram Theater engagement, 148; "Morning Hour Blues," 136; as "Mother of the Blues," 3; "Mystery Record" competition, 119; original material of, 108, 112; Pine Top Smith accompanies, 168; Bessie Smith and, 107, 108, 204; on T.O.B.A. circuit, 140; Williams produces, 3, 106, 107–11, 113, 119–20, 122, 136, 247, 252, 253; among Williams's favorite artists, 214; Wilson's *Ma Rainey's Black Bottom*, 2–3, 252
Rainey, William "Pa," 108
record collectors: as fixated on the obscure, 255; on Robert Johnson, 245; Lomax's list and, 207; as nonconformist, 255; on recording officials of 1920s, 243–44; shape narrative of blues, 236, 241–42, 243, 258; on Williams, 196; on Williams and Ma Rainey, 252
Redding, J. Saunders, 52, 183–84, 185
Redding, Louis Lorenzo, 52, 55, 183
Reed, Long Cleve, 146
Reeves, Dan, 224, 238
rhythm and blues (R&B), 193, 229, 232, 253, 256
Rickey, Branch, 79, 225, 238, 271n11
Robeson, Paul: as All-American, 36; in Alpha Phi Alpha, 51, 230; blacklisting of, 231; in Blake's *Shuffle Along*, 85–86; with Colored Giants, 147; on Dreamland Cabaret team, 272n35; *The Emperor Jones*, 217; on football at Rutgers, 25; friendship with Pollard, 27; friendship with Williams, 27, 34, 213, 239–40, 254; with Fritz Pollard's All-Stars, 85; Sidney Jones as friend, 192; at Narragansett Pier, 34; newspapers' racialized descriptions of, 52; in NFL, 73, 74, 76, 84, 85–86, 139, 238, 240–41; political activities, 230–31; and Pro Football Hall of Fame, 248;

sports and music of, 255, 256; Sullivan on, 167; visits brothel while in college, 99; Williams compared with, 256–57; Williams in *Chicago Whip* on, 64
Robinson, Bill "Bojangles," 68, 186
Robinson, Ed "Robbie," 25, 29, 43, 44
Robinson, Jackie: in integration of baseball, 3, 222, 233, 238, 252, 271n11; at UCLA, 222, 225
Robinson, Mabel, 213
Rockefeller, John D., Jr., 20, 36, 182
Rooney, Art, 175
Rooney, Art, Jr., 175
Rooney, Dan, 175
Rooney, Jim, 175
Roosevelt, Franklin D., 187, 227
Roosevelt, Theodore, 18, 32, 41
royalties: Basie not paid by Decca, 197, 198; Black Patti does not pay, 145; Blackwell collects, 162; Dorsey on, 165; gospel quartets not paid by Decca, 212; Nixon not paid by Decca, 194; Williams does not offer, 97; Williams takes songwriters, 116–19
Rushing, Jimmie, 174
Russell, Bill (musician and historian), 191, 241, 244, 255

Sachs, Len, 123, 125
Satherly, Art, 89, 243
Saunders, Red, 249–50
Schissler, Paul, 222, 223
Scholz, Jackson, 45, 46
Scruggs, Irene (Chocolate Brown), 1–2
segregation: in the Army, 37; at Brown University, 50; as economic idiocy, 104; in Green Bay, Wisconsin, 123; individual agency in, 221; in Missouri, 103, 120; in Monmouth, Illinois, 8; in music business, 98; of NFL, 3, 80, 104–5, 135, 138–39, 186–87, 219–23, 258; in Pine Bluff, Arkansas, 6; in record business, 69, 193, 210; in the South, 14, 15; in sports and music, 254; in Wilson's policies, 16; of Yale football, 28. *See also* Jim Crow
separatism, 63
Sharpe, Albert "Doc," 42, 43, 137

Shelburne, Johnny: at Dartmouth, 44, 64; with Fritz Pollard's All-Stars, 85; with Hammond Pros, 80, 83, 84, 85; at Penn Relays, 56; on white players and integration, 139
Shurtleff, Bert, 126
Simmons, Ozzie, 220–21, 222, 223, 234
Sissle, Noble, 199, 202, 203, 249
Slater, Duke: amateur 1933 track meet officiated by, 186; Black newspapers on, 48; with Chicago Cardinals, 138, 186; coaches Negro All-Stars, 220; with Colored All-Stars, 179, 181; with Fritz Pollard's All-Stars, 85, 175, 176; Harding's connection with, 224; in integration of sports, 181, 233; Kerner supported by, 235; in NFL, 139, 223, 238, 240; in Pro Football Hall of Fame, 248; with Rock Island Independents, 103, 106, 120, 179; Sullivan on, 167; in Varsity Club of Chicago, 234
Smith, Bessie: Black Swan turns down, 88; Charters's *The Country Blues* and, 242; classic blues of, 131; Davenport plays with, 161; Dorsey and, 163; "Down Hearted Blues," 92; "From Spirituals to Swing" concerts and, 204; Rainey and, 107, 108, 204; among Williams's favorite artists, 214
Smith, Clara, 131
Smith, Clarence "Pine Top," 167–68; in boogie-woogie development, 206, 256; death, 168; Lewis and Ammons and, 168, 205; "Pine Top's Boogie-Woogie," 167, 168, 205; Williams owns rights to music of, 206; Williams records, 167, 205, 253
Smith, Harry, 242
Smith, Jabbo, 169
Smith, Joe, 119
Smith, Mamie, 48, 68, 131
Smith, Reverend Nathan, 207
Smith, Trixie, 88, 90, 118, 131, 200, 253
Southard, Harry, 180–81
South Side Boys Club, 230
Spand, Charlie, 135
Speckled Red, 170–71, 185, 206, 256
Speir, H. C., 159, 170

Spellman, Jack, 126
Spelman College, 182, 184–85
Spivey, Victoria, 190
State Street Music Company, 142–43, 160, 280n3
Stokes, Julia (mother-in-law), 114, 180, 187
Stokes, Pearl (sister-in-law), 114, 180
Stokes, Stella (sister-in-law), 114, 213
Strickler, George, 220
Strode, Woody, 3, 222, 225, 241
Sturgis, Rodney, 211
Sullivan, Ed, 167, 221
Sunnyland Slim, 229, 233, 249
Supper, Maurice A.: Black Patti hair-straightener of, 94, 145, 191; Black Patti's market access blocked by, 147–48; on blues selling well, 89–90; Chicago Music dissolved by, 113; Chicago Music established by, 92, 94; Mello Brown Company of, 192; on Williams and success of Paramount, 132–33; Williams on Calt and, 245; Williams remains close to, 191–92
Sweet, Fred, 127
Sykes, Roosevelt, 191, 199

Taggart, Blind Joe, 148–49, 190, 207
Tampa Red, 164; on field trip with Williams, 171; Georgia Tom and, 164, 173, 176; in Hokum Boys, 164; "It's Tight Like That," 164–65; Robert Johnson compared with, 245; on "List of American Folk Songs On Commercial Records," 207; at T.O.B.A. theater in Memphis, 171; Williams and, 169, 235
Tapscott, Horace, 180–81
Taylor, Yack, 213
Temple, Johnnie, 190, 191, 200, 209
Temple, William H., 115, 142, 187
Terkel, Studs, 81, 231, 239–41, 248, 254
Terry, Sonny, 204, 229
Tharpe, Sister Rosetta, 200–202, 253
Thomas, Henry "Ragtime Texas," 159, 160, 246
Thorpe, Jim: Abbott on, 236; on All-American Pro First Team, 105; on Canton Bulldogs, 76; at Carlisle Indian Industrial School, 18, 79, 103; with Hammond Pros, *157,* 166; with Hammond Semcos, 166–67; as NFL president, 75, 166; at Olympics of 1912, 20; preeminence of, 44; rivalry with Pollard, 219; with Rock Island Independents, 119, 120; Williams and, 253, 256–57
Titon, Jeff Todd, 258–59
T.O.B.A. (Theater Owners Booking Association): Davenport and, 161; as declining, 148; Georgia Tom and Tampa Red at, 171; in Overton Building, 92; Price and, 172; Rainey and, 140; Pine Top Smith on, 168; Williams and, 99, 112
Tolan, Eddie, 186
Tolsen, Melvin B., 179, 224
Trigg, Joseph Edward, 64, 270n5
Turner, E. C. "Pop," 221, 223
Turner, Joe, 204
Twilight, Alexander Lucius, 15

Varsity Club of Chicago, 234–35
Victor (record label): American Federation of Musicians and, 212; as competition for Black Swan, 87; as competition for Paramount, 89; Ink Spots record for, 198; Mississippi Sheiks record for, 165; Peer at, 91, 93; race records of, 232; records demeaning to Blacks of, 68

Wald, Elijah, 255, 284n34
Warner, Glenn "Pop," 18, 79
Wartman, Maynard Jones, 38–39, 40, 48, 57
Washington, Booker T., 16, 17, 19, 68, 70
Washington, DC, 16, 95
Washington, Kenny "Kingfish": in integration of NFL, 3, 224–25, 233, 238, 241; at UCLA, 222
Waters, Ethel: Blake on, 93; classic blues of, 131, 177; records for Black Swan, 71, 90, 91; records same material for different labels, 117
Waters, Muddy, 226, 227–28, 249, 253
Webb, Chick, 210, 211
Wesley, Charles, 37, 38, 266n1

Wheatstraw, Peetie: boogie-woogie of, 206; Ellison's *Invisible Man* and, 214; Robert Johnson and, 204, 242, 245; Price books, 200; Williams produces, 178–79, 190, 191

White, Georgia, 189, 190

White, Josh, 149–50, 195, 207

whiteness, 210, 246

white supremacy, 3, 37, 58, 222, 259

Wilkins, Robert, 170, 171

Williams, Aleta Carolyn Stokes (wife): at Chicago Music Company, 142; death, 237; little is known about, 254; marries Williams, 114–15; mother dies, 187; moves to Washington Park area, 174; at Poro College event, 192; as socially connected, 141, 214; style of living, 233–34; Josh White stays with, 149; on Williams as "man-about-town," 213

Williams, Bert, 33, 68

Williams, Big Joe, 178, 227

Williams, Clarence, 122, 161, 196, 209–10, 232

Williams, Dan (father), 5–6, 98, 252

Williams, J. Mayo ("Ink")

—in the Army, 37–41; commissioned as second lieutenant, 41; discharged from service, 41; machine gun training, 40; at Officer Training School, 37, 38–39, 40; registers for draft, 38; withdraws from Brown, 39

—at Black Patti Records, 141–47; Gennett and, 142, 145, 146; interest in his time at, 254; Reed and Hull recorded by, 146

—at Black Swan Records, 66, 71–72, 87–89, 119; on Bibb's embezzlement, 72, 88–89; downfall foreseen by, 90; never visits offices, 91; on Pace and Black Swan, 90

—blues revival and, 235–36, 249; *Anthology of American Folk Music* and, 242; blues researchers contact, 241; Charters's *The Country Blues* and, 242; and "List of American Folk Songs On Commercial Records," 207; on skewed understanding of blues history, 205

—at Brown University, 23–36; clothes-pressing shop of, 26, 27, 34, 35, 36, 48, 57; course load, 26, 30, 35, 43; football at, 24–27, 29–30, 35–36, 42–49, *152, 153, 154,* 253; grade point average, 34, 36, 56; graduation, 56; job offers after graduation, 57, 62, 182; knee injury, 45, 49, 50, 56; on McMillan, 53–54; in minstrel shows, 31–32, 48, 50, 53; at Narragansett Pier during summer, 34; newspapers' racialized descriptions of, 52; off-campus social life, 26; only touchdown of college career, 49; reported to have been in Missoula, Montana, 31; returns after service, 41; senior yearbook entry, 56–57, *155*; track at, 27, 30, 31, 33, 45–46, 50, 55–56, 66, *155,* 253; transfers to, 21, 259; works at Sunnyside Hotel summers, 9, 12

—at Brunswick/Vocalion, 150, 159–79, 190; assistants, 160; Carr and Blackwell produced by, 161–62, 165, 169, 173, 253; Bo Carter produced by, 165–66; Davenport produced by, 161, 165, 169; field-recording trips, 169–75; on Georgia Tom-Tampa Red split, 176; Jim Jackson produced by, 169, 170, 171, 172; Memphis Minnie produced by, 174, 253; scouting trips, 162; Pine Top Smith produced by, 167–68, 205, 253; Wheatstraw produced by, 178–79, 253

—in Chicago: to Chicago after graduation, 62; Drexel Boulevard residence, 237; East 47th Street residence, 237; East 51st Street Residence, 233–34; Michigan Avenue apartment, 141

—death, 250

—at Decca Records, 190–204, 209–18, 254; American Federation of Musicians tries to have him fired, 212–13; assistants, 198–200; Coles Brothers produced by, 202–4; daily schedule, 200; gospel quartets produced by, 212; John Hammond and, 196, 198, 205, 208, 243, 258; Harlem Hamfats and, 209, 211; Ink Spots signed by, 198–99, 202; Mahalia Jackson produced by,

Williams, J. Mayo ("Ink") (*continued*)
202, 253; Louis Jordan produced by, 211, 212, 213, 214, 215–16, 217, 232, 253; McTell produced by, 189, 191; Memphis Minnie produced by, 190, 253; Montgomery and Scruggs meet with, 1–2, *158*; Nixon and Estes produced by, 193–94; regular trips to New York headquarters, 196; replaced with Jordan by Gabler, 216; in signing of Basie for Decca, 196–98; Tharpe produced by, 200–202, 253; Wheatstraw produced by, 190, 191; works with Kapp brothers, 173–74

—early life, 5–13; birth, 6; birthplace, 6–7, 261n2; Chicago trip of 1910, 9; on debate team in high school, 10, 11, 58; father's death, 6; football in high school, 9, 10, *151*; high school transcripts of, 263n7; high school years, 8–12; junior class picture, *151*; stepfather Miles Magruder, 8; track in high school, 9–11

—at Ebony Records, 231–32, 235; "Black Is Beautiful" of 1972, 249; hopes to sell some 45s to Calt, 244; label folds, 237; ledger of, 237; overdubs of original records released, 236; Sunnyland Slim produced by, 233

—historical assessment: autobiographies proposed, 247, 250, 255; as erased from history, 251; as erased from NFL history, 248; facts of his life as inconsistent and incomplete, 257–58; as forgotten, 3, 259; Jarrett and Saunders program on, 249–50; life intersects a far-ranging cast of characters, 253–54; on setting the record straight, 237, 249

—at Howard University, 14–22; football at, 17, 19, *152*; immersion in majority black life, 17; NAACP involvement, 16; rarely mentions Howard, 21–22, 31; track and field at, 19

—interviews of, 254–55; Calt interview, 243–44, 245–47, 254, 255, 259; Mackenzie interview, 244, 245, 254; O'Neal interview, 247–48, 249, 254, 255; Russell and Steiner interview, 244, 254, 255; Terkel interview, 239–41, 254, 255

—musical opinions of: on blues, 98, 101–2, 246; on dance music, 92, 102, 216, 247, 256; favorite blues artists, 214; on vernacular Black cultural forms, 17, 92, 97, 98, 112, 202, 204, 212

—at Paramount Records, 91–122, 129–35, 140, 147–50; assistants, 96; Blind Blake produced by, 133–35, 140; Chicago Music run by, 92–102, 113, 116, 119, 133; as "company man," 115; "coon songs" rejected by, 100; deal with Paramount, 91–92; deal with railroad porters, 100; "de Mayo 1923" on Paramount labels, 133; finding artists, 99, 178; Papa Charlie Jackson produced by, 112–13, 140, 247, 253; Blind Lemon Jefferson produced by, 129, 130–33, 140, 242, 253; Guy B. Johnson correspondence, 121–22, 124–25, 127–28; jukeboxes installed in bordellos by, 99; Laibly undermines, 120, 133, 141–42, 148, 196; leaves Paramount, 150, 160, 162, 196; *Ma Rainey's Black Bottom* and, 252; Jelly Roll Morton produced by, 100, 180, 253; as not on equal footing with white executives, 133; King Oliver produced by, 180, 253; pen name of, 18; Ma Rainey produced by, 3, 106, 107–11, 113, 119–20, 122, 136, 247, 252, 253; remains close to Supper, 191–92; seeks to buy old Paramount masters, 191, 241; song rights purchased by, 116–19; Blind Joe Taggart produced by, 148–49; visits Paramount headquarters, 90–91

—personal characteristics: Afrocentric experience sought, 14–15; antisemitism, 115, 146; build, 95; carefully presents himself, 214; character, 20, 91, 150, 251, 252; code-switching, 189, 246; compartmentalizes his unsavory practices, 101; congenial nature, 246; drinking, 113, 115, 185, 214–15, 216, 233; focus and fortitude, 253; gambling, 20, 53, 101, 178, 185, 215, 216;

as gifted athlete, 8, 20; home-brewed gin, 72, 214; Kerner supported, 235; nickname "Ink," 9, 257; as no "great man," 252; as political moderate, 231; rarely wears helmet in football, 82, 105, *154,* 253; religious beliefs, 144–45, 237, 254; as socially connected, 141; sports and music in life, 221, 255–56; style of living, 233–34; as success oriented, 246; switches party affiliation, 187; as well-traveled, 9, 185

—personal relationships: Dorsey's relationship with, 163–64, 178, 239; friendship with Annan, 26–27; friendship with Blackwell and Carr, 195–96; friendship with Robeson, 27, 34, 213, 239–40, 254; Jewish friends, 115; Los Angeles connections, 180–81; marriage to Aleta Carolyn Stokes, 113–15; Pollard as lifelong friend, 11

—philanthropic activities: in "Keep 'em Smoking" campaign, 217; in South Side Boys Club campaign, 230

—professional characteristics: advances in recording technology and, 202, 226, 232; boogie-woogie associated with, 168, 206, 253, 256; "Corrine Corrina" associated with, 165; failures in spotting talent, 201–2, 228; line through his catalog as producer, 256; predatory business practices, 97, 101, 115–19, 191, 194, 195, 212–13, 245–46; seen as entrepreneurial failure, 234

—race and civil rights and: in Alpha Phi Alpha, 50, 51, 52, 85, *156,* 185, 230, 239, 246; Harlem Renaissance and, 213, 214; as pace setter, 235; at Poro College event, 192; race consciousness and, 246; as race "pioneer," 48; role in integration of sports, 233; sports and civil rights in life, 256–57; in Varsity Club of Chicago, 234; on white players and integration, 139

—small independent labels of, 226–31; Lee Brown recorded by, 227; gospel music recorded by, 229–30, 253; loses place in Chicago's Black music community, 228, 230; Stick McGhee recorded by, 229, 231; Muddy Waters recorded by, 227–28, 249, 253

—sports after college: and All-American designation, 36, 41, 44, 49, 50, 188; on All-American Pro First Team, 105–6; amateur 1933 track meet officiated by, 186; in article on early NFL, 236; as Black athlete of 1921, 82; with Chicago Black Hawks, 162; with Cleveland Bulldogs, 123, 125–26; coaches at Morehouse College, 182, 187–88; coaches at Paul Quinn College, 131, 150, 162, 167, 169, 179, 224; coaches Negro All-Stars, 220, 224; with Colored All-Stars, 179–80, 181; with Colored Giants, 147; ends regular involvement in football, 190; final NFL game, 136; as first Black NFL official, 74, 75, 79, 81, 82, 139, 253; with Fritz Pollard's All-Stars, 85, 175–76; with Hammond Boosters, 147; with Hammond Pros, 76–77, 80–84, 102–6, 119–20, 122–24, 125, 135–38, *157,* 239, 254; with Hammond Semcos, 166–67; indoor football league developed by, 83; never considered for Olympics, 46; in NFL, 3, 74, 139, 223, 238, 240, 253, 258; only touchdown of NFL career, 103; out of NFL, 138, 186, 187; on Pittsburgh Independents track team, 34; and Pro Football Hall of Fame, 248; Rock Island Independents try to sign, 106; with Sunlight Laundry team, 172

—writes for *Chicago Whip,* 64–66, 83, 184, 246

Williams, Luther (brother): birth, 5; in Chicago, 61, 62; death, 104, 252; father's death, 6; as Pullman porter, 8, 58, 100

Williams, Marc, 207

Williams, Marie (sister), 6, 7, 252

Williams, Mary Lou, 173, 197

Williams, Maurice "Sam/Sambo" (brother): birth, 6; at Chicago Music Company, 142; death, 196, 252; legal difficulties, 57, 58–61, 62, 98; as railroad porter, 100; stepfather Miles

Williams, Maurice "Sam/Sambo" (brother) (*continued*) Magruder, 8; and Williams's home-brewed gin, 72; Williams visits in Chicago in 1910, 9; works at Sunnyside Hotel summers, 9, 12

Williams (McCoy), Joe, 169, 170, 171

Williams, Millie (mother): at Chicago Music Company, 142; as domestic, 98; home in Monmouth, Illinois, 7, 12; husband Dan's death, 6; marriage to Dan Williams, 5; marriage to Miles Magruder, 7, 8; moves to Chicago, 57, 61; tells Williams to stay in Chicago, 64; Josh White stays with, 149

Williams, Virgil, 63

Wills, Harry, 82, 104

Wilson, August, 2–3, 252

Wilson, Leola, 136

Wilson, Sox, 211

Wilson, Wesley "Kid," 200

Wilson, Woodrow, 16, 24, 27–28

Winchester, Daisy, 213

Wisconsin Chair Company: Depression affects, 191; headquarters of, 90; Williams appeals to executives of, 91; Williams's furniture from, 115. *See also* Paramount Records

women: early blues as mostly all female, 112; female guitar-based musicians, 174; "List of American Folk Songs On Commercial Records" and, 242; Memphis Minnie as strong female blueswoman, 177; Sampson and, 141

Work, John, III, 227

Work, John Wesley, Jr., 107

Wray, Rex, 49

Yale University: football at, 18, 28, 42, 78, 253; interracial socializing among athletes at, 47, 53; Pollard in 1916 game, 28–29, 43; racism at, 42; ringers used at, 79; Williams on Black athletes at, 65; Williams vs., 42–49

Yazoo Records, 243, 246, 247

Young, Alvah Andrew "Doc," 77; on Akron game, 136; Black players hired by, 80, 102, 123, 238–39; gambles with Williams, 214; as Hammond Pros owner, 77, 139; on KKK and Kokomo game, 105; on local players, 83

Young, Frank, 104

Young, Harry, 77, 80, 102, 105, 122, 139, 246

Young, Lester, 200

CLIFFORD R. MURPHY is a musician and ethnomusicologist. He is a founding member of the rock band Say ZuZu, the director of the Smithsonian Center for Folklife and Cultural Heritage, and the author of *Yankee Twang: Country and Western Music in New England.*

The University of Illinois Press
is a founding member of the
Association of University Presses.

———————————————

Composed in 11.5/13 Adobe Garamond
with Gotham display
by Jim Proefrock
at the University of Illinois Press
Manufactured by Versa Press, Inc.

University of Illinois Press
1325 South Oak Street
Champaign, IL 61820-6903
www.press.uillinois.edu